【2013 版】

MAGIC XIAMEN

—— GUIDE TO XIAMEN

魅力厦门

By Dr. William N. Brown

厦门大学出版社
XIAMEN UNIVERSITY PRESS
国家一级出版社
全国百佳图书出版单位

Magic Xiamen

Color photos courtesy
of Mr. Zhu Qingfu

Good morning, Xiamen!

Bailu Zhou, cultural heart of Xiamen

Welcome to Amoy

Egrets--our city bird

Poetry in motion

Xiamen Botanical Garden

The Mandarin--garden hotel for a garden city

Picture perfect: Gulangyu Islet in foreground, Xiamen Island across the harbor

Gulangyu beach: popular a century ago--and today.

Seaside garden

Smooth sailing

19th and 20th century China had only 2 international settlements: Gulangyu and Shanghai

Gulangyu (Drum Wave) Islet

**"Richest square mile on earth"
in the early 20th century.**

Asia's largest piano museum

Gulangyu nightscape

Gulangyu's Huang Family Villa--most beautiful villa in China in the 1920s (Nixon stayed here)

Gulangyu Islet (Haicang is behind Gulangyu)

It's not hard to

Enjoy Amoy...

The banks of Yuandang lake

Enjoy cross-strait festivals and celebrations

International cuisine street

Riyuegu -- 1 of Asia's Top Ten hotsprings resorts

Haicang in the distance (Sun Yat-sen's "Oriental Mega-port")

Ancient Amoy Harbor

Now bustling day and night, 24/7

The entrance of that port was a fine sight... it was very safe, clean and deep; and from the entrance, it is divided into three arms of the sea and so many ships were cruising under sail on each one of them that it was an amazing thing to see....

Father Martin De Rada, July, 1575

Celebrating Xiamen--Taiwan direct flights

Cross-strait Development

Beautiful Xiamen Int'l Airport--the world at our doorstep

Xiamen's Taiwan Folk Village

Xiamen International Exhibition Center

Home of China International Fair for Investment and Trade (CIFIT)--world's largest!

Sept. 8-12

Health is Wealth

Amoy Mascot
(Haihai 海海)

Carnivals draw the crowds

Orient Golf Resort, Haicang
China's 1st PGA course and tournament

One of China's 4 strategic cities for yachting

Xiamen Int'l Marathon

Xiamen Olympic Museum

Jimei's annual dragonboat race

Xiamen--Home of pioneering educators

Xiamen Univ., founded 1921 by Tan Kah Kee,"Henry Ford of Asia"

Photo by B.B. Xiamen Int'l School (XIS)
400 students, 34 countries and regions

Xiamen University--rich heritage, richer future

Xiamen University Beach--the best classroom on campus

Jimei University

Mr. Tan Kah Kee's College Town (Jimei)

Magic Xiamen©2013

Guide to Xiamen

魅力厦门--厦门指南

Hundreds of Readers have sent letters, some of which are included in the back.

We are reprinting the book anyway.

Comments? E-mail: amoybill@gmail.com
Snail Mail: Dr. Bill Brown, Box 1288, Xiamen Univ.
Xiamen Fujian, PRC 361005

Complaints? Write my wife, Susan Marie..

Warning: Xiamen changes daily. ***Phone ahead***, or check our websites:
www.Amoymagic.com (outside China)
www.Amoymagic.mts.cn (in China)
www.Xiamenguide.com

Enjoy Amoy! 爱我厦门!

Dr. Bill 潘维廉
Xiamen University
School of Managtement

① This page's artwork from "*Story of the Amoy Mission after 100 Years—1842-1942.*"

Contents

① "Run your family like you cook small fish: very gently." Chinese Proverb

Highlights This Edition

More historical (some hysterical) insights, such as proof that Chopin, Bach and Mozart were Chinese (Parks chapter); why cars roll up hill on Wenyuan Road's "Spook Hill"; the true story of how an intrepid Scotsman discovered the deadly Amoy Vampires in the 1870s; the secret to surviving Darwinian driving, etc. We also have more info on the best travel spots in our Fujian province.

AXE (All Xiàmén Expatriates) will help you keep your edge with a Laowai (foreigner) welcome packet for members, help finding accommodation, monthly coffee meetings, sports activities, shopping & cultural trips, book club, etc.

AXE E-mail axe.xiamen@gmail.com
AXE Blog: http://allxiamenexpatriates.blog.com
AXE Facebook: facebook.com/allxiamen.expatriates

外籍鹭荟 AXE All Xiamen Expatriates

Orient Plus 恩加 eunice.orientplus@gmail.com

Still dis*Orient*ed? OrientPlus（恩加）is a lifesaver for Expats and foreign firms, helping with home searches, investment project coordination, orientation services, settling-in assistance, etc. Contact Eunice Chao:

Tel: 5811891 13906028020
E-mail: Eunice.orientplus@gmail.com

Xiàmén Shopping! Gone are the days when our sons ground our flour on the 100 pound granite mill I lugged by bike and boat on a 2-day trip to the countryside. Susan Marie says she can get virtually everything she needs from Metro (German), Carrefour (French), Wal-Mart (Arkansan), and the Restaurant Supply (Chinese—and the best prices on Italian olive oil, Australian butter, baking chocolate and vanilla, etc.).

Please see Shopping Chapter.

Back to the Grind, early 1990s

Warning! Phone ahead! Chinese businesses are like mushrooms—springing up overnight and vanishing just as quickly. Phone ahead to make sure they are still there, and ***visit www.amoymagic.com*** for more info and 100s of pages of additional information and photos—or **refer to the E-books**.

Explore Xiamen & Fujian!

Books by Bill Brown[①]

Old Xiamen—Cradle of Modern Chinese Business & Business Education
《商业老厦门——现代中国商业与工商管理教育的摇篮》
Bilingual (Xiamen Univ. Press)

Old Gulangyu in Foreigners' Eyes 《老外看老鼓浪屿》
Bilingual (Xiamen Univ. Press)

Magic Xiàmén—Guide to Xiàmén 《魅力厦门》
English and Chinese versions (Xiamen Univ. Press)

Discover Gǔlàngyú 《魅力鼓浪屿》
Bilingual (Xiamen Univ. Press)

Discover Quánzhōu 《魅力泉州》
Bilingual (Xiamen Univ. Press)

Magic Fújiàn 《老外看福建》
Bilingual plus MP3 CD (Xiamen Univ. Press)

Magic Haicang 《魅力海沧》
Bilingual (Xiamen Univ. Press)

Fújiàn Adventure 《魅力福建》
English and Chinese versions
(Lujiang Press and Straits Publishing)

Magic Sīmíng 《魅力思明》
Bilingual (Xiamen Government Publication)

Xiàmén University—Strength of the Nation 《魅力厦大》
Bilingual (Xiamen Univ. Press)

The Art of Business Warfare 《企业兵法》
Chinese only (Beijing Univ. Press)

Organizational Behavior 《组织行为学》
Chinese Only (Jiangxi Province People's Press)

E-books online in 2013
Over 1,000 pages of additional texts and photos on Xiamen and Fujian Province online at Amazon.

① Only in cold weather do we know the pine to be an evergreen. Chinese proverb

Acknowledgements

Susan Marie I violate protocol by thanking my wife before President Xi Jinping and Cao Fang, but ancient "Henpecked Chinese Jokes" (p.11) suggest they'll understand my plight. I hope their wives understand.

Sue knew nothing about the internet when Sue started Amoymagic.com (she thought HTML was a health plan). Thanks for persevering, Sue. Visit the 500+ pages of Amoymagic.com.

President Xi Jinping. In 2002, when he was Fujian's Governor, Xi Jinping said at a dinner, "You've written about Xiamen, your '2nd home'; why not write about Quanzhou, your '3rd home'? It was just a casual comment, but that bit of encouragement helped lead me to write almost a dozen books on Fujian. Thank you President Xi.

Mr. Cao Fang, "Master of Gulangyu," helped with this book and even penned the cover's elegant calligraphy. Thank you, Master Cao Fang! Read more about Gulangyu government's new young leader at the end of this first section.

Frank Wei & MTS. A good translation can make or break you, especially in China, so MTS has been my translator and website partner for a decade. Frank is chair of the Translation Service Committee of Xiamen Translator Association. MTS was accredited by China Translator's Association as "The Most Trustworthy Translation Company", and now has a new office in Santa Clara, California.

Frank's also a web wizard. In 1996 he created China's 2nd English website, the award-winning Chinavista.com, and in 2007 helped us launch www.xiamenguide.com Thanks, Frank.

Zhū Qìngfú (朱庆福) Another old friend, award-winning photographer Zhū Qìngfu, has provided the color photos in Magic Xiamen since the first edition over 10 years ago.

Read our online bio about him and his 3,000 published works, 300 of which landed domestic and international awards: See: http://www.amoymagic.com/zhuqingfu/zhuqingfu.htm

Veteran Bushwalker Trish Boman, an Aussie teacher at Xiàmén Int'l School, wrote the Bushwalks chapter. Thanks, Trish!

Joshua Kellard edited 1/3 of the book, though being from England, standard American was a challenge for him. Still, he bid his dest fixing the nistakes. Thanks Josh!

Thanks to Mr. Stephen Potter, who provided many B/W and color photos.

And thanks to the 5,000+ Laowai who are helping put Amoy back on the map.

Enjoy Amoy!

①

① **Multilingual Technologies, Inc**. 4633 Old Ironsides Drive #230, Santa Clara, CA 95054
Tel: 408-970-9586 Toll-Free: 1-800-906-9189 www.multilingual-tech.com

Supplement

Amoy's Gold in Livcom① 2002!

In 2002, I was honored to be on Xiàmén's team in Stuttgart at the Livcom Awards—the "Oscar of Livable Communities." (And proud that Xiamen will host the 2013 competition). With 40+ cities from around the world, Xiàmén had such stiff competition as Chicago, Phoenix, & Hángzhōu (杭州). Each had formidable advantages but none matched the sheer speed and comprehensiveness of Xiàmén's metamorphosis. Over a 20 year period, Xiàmén was China's #1 city in economic growth, and #2 in environmental sustainability, an amazing feat—and she started from scratch!

Xiàmén prospered 700 years ago as part of Quánzhōu, the start of the Silk Road of the Sea, and in the 1920s, several foreigners wrote that Gǔlàngyǔ was "the richest square mile on earth." But the Japanese razed us in World War II, and Táiwān bombed us after Liberation (1949)....

In the 1950s and 1960s, Xiamen Univ. had the only students in China with the slogan, "Pen in one hand, gun in the other!" Until the 1980s, Běijīng put little money into developing Xiàmén or Fújiàn (why build only to have Táiwān bomb it?).

When Susan Marie, our small sons, and I disembarked the slow boat to China (24 hours from Hong Kong to Xiamen) at Hépíng Port in 1988, Xiàmén had only one tall building—the harbor's Seaview (it now has Pizza Hut on its 24th floor). Electricity was off several days a week, water was off days at a time, dirt roads were potholed, the city itself was dirty and grimy with coal soot. The beach patrolled by gun-toting Xiamen Univ. students in the 1960s was still covered with tank traps and military camps, and was off limits to foreigners (as were the hills behind Xiamen Univ.)

July 4th, 1921, Celebration on Gulangyu
"Richest Square Mile on Earth!"

---

① Livcom: the "Oscar of Liveable Communities," recognizes environmental excellence in international communities. Visit: **www.livcomawards.com**

Within one decade, Xiàmén was a delightfully open city, and China's cleanest city! Xiàmén was first to broadcast air quality reports, and one of the first to adopt international standards in quality and pollution control. But only after working for 8 months on our Livcom presentation did I fully grasp the magnitude of Xiàmén's achievement. When I gave our presentation in Stuttgart, I was proud to be "Xiamenese"—and proud we won the gold in the "Oscar of Livable Communities."

Xiamen University Students Enjoy the Beach! (1950s)

A special thanks to Livcom founder, Mr. Alan Smith, who has since become a dear friend, and who wrote a special intro to Livcom, which you can view on our website.[1]

J. Nienhuis

#1 Destination in China![2] Chinese New Year, 2011—Xiamen was mainland China's #1 tourist destination (Beijing was #2). I hope this little book helps you understand why Xiamen is magic—for both Chinese and foreigners.

Enjoy Amoy!

Dr. Bill

① Livcom article: **http://www.amoymagic.com/NationsinBloom2002.htm**

② "Great souls have wills; weak souls only have wishes." Chinese Proverb

Supplement 1

Thanks to Cao Fang—the "Master of Gulangyu"

Xiamen's amazing changes the past 25 years owe a lot to both our visionary leadership and residents who haven't been afraid to act on those visions. But what about the next 25 years? My old friend, Cao Fang, the new "Master of Gulangyu", is confident that the best is still ahead of us. To help you better understand Xiamen, let me introduce to you one of the many special people behind our island's success.

Gulangyu residents fondly call its highest-ranking executive officer "Master of the Islet", and the new master is Cao Fang, an old friend of mine—though he's actually quite young (he entered college at age 15 and hasn't slowed down since).

Gulangyu opened to foreigners in 1840 during the first Opium War and by the early 1900s was called the "richest square mile on earth." It sank into obscurity after the Japanese invasion in 1938, but today Gulangyu shines again as one of China's top tourist spots. At Chinese New Year, 2011, Xiamen was mainland China's #1 destination (Beijing was #2), and Xiamen's top spot was the tiny islet of Gulangyu.

Unfortunately, the crowds of tourists have also been accompanied by throngs of illegal street merchants, as many as 300 to 400 a day, hawking inferior or even dangerous products. They often cheat shoppers, and when Gulangyu officials once tried to intervene, the hawkers attacked with knives, actually injuring some officials.

Gulangyu is applying for UNESCO World Heritage Status, but some historic villas have been rented out as small hotels, many torn down and rebuilt with no thought to their value. No wonder that many of the islet's original residents—professors, musicians, doctors, bankers—have fled the islet.

But some are fighting back. Fujian governor Su Shulin was frustrated when he witnessed the madness and said, "We must protect Gulangyu Islet!" He urged the local government to take charge and to appoint a new "master of Gulangyu"—and not surprisingly, they turned to young Mr. Cao Fang.

I met Cao Fang about ten years ago when he was vice secretary-general of the Xiamen Municipal Government. At that time, a program on CCTV, entitled "Meet China", introduced to global audiences China's most enchanting cities, including Beijing, Shanghai, Guangzhou, Xi'an, Hangzhou and Xiamen. In the summer of 2002, then then-mayor of Xiamen, Zhang Changping and the black mayor of San Francisco Willie Brown were interviewed in a phone conversation by CCTV to promote Xiamen to the world. I was also invited to talk about my impressions of Xiamen from an American perspective (they had me speak in Chinese and translated it into English—which rather surprised Mayor Brown). The program was a great success and made a big impact in China and the U.S., and Cao Fang was the chief planner of the program. I was quite impressed that someone of his relative youth had such knowledge not only of politics and economics but also of our local history and culture. Cao Fang and I kept contact over the ensuing decade. Frankly speaking, he's not one who would catch your attention on sight. He isn't tall, and he seems rather quiet—but he's strong (and stubborn—though he'd prefer being called persistent), learned, and visionary—a modern version of what I imagine the old Confucian masters to have been.

Cao Fang went to college at age 15 (almost unheard of in China), majoring in Chinese literature, but he is also passionate about philosophy, journalism, sociology, management science, and art. He has visited Russia, France, Austria, Switzerland, Egypt, South Africa, Argentina, Brazil, Singapore and Canada, and studied in Australia. He has also been to the U.S. and has a keen interest in and respect for American culture. His favorite American novel is "Gone with the Wind"; his favorite movie is "The Godfather". He admires Abraham Lincoln and can even recite the Gettysburg Address—something few American students can do nowadays.

It is no wonder that Xiamen made Cao Fang the "Master" of Gulangyu. He goes after problems like a bulldog. When he was vice magistrate of Xiajiang County in Jianxi Province at age 26, a 26-kilometer segment of the planned railway from Beijing to Hong Kong needed to pass through his county, along the foot of the Jinggang Mountain, where Mao Zedong once had a peasant guerrilla army. But local villagers refused to move their ancestors' tombs to make room for the railway. So Cao invited the village chief to a big dinner. He reasoned with the chief while they drank wine and ate meat to their hearts' content. Before long, they were both tipsy, and the village chief patted Cao on his shoulder, exclaiming: "I'm an uncouth fellow, but you take me as your brother. What you have said makes sense." The following day, he led the villagers to move their ancestors' tombs for the railway.

Cao Fang later transferred from Jiangxi to Xiamen to help investigate the infamous Lai Changxin smuggling case (the most serious corruption case in modern Chinese history). Lai fled to Canada for over 10 years, leaving vacant his headquarters, the Red Mansion. Many proposals were made to use the place, but all were controversial. In the end, Cao led the move to turn the building into a school and popular lecture venue for the over 800,000 migrant workers on Xiamen.

Cao Fang was also the spokesman for the Lai Changxin investigation, responding calmly to the barrage of questions posed by journalists from the Associated Press, Reuters and Taiwan. His answers were not entirely free of the diplomatic rhetoric of the Communist Party, but he still managed to win over the journalists with his wit.

When in charge of the Emergency Response Bureau, Cao Fang taught students how to cope with earthquakes and tsunamis. The devastating earthquakes in Wenchuan and Japan compelled him to organize annual drills. As the sirens wailed, 400,000 students evacuated from their classrooms to the playground. The lessons took hold. When an earthquake shook the Taiwan Strait in March 2010, Xiamen students fled to safety with little direction from their teachers.

When Cao Fang was appointed "master of Gulangyu islet," Xiamen municipal leader Yu Weiguo said, "Cao is knowledgeable, capable, competent, and accomplished in the arts. His calligraphy has been lauded by such leaders as Beijing mayor Liu Qi (who helped Beijing land the 2008 Olympics) and Nan Huaijin, a leading scholar on Chinese culture. My own home has a Cao Fang calligraphic work, which reads "Xiamen shelters guests from the five continents and embraces vast stretches of the sea." In addition, Cao Fang penned the Chinese characters for "Magic Xiamen" on this book's cover. Shortly after Cao came to Gulangyu, the former Prime Minister of Hungary, Medgyessy Peter, paid him a visit. Cao arranged for a pianist to play *Hungarian Rhapsodies XI*, a masterpiece of Hungarian musician Liszt. Mr. Medgyessy was amazed, and told Cao, "I never imagined that in a place so far away from Hungary, there would be such a beautiful islet of pianos and an islet master who admires Liszt and Hungary!"

Cao greeted me once while friends and I were playing the mooncake game near the Koxinga statue and shared how busy he'd been since becoming the "master" of Gulangyu. Only40 days after he took office, Governor Su Shulin visited Cao to hear his ideas on managing Gulangyu. Cao plans to return the islet to its former grace and beauty by introducing more democratic decision making, and bringing together government, NGOs, residents, merchants and the press to join forces in managing the islet. The most important step, Cao says, is to establish rules by which everyone plays the game and to safeguard everyone's legitimate rights and interests. Governor Su was pleased, and said, "Great! I trust you. Make your mark here!"

A gifted Qing Dynasty scholar, Zhen Banqiao, once wrote in a poem, "The bamboo stretched its root to the ground", which means that perseverant adherence to goals always leads to success. China's new President, Xi Jinping, when he was the newly-elected CPC Secretary-General and transferred from Fujian to Zhejiang, inscribed for Cao Fang, "Cao, my dear friend, best wishes to you and Gulangyu!" After 25 years in Xiamen, I've seen that what makes Xiamen special is the people—good leaders with vision, and good residents to act upon the vision. I look forward to seeing how the next 25 years unfolds not just for Gulangyu but for all of Xiamen under the leadership of the next generation of leaders—people like Cao Fang, "Master of Gulangyu."

Cao Fang and Mr. & Mrs. Alan Smith, Livcom founders

(1655 Map of Fujian Province)

Chapter 1

Welcome Lǎowài!

Lǎowài! Get used to hearing, "Lǎowài（老外)!" This is Chinese for "venerable outsider" (foreigner). I just yell back, "Lǎonèi! "（老内，"venerable insider").

When Chinese protest, "No such word!" I reply, "There is now."

In the Blood Fortunately, Chinese see us not just as Lǎowài but also as Péngyǒu (朋友, friend), and sometimes as family. Chinese hospitality is one reason China gets in your blood for life (like malaria—but who courts mosquitoes?①)

Our family fell for China, and especially for Xiàmén (former "Amoy"). Whether you are passing through or staying awhile, we hope you too enjoy our enchanting island, which for centuries has woven her spell over Lǎowài and Lǎonèi alike with her balmy climate and her rolling green hills dotted with gardens and pagodas and temples.

> **No Xiàmén, no U.S.A?**
>
> A few years ago, I emceed a Xiamen government luncheon in Guangzhou for 400 American business people from throughout S.E. Asia. A U.S. rep scheduled to give a 5 minute greeting instead spent over 30 minutes regaling us with how America was changing Asia, leaving me no time for my own 30 minute scheduled intro to Xiamen (the whole point of the luncheon, which we paid for). So I axed my talk from 30 min. to 2 min.
>
> "I'm so thankful to hear my homeland is changing the world," I said, "but you should know that had it not been for Xiamen, there would not even have been a U.S.A." Dead silence, as 800 eyeballs glared at me.
>
> "You've heard of the Boston Tea Party?" It was hard keeping a straight face as I continued, "The tea tossed in Boston harbor was our local Anxi tea, and the three ships were from Xiamen, then known as Amoy.
>
> "So had it not been for Xiàmén, the good old U.S. of A. would still be a British colony, we'd be eating fries with malt vinegar instead of vinegar and ketchup (clarifed by Josh K.!) and our lawyers would be wearing powdered wigs."
>
> My 2 minute talk was probably better than the 30 minute one I'd planned. After the laughter subsided, several gathered to question me about Xiamen.

Why "Magic Xiamen?" In the early '90s, I spent one afternoon hastily improvising a 24-page "Xiamen Survival Guide" for new Lǎowài who staggered about intoning the **Lǎowài Litany**:

"Where can I buy cheese?" (There wasn't any).

"Which toilet paper won't burn buns? (TP was like recycled sandpaper).

---

① Speaking of mosquitoes—Amoy is the "Cradle of Tropical Medicine," where Sir Manson discovered the link between malaria and what is officially the deadliest creature on the planet—the mosquito. (No malaria today). See Wildlife Chapter.

"Where are sit-down toilets?" (Read "Dethroned" at end of chapter).

But today, Xiàmén's 5000+ Lǎowài no longer need a "Survival Guide" because life on the Garden Island is not a struggle but fun and rewarding. Yet newly arrived Lǎowài, and even old hands, still wonder where to shop, or eat, or beat a weekend retreat. I hope *Magic Xiamen* helps.

Explore Amoy—but *Double Check*[1] Our magical little island changes daily; this book cannot change (though I hope to update the E-version often). So ***Call before you go***, because restaurants, shops and tourist sites spring up like mushrooms overnight, and some disappear just as quickly. And visit our websites for more information:

www.amoymagic.mts.cn (in China) www.amoymagic.com (back on earth)
www.xiamenguide.com (in cooperation with MTS—Master Translation)

Hopefully, the books (and online E-books) and websites help you better appreciate our city's rich history, culture, and traditions, as well as guide you to restaurants, stores, tourist traps, etc.. But the best way to know Amoy is to explore it on foot, or by bike or bus (check out our double-decker tour busses in "Transportation" chapter). \

Pop Quiz What Chinese city did a 1999 U.S. Embassy report in Běijīng say was "Greener than Green, a Model of Environmental Achievement?" Which Chinese city won the gold medal in Stuttgart at the 2002 Livcom[2] competition? What was the planet's only city to receive the 2004 UN Habitat Award? What city was #1 in economic growth while at the same time #2 in environmental protection? What city has idyllic weather, clean air (we had China's first air quality forecasts), beautiful beaches and gardens, sumptuous seafood, a unique marriage of Chinese, European colonial and modern architecture, a good international airport (soon with direct flights to California), one of the world's best harbors, China's only key university in a Special Economic Zone—and unlimited business opportunities so you can afford to enjoy all of the above?

Beautiful Amoy. Stephen Potter

Nowhere but the "Garden Island" of Xiàmén.

① Chinese Proverb: "Fix your roof *before* it rains; dig your well *before* you are thirsty."
② Livcom: The "Oscar of Environmental Awards" www.livcomawards.com

Why "Amoy" instead of Xiamen?

After my lecture on Fujian history to 300 Zhangzhou Univ. students, a youth leaped to his feet, glared at me like a Red Guard about to plant a dunce cap on a teacher guilty of "old thinking," and demanded, "Why do you say 'Amoy'? Why not 'Xiàmén'? The right name is Xiamen! Huh? Huh?"

Chinese often ask this, but seldom so indignantly. I replied, "Why do Chinese say Jiù Jīnshān" (旧金山) instead of "San Francisco"? Huh? Huh?"

"Because Chinese can't pronounce "San Francisco"!" he retorted.

"Enough said," I replied.

The name "Amoy" appears on maps as early as the 1600s (though spelled in many ways—Emoy, Emowie, etc). Xiamen's name in the local dialect was "Ah Mo" (like "Amen" spoken through the nose). "Amoy" was as close as foreigners could get. Even today, Overseas Chinese boast they are from Amoy, not Xiamen, and Chinese throughout Asia speak Amoy Dialect, not Xiamen Dialect.

Though I hope foreigners learn the "proper" name, Xiamen, I use "Amoy" throughout this book because 1) Xiàmén is still hard for foreigners to pronounce, 2) even Overseas Chinese call Xiàmén "Amoy", and 3) virtually no Western history books use the name "Xiamen," but Amoy goes back centuries. For those with a bit of Chinese history under their belt (as opposed to a lot of Chinese cuisine *over* their belt), the very word Amoy conjures up exotic vistas and tales. And even today, the world uses "Amoy Soy Sauce," not Xiàmén Soy Sauce. In Hong Kong, bird flu first appeared on Amoy Street, not Xiàmén Street. Malaysia's Equator Academy of Art is on Amoy Lane, not Xiàmén Lane. And last but not least, the Latin seal of Xiàmén Univ., founded not by foreigners but a Chinese, bears the inscription "Universitatis Amoiensis"—not "Universitatis *Xiamen*ensis".

So Amoy is not a vestige of foreign imperialism. Amoy is as much a Chinese word as a foreign word, and it sounds a lot more like "Ah Mo" than "Jiù Jīnshān" sounds like San Francisco, so Chinese purists, give us a break. But, out of deference to my Chinese hosts, I usually refer to our island as Xiàmén, not Amoy.

As for that minority that still take umbrage at my sparing use of Amoy, I throw down the gauntlet. When Chinese start saying "Washington" instead of "Huáshèngdùn" (华盛顿), or California" instead of "Jiālìfúníyà" (加利福尼亚) or "Jiazhou" (加州), I will axe Amoy from my vocabulary. Until then—get a life, folks, and be glad that visitors from all over the world are once again flocking to our beautiful little island, regardless of what you call her. In summary...

Enjoy Amoy!

Xiàmén at a Glance

Location: S.E. China in Fujian Province, facing Táiwān, between H.K. &Shanghai: 117°53'—118°25' E. longitude, 24°25'—24°54' N. latitude

Population: 3.61 million, including about 1 million non permanent residents

Nationalities: Hàn（汉）, Shē (畲）, Miáo（苗）, Huí (回）,
Manchu (Mǎn, 满）, Gāoshān （高山）, Lǎowài (老外).

Languages: Mandarin, Mǐnnán (S. Fújiàn Dialect), Chinglish

Climate: Subtropical Marine Monsoon

Avg. Winter Temperature: 55°F Avg. Summer Temperature: 82°F

Avg. Annual Rainfall: 1.315mm

Total Land Area: 1,700 km^2 **Island's Area**: 130km^2

Sea Area: 300+ km^2 **Coastline**: 234 km

Green Coverage of Developed Areas: 42%

Green Space Per Capita 13.57m^2

Average Lifespan: 78.23

Avg. Income of XMU Teachers: enough to pay taxes, but not enough to avoid taxes

Sister Cities: Cardiff Shire, UK; Sasebo, Japan; Cebu, Philippines; Baltimore, US; Wellington, New Zealand; Penang, Malaysia; Sunshine Coast, Australia; Kanaus, Lithuania; Guadalajara, Mexico; Zoetermeer, Netherlands; Kuching Sarawak (Malaysia); Surabaya, Java, Indonesia; Mokpo South Korea; Sarasota, U.S.; Marathon, Greece; Trier, Germany; Richmond, B.C. Canada

Number of Italian Restaurants: 40+

Diamond[1] in the rough—Xiàmén then and now

Hexiang Xi Lu, 1988

Earth to China? No wonder the Chinese plaster walls and buildings with "Go into the world!" banners. That Chinese even admit the need to go ***in*** to the world is proof enough the whole country is ***out of this world***. When we arrived in 1988, we did feel we were on another planet. Xiamen little resembled the beautiful island we take for granted today. In 1988, an American with 30 years experience in Asia visited us and solemnly declared, "With the whole country to choose from, you chose the armpit of China!"

[1] Chinese Proverb: A flawed diamond is better than a perfect but common stone.

Shannon and Matthew man the fort (Xiamen, 1993)

Garden Under Guard Chinese argue, "But Xiàmén *scenery* was beautiful, even in 1988!" Maybe, but how could we have known? Beaches were fortified camps lined with tank traps and off limits to foreigners. Hills were also off limits; even our two small sons were detained by soldiers who demanded to know, "Why are they dressed in military uniforms?"

"New American secret weapon," I replied. "Miniature solders can sneak in anywhere." The soldiers laughed heartily, had their photos taken with my little warriors, and let us go our way.

Not only was our travel restricted but so was our diet. In fact, technically, XMU's foreign teachers were not allowed to eat. We had to eat in the cafeteria, but they refused cash. We could only use ration coupons for meat, veggies, flour and oil. Foreign teachers were not allowed to receive ration coupons.

We survived by purchasing coupons "under the table[①]" from Chinese teachers.

Gone Postal Our sense of "Far Side" isolation was compounded when it took two months to receive a letter from back on earth, only to find they had been ripped open and stapled or glued shut—letters hopelessly glued to the envelopes. Some mutilated envelopes were unsealed and empty, and stamped in bold Mainland Red with, "Received These Condition." Happily, China's mail service today is even better than back home—7 days a week, rain or shine.

And either they quit opening mail or they've learned to reseal it nicely.

Giving us a Line Phones were worse than mail. We made only one phone call during our first year—from downtown to Xiàmén University (XMU). The XMU operator, who routed all calls, said "No such number," and hung up. I made two calls my second year. Only one call got through. I finally spent over $400 USD for a home phone, which was installed three years later.

Today, $6 gets same day installation—though why bother when cell phones are as cheap, and unlike back home, no contract needed.

We now have the world at our fingertips. Between the landlines, cell phones, emails, texting, blogging, podcasting and Skyping, we're too well connected.

Phoneless cord, perhaps?

Current Events In the early 1990s, Xiamen's skyline barely broke the waterline, but frequent blackouts made tall buildings with elevators impractical, if not downright scary. Power outages were scheduled (one day a week) and unscheduled (almost daily). When we *did* have power, the current was so weak it could drop from 220 to 160 volts when a neighbor half a block away fired up an electric teakettle, and surge to 280 volts when they unplugged it. We fried more electronics than fish and vegetables, and I often browsed Xiamen's shops and bookstores by candlelight.

We now have all the electricity we could want—and the bills to prove it.

① For "under the table", Chinese say "use the back door" (zou hou men, 走后门)"

Backroom Books Next to cheese, early Laowai most craved English reading materials, but the only foreign books for sale were pirated volumes in bookstores' backrooms, behind the drawn curtains and the "Foreign friends not allowed" signs. Today, thanks to mutually beneficial agreements with foreign publishers, we can buy foreign books and magazines (and online orders are a cinch; we've no problem receiving orders from Amazon, eBay, etc.).

Our First "Car"

In 1988, it took us two months to get permission to buy a 3-wheeled pedicab! "No! Foreigners cannot buy commercial vehicles!"

"I didn't come all the way to China to run a rickshaw! It's for family use!" I argued.

I had to get an official letter from Foreign Affairs, and signed a contract swearing I would not use the vehicle for profit.

As I proudly pedaled out of the bike shop and down Sīmíng Rd back to XMU, a youth walking with his girl friend pointed at me and yelled, "Heh! How much to take us to Zhōngshān Park?"

In 1993 I applied for a van. "No! Foreigners can't buy commercial vehicles!"

Of course, we were finally allowed to buy **Toy Ota**, the 15-passenger van, that we drove to Tibet and back, but that's another story**...**

(see www.amoymagic.com)

The Diamond Shines In spite of challenges, we quickly fell for Amoy, which in hindsight we see was a diamond in the rough—though it took two decades of polishing to make it sparkle.

Xiàmén was one of China's less clean cities in the late 1980s; by the mid '90s it was China's cleanest and most livable city. Xiàmén has changed so much, in fact, that visitors from abroad no longer pity us for having to rough it in a developing country. (Increasingly, visitors don't want to leave![1])

Growing but Green Xiàmén's core guideline has been, "Don't sacrifice environment for prosperity." Since 1997, Xiàmén has invested at least 3% of GDP on the environment. In 2002, when we won the Gold at Livcom in Stuttgart, one international judge exclaimed, "I had no idea such cities exist in China."

In 2004, Xiàmén was the only city to receive the UN's Habitat Scroll of Honour. The Under-Secretary-General Anna Tibaijuka praised Chinese cities' balanced emphasis on development and decent living conditions. And happily for us, those "decent living conditions" now include excellent services.

---

①**Want a job in Amoy?** Check www.amoymagic.com/jobconn.htm But please note, again, that phone numbers & sites frequently change.

Healthy Life Xiamen's average lifespan is 78.2 years. We have 895 medical institutions, including 27 municipal hospitals, Fújiàn's best Blood Center and Research Center for cardiovascular disease, and two facilities opening soon as joint ventures with Harvard Medical School and Johns Hopkins. You can even get laser eye surgery in our Eye Center (see Medical chapter).

Geography & Weather Xiàmén lies about a mile off. Fújiàn's serpentine coastline and faces Táiwān. We are 695 nautical miles south of Shànghǎi, 287 nautical miles north of Hong Kong, 816 nautical miles from Nagasaki, and a few thousand nautical miles from Tom's No. 5 Chīlǐ Bùrgěrs in Lǒs Āngělès.

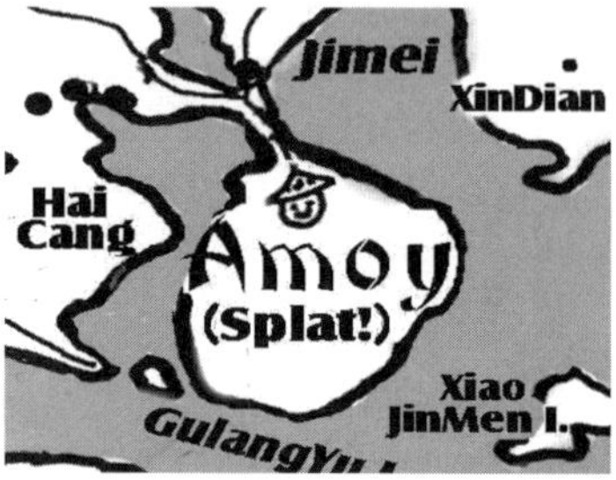

Locals claim Xiàmén is shaped like a flying egret but I don't see the resemblance. Amoy is almost round: 13.7 km north to south, 12.5 km east to west—more like an egret after crash landing. ***Splàt!***

The northern reaches of this ***Splàt!*** are mounds of volcanic rock piled 150m above sea level; the hilly south is crowned by Yúndǐng Hill (Yúndǐng Yán, 云顶岩) which towers all of 339.6 m. above sea level. Xiàmén is so stable geologically that even Taiwan's frequent shakes don't faze us.

Our only shake ups are from Susan Marie's driving.

Amoy's gardens bloom year round, thanks to an atmospheric alchemy that keeps the mercury at about 20.8ºC—except July to September, when it soars to 28℃ or more, and the humidity is so high you can suck the air with a soda straw. Three or four typhoons per year, usually between July and October, liven up an otherwise boringly nice climate and help blow away some of the hot air that accumulates, though 1999's Typhoon Dan blew away more than hot air…

Typhoon Dan dumps on us As Typhoon Dan descended upon Xiàmén in October, 1999, newly arrived Kodak engineer Rick Huntington asked, "Are typhoons bad here? We've never seen one."

"Nah," I said. "They fizzle out over Táiwān, which blocks them. Locals say Koxinga's (Zhèng Chénggōng, 郑成功) statue guards the harbor. So tell the Kodak folks to relax and just see what develops."

Koxinga must have been out to lunch. Dan was the worst typhoon in 50 years, whipping rain about like a laser light show. Giant banyans toppled, power poles and lines fell; wooden window frames flew right out of neighbor's walls.

In spite of the devastation, utilities were quickly restored, even at hard-hit Xiàmén University (XMU), but we'll no longer take warnings so lightly.

Fortunately, Xiamen government responds quickly and efficiently, and even Typhoon Dan didn't affect the phones or internet, so you can probably check for updates at http://www.weather.com.

Xiamen Weather

Average Data	Jan	Feb	Mar	Apr	May	June	July	Aug	Sep	Oct	Nov	Dec
Average High (°F)	61/64	60/63	64/67	71/74	78/82	83/87	88/92	88/92	86/89	80/84	73/76	65/69
Average High (°C)	16/18	15/17	18/20	22/24	26/28	28/30	31/33	31/33	30/32	27/29	23/25	19/21
Average Low (°F)	49/52	49/52	52/56	60/63	68/71	73/77	77/80	76/80	74/78	68/71	60/64	53/56
Average Low (°C)	9.0/11	9.0/11	11/13	15/17	20/22	23/25	25/27	25/27	23/25	20/22	16/18	12/14
Rain (in)	1.4/1.5	3.0/3.1	3.7/3.8	5.5/5.6	6.4/6.5	7.6/7.7	5.5/5.6	5.9/6.0	4.4/4.5	4.0/1.1	1.2/1.3	0.9/1.0
Rain (mm)	35/40	75/80	90/95	140/145	160/165	190/195	140/145	150/155	110/115	25/30	30/35	20/25

Supplement

How We Got Here

Seeing Red I had zero interest in China or Asia until I was 20. I'd never met a Chinese and never held chopsticks or eaten Chinese food. But the U.S. Air Force *orient*ed me.

In 1976, I volunteered for two years of solitude on the world's largest island, icy Greenland, population a trifling fifty eight thousand. So Uncle Sam of course packed me off to Formosa, a small island of twenty million (twenty million and one, including myself).

I was intrigued when the captain in my orientation course said that Formosa, the Portuguese name for Táiwān, meant "Beautiful Island," but I snickered when he said 1 in 4 people in the world were Chinese.

"Do you think that is funny?" he demanded.

"Sir, no sir!" I said. "But our family has 4 people, and none of us are Chinese."

He was not amused, and off I went to Taizhong, Taiwan, just 100 miles across the sea from Amoy and the Apocalyptic Yellow Peril of Communist China.

I wrote my will and gave my sister my car (true story!).

Taiwan, 1977

A Sign from the Heavens. Fortunately, by 1976 the two sides of the Straits were launching words, not weapons. And one fine spring day, a batch of colorful leaflets from a mainland balloon descended like colored snow upon C.C.K. Airbase. Frantic Taiwanese soldiers scurried about like ants on the scent of sugar, stuffing the leaflets in sacks. "Don't look at them!" they yelled.

They were in Chinese, which I could not read, so I had zero interest in them until they forbade me to look at them. When they added, “Touch them and you go to jail,” I knew they had to be good. After all, as Confucius would have said had he raised American teens, “Forbidden fruit is always sweeter.”

I stealthily stuffed my pockets with contraband propaganda[①] and hurried home. I pulled the curtains, and for hours pored over photos of blissful Chinese farmers, and acrobats performing improbable feats. I knew, of course, the Communists viewed the world through Red-tinted spectacles, and didn’t believe a word (or a photo), but my curiosity was piqued….

Island Fever I fell in love with Táiwān and her people, and for two years hiked and biked the length and breadth of the island, both exploring and raising money for a children’s hospital. But like most gems, the Jade Island is small, and island fever coupled with curiosity about the contraband leaflets hidden in my room led me to sit on the beach for hours, wondering what the enemy on the other side of the Dire Straits was really like. I’d have never imagined that a decade later I’d move to Amoy, just 100 miles away, with two infant sons and a “Made in Táiwān” wife (blonde and blue-eyed Susan Marie was born and raised in Táiwān).

Given my love of Táiwan, it was no surprise that I also fell for Xiàmén; 75% of Taiwanese’ originate from South Fújiàn. Both sides of the straits share the same culture, customs, arts, crafts, “etc.” And the Strait narrows daily.

A few years back, a mainland film studio shot part of a TV series on a Táiwān-occupied island 3 miles from Xiamen. Upon their return to Xiàmén the director found they’d left some things back on the Táiwān-controlled island. “We’ll lose days,” he moaned, as he envisioned a crew member retracing their steps via Hōng Kǒng, Táiběi, Táizhōng, Jīnmén, and back to Xiàmén.

A local fisherman said, “Bú Yào Jǐn” (不要紧, “No worries, mate”). I have relatives there.” And under cover of darkness he put out in his little sampan and returned with the missing items the next morning.

Angling, not Wrangling In September 1998, we held our 1st annual Táiwān-Xiàmén fishing contest. Afterwards, like fishermen the world over, both sides headed home to exaggerate the size of their catches and bemoan the big ones that got away.

It was nice to see both sides angling instead of wrangling. Nowadays, 15% of residents on Táiwān-controlled Jīnmén Island have apartments in Xiàmén, and tens of thousands take ferries, ships and planes each month between Xiamen, Jinmen, and Taiwan Island.

① I still have the leaflet in the photo

Historical Supplement

Míng Dynasty Tales of Henpecked Hans

These Míng Dynasty (1368-1644) tales suggest Lăowài and Lăonèi have a lot in common. I just hope Susan Marie doesn't read them....

When I'm Ready A man badly beaten by his wife fled for his life and crawled under the bed. His wife screamed, "Come out this instant!"

"I'm the head of this house," he said. "And I'll come out when I'm good and ready."[①]

Till Death Do Us Part A group of henpecked men held an emergency meeting to discuss ways to regain their dignity. A bachelor prankster walked into their midst and said, "Your wives heard of this gathering and are all on their way here to deal with you." All but one man panicked and dashed out the door.

"He's the only one with courage to stand up to his wife!" the bachelor exclaimed.

But closer examination revealed he'd died of fright.

Grapes of Wrath A magistrate asked his court clerk how his face got scratched. The embarrassed clerk said, "Last night, I was walking in the yard, taking in the cool night air, when a grape trellis fell and scratched my face."

The magistrate declared, "Only a wife could do this. Bring her here right now!

But the magistrate's own wife had been hiding in the next room, and hearing this she stormed into the court. The terrified magistrate shouted, "Court's in recess! Clear the court! My own grape trellis is falling down!"

Nighty Nightsoil Two men, both terrified of their wives, were moaning to one another. One said, "My wife is so strict she even makes me empty the night soil."

"What?" said his friend. "Why, if I were you –"

"—If it were you, what would you do?" came his wife's voice from behind him.

"If it were I, I'd go empty it."

Supplement: Dethroned

(Written with hindsight)

I love China, but she can throw us Lăowài for a loop with the most mundane things—like toilets. Chinese invented sit-down flush toilets 2,000 years ago, but today they use what is little more than a ceramic hole in the ground.

"Where on earth do I sit?" I asked my better half.

"You don't sit," Susan Marie explained. "You plant your feet on the raised shoe-shaped platforms and squat."

---

① Ancient Chinese saying, "Man head of house; woman neck that turns head."

"You're kidding!" I tried, but could only manage when holding a pipe for dear life. Sue said, "You can't squat? I can! Your sons can! You're the only one in the world, Bill Brown, who can't squat!"

"Easy for someone born and raised in Taiwan," I said. "And Shan and Matt grew up in Xiàmén. But I'm American. Barbie, Ken, and G.I. Joe are fully bendable, but I am not."

East meets West; goes to pot

Of course, squat toilets do have advantages. Not much can go wrong with a ceramic hole, and there are no lids or seat to clean or fix, as happens in hotels when unenlightened souls squat atop Western toilets. But practical or not, I miss the days of sitting upon the throne with a good read.

Happily, some places—such as airports—now offer a token Western toilet, but Chinese are careful to make sure foreigners know what they think of unbendable barbarians by posting a sign, "For the weak only." But I don't care. I ignore the stares and snickers and use the weak folks' potty.

And I'm usually already ensconced upon the throne before I remember that most of them still don't have toilet paper.

On a good note, toilet paper (Wèishēng Zhǐ, 卫生纸) has improved immensely. This is not surprising, given that Chinese invented not only sit down toilets but toilet paper as well. Almost 1,000 years ago, imperial households employed petit squares of perfumed paper upon their royal rears. Even commoners used recycled paper upon their posteriors—though one scholar famously objected to using paper with poetry upon it on one's buttocks, be it royal or common. But in 1988, Chinese TP felt like recycled sandpaper, and it was months before our tender bourgeois bottoms could cope.

Fortunately, Xiàmén firms now put out quality TP, and we soon learned that it was not just foreigners' behinds that were ready for pampering. Chinese themselves also prize the new TPs, many of which have fragrances, and delicate prints. An American lady in Quánzhōu told me that her favorite brand is "Mind Act Upon Mind." The ad boasts, "For soft and comfortable life you can really feel good."

Nice. But for me, a soft and comfortable life still requires a sit-down toilet.

Susan Marie's disdain notwithstanding, I'll go to pot if forced to squat.

Supplement 3

A Few Miracle Amoy Photos

Boot Kids 1926: Wilbur, Beatrice, Marian, Raymond, Harriet, Ethel Boot family in Amoy from 1903-1940.

Below are 3 of the many happy "coincidences" I've had while researching Amoy history.

Wilbur Boot's Broken Arm I found a 1920s photo of 6 foreign children on Gulangyu and wondered who they were. Five days later, a Michigan lady emailed that to celebrate her dad's birth on Gulangyu 90 years earlier to missionary parents, she had downloaded our website's Amoy Mission materials for him, and asked if I had more material. I sent old letters and photos, and also asked if her dad knew these 6 children.

The boy on the left was her father! Wilbur had never seen the photo, but 90 years later still remembered he'd fallen from a tree two hours later and broken an arm.

But Wilbur was wrong. He broke **two** arms, not one, because I just happen to have the original letter by nurse Tena Holdkeboer describing "little Wilbur's" accident.

Ebay Miracle In May 2005, I saw a postcard of the Freemasonry Hall on Gulangyu. The next day, I confirmed it was still for sell and registered with eBay to buy it (I'd never used eBay before). And during the 15 minutes it took to register, someone else bought it. I was disappointed, to say the least. But the next day, I received an email from a freemason, Mr. Ashley B. in Hong Kong, and he said he'd seen my website and that the day before he'd bought a postcard from eBay of the old Amoy Freemasonry Hall, and asked if I'd like a copy. He not only scanned the postcard for me but also the deed and other material.

Picture Perfect I saw a color 1950s photo of 3 unknown women on a couch in the U.S. and on the wall behind them was an oil painting of what resembled Gulangyu's missionary Hope Hospital. I scanned and enlarged it, and saw the John Otte memorial. How I wanted to find who the people were and have the painting photographed, but it was a 60-year-old photo. Hopeless?

A week later, a man in the U.S. wrote that while emptying his basement to move to another state, he'd found a 1930s oil painting of Gulangyu's Hope Hospital, and a letter by the Chinese artist (a Hope patient). He mailed them to me, and they will be part of the Amoy Mission museum we hope to get going.

Chapter 2

5,025 Years of Amoy History

Fújiàn province's history extends back before the dawn of Chinese civilization 5,025 years ago.[1] In fact, Chinese claim that scientific records prove the cave relics in Sānmíng's Wànshòuyán（三明万寿岩）are 180,000 years old.

Leave it to Chinese to keep scientific records for 180,000 years.[2]

Little is known of such ancients as the Mín（闽）, who left no written records, other than some Shāng Dynasty（商代 16th-11th century B.C.) pictographs carved into a rock in a Huì'ān（惠安）village.

An ancient Chinese wit eventually discovered writing, or at least how to draw better (Chinese characters are pictographs), and began recording Fújiàn's history in the Warring States Period (475 – 221 BC).

Ancient Fujianese left some fairly strange relics, such as the 4,025-year-old boat-shaped tombs perched hundreds of feet up the vertical cliffs of Wǔyí Mountain (Wǔyíshān, 武夷山). I've been dying to know why they did it—and how.

Extraterrestrial stopping by for Chinese take-out? NASA seems to think so....

NASA Seeks Mǐnnán on the Moon

After failing to find intelligent life on earth, NASA began to seek it in space by sending interstellar greetings in many languages. Their message in Amoy dialect was, "Friends of space, how are you all? Have you eaten yet? Come visit if you have time."

If the Mǐnnán message doesn't get a response, nothing will, because Amoy life is indeed out of this world.

Ancient Fújiàn's Mǐnyuè were joined by such tribes as the Shē clan（Shēzú, 畲族）and the Miáo tribe（Miáozú, 苗族）. Originally from the Yangtze River Valley, the Shē claim descent from a legendary emperor—hence their unique 'phoenix clothing' and 'phoenix hairstyles' (The phoenix implies royalty).

We also have the Dan Tribe (Dànzú, 但族), whose Mongol ancestors made the long trek to Fújiàn about 700 years ago. They are unrelated to the Israelite tribe of Dàn, though China does have so many Chinese Jews scattered about that some experts claim they are remnants of Israel's Lost Tribes.

After using Chinese maps to drive around China, I can see how they got lost.[3]

---

① A university Prof. said China had 5,000 years of history—but that was 25 years ago.

② Chinese first invented paper, and then paperwork; Red tape, in other words.

③ Actually, ancient Chinese invented maps with grids, as well as the so-called Mercator projection map. And today we have GPS.

The Legendary Chinese Jews

Jews probably first made their way towards China during the Babylonian exile 2500 years ago, when trade with China was already well established, but a 718 A.D. business letter, written on paper in the trade language of Judeo-Persian, is the first proof on paper (paper was produced only in China).

In the late 9th century, ibn Khurdadbih, the "Postmaster of Baghdad," spoke of Jewish traders (Radanites) who traveled from Spain and France to China and back via land and sea. Marco Polo met Chinese Jews in Běijīng around 1286, and in 1346, the Muslim traveler ibn Battuta entered Hángzhōu through the "Jew's Gate. He wrote of "Jews, Christians and sun-worshiping Turks, a large number in all."

During the mid 16th century, a Portuguese traveler wrote of China's "Moores, Gentiles, and Jewes, have all theyr sundry oathes," and that China's judges had them swear in courts "by the thynges they do worshyppe."

Matteo Ricci (Lì Mădòu, 利玛窦), famed Catholic missionary, is credited with discovering the Jewish community in Kāifēng (开封, N.E. Hénán 河南 Province). In truth, the Jews found Ricci—and thought he was a Jew!

A Jewish Chinese mandarin, Àitián (艾田), left Kāifēng in June, 1605, seeking a better post in Běijīng and a meeting with Ricci. Ài had read about Ricci's monotheism, and since Ricci stubbornly denied being a Moslem, the Chinese Jews concluded he must be a Jew.

Ricci was thrilled to meet Ài, and since Ài was a monotheist but stubbornly denied being a Moslem, Ricci concluded he was a Catholic. Ricci led him into the church, which Ài thought was a synagogue, and knelt before paintings of Mary, the baby Jesus, and a young St. John. Ài decided they must be Rebecca, Jacob and Esau, and the ever courteous Chinese politely knelt. He did remark that his people did not genuflect, but he had no objections to Ricci's peculiar method of honoring ancestors.

Ài asked why a painting of Matthew, Mark, Luke and John didn't include Jacob's other sons. In the end they cleared up the misunderstanding, to both party's delight, but it seems the Jews still considered Catholicism a mere offshoot of Judaism. In a 1608 letter to Ricci, the elderly rabbi of Kāifēng's synagogue (built in 1163) objected to Ricci's insistence that the Messiah had already come. But he said their other differences were minimal, and he suggested that Ricci succeed him as chief rabbi of Kāifēng—provided that Ricci first quit pigging out on pork.

Kāifēng's Jews are thought to have originated from either Persia, India, Bukhara, or Yemen. The fact that Quánzhōu and other coastal cities had Jewish communities suggests they arrived as traders by sea, rather than overland. But the Míng shut down the silk road and the silk sea, and the Jews succumbed to isolation (though they were never persecuted by the Chinese, as they were in most nations). Today, hundreds of Chinese Jews still dwell on the Kāifēng street named, "Lane of Sect that Teaches the Scriptures" (Jiàojīng Hútong, 教经胡同). Alas, no lox and bagels.

Whether the Lost Jews did come to China or not is debatable, but we did have lots of Lost Arabs, with at least 40,000 in ancient Quánzhōu. Their descendants today include the Dīng（丁）and Guō（郭）clans, some of whom have curly hair and hooked noses, and look more Lǎowài than Lǎonèi.

And it appears that some Chinese Arabs are as zealous as their Middle Eastern cousins. Back when Iran was after Salman Rushdie's hide for writing "Satanic Verses," N.W. China's Moslems were after a Chinese writer for heresy.

With so much running after folks, I can understand why back in 1935 they changed Persia's name to "**Iran**."

China—Ancient and Ageless

The weight of China's past is mind boggling. For Americans, an antique is a Barbie doll from 1959; for Chinese, it's a 2,025-year-old brass horse, or ancient woks and pans—or even ancient sauces!Sichuan sauces get tastier over time because saucepots are never washed. Xiàmén Univ.'s famed artist Táng Shǎoyún (唐少云) told me that his family's sauce is 14 years old, and that a Chéngdū family's sauce has been seasoning for over 200 years. The saucy rascal grinned slyly and said, "Their sauce is older than your country!"

An ancient nation has different views of "youth." On August 11, 1990, *China Daily* announced, "China's Ten Outstanding Young People." One of these ten outstanding youth was "go chess" world champion Niè Wèipíng (聂卫平). This "youth" was 39 years old.

Ponce de Leon, eat your heart out.

The Guest People Over 1,000 years ago, entire villages of "Guest People" (Kèjiā, 客家) migrated from the Central Plains to remote areas of Fújiàn. They have so faithfully preserved their ancient language and customs that many people mistake them for a minority, but they are Han and proud of it.

But even after 1,000 years, they still call themselves "Guest People". I have had guests wear out their welcome in one weekend. If I had a bunch stick around for 1,000 years, I'd shred the welcome mat and show them the door.

To avoid being shown the door, these gutsy "guests" built the giant earthen fortresses that have fascinated architects the world over, and which UNESCO dubbed. "The World's 8th Wonder".

The C.I.A. was as intrigued as UNESCO, though for different reasons.

Ready, Aim, Fire!

Hakka Silos? I told some Hakka friends that their homes were round so their wives couldn't corner them, and some agreed with me! But back in 1985, President Reagan and the CIA had a different explanation.

A CIA intelligence report warned,

"We are not joking here to use 'group'. The group nuclear base is likely to be a fact. According to our report through the KH22 satellite hovering, there are over 1, 500 unidentified huge mushroom-like buildings in Fujian Province of China, which are extremely similar to nuclear equipment. New penetrative satellites can observe through high buildings, but failed in front of the 1, 500 high-rises, in which China's sophistication of nuclear research can be seen. Therefore, it is necessary to grasp the nature of the buildings."

Quoted in *People's Daily*, April 7, 2004

In December, 1985, a couple from the New York Institute of Photography visited China to take photos—ostensibly of scenery and culture, but their real goal was to spy out the "silos." To their surprise, Zhāngzhōu's Federation of Literature & Art warmly welcomed them and proudly showed off the World's 8th wonder. Thus the CIA learned the "sophisticated" silos were earthen fortresses, some many centuries old.

NASA, meanwhile, is probably wondering if the saucer-shaped dwellings aren't proof that the ancient Min really did come from outer space.

Bombed

I saw a satellite dish on a remote roundhouse and I hacked off a Hakka elder by asking, "For tracking missiles?"

He didn't laugh. "No! Not missile! For TV! Basketball!"

That joke bombed.

Vertical Fújiàn—Home of Overseas Chinese There is one good reason that Fújiàn is home to most overseas Chinese around the world: geography. We have greater geological and botanical diversity than Eden, and I doubt even Eden's serpents could have matched our 33-foot pythons. (Fújiàn's nickname was "Serpent Kingdom").

What we do lack, however, is flat land.

Locals say Fújiàn is "8 parts mountain, 1 part water, 1 part field." (bāshān yìshuǐ yìfēntián, 八山一水一份田). Fújiàn would easily be China's biggest province if an ancient immortal flattened the place.

Farmers coped by terracing mountains top to bottom, and 1,000 years ago engaged in a massive coastal land reclamation project—but still not enough land. So famished Fujianese cut their apron strings and sought their fortune abroad, in spite of the Emperor's decree of death for anyone caught emigrating.

The descendants of those fleeing Fujianese now number only 3 to 4% of the population of many Asian countries, but they dominate 80% of the economy. Those who stayed home also made their mark.

Alexandria of Asia South Fújiàn's Quánzhōu, about 70 km. up the coast from Xiàmén, was the greatest port in the ancient world, rivaling Alexandria, Egypt. It was the start of the Maritime Silk Route（Hǎishàng Sìzhōu Zhīlù, 海上丝绸之路）and legends claim Sinbad himself visited this legendary port which Arabs called Zaytun (the origin of our word 'satin'). Marco Polo wrote:

> "And I assure you that for one shipload of pepper① that goes to Alexandria or elsewhere, destined for Christendom, there come a hundred such, aye and more too, to this haven of Zaytun; for it is one of the greatest havens in the world for commerce."

Jerusalem of Asia UNESCO called Quánzhōu a "World Museum of Religion" because it had virtually every major world religion. A Míng Dynasty stele in a Fúzhōu mosque records that 2 of the 4 disciples Mohammed sent to China went to Quánzhōu, which in its heyday had 7 mosques and 40,000 Moslems, as well as Nestorian Christians, Jews, Hindus, Tibetan Buddhists, Franciscans (the Chinese emperor himself funded three Franciscan cathedrals), Jews, and Jains.

Today, Quánzhōu has the planet's only surviving temple to Manichaeism, the ancient Persian religion that claimed people were but blameless pawns in a battle between Light and Dark forces. (This appealed greatly to St. Augustine, who followed Mani for ten years, partying heartily while famously praying , "Lord give me chastity—but not yet."

Babel of China (Pǔtōnghuà or Bùdǒnghuà? 普通话或不懂话?) Fújiàn's vertical topography influenced not just economics and politics but culture. Our mountains, valleys and rivers isolated villages so effectively that Fújiàn developed more idioms than any other province in China. In 1878, the missionary J.E. Walker wrote,

> "A native can hardly pass the limits of his own village but his speech will betray him... The tones seem utterly lawless."

Over a century later, in 1993, Qiū Huángxīng (邱煌星) wrote in *A Cultural Tour Across China*,

> "The dialects in Fújiàn count as the most complicated in China. The twenty-six million people in Fújiàn speak dozens of dialects, including the Mǐnnán dialect and the Púxiān (莆仙), Mǐndōng (闽东), Mǐnběi (闽北) and Hakka (客家) dialects, among over thirty minor ones. As for the different dialects within each county, they are simply too many to count. A friend from Fújiàn told me that once when somebody in his village got married, he was asked to go and borrow some dishes from a neighbor living in a village 1.5 km. away separated only by a hill and could neither understand nor make himself understood."

Amoy—the Original Chinese? Interestingly, research by missionary linguists back in the 1850s revealed that Fujian not only had the most dialects but that the Amoy Dialect (Minnan, or S. Fujian) was most like the ancient Chinese language of 2,000

① Some scholars doubt that Polo ever visited China. I think their greatest argument should be that he mentioned pepper but not MSG.

years ago. This is why many Korean and Japanese words (which originated from ancient Chinese) resemble Minnan Dialect. Examples:

English	Mandarin	Minnan	Korean	Japanese
Bridge	qíao	kio	kyo	kankyo
Book	shū	chheh	chaek	chosaku
Student	xuéshēng	hak-sing	haksaeng	gakusei
Dangerous	wēixián	gui-hiam	wiheom	nuclear power

Minnan Dialect Brought the World to Amoy Before the Opium Wars opened China to trade, merchants and missionaries worked with Chinese in other Asian countries. Since most were from Amoy, the foreigners learned the Amoy Dialect. Naturally, after China was forced open, foreigners came to where they did not have to learn a new language. Thus geography, and language, are the reasons that Xiamen had China's first Protestant church and missions, the earliest Protestant medical missions, and is known for its pioneering modern medicine, modern education, modern art and literature…. Xiamen, and especially Gulangyu, the "richest square mile on earth," had more influence on China, as well as other nations, than any other place its size. Amoy was a miniature Hong Kong on steroids—but that was a thousand years after the legendary battle between Amoy's egrets and serpents…

Xiàmén on the Rise While Jews, Arabs, Mongols and Chinese were wheeling, dealing and double dealing, Xiàmén Island was in the throes of a deadly battle for supremacy between egrets and poisonous snakes—or so the legend goes. The Egrets won, earning Xiàmén the nickname, "Egret Island" (Lùdǎo, 鹭岛). Some serpents must not have gotten the message, because I've come across a few slithering outside our XMU apartment. But neither snakes nor egrets kept away Sòng Dynasty (Sòngcháo 宋朝, 960-1127 A.D.) farmers who nicknamed Xiàmén "Jiāhé Island" (嘉禾岛), meaning "Isle of Abundant Crops." At that time, Amoy was under the jurisdiction of Tóng'ān County, Quánzhōu Prefecture. Nowadays the tables have turned, and Tóng'ān is part of Xiàmén, and probably glad of it, given Xiàmen's deep pockets.

The Citadel of Amoy

"Amoy is situated on an island of the same name. The city proper or citadel is about one mile in circumference. Its form is nearly that of a rhomboid or diamond. It is surrounded by a wall about twenty feet in height, and eight or ten feet in thickness, built of large blocks of coarse granite. It has four gates. The outer city, or city outside of the walls, is much more extensive. Its circumference, I suppose, is about six miles."

Rev. Talmage, Amoy, 1847

Imperial troops were stationed on Xiàmén back in 1058 (Sòng Dynasty). In 1282, one thousand soldiers oversaw political and military affairs in the "Thousand Households District."

Prince Zhōu Déxìng (周德兴) reinforced Xiàmén against the perennial plague of "pigmy bandits" (the Chinese term of endearment for Japanese pirates). The 4,000 households were divided into 22 wards governed by a city council, and the town was enclosed by miles of heavily fortified walls that survived the pigmy bandits but were razed in 1928 to make room for modernization. Oh well, life is still off the wall even if not within them.

China kept the pigmy bandits at bay but European Lǎowài were another matter. After Portuguese commenced trading with Xiamen in 1516, Zhāngzhōu and Quánzhōu merchants took up smuggling with foreign devils at the entrance to Xiàmén harbor on Wu Islet (浯屿).

In 1575, the Spanish sent a mission from Manila to Fúzhōu, but Fúzhōu showed them the door, so they turned their wills and wallets to Xiàmén, where locals would do anything for a peso—or dollar, or cowrie shell, or a …

Mad About Money in Amoy

"The currency question in Amoy is almost sufficient to turn one's hair grey... There are at least six or seven different kinds of the dollar coin in circulation at this port, viz, the Yen, Mexican, Hong Kong, French, Straits, and Hupeh dollar and some Manila pesos... None of these enumerated here pass for the standard dollar at this port. The Spanish dollar remains the standard tho it is not in circulation."

Rev. Pitcher, *In and About Amoy*, 1912

8 pounds of cash

The Dutch followed the Spaniards, and after seizing Táiwān in 1624, they smuggled silk and sugar between Táiwān and Jīnmén Island (the Táiwān-controlled island about 3 miles off shore). But the silk and sugar trades proved neither smooth nor sweet once Koxinga came aboard.

Koxinga (Zhèng Chénggōng, 郑成功) **Made-in-Japan Chinese Hero**[①] Ships entering Xiàmén Harbor are greeted by a massive statue that locals claim shields our port from rough seas and weather. The statue is of Zhèng Chénggōng (1624-1662), whom the Dutch called Koxinga and Japanese called Kokusen'ya or Tei Sēikō. (So Seiko was a watchman?)

Koxinga was born in 1624 in Hirado (Nagasaki) Japan, of a Chinese father, Zhèng Zhīlóng (郑芝龙), and Japanese mother (Tagawa Matsu). The last hero of the Míng Dynasty to stand against the Manchus, and the man who ousted the Dutch from Táiwān, Koxinga is today revered on both sides of the Táiwān straits, as well as in Japan, where 19th century plays about his exploits were as popular as Shakespearean

① Read about Koxinga & Dutch Taiwan governor Coyett in *Discover Gulangyu* plays in England.

Koxinga's father studied foreign trade in Macao. While applying Portuguese trade principles to piracy in Japan, he married Miss Tagawa Matsu, who bore Koxinga. Japanese legend has it that on the night of his birth the stars fell from the sky and the earth shook.

Like most fathers, Zhīlóng wanted his son to have what he had lacked as a youth—namely, lots of homework. He sent 7-yr-old Koxinga to school in their ancestral hometown of Nán'ān (南安, "Southern Peace"). Koxinga survived school and homework, and at age 21 headed off to Nánjīng State College, but his future lay not in scholastics but war.

I said "IRON" Apron!

After a peasant army overthrew the Míng, the Manchus waltzed into the power vacuum and created the Qīng (清) Dynasty. The Manchu's arrogance angered the Hans, who like most folk resented any arrogance but their own. They rebelled, and after a defeat in Fúzhōu in 1646, Koxinga's mother Tagawa committed suicide and Koxinga's father surrendered.

Filial piety dictated Koxinga also throw in the towel, but to his father's surprise he remained loyal to the Míng. He chose Xiàmén as the base for Ming's last anti-Qing army, and renamed the island Sīmíng (思明, "Remember the Míng"). Even today, one of Xiàmén's main streets is Sīmíng Rd.

Koxinga trained his legendary fighters from the heights of Gǔlàngyǔ's Sunlight Rock (Rìguāngyán, 日光岩). To qualify as his personal "Tiger Guard," soldiers had to heft a 600 pound iron lion. These hernia-proof warriors wore iron masks and iron aprons, wielded green bows and arrows, and used long handled swords for killing horses—a brilliant strategy Koxinga had learned in school while studying about the Great Wall, which was meant to keep out not barbarians but their horses. While Tartars on horseback were well nigh invincible, when on foot the Chinese made Tartar sauce out of them.

In April, 1661, Koxinga sailed from Xiàmén with 25,000 men and 100s of war junks to drive the Dutch from Táiwān and make it his base for anti-Qíng operations.

Chinese on both sides of the straits celebrated Koxinga's victory, and his men kicked back and played the "Mooncake Gambling Game" (you will too if you're in Xiàmén or Táiwān during Mid-Autumn Festival; see the Festivals chapter). But patriotism had taken its toll on Koxinga, who died five months later on June 23.

Táiwān's Last Dutch Governor Describes Koxinga's Troops

Neglected Formosa, by Coyett; quoted in *Discover Gǔlángyǔ*, by Dr. Bill

"The archers formed Koxinga's best troops, and much depended on them, for even at a distance they contrived to handle their weapons with so great skill, that they very nearly eclipsed the riflemen.

"Every 10th man of them is a leader who takes charge of and presses his men on to force themselves into the ranks of the enemy. With bent heads and their bodies hidden behind the shields, they try to break through the opposing ranks with such fury and dauntless courage, **as if each one had still a spare body left at home.** They continually press onwards, notwithstanding many are shot down; not stopping to consider, but ever rushing forward like mad dogs, not even looking round to see whether they are followed by their comrades or not".

A Chinese historian recently argued that Koxinga "died of overwork." May that be a sobering lesson to all.

Táiwān's return to the motherland was a windfall for traders in Xiàmén, just 100 miles across the Strait. Amoy became the choice port of call for both Chinese and foreign merchant ships. In 1684, the Qīng legitimized Xiàmén's claim to being the "Southern Gateway to China" by establishing a customs house. The British and Spanish flooded into Xiàmén, and by the early 1700s, even the once reviled Dutch had won a warm reception.

While foreign devils flooded in, the Sons of the Dragon flooded out, much to the Emperor's dismay. In 1728, the Emperor tackled Fujianese' mass emigration by warning that Chinese who did not immediately return to China would be banished or, if caught, executed. But nothing stemmed the tide. By the mid 19th century, there were 2½ times more overseas Chinese of Xiàmén origin than there were actual Xiàmén inhabitants.

Amoy coolies packed for shipment, Amoy. Rev. Pitcher, 1912

Paul Hutchinson wrote in 1920,

> "...About 60,000 people go out through Amoy each year on their way abroad, mainly to the Straits Settlements, Java, Borneo and the South Sea Islands... Amoy was the center for foreign trade almost earlier than any other city in the whole of China. The Dutch and the Portuguese traders came here as early as 1300. There are some graves of foreign men that date back to 1698, 1702 and 1710."

Today, Xiàmén is an ancestral Mecca for 350,000 overseas Chinese, and over 70% of Táiwān residents trace their origins to South Fújiàn – which helps explain why folks on both sides of the Táiwān Strait are so alike in dialect, dress, customs and cuisine.

The "Piggie" Trade

"Most coolies came from the southern, coastal provinces of China, especially Fukien...large numbers of men where shipped out through Hong Kong, Macau and other ports such as Amoy. They were, from the very start, exploited by Chinese coolie shipping agents and ships' captains – over a third of whom were Americans – then abused and treated atrociously by their employers.

"The trade in these unfortunate souls was known colloquially as the 'Pig Trade': the 'Poison Trade' was slang for the opium business. Crowded into corrals like slaves they were, as the British Consul in Canton observed in 1852, frequently painted with letters such as P, C or S meaning Peru, California or the Sandwich Islands.

"Whilst some were convicts on release or kidnap victims (we still use the contemporary expression, 'shanghaied'), over 95 per cent were indentured workers who, having had $50 paid for their sea passage on their behalf by would-be employers who regarded it as a loan against future income, were offered a wage they never saw for their loan and deductions for living expenses exceeded their earnings. Their traveling conditions were grim but because money had changed hands they were not legally slaves so no action could be taken against their shippers. Many died en route: one British-owned vessel, the John Calvin, lost 50 per cent of its passengers whilst American ships were often known to have 40 per cent mortality rates.

"Women were sometimes part of 'Pig Trade' cargoes. Under Chinese law females could not emigrate but coolie employers overseas wanted women: the aim was to make their indentured coolies settle in their new countries, thus alleviating the need to import more. The women were mostly either kidnapped or purchases under a Chinese system, known as mui tsai, which allowed for the sale of young girls as servants or concubines-in-training. This aspect of the trade was invidious: in 1855, the British vessel, Inglewood, hove to off Amoy with a cargo of female children all under the age of eight. The crew, disgusted at what comprised their cargo, reported it to the British consul who arranged for the children to be returned home."

Martin Booth, *Opium – A History,* 1996

Gulangyu Int'l Settlement, "Richest Square Mile on Earth!" (in 1920). In 1902, a Gŭlàngyŭ municipal council of six foreigners and one Chinese was elected. The new Int'l Settlement had consulates or consul offices for sixteen nations, including the U.S., Britain, France, Japan, Germany, Spain, Denmark, Portugal, Holland, Austria, Norway, Sweden, the Philippines, Belgium, etc.

Amoy Harbour in 1873, from Koolongsu. Photo by Thomson

Today, Gŭlàngyŭ's hundreds of colonial-era mansions (over 1,000) is a reminder of Old Amoy's immense wealth and talent. Only in Xiamen did Chinese and foreigners pool their efforts so closely to pioneer everything from modern medicine, music, literature and education to sciences, arts, and sports.

Gulangyu—Cradle of Tropical Medicine. Sir Patrick Manson, "Father of Tropical Medicine," made his monumental discoveries on tiny Gulangyu islet. It was on Gulangyu that Manson discovered the deadliest creature on earth, the "Amoy Vampire" (true story! Read the "Wildlife" chapter supplement).

It was not easy for the intrepid Scotsman to earn the trust of Chinese who for decades had heard that foreigners ate Chinese babies and used their eyeballs to line mirrors. When Dr. Manson insisted he'd come to 'serve' them, they may have thought he meant to serve them on a platter. He put their fears to rest by working from an open-air clinic to prove that his surgeon's scalpel didn't come in a set, with knife and fork. But Manson was lucky that Chinese never caught him on his midnight forays into graveyards, knife in hand…

Manson sought to understand Amoy's unusual ailments by dissecting everything from miniscule mosquitoes to corpses, but he dared enter the graveyards only in the dead of night because Chinese frowned on carving up corpses, particularly of loved ones. Manson's perseverance paid off. He was first to link mosquitoes with malaria, improved surgery for elephantiasis, and invented surgical instruments in use to this day.

Manson was loved by Lǎowài and Lǎonèi alike by the time he left to set up a school of medicine in Hong Kong, where one pupil was none other than Sun Yat-sen, the 1st President of China.

Nobel Laureate Laowai

Dr. Walter H. Brattain, born in 1902 on Gulangyu to missionary parents, obtained his Ph.D. in 1929, worked his entire life with Bell Laboratories, and was a co-winner of the Novel Prize for inventing the transistor, which made possible the laptop on which I am now typing.

Fall of Amoy Japan took possession of Gulangyu in 1938, and over 60,000 Chinese refugees crowded on the tiny island when Japanese bombed Amoy.

Britain had already surrendered her Gulangyu concession back in 1930 (while retaining rights n the International Settlement). Japan surrendered her concession in 1945, after losing the war, and the last foreign rights were relinquished by 1946. And then came Chairman Mao.

The Great Helmsman gained fame after leading thousands along the Long March (which was followed by the lesser known Short April). And then in 1949, Chairman Mao ousted us Lǎowài forever. Well, not quite forever.

We're back—but happily, this time we're not crashing the gate, but being warmly welcomed as Wàiguó Péngyǒu! (foreign friends, 外国朋友).

Village train stop, 1934. JeanetteVeldman (Hope Hospital nurse)

Amoy Bullet Train, 200+kph (2012)

Just 80 years ago, the Xiamen to Fuzhou trip took 5 days. In 1993, it once took me 15 hours to drive it. It is now only 3 hours by car or two hours by bullet train.

Post Liberation Xiàmén After 1949, one of Běijīng's first steps was to end Amoy Island's age-old isolation by connecting it to the mainland with a causeway and railway (see Jīměi chapter).

By the late 1950s, Xiàmén was producing advanced electrolytic capacitors, carbon resistors, and fish detectors. It had a booming chemical industry, and the textile industry produced synthetic and natural fibers. The Municipal Grain Bureau oversaw factory production and export of every conceivable foodstuff to dozens of countries.

Beijing also learned Amoy folk had banking in the blood. In the early 1900s, Xiamen bankers trotted about with baskets of money slung over their shoulders. In the 1920s, these "basket bankers" expanded operations to over 100 "Money Shops."

No wonder 1920s Gulangyu was the richest square mile on the planet, and Sun Yat-sen dreamed of making Xiàmén and Hăicāng an "Oriental Mega-Port." But the dream ended all too quickly.

While Běijīng worked at building a "New China," Chiang Kai Shek (Jiăng Jièshí, 蒋介石) worked to recapture the Old China, which included bombing Xiàmén back into the Stone Age. Běijīng finally put further construction on hold and beat the plowshares back into swords. While the rest of China forged ahead economically, Fújiàn Province, and especially Xiàmén, became a frontline defense against Táiwān.

By the late 1970s, once glorious Fújiàn had become one of China's poorest provinces. Xiàmén was no longer the Gateway to China but one giant bomb shelter, and Xiamen University students were going to class with "gun in one hand and pen in the other." Of course, by the mid-60s, Táiwān was all but forgotten anyway, as the Cultural Revolution (1966-1976) raged for an entire decade, wreaking havoc throughout China. Xiamen not only had to face U.S.-backed Taiwan but doing it while coping with angry Red Guards right at home.

Resurrecting Yúndāng Lake (筼筜湖). With one of the world's top ten natural deep harbors, Amoy was once a great haven for ships (Germany's favorite Asian port in the late 19th century), as well as one of Xiàmén's major aquatic production centers. But the Cultural Revolution brought development to a standstill. As the once scenic Yúndāng Lake choked with silt, some so-called experts suggested it be filled in and used as fields rather than a harbor.

Only during the early 1980s did China finally come to grips with the forces that had almost torn it apart, and Běijīng once again pursued its dream of making Xiàmén an economic powerhouse.

Thanks to a 400 million Yuán face-lift, the once squalid and noxious Yúndāng Lake is now the cultural center of Xiàmén, attracting tourists, real estate developers, and the wildlife that had fled over the previous few decades. The lake has hosted international aquatic sporting events, and weekend crowds throng the lakeside parks, watching the colorful Musical Dancing Fountains.

The Yúndāng clean-up received not only praise from the Central Government, but was also chosen by the Development Program of the United Nations as a demonstration site of the "Regional Program for the Prevention & Management of Marine Pollution in the East Asian Sea."

Amoy Reborn! In the early 1990s, Xiàmén was still considered one of China's less clean major cities. By the late 1990s it was recognized as China's most livable city—and the transformation was not just skin deep. Xiàmén is now idyllic not just for tourists but for residents, whether teachers, students, or business people.

Supplement

Getting a Bead on Business

Chinese have been boing up on business for thousands of years, and they have that beaded bone wonder, the abacus, to prove it.

While Xiàmén folk wholeheartedly embrace the future, they still cling to their cheap, energy-saving, immensely practical and highly accurate abacuses (or abacus), which in skilled hands are faster, and deadlier, than an electronic calculator.

I marvel every time a businessman or clerk flicks the black wooden beads up and down the brass rods faster than a Buddhist monk fingering his rosary. And when they present it to me for my verification, I never let on it's Greek to me.

I bought my first of many abacuses in Los Angeles' China town, and set about relearning the skills my first grade teacher, Ms. Magruder, had allegedly imparted to me decades earlier. And after reading the foolproof instruction booklet 3 times, I shelved the beaded bane. Years later, in Xiàmén, I bought a miniature abacus in the hope that smaller ones were easier, but it was still worse than Rubik's cube. No wonder they were invented by ancient Babylonians. Who but Saddam Hussein's ancestors would have dared?

The abacus began as a sand-covered board for scratching merchants' ciphers. Eventually someone scratched out some lines and added counters for tens, hundreds, and *deng deng*. Then the Romans added grooves to make it easier to slide the counters. Modern Chinese merchants now use wires to string up the counters and to string along their customers. And to this very day, the abacus beads are still pushed by Middle Eastern, Chinese and Japanese businessmen and schoolchildren, and by desperate economists.[1]

I still can't figure out the abacus, but I have a nice collection of them. In fact, I have a whole case of the miniature brass and jade versions, packaged in Chinese silk boxes. I present them to friends, along with the idiot-proof instruction booklet so they will have no excuse for failure.

Misery loves company.

[1] After countless economists telling him, "On this hand…" and "On the other hand…", President Roosevelt allegedly said, "I would give anything for a one-handed economist."

Chapter 3

Enjoy Amoy—First Steps

In love with Amoy!

"Boredom is always counter-revolutionary.
"Always."
Guy Debord, French philosopher

1988—Escape *from* Xiamen Xiàmén was so boring in the early 1990s that we escaped every chance we could to Hong Kong, or even to neighboring Zhāngzhōu, which though a backwater town had better shopping than Xiàmén. (On one excursion to Zhāngzhōu we bought two cases of excellent strawberry jam from Shānghǎi, which we rationed so carefully that they lasted us 3 years. We had no choice. Products were not marketed but distributed, and you might never see them on the shelves again).

By 1993 we had island fever, so we bought our van, Toy Ota, and began exploring China. After traveling around Fujian and neighboring provinces, in 1994 we drove 40,000 km to Tibet and back via Mongolia and the Gobi Desert. And the more we traveled the more we came to appreciate our home province of Fújiàn—especially Xiàmén. And over the years Xiàmén has changed so dramatically that we no longer seek escape from Xiàmén but ***to*** Xiàmén.

Toyota in Lhasa! (August, 1994)

China's #1 Destination! Chinese New Year, 2011, Xiàmén was China's #1 destination; Beijing was #2. Xiamen is now such a treat that Sue and I sometimes pretend we're on vacation right here in Amoy and spend a weekend enjoying local international restaurants (Greek, Turkish, Italian, Texan), and exploring the hilly lanes of Gǔlàngyǔ Islet, the former Int'l Settlement. We love Xiàmén's dozens of parks, or cycling the beautiful island ring road, which now has granite sculptures instead of granite tank traps, and facilities for windsurfing, sailing, sunning and swimming. And our 6 km. Xiamen Boardwalk is one of the best on the planet (see Parks chapter).

Xiàmén theaters show the latest films in both 3D and IMAX. We have several PGA class golf courses (one designed by Greg Norman), bowling alleys, museums and libraries, a water park, one of China's best marine aquariums, and a Táiwān Folk Village. We are also one of China's few cities to have our own Philharmonic Orchestras, and weekly performances of both homegrown and foreign talent.

I've given up counting how Xiamen malls. We have Germany's Metro (Màidélóng, 麦德龙), France's Carrefour (Jiālèfú, 家乐福), and Wal-Mart Supercenters (Wòěrmǎ, 沃尔玛) even across the street from each other. See the Shopping Chapter for details.

Today, there is no longer any excuse for suffering counterrevolutionary boredom in Xiàmén.

Amoy, 1900 (John Otte)

Suggestions for Exploring Amoy

1. Buy a bus pass: see Transportation chapter. Cheap, efficient; easy to use.

2. Buy a bilingual Xiamen map with latest bus routes from bookstore or map hawker near Gulangyu Ferry. Check our website for a printable 30-page bus route supplement.

3. Some of Xiamen's most popular sites include:

a. Gulangyu Islet: see Gulangyu chapter, or my book *Discover Gulangyu.* Xiamen University: see Cradle of Modern Chinese Education chapter, or my book, "*Xiamen University—Strength of the Nation.*"

c. Zhongshan Rd. (old downtown, 1920s); no cars so fun to stroll, especially at night when lit up; good shopping, dining, people watching' periodic exhibits.

d. Xinjie Church, China's 1st Protestant church, circa 1848; see Birthplace of Chinese Protestantism chapter.

d. Nanputuo Temple, circa 686 A.D., near XMU; "Chinese" Religions chapter)

e. Botanical Garden, 6 km. Boardwalk, 8 km. Railroad Park, Yundang Lake Dancing Musical Fountains, Music Park, etc.; see Parks Chapter.

f. Boat ride to Taiwan-controlled Jinmen Island: see Tong'an & Jinmen chapter

4. Enjoy Chinese and foreign cuisines. The "Living on Amoy" section includes an extensive bilingual menu so those who can't speak Chinese can just point and pay.

5. Join in on both Chinese *and* foreign festivals: see Festivals & Culture Chapter.

6. Visit world-class attractions (several UNESCO World Heritage Sites) in our Fujian Province. I have spent months driving around Fujian, and wrote and filmed a 62-part mini documentary about Fujian sites. Endless attractions include: Hakka round houses, Amoy tigers, Quanzhou (Marco Polo's celebrated start of maritime silk route), Anxi (China's great tea center), Dehua (ancient porcelain center), Sanming (China's largest sleeping Buddha, gem mines, etc.), Baishuiyang (where locals literally walk on water), Zhouning (carp worshippers), Quanzhou marionettes (world famous), Zhangzhou hand puppets, Longhai basalt volcano, etc.

See "Favorite Fujian Destinations" on Amoymagic.com for more ideas.

Supplement: Fallen Arches

Explore Old Amoy—while you still can

Collections of 19th and early 20th century photos of Xiàmén often include photos of magnificent stone memorial arches built over 300 years ago in memory of two great Chinese generals. But they were partially destroyed by the Japanese during the war, and after Liberation razed so completely for new construction that it took years to find their location.

The grand memorial arches once stood at the intersection of Tácuòshé Rd. (塔厝社路) and #50-58 Jiāngjūncí Rd. (将军祠路50-58号), near Xiamen City Hotel (Xiàmén Bīnguǎn, 厦门宾馆). The arches are long gone, but this site still has remnants of artwork unlike anything I have seen in China.

Rider on Chinese Elephant

Just inside the gate are two small doorways to the left. The small courtyard just inside the rear doorway has old columns that are a century or more old, but the real treasure is the artwork below the eaves and above the windows. I was astonished to see a bas-relief of a bushy bearded foreigner in high hat riding a Chinese tiger (symbolic of foreigners running roughshod over China?). To either side of this foreign daredevil were flying deer, replete with antlers and wings; evidently Santa Claus was not the first to get about by reindeer.

Another carving was of a rider on what Prof. Chau Tam Luan, a visiting Vietnamese Overseas Chinese, said was a Chinese elephant.①

I joked with my Chinese friends that the elephant's eyes looked Western, but the Chinese professor explained that the ears, not the eyes, made it Chinese. However, whether the rider was Chinese or foreign no one could say since the face was disfigured so badly-and the few remaining historical treasures will also vanish if we do not take protective measures.

Much of Xiàmén's history has been lost through neglect or wanton destruction. Two stone lions in front of the nearby bike repair shop are so weathered I could barely discern what they represented.

We can't save everything from the past. If we did, there'd be no room for the present (especially in China, which has so much past). But it's a pity that the only arches left in Xiamen today are McDonald's golden arches. I hope Xiamen will take measures to protect the few remaining historical sites, and to put up bronze plaques explaining their historical significance.

Over the years, officials in nearby Quánzhōu have told me, "Xiàmén, unlike Quánzhōu, has no history-only 600, 700 years." But while Xiàmén's history is relatively short—by China's standards—it is rich, and we should treasure our past, so

① The mind's like a horse on a plain; easy to let loose but hard to stop. Chinese Proverb that our future generations may learn from it and build upon it.[①]

Supplement

Origin of Xiamen Street Names

by Robin (fèifēi, 费菲)

Amoy street, 1930s

Street names have two sources:

1) traditional and custom, or
2) government decree.

Traditional names have 5 sub-categories

1. Roads named for industry or avocation:
   dǎtié jiē (打铁街): "Forge iron and steel" Street
   dǎxíbó xiàng (打锡箔巷): "Forge tin & oil" Street
   màijí xiàng (卖鸡巷): "Felling chicken" Lane
   shúròu xiàng (熟肉巷): "Selling cooked meat" Lane
2. Roads named after local features:
   shíbì Jiē (石壁街): "Stone Wall" Street
   túdui xiàng (土堆巷): "Dirt Pile" Lane (teacher's dorm?)
   kuàngzǎi jǐng (矿仔井): "Mine" Well
   mángguǒ jiǎo (芒果脚): "Mango" Lane
   Liǎohuā lù (蓼花路): "Polygonum Flower" Rd.
3. Roads named after temples or palaces:
   měirén gōng (美仁宫): "Beauty & Benevolence Palace
   māzǔ gōng(妈祖宫): "Mazu Palace
   chénghuáng miào (城隍庙): "Chenghuang Temple"
4. Roads named after prominent families who lived there:
   Sūcuò xiàng(苏厝巷): Sucuo Lane
5. Roads named after famous personages' tombs:
   báicuò mù (白厝墓): "White tomb"
   mǎ mù (马墓): "Ma's tomb", etc.s

Government-named Roads have two categories

1. Names borrowed from other places: Fúzhōu Lù (福州路), Zhāngzhōu Lù (漳州路), Tàishān Lù (泰山路)
2. Names reflecting desirable qualities or attributes: Tàipíng Lù (太平路, "peace"), Zìqiáng Lù (自强路, "self-improvement") and Xìng'ān Lù (兴安路, "prosperity and peace")

Note: Many cities have names such as Zhōngshān Lù (中山路—Sun Yat-sen), and Sīmíng Lù (思明路), "Remember the Ming!" (Koxinga's patriotic war cry)
lù (路), jiē(街), and dào (道) = Street; xiàng (巷) = lane

---

① Those who retreat 50 paces laugh at those who retreat 100 paces. Chinese Proverb

Supplement 2
A Laowai's Life in Xiamen

Stephen Potter, Xiamen businessman and photographer
(Thanks, Stephen, for supplying some of this book's photos)

I've lived and worked in China for over 12 years, with 4 in Quanzhou and the rest in Xiamen.

I first came to China in January, 1999, to set up an inspection office for containers shipped from China. I'd tried to hire Chinese for this but it didn't work because most used the opportunity to go into business for themselves. I had no choice but to run the business from a China office—but over the years I've learned much about Chinese culture and working with Chinese.

China is not the same country it was 10 years ago. Back then, no one stopped at stop lights and people walked down the middle of streets in Quanzhou or Xiamen without encountering any significant traffic. Even people's attitudes were different, as was their clothing, and the way they walked. People from Taiwan or Hong Kong stood out like a sore thumb, though today it is the mainlanders who dress better, as they compete to outspend and outdo each other.

Living and working in China, especially as the owner of a company, gives a much different impression of Chinese than you'd get from touring or teaching. It gets down to the nitty gritty of daily life with everyone competing to find a way to make a living or build a business. Chinese are fiercely competitive in the background and very friendly in the foreground. This is the accepted and expected way of life. I tell people who want to do business in China to expect it to be much like the driving. There are loosely followed rules but if someone has a chance to cut in front they will. There are no real "right of ways" – just opportunities to be grabbed to get ahead.

I lived in Quanzhou, Song Yu and Hai Cang: all the areas I had factories. Those places have their own type of energy but it takes a bit of getting used to. I later moved to the better part of Xiamen when my daughter came to stay with me; after she left, I just stayed on in the city where it was more convenient. It is easy to get spoiled.

In my first year, I was in an outdoor street restaurant and saw a group of men sitting around the tables arguing violently. They even jumped up and gave each other rude gestures, shaking their fists and shouting even louder. Eventually they seemed to settle the argument, have a drink and sit back down—and then they went at it again. I really expected a fist fight but it never got that far. Later, I learned they were only playing a popular drinking game, but at the time it was certainly confusing. It takes patience to understand Chinese and their way of life, and a willingness to let them work out situations in their own way. I learned to not get excited when things don't go right – to learn from it, and learn to be a good observer of the different types of characters involved.

I enjoy many things in Xiamen, especially parks. The 10,000 Stone Botanical Garden is a favorite place for a hike. It takes a while to discover all of the park's side trails and mini hikes. Zhong Shan Park, Fox Tail Hill and others can keep a nature lover occupied. A very good hike is from the Botanical gardens over the top of the hill and down into Nan Putuo Temple. Yun Dang Lake and Egret Park can take a few hours to walk around—or you can take a shortcut by using one of the many bridges. And little Gulangyu islet, just off Xiamen island, has many interesting buildings and shops, photo opportunities, interesting places to eat, and best of all—no cars! The crowds are a bit much at times, but there are still many places where a person can walk quietly and enjoy the surroundings.

One of the things that kept me sane was my camera. I visited many places, often stopping to take pictures of things most tourists would never see. These may not be highlights of life or fantastic scenic views but they are views of everyday life, of old people with young children, harvests spread on the roads, people working in the fields, daily life on back street noisy markets in small towns, and the small dirty roads with the small shops where all the real activity goes on.

I take photos wherever I go, looking for the ordinary things in life that can be isolated into an interesting and hopefully artistic composition.

My favorite photo subject is flowers of all kinds, and Xiamen is one of the best places for flowers. There doesn't seem to be a season when there aren't any flowers. Even in the winter there are flowers somewhere. In spring there is a constant succession of different trees each lining up one after the other to show off their many blooms. This year was one of the best. It had rained a lot during the spring and the trees outdid themselves with their blooms.

Each flower is unique with interesting and beautiful features. It might seem crazy to keep taking pictures of the same types of flowers over and over but each time I look for a new composition, prettier flower, different lighting, better background, different depth of field – there is always a better picture to find.

The climate in Xiamen is sub-tropical, with the weather tending to get hot in the summer but early mornings are refreshing and the evenings cool off. For spring and fall it is hard to find better weather anywhere. One of my favorite ways to relax is in a coffee house sitting under the shade of trees and shooting the breeze with people foolish enough to listen. Xiamen is one of the most comfortable cities to live in – not just as a city in China but generally for quality of life. There may not be a huge variety of entertainment and fantastic artistic venues but for daily life, and what a person does in their regular life, it is a good city to live in.

Xiamen after a storm. Stephen Potter

Chapter 4

Gŭlàngyŭ Islet① Overview

"Across a narrow channel—then an hour-and-a-half distant by slow junk [1/4 mile] —lay Kulangsu [Gulangyu], a place of comfortable retirement for the more affluent merchants and at one period a competitor for the reputation of being the "wealthiest square-mile in the world." Norman Goodall, 1920

"The foreigners generally live on Kulangsu, a small island in Amoy Harbor, with a shore line of about 3 miles, and one of the most picturesque places to be seen on the whole coast of China. Incidentally it might be states that there are more wealthy men living on Kulangsu than in any other spot in the world, with the exception of Pasadena, California." Hutchinson, 1920

#1 in China! Chinese New Year, 2011, Xiamen was mainland China's top tourist spot (Beijing was #2), and Amoy's crown jewel is the 1.77 km^2 Gŭlàngyŭ Islet (鼓浪屿 "Drum Wave Islet"). In the early 20th century, the "richest square mile on earth" had 14 consulates. Today, the hundreds of "Amoy Deco" mansions make the islet an unparalleled open-air museum of international architecture (we are applying for UNESCO World Heritage Site status).

Why the wealth? Unlike anywhere else in China, Amoy's rich and talented Chinese and foreigners pooled their brains and bank accounts to pioneer modern education and medical work.

The islet had China's first Protestant missions and medical work, and where Sir Manson, "Father of Tropical Medicine," first linked mosquitoes to malaria. Tiny Gulangyu had 20 pioneering educational institutions, and was home to leading educators, scientists, artists, writers, and over 100 famous musicians.

① *Discover Gulangyu* 《魅力鼓浪屿》& *Old Gulangyu in Foreigners' Eyes*《老外看老鼓浪屿》

Gulangyu (Kulangsoo), 1897

"By the treaty of Nanking which followed, Amoy was thrown open to foreign trade, and since that period residents have enjoyed a complete immunity from any attempts on the part of the Chinese authorities to dislodge them. It is the most accessible of all the Consular ports in China...Amoy has been celebrated as a trading town for more than a thousand years, and was one of the earliest seats of European commerce in China. The Europeans engaged in trade here have their residences on Koo-lang-soo...This may be considered one of the healthiest ports in China, and is seldom visited by epidemic sickness, as the cemetery can show. Compared with other ports, Kulangsoo may be said to be exceptionally healthy, and may be denominated the 'beautiful isle of the sea.'...The climate of Kulangsoo is one of the finest in China...

"The total number of foreign residents of all nations including Customs employees is about 300...

"Kulangsoo boasts of a Club, which is an admirable institution, and largely patronized by the residents. There are also Race, Cricket and Lawn-tennis Clubs, formed of the leading members of the community, and two Masonic Lodges." *Amoy — Physical Features, Monuments, Temples, &c.* by J. S.

The China Review, Vol. 22 No. 5 (1897)

Gulangyu: China's 1st Protestant Medical Missions "The year 1844 is a noted one in the history of medical missions. In January Drs. Hepburn and Cumming opened a hospital in the city of Amoy..."

Chinese Recorder, Vol. 5, Shanghai

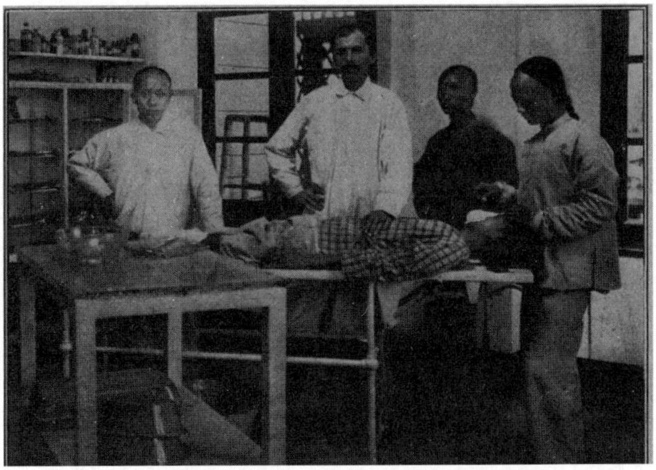

Dr. Otte operating with Chinese assistants

"The only local records of these early [foreign] traders are the tombstones on Kolongsu which mark their last resting place. Recently [1905] they were taken up and placed in the Foreign Cemetery. On their tombstones are these dates 1698, 1700, and 1710. Even tradition has failed to leave any trace of the site of the English factory." Pitcher 1905, p.43

Girl students, Gulangyu, 1921
Photo by Jean Nienhuis (Head nurse, Hope Hospital)

Gulangyu's Pioneering Women's Education In 1845, Rev. Lyman Burt Peet (弼来满) started China's first day-school on Gulangyu, and William Young (养为霖) opened Fujian's 1st school for girls about the same time. One of China's first kindergartens, Gulangyu Huaide Kindergarten (鼓浪屿怀德幼儿园), was built in early 1898. (Read "Cradle of Modern Chinese Education" chapter).

Famous Gulangyu residents have included:

Dr. Lin Qiaozhi （林巧稚）， "Mother of Modern Chinese Medicine"
John Ma （马约翰), "Father of Modern China's Sports"
Teng Hiok Chiu （周廷旭), internationally famous artist and first Chinese to win an Olympic medal (with British basketball team, Paris, 1924)
Yu Qingsong (余青松), famous astronomer
Lin Yutang（林语堂), globally respected Chinese writer
Lu Zhuangzhang（卢戆章), "Father of Pinyin"
Yin Chengzong（殷承宗), "China's best pianist" (New York Times), and over 100 other famous Chinese musicians
Sir Patrick Manson, "Father of Tropical Medicine"
Walter Brattain, Nobel Prize for co-inventing the transistor.
Horace Talmage Day, famous American artist born and raised on Gulangyu (painting of Amoy, age 8, influenced his style).

...And literally hundreds of other Chinese and foreigners who worked together to make Amoy perhaps the only place in 18th and 19th century China that was truly international.

Read more in the education chapter.

Getting to Gulangyu

The Xiamen-Gulangyu Ferry The ten minute ride, at this writing, costs 8 Yuan roundtrip. It's a bargain. Wartime inflation in the 1940s jacked the price to over 6 million dollars—one way!

Buy a token at the ticket office on the Xiamen side (end of Zhongshan Rd., facing Lujiang Hotel). Scan the token but keep it, as you will need to insert it in the turnstile slot when you return from Gulangyu. Or you can swim.

6 million Yuan ferry ride, 1940s

The 8 Kilometer Round Islet Cruise is inexpensive and offers glimpses of Monkey Isle, Pearl Isle (Băozhūyú), and Burning Isle (Huŏshāoyú), an extinct volcano.

Getting About Gulangyu Cars, bikes and skateboards have long been banned on Gulangyu, so wear good walking shoes. Electric tourist carts (60 Yuan for pick up or drop off at five places, once each place) are nice on a hot, muggy day, but I love exploring the quaint narrow lanes. A bit of imagination can transport you back a century to the heyday of "the richest square mile on earth."

Gulangyu Turkish Ice Cream Cone

Gŭlàngyŭ Shopping Gŭlàngyŭ has Xiamen's best selection of handicrafts, arts and souvenirs—and some of the best prices.

Laowai favorites include Chinese cultured pearls (best prices and quality at Pearl World, on Lóngtóu Rd.), glass bottles and globes hand painted from the inside (Jimmy Carter said they were "Miraculous!"), oil paintings (Xiamen is the world's greatest production base; our artists can copy anything from a van Gogh to a family photo), Chinese fans, Minnan tea sets and tea, paper parasols (Japanese got them from us, and refined them; they even have paper beach umbrellas), seashells (amazing variety), and of course strange dried Chinese fruits and meats--seahorse, starfish, scorpion, shark's fin. Chinese eat anything. If it is truly inedible, they process it, call it Chinese medicine, and eat it anyway.

Gŭlàngyŭ Mall, facing the Ferry (can't miss the McDs and KFC) looks colonial but was finished in 2001. I like the "Gentle Reminder" at the top floor's Nana Inn: "Please stop if you aren't living….!"

Not a problem. When I cease living, I will certainly stop.① But not before.

The square often has performances of traditional music, and popcorn and candy. Also try the traditional snacks (fish ball soup), as well as treats like Turkish ice cream, sold up Longtou Rd. past the beef jerky stall (family-owned since 1842!).

And take a moment to chat and have tea with the merchants, who will invited you to "He cha!" "Have some tea!" (Our word "chai" comes from Mandarin's "cha," but "tea" comes from the local dialect's word for tea, "dei.").

---

① A Chinese reporter asked if I'd stay in China until I die. "Yes," I said, "and put my ashes in a coffee can, not a boring old urn—but *decaf*, so it doesn't keep me awake."

Dragon Head (Longtou) Rd., Gulangyu, 1942 J. Anderson

Dragon Head St.(龙头街), which winds past the Mall, has been Gulangyu's Main Street for a century. Both sides have shops selling tea and teapots, Chinese art and handicrafts, a bookstore, puppets & marionettes, etc.

Sleight of Hand-Puppets

Marco Polo's fabled port of Zaytun, 60 miles north of Amoy, has long been China's marionette capital, and Zhāngzhōu (漳州), to our west, is famous for hand puppets. But you can enjoy performances right on Gŭlàngyŭ.

These aren't like my childhood toys, or the cheap plastic George Bush and Saddam Hussein "boxing puppets" sold in some Gŭlàngyŭ shops. In the hands of a Chinese master puppeteer, they are pure magic—the closest thing in this life you'll find to real little people (elves, fairies, leprechauns, lame duck presidents, non-tenured professors…).

Some puppets puff long pipes and blow more smoke than politicians in a primary. Others pour tea from tiny pots into thimble-sized cups. Still others dance, juggle, or perform astonishing comic and acrobatic routines, tossing spinning plates and catching them on poles, juggling a barrel on their heads—or even tossing and flipping each other!

One Chinese sagely observed of foreigners laughing at puppets, "It's because foreigners don't have puppets." He reminded me of the farmer who said, "Foreigners don't have fireworks." Actually, we have both fireworks and puppets. But few folks wield the magic to bring the creatures to life. I once snuck back stage to see if they might not be using real little people, but nary a lame duck president in sight.

Take in a Zhāngzhōu puppet show, and then take home a handcrafted puppet for only 50 to 100 Yuan. Arrange a private show by contacting Mr. Hong Mingzhang (洪明章). Tel: 206-9933, or 897-3331. Mobile: 13666008151 Address: #2 Zhōnghuá Rd (中华路二号) Gŭlàngyŭ.

Top Gŭlàngyŭ Sites Chinese cities' glossy brochures make boasts like, "1,043 Scenic Sights famous home and abroad." Quánzhōu claims over 2,000. But with Gŭlàngyŭ, it's no brag, just fact. Sites include the hundreds of Amoy Deco villas, plus relics of foreigners' three centuries of occupation and trade.

For more in-depth information, refer to *Discover Gulangyu*.

1. Ferry Quay
2. Former English Consulate (1844)
3. Underwater World
4. Book Store
5. Former Spanish Consulate (1850)
6. Xiamen # 2 Hospital
7. Catholic Church, Japanese Consulate
8. Piano Island Hotel
9. Beautiful Island Hotel
10. Bank of China
11. Concert Hall
12. Xiamen Music School
13. Marine Environmental Center
14. Library
15. Former Dutch Consulate
16. People's Stadium
17. Gulangyu Hotel
18. Dragon Head Hill
19. Sunlight Rock
20. Zhengchengong Museum
21. People's Primary School
22. Xiamen Trinity Christian Church
23. Qin Dynasty Statuary Exhibit
24. Gulangyu Local Government
25. Cavern of Horror
26. Bishan Park
27. Xiamen #2 Middle School
28. Stadium
29. Xiamen Museum
30. Longshan Cave
31. Former U.S. Consulate (1865)
32. Former Salvation Hospital (1898)
33. Yanwei Hill
34. Xiamen KLI Cactus Park
35. Post Office Training Center
36. Jide Palace
37. Fujian Arts & Crafts School
38. Gulangyu Experimental Ctr. of Fujian Prov. Agric. Res. Instit.
39. Langdong Hill
40. Gulangyu Fishery Shipyard
41. Gulangyu Villa
42. Gulangyu Villa Ferry (C.T.S.)
43. Gulang Rock
44. MeiHua Beach
45. Xiamen O.C. Subtropical Garden
46. Bird Garden
47. Piano Garden
48. Cable Cars to Sunlight Rock
49. Gulangyu Naval Sanitorium
50. Gulangyu Army Sanitorium
51. Gusheng Tunnel
52. Gangzaihou Beach
53. Gospel Hall
54. Yanping Park
55. Shuzhuang Gardn
56. Cadre's Sanitorium
57. Seaview Garden Holiday Resort
58. Former Denmark Telegraph Offic
59. Seaview Villa Ferry
60. Seaview Villa Beach
61. Yu Garden
62. Former Yude Girl's School (1880)
63. Dadeji Beach
64. Cadres' Econ. & Trade School
65. Lodge Cabin
66. Koxinga Stone Statue
67. Bright Moon Park
68. Fuding Beach
69. Flag Raising Hill
70. Just getting started....

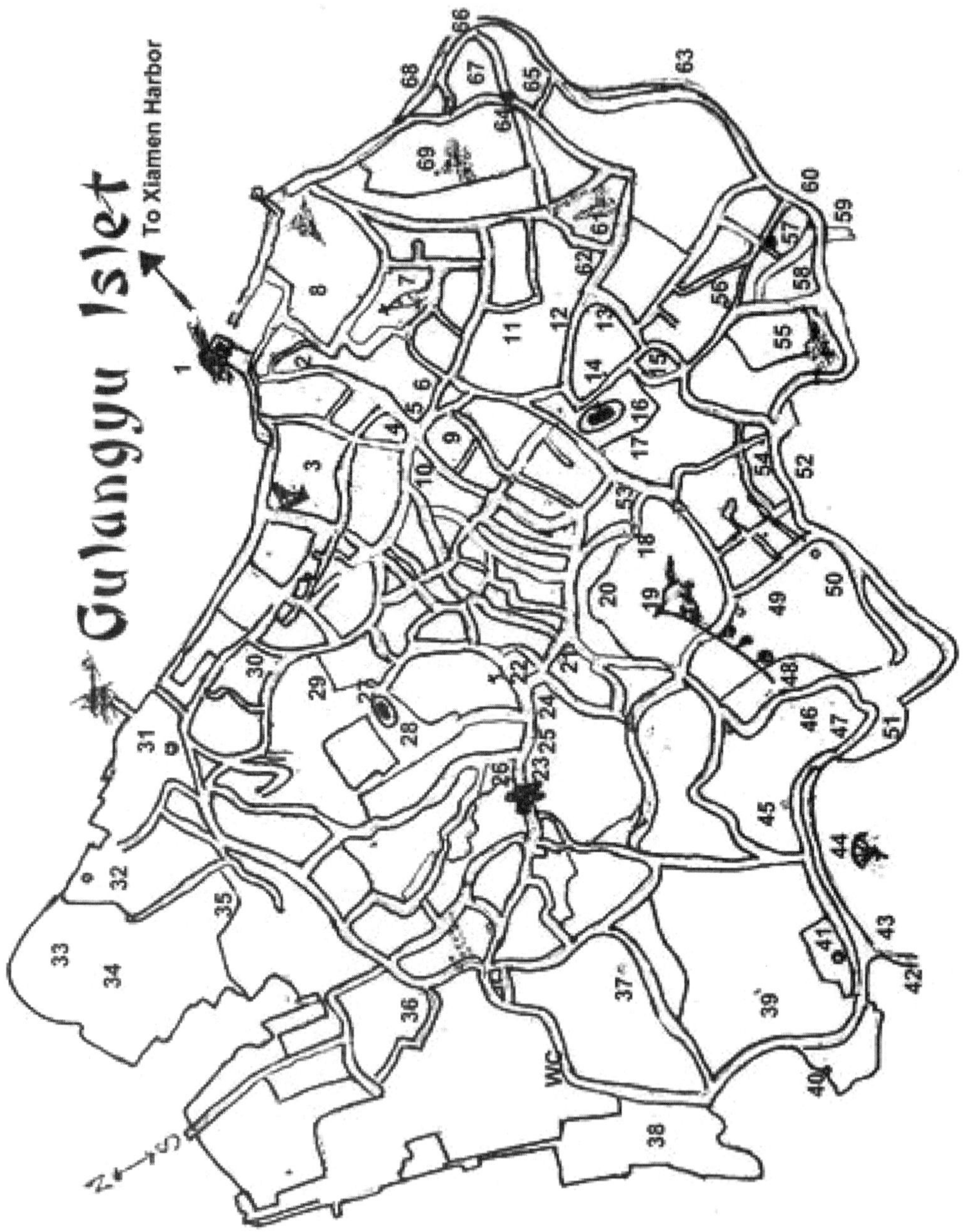
Gulangyu Islet
To Xiamen Harbor
WC

Isle of Music You'll soon see—or *hear*--why Lǎowài loved this little isle. Even today, it has one asset rare in China: **quiet!** Cars and bikes have always been forbidden, so the islet is blissfully quiet (except on holidays), but one sound you *will* hear is pianos.

Chinese band, Amoy, 1900. John Otte

South Fújian has many indigenous music forms, including the popular 1,000-yr.-old "Nányīn Opera." But Xiàmén also excels in modern music. Gǔlàngyǔ has produced over 100 famous musicians, and now has more pianos per capita (one for every five families) than anywhere else in China.

Pianos & Preachers In the 1840s, missionaries came with Bibles in one hand and pianos in the other; very big hands.

Amoy had China's first Protestant Church① (1848), and in 1862, foreigners chipped in to build Gulangyu's Union Church (try their Saturday night music performances). The Doty family had Gulangyu's first piano in the 1850s, and Gulangyu folk have been hooked on pianos ever since.

Famous Gulangyu pianists have included Zhōu Shǔ' ān (周淑安) in the '20s, Lín Jùnqīng (林俊卿) in the '30s, Wú Tiānqiú (吴天求), in the '50s, Xǔ Fěixīng (许斐星) in the '60s, Xǔ Fěipíng (许斐平) in the '80s, and Chén Zuǒhuáng (陈佐湟) and Xǔ Xīng (许星) in the '90s. And we're still churning them out today. Not an evening passes that some family's budding pianist is not holding a recital. Many go on to study in the Amoy Music Academy, and from there to play in London, New York, Paris—or the local churches from whence the pianos came in the first place. It's no wonder that Gǔlàngyǔ has **Asia's largest piano museum,** as well as one of the world's best Organ Museums (see "Museum Chapter").②

---

①Catholics were also busy. The Vicariate Apostolic of Amoy—Dominican, circa 1883—included Taiwan, & oversaw 11 European and 8 Chinese priests, 32 churches or chapels, 3 orphanages, and 13 schools.

② Chinese Proverb: To prosper 1 year, grow grain; to prosper 10 years, grow trees; to prosper 100 years, grow people.

Xiamen Philharmonic Orchestra was established in 1998 by internationally renowned conductor Prof. Zhèng Xiǎoyīng (郑小瑛). In spite of their motto, "Highbrow art will be increasing popular," lowbrows like myself enjoy their over 100 works. Zheng is well loved because she not only conducts the music but also takes time each performance to explain the music, making each event both enjoyable and educational.

"I have cooperated with other Chinese orchestras like the National Symphony Orchestra, Běijing Symphony Orchestra and Shanghǎi Symphony Orchestra. The one in Xiàmen is quite different though because the members are so young and surprisingly, so well disciplined." Eric Lederhandler [Belgian conductor] said.

Vivian Zhang, Xiamen Daily's Common Talk, Nov. 2004

Chinese Opera

Just past Húlǐ Hill Fort (***not*** Gǔlàngyǔ, but on the Island Ring Rd.) is an open-air stage where you can catch one of the locals' favorite pastimes: a unique version of Chinese Opera that has resulted from centuries of collaboration between artists in Táiwān and Southern Fújiàn.

After Koxinga's unpeaceful liberation of Táiwān from the Dutch in 1662, Fujian folk migrated to Táiwān and introduced their folk music, which developed into Gezi Opera (which in turn was influenced by Liyuan Opera, Gaojia Opera, Peking Opera, and Opera Winfrey). Gezi Opera then recrossed the Táiwān Straits to Xiàmén and Southern Fujian, and after some innovation it was renamed "Xiang Opera."

In town and country alike, audiences are enthralled by the lively, melodic stories told in simple language. Favorites include "Liang Shanbo and Zhu Yingtai," which is China's version of "Romeo and Juliet." Others include "Dumb Girl Sues," "A Tale of the White Snake," "True and False Princes," and "Five Daughters Offer Birthday Felicitations."

Xiàmén folk also enjoy Gaojia Opera. This lively combination of singing and acrobatics originated over 200 years ago in Quanzhou, and used to be called Songjiang Opera because it is about Song Jiang, chief hero of the classic "Outlaws of the Marsh." Clowns are the heart and soul of this cynical yet comical opera.

More music? Try…

Xiàmén Piano Museum (Asia's Largest) and **Organ Museum** (soon to be the world's largest; see "Museum" chapter).

Xiàmén Music Square—open-air music museum, performances (see "Parks" chapter). Location: Island Ring Road.

Savour Gŭlàngyŭ's silence, punctuated by preschoolers practicing scales or "Chopsticks,"[1] then steal a glimpse of the ancient harbor and skyline from Gŭlàngyŭ's Sunlight Rock, where the hero Koxinga drilled his troops before retaking Taiwan from the Dutch. The admission price also includes the cable car, aviary, Koxinga Memorial, and heat stroke.

After your sweaty ascent of Sunlight Rock (formerly Camel Rock), cool off in a coffee shop, or with a speedboat tour around the island. Then visit Dragon Hill, Hoisting Flag Hill, or parks where Chinese will eagerly point out ancient engravings.

For most of its 5,025 years, China lacked TV and internet, so folks watched rocks instead (eminently patient people). They eulogised every rock, boulder and mountain in China with calligraphic inscriptions,[2] which to the uninitiated (like me) are essentially ancient graffiti sanctified by time.

Just kidding. Sort of.

Conquering Camel Rock, Gulangyu, 1920s

Underwater World Xiamen（厦门海底世界）, just to the right as you exit the Gŭlàngyŭ Ferry, has more fish than most Xiamen restaurants. Over 10,000 finned folk of 350 fresh and salt water species swim in 17 large and small tanks, a rock pool, a cylindrical tank, and two immense shark and reef tanks.

Two 80-meter tunnels allow you to walk under the tanks (and sharks) without getting soaked by one million liters of water. Visit the Penquin and Freshwater Fish Hall, Ocean Fish Hall, Sperm Whale Hall, and Dolphin and Sea-Lion Performance Hall.

A joint-venture with Singapore Xingwang Holding Limited Company and Gŭlàngyŭ Beauty Spot Construction Company, the facility is open daily, 8:30 AM to 8:00 PM. Present a valid student card for a discount.

Swimming in Amoy, 1920s J.N

Add: Gŭlàngyŭ, #2 Dragon Head Rd. (鼓浪屿龙头路 2 号.) Tel: 2067668

---

① Chopsticks: Waltz written in 1871 by English composer Arthur de Lulli

② Chinese Proverb: Jade is useless until polished; man is worthless until educated.

Gulangyu Gardens (adapted from *Discover Gulangyu*)

Li Qingquan Villa

Gulangyu is a riot of floral colours and scents, of gardens large and small at every turn. Even the smallest household displays choice potted plants on balconies and rooftops, while larger villas boast finely sculpted trees, roses, and azaleas, and bougainvillea in blazing hues of red, pink and purple.

Gulangyu gardens reflect owners' tastes, temperaments, and education—or lack thereof. Some gardens' intricate detail overpowers the senses, while some are elegantly simple—almost Zen. Still others are simply in bad taste, though even the gaudiest gardens are worth a gander—at least once.

Shuzhuang Garden's "9 Bend 44 Bridge" snakes across the water likc a bcfuddlcd bamboo viper.

Shuzhuang (bean plantation) was built by a Taiwanese businessman who moved here with his family during the Sino-Japanese War of 1894—1895.

With its stone bridges and walkways zigzagging over the sea, Chinese say it is "a garden in the sea and a sea in the garden."

After enjoying the delightfully diverse flowers and shrubs, savor some Anxi tea in the tea house and enjoy the sea view, or the golden beach. ① And don't forget to take in Asia's largest Piano Museum (on the hill above the zigzag bridge)

Add: No. 45 Huangyan Rd., Gǔlàngyǔ (鼓浪屿晃岩路 45 号) Tel: 2063744

Website: www.shuzhuang.com.cn

① Chinese Proverb: Make those nearby happy, and those far away will come.

Popular Gŭlàngyŭ Gardens and Parks at a Glance

Adapted from *Discover Gŭlàngyŭ*

Gŭlàngyŭ Sunlight Rock (Rìguāngyá, 日光岩) Former training ground for Míng hero Koxinga (Zhèngchénggōng 郑成功). Great view from peak. Admission includes aviary, cable car. Tel: 2026851

Shūzhuāng Garden (Shūzhuāng Huāyuán, 菽庄花园)—Gulangyu's largest garden, including Asia's best piano museum (Gangqin Bowuguan, 钢琴博物馆). Read about the Piano Museum in "Discover Gŭlàngyŭ," Arts & Music chapter.
Tel: 2063744, 2063722

Piano Garden (Qīnyuán, 琴园) Inside Shūzhuāng Garden

Bright Moon Garden (Hàoyuè Yuán, 皓月园) & Koxinga Statue
Tel: 2063401, 2063930

Yánpíng Park (Yánpíng Gōngyuán,延平公园) & Koxinga's Well

Gŭlàngyŭ Aviary (Báiniăo Yuán,百鸟园) Beautiful tropical foliage, over 100 types of birds, bird performances, large-screen theater

Zhāngzhōu Lù (漳州路) Gulangyu's "most garden-like" road

Xiàmén Overseas Chinese Subtropical Plant Nursery

Yùyuán Memorial Garden (Yùyuán Jĭnqū, 毓园景区) Memorial to Prof. Madame Lín Qiăozhì (林巧稚教授), mother of modern Chinese gynecology. Add: from Bright Moon Park (皓月园), walk up Zhāngzhōu Lù (漳州路) or Fùxìng Lù (复兴路)

Xiàmén Underwater World, Gŭlàngyŭ (Xiàmén Hăidĭ Shìjiè, 厦门海底世界) To right of Gŭlàngyŭ ferry behind giant octopus sculpture. Tel: 2067668

Tea Garden, Gŭlàngyŭ Free Mĭnnán "Gongfu" tea ceremony (perhaps precursor to the Japanese tea ceremony). Add: #8 Tiánwĕi Lù (田尾路) Tel: 2069917

Some Private Parks and Gardens

Lĭ Qīngquán Villa (李清泉别墅) Delightful garden & rockery

Huáng Róngyuán Villa (黄荣远别墅)—#32 Fújiàn Lù
Expansive garden; rockery, best view of Catholic Church.

Yáng Family Garden (杨家园)—#4-8 Ānhăi Lù

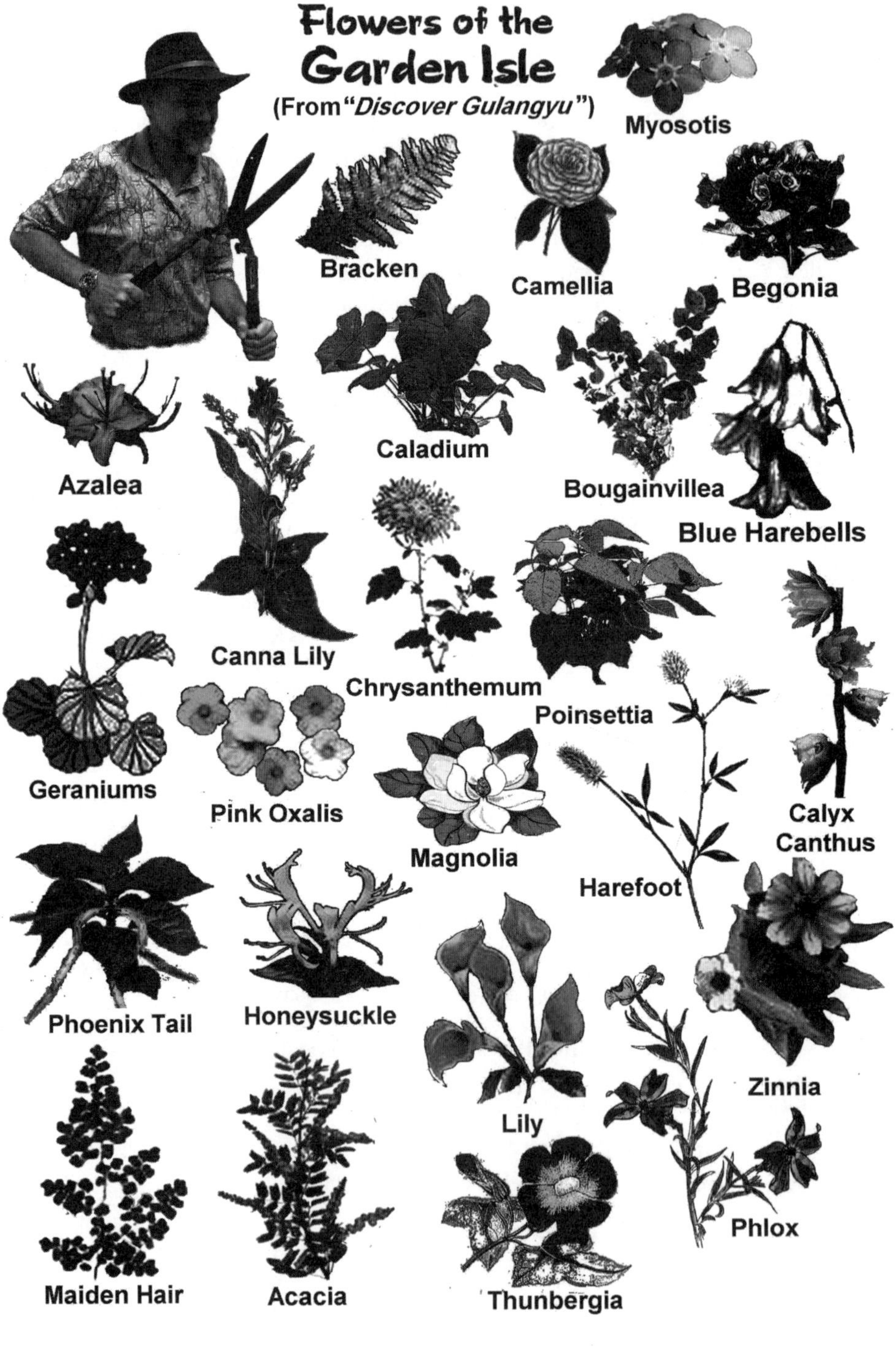
Flowers of the
Garden Isle
(From "*Discover Gulangyu*")
Myosotis
Bracken
Camellia
Begonia
Caladium
Azalea
Bougainvillea
Blue Harebells
Canna Lily
Chrysanthemum
Poinsettia
Geraniums
Pink Oxalis
Magnolia
Calyx
Canthus
Harefoot
Phoenix Tail
Honeysuckle
Lily
Zinnia
Phlox
Maiden Hair
Acacia
Thunbergia

Gulangyu's Endless Parks

(From "*Discover Gulangyu*")

Bishan Park (Gulangyu's Wilderness)

Bright Moon Park

Jishan Christian Cemetery
(A very peaceful park!)

Dr. Lin Qiaozhi Memorial Garden

Seaside Garden and Sculpture

Cable Car Between
Sunlight Rock and Aviary

Supplement

Xu Manke – a Daughter of Gulangyu

Note: thanks to "Gulangyu Master" Cao Fang for introducing me to Ms. Xu.

As she strolls Shuzhuang Garden wearing an elegant, form-fitting cheongsam, artist Xu Manke evokes images of early 20th century society ladies such as Madam Soong May-lin, or the demure debutantes of Gulangyu's Roaring 20s.

Dr. Lin Qiaozhi

Although Gulangyu Islet was famed as the early 20th century's "richest square mile on earth", it was known equally for its cultural, artistic and educational attainments—and for the Daughters of Gulangyu who helped shape modern China.

Lin Qiaozhi, China's "mother of modern women's medicine," was born and raised on Gulangyu, and after study in the U.S. served as the director of obstetrics and gynaecology at the Peking Union Medical College Hospital. She delivered over 50,000 babies, earning the nickname "Mother of Tens of Thousands of Babies".

Ms. Shu Ting

The famed poetess Shu Ting, who penned the immortal "*Ode to the Oak*," has lived on Gulangyu. She was once quoted as saying that "she [Gulangyu Islet] can't break with me, and I can't go without her". Gulangyu was also home to renowned female Chinese pianist and educationist Zhou Shu'an, and Zhuo Yilong, wife of pianist Fu Cong.

Ms. Xu Manke

And today, one of Gulangyu's favorite daughters is Xu Manke, whose life embodies the world she paints.

Manke's father, Prof. Xu Wenhou, was a distinguished professor at the Gulangyu Art School, which is famous for its painters and sculptors who have produced works now displayed in the People's Hall in Beijing and the mansion of the Chief Executive of Hong Kong. Professor Xu breathed life into traditional Chinese paintings of everything from South China maids to Northwest cowboys and ancient poets, hermits and warriors. Xu's portrait of the fierce Zhong Kui, China's favorite "ghost buster," hangs in the office of Cao Fang, Director of Gulangyu Government.

The angry painting isn't something I'd care for in my own office, but Cao said, "I put it here to strike fear into evildoers and bring peace to the islet."

Maybe he should put a copy of Ghostbuster by the ferry where more will see it?

With a father like Prof. Xu, and practically born and raised on the Art School campus, it is no surprise Manke is also an artist, and that her perspective on life has been shaped by Gulangyu life and art. She was strongly influenced by European art while at Gulangyu primary school and No. 2 Middle School, both of which were run by Christian missions before Liberation. But when Manke left Gulangyu to study at XMU, she majored not in art but journalism, coming out top in every subject. But perhaps the beauty of XMU, widely known as one of China's most beautiful universities, reawakened the slumbering artist within. After the success of her exhibit of paintings of flowers and birds, and her first prize in a nationwide art competition, Xu abandoned journalism and, like her famous father, became a professional painter.

The Imperial Palace Press published her two-volume "The Picture Album of the Forbidden City", and both Jiangsu Fine Arts Press and Anhui Fine Arts Press are publishing her work. Yu Jigao, vice president of the *Chinese Elaborate-style Painting Society* said, "Xu's paintings are a relentless pursuit of beauty and fullness of life—simple and surreal, classic while bearing the mark of the times."

In Miss Xu's foreword to her book *Painting Realm*, she shares what goes through her mind when she starts out to capture a Xiamen scene on canvas—or, more accurately, when the scenes capture her.

Ms. Xu's Foreword to her "*Painting Realm*"

It is a pleasant morning in May. Normally, Xiamen is already pretty hot in May, but we have this refreshingly cool 21°C morning sandwiched between two rainy days and an imminent rainstorm forecasted. I sit in the rattan rocking chair on the balcony, drifting away into a trance. The need to write up an article and to describe the process for *Painting Realm* weighs heavily on my mind, so I let it go and loose myself in studying the elegant, moist Areca palms lush orchids, dignified in their earthen pots. The rain drops are redolent of evening primrose; and glisten like oval emeralds on the leaves of the lotus which has stood in its jar for ten years. The floor-to-ceiling glass window overlooks Yundang Lake, and a pair of egrets glide leisurely over the lake. Across the lake, the verdant Xianyue Hill looms over the buildings. The graying sky betrays its resolve to rain, but the day is still bright, and the air refreshing and clear. I forget myself in a scene that is both familiar and novel, changing with seasons and moods.

Time ticks away, and my emotions calm—the calm of a breeze skimming the lake surface, lingering on the banks, loitering about the flowers and trees, leaping over towering buildings and vanishing in the distance. The hustle and bustle of reality fade, the noise of flowing traffic recedes, and the heat of candlelight disperses the delicate and fresh aroma of jasmine flowers and mint in the glass jar of water. The small blue-and-white teapot on the table looks all the more elegant; the floral-patterned back cushion on the reclining chair seems to slouch lazily; even the marquisette curtains on the floor-to-ceiling window are captivating. I often capture these details with my pen, and as pen touches paper, I often feel as if I've become a person that I don't really know.

I attempt to see scenery with new eyes, from another person's perspective, taking in the violet and the yellow carnations blooming boldly in their vase. The windows and balconies across the lake seem to loom against the leaden sky. An angler tosses his line into the lake. The beauty of the world has its own reason to show off, but it withers so quickly. This fleeting beauty fascinates yet saddens me. This ancient foreordination lies beneath the complicated reality and appears in new masks before us from time to time. Such spaces frequently appear in my drawings. I pay more attention to space than time. Beneath its veneer of calm and composure lies a different cognition and realm: a light and clear space, or a dim and chaotic space, a closed, serene and solidified space, or an open, flowing space like a running stream. We live in space, where our selves expand and life disappears.

A couple of heavy clouds drift from afar, floating behind twin silver-gray towers across the lake. The lakeside scenery dims, and the bright lushness at the turn of spring and summer darkens as well; the heavy rain may fall any time. But the candlelight heating the jasmine flowers and mint glows brighter and warmer. The flower tea in the glass pot exudes an emerald green. But the wind is capricious, perhaps wanting to play a small trick with the weather forecast. The clouds are gently blown to the horizon, thin sunbeams stream down like theater lights after the curtains open. Everything under the sky comes back to life. It is still a southern spring and summer with exuberantly blossoming flowers. The flame trees, mulberries, oleanders, palm trees, frangipanes, redbuds, bougainvilleas, and flowers and shrubs whose names yet escape me dot the lawn by the lake; they are golden yellow, bright red or emerald green—a sparkling sea of colors.

Yes, the colors. I'm infatuated with colors! They bear my life experience and the emotions in my memory. This infatuation leads me to leap for joy at seeing apt descriptions of colors. Even simple green comes in a great diversity of forms: tangerine-green, tea-green, moss-green, vivid-green, apple-green, bean-green, lake-green, bright oil-green, olive-green, emerald-green, stone-green, water-green, onion-green, dark green, patina green… All sorts of colors with delicate changes in hues, and the density and size of the colors in the paintings, make the relations among the paintings all the more changeable, compelling me to add colors and to adjust the new colors and the relationship between their brightness and darkness. Therefore, although the sketches of paintings are definitive, their final images are unpredictable, as they take shape slowly in the painting process.

The sky begins to turn silver-gray again, sunlight has vanished without my knowledge, and raindrops fall. I close the window, continuing my game with space and colors.

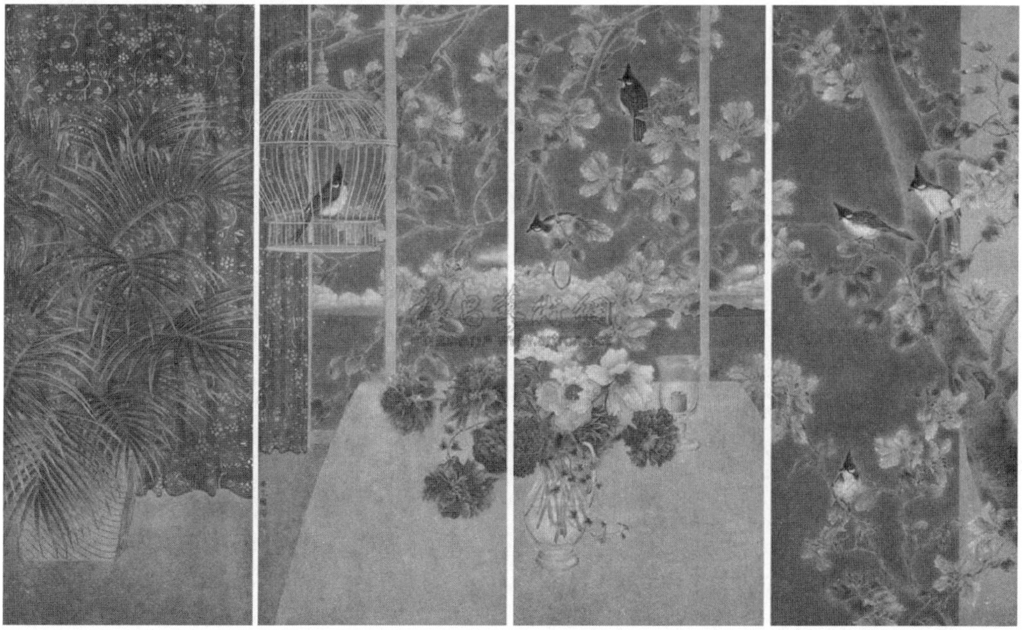

Chapter 5

Gǔlàngyǔ "Amoy Deco" Architecture

(Adapted from *Discover Gulangyu*, Bill Brown, Xiamen Univ. Press)

A leisurely two hour stroll along Gǔlàngyǔ's paved 4 km. ring road allows you to enjoy the beach on one side and the eclectic architecture on the other—bungalows built in English, French, German, Japanese, Spanish and Chinese styles—or even the unique "Amoy Deco."

In 1972, Nixon stayed in Gǔlàngyǔ Guesthouse. One of China's finest foreign villas, this estate has been the setting for many films and TV programs

Another elegant edifice is the former U.S. Consulate, at #26 Sanming Rd. It was built in 1938 with imported American red bricks to replace the former consulate, which had burned to the ground. Since 1949, it has been used as an oceanographic institute, foreign affairs office, and hotel, and will soon be used as a museum.

Xiàmen has spent tens of millions of USD on our Gǔlàngyǔ Islet Architectural Protection Plan to preserve sites like the French-style Lin House, neo-Gothic Catholic church, geometric Art-Deco court building, Filipino Huang Mansion, and Gǔlàngyǔ Shifan University, which was designed by American Henry Murphy (famed for marrying Chinese and Western architecture).

Former U.S. Consulate

Amazed at the Maze? Gulangyu architecture is amazing—and a maze.

"Umbrella lanes" (19th century foreigners' term because too narrow for open umbrellas) twist and turn up and down hills. To confuse things, six or eight lanes may share the same name if they intersect at any point. I have counted at least eight Anxi roads.

Decipher the maze with *Discover Gulangyu*, which has chapters for each road and its architecture, sites, and stories of the people behind them (such as the infamous Cat King warlord).

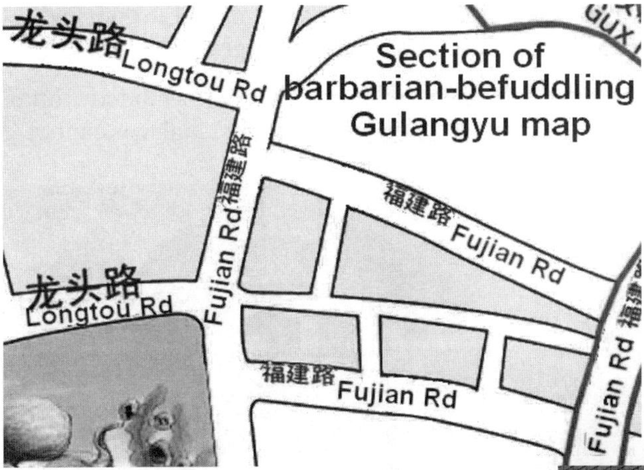

Zhonghua Rd.--every way but up

Getting About Electric carts serve the main routes, but the best way to savour the scenery and sites is a leisurely stroll with frequent stops for some of the tea that changed American history.①

Take the 4 km. ring road for a scenic view of bay and beaches, then cut inland anywhere to enjoy the architecture, paying close attention to the delightful variety of gates, windows, verandas, roofs, columns, pillars…

① The tea dumped overboard during 1773's Boston Tea Party was our Anxi tea, shipped from Xiamen. So had it not been for Xiamen, there would be no U.S.A., we'd be speaking the Queen's English, we'd be eating chips with malt vinegar instead of fries with ketchup, and our judges would be wearing funny white wigs like the ones in England and Hong Kong. So thank you, Xiamen.

How "Amoy Deco" Got This Way Gulangyu's architecture so defies categorization that experts finally gave up and dubbed it Amoy Deco. But Amoy Deco did not debut without resistance, even ridicule by pontificating purists who felt the madcap marriage of East and West mirrored a divorce of reason, or at least poor taste.

This hodgepodge of houses was born of foreigners schizophrenically grasping at the East while clinging to the West, and of Chinese clinging to their roots while grasping at all things "modern." The upshot was what Laura Wild called "hideous duplication of the ugliest kind of brick structures America can produce."① Walter A. Taylor② wrote in 1924 that the missionaries who built churches, hospitals and schools, were,

> "the same people [who] fill their homes with all manner of thing Chinese [to] adapt themselves to Chinese customs...[but] ornament the outside of their buildings with poor copies of details ten generations removed from Europe, and 'milk bottle' columns which would make Vignola③ turn in his grave."④

Taylor encouraged modern architects to blend Chinese style with modern foreign construction but warned, "We cannot carry on in the foreign 'rut' and we cannot go over into the Chinese 'ditch.'"

Henry Murphy, the American designer of Gulangyu Shifan University, avoided both rut and ditch with his Ginling College for Girls in Nanjing, which opened October, 1923. Laura Wild wrote, "Buildings well adapted to modern laboratory work and furnished with the conveniences of life have been crowned with beautiful roofs and decorations characteristic of China."

#14 Yongchun Rd. (One of my favorites)

Tan Kah Kee followed Murphy's lead in designing Xiamen University, claiming his own marriage of East and West represented his vision of modern education rooted in traditional Chinese values.

---

① Laura H. Wild, "Higher Education for Women in China," China Christian Advocate October, 1923, p.5 (she was not writing on Gulangyu but in general).

② Walter A. Taylor taught at Ohio State University's College of Engineers from 1920-21, and then attended the Harvard-Yenching School of Chinese Studies in Beijing.

③ Giacomo da Vignola, 1507-1573, influential Italian architect best known for writing the "Rule of the Five Orders of Architecture in 1562

④ Chinese Recorder, October 1924

Overview of "Amoy Deco" Windows, Gates, Verandas, & Roofs

Huang Rongyuan Mansion

Gulangyu has an astonishing variety of intricately detailed roofs, porches, windows, verandas, columns, pillars. Some have compiled entire albums of just windows, gates—even pillars!

Amoy Deco Verandas (廊) Most villas have colonnaded verandas enclosing one or more sides. With ornate pillars, columns and arches, these verandas were both decorative and practical, protecting residents from the pounding sub-tropical rains or the blazing sun—at least those with sense enough to avoid the sun and rain.

> **Feeble Foreign Brain Couldn't Take the Heat**
>
> "Without common-sense, a missionary will neglect his own health and become a burden to his colleagues, his friends, and himself, as did a certain young man, who on being urged to wear a sun-hat and carry an umbrella, smiled serenely, and quoted [the Bible], 'The sun shall not smite thee by day.' The recorder says that he is now at home with an enfeebled brain, which, one surmises, can never have been very strong." Soothill, 1907

Single-Sided Verandas—Yang Home, #4 Anhai Rd. (杨家园) and Liqing Quan Villa（李清泉) on Flag Hill Rd. ("Discover Gulangyu," Fuxing Rd. chapter).

Two-Sided Verandas—Foreign Mother-in-law Lady Bldg, #36 Anhai Rd. (番婆楼). Two-sided verandas were usually on the east, south, and southeast to maximize shade in summer and sunlight in winter.

"Foreign Mother-in-law Bldg." #36 Anhai Rd.

Three-sided Verandas—Seaview Villa (观海别墅), Huifeng Residence (汇丰公馆) and Yanhuo Building (验货楼).

Four-sided Verandas—Huang Family Mansion (Huángjiā Huāyuán, 黄家花园) and Eight Diagram Building (Bāguà Lǒu, 八卦楼). Bagua Bldg's largest column reaches almost one meter in diameter.

Amoy Deco Attached Buildings (陪楼) Extended Chinese families prefer large homes, but Gulangyu homes took it to extremes because the rich Chinese not only had many children (and wives) but also welcomed (or endured) an influx of rural relatives who wanted to live in the elite Gulangyu International Settlement.

They also needed quarters for the small armies of servants who undertook domestic and business affairs. Most mansions had separate kitchens, laundry rooms, and storage rooms. These annexes were usually similar architecturally, at least externally, to the main building, though internally they were much simpler, reflecting servants' lower status in Gulangyu's highly stratified society.

Yang Villa servants' alleys

Yang Family Villa, childhood home of photographer Bai Hua, has attached buildings similar externally to the main building, but rooms are small and narrow. The narrow alleyways between buildings were used mainly by servants and "little wives" (wives or concubines, excluding the oldest wife), who were expected to serve as unobtrusively as possible.

Amoy Deco Roofs Sunlight Rock's peak affords an excellent view of the orange and red Jiageng roof tiles (嘉庚瓦) that contrast yet oddly harmonize with the deep green forested hills of Gulangyu Islet. The most unusual roofs are:

Sunlight Temple (Rìguāngyán Sì, 日光岩寺) Part of the roof's a rock!

Eight Diagrams Building at #43 Guxin Road (Bāguà Lǒu, 八卦楼). Gulangyu's most conspicuous roof was inspired by Middle Eastern mosques.

Golden Melon Building (金瓜楼), at #99 Quanzhou Road. Some say the "Golden Melons" reflect Romanesque influence; others say they are Chinese. A place in Kangle Village (康乐新村) has two similar golden melons.

Lin House, #82 Quanzhou Road (Línwū, 林屋) Intricate, steeply sloping red and orange roofs seem Dutch to me but experts say they are North European. The designer, Lin Quancheng (林全诚), also designed the roof of Gulangyu Island Water Supply Company to resemble an unfolding red tulip bud (suggesting to me Dutch influence).

Photo by Lily Wang

Catholic Church (天主教堂), #34 Lujiao Rd., has a beautiful neo-Gothic roof, the white steeple contrasting starkly with the deep greens of the magnificent old trees guarding its perimeter (see "Birthplace of Chinese Protestantism" chapter).

Sea & Sky Palace Complex, #38 Fujian Road (Háitiān Tánggòu, 海天堂构), is said to be like no other building in China. Notice the carved phoenix and other mythical creatures on the rooftop of the intricately detailed central building.

Scenic View Villa (观彩楼), #6 Bishan Rd. —my favorite, this Dutch designed roof is said to resemble a Chinese sedan, hence the nickname "bride's sedan," but the windows look to me like Pluto's house in Disneyland.

Amoy Deco Gates Chinese, whether in city or country, love gates—the grander the better. But Gulangyu gates are in a class of their own.

Some gates boast Greek columns embellished with 19th century European artwork, mythic Chinese dragons and phoenixes, capped by Chinese "flying sparrow" eaves and, for good measure, crowned with Art Deco lintels right out of 1930s' Chicago.

Art Deco (Amoy Deco) Gate, 1935, #18 Guxin Rd.

Many gates retain traditional double central doors flanked by smaller doors. Side doors were for daily use; central doors were for dignitaries or special occasions (or perhaps extremely large foreign guests).

My favourite gates are on Fujian Road（福建路), Anhai Road（安海路), Lujiao Road（鹿礁路), Brush Mountain Road（Bǐshān Lù, 笔山路) and Chicken Hill Road (Jīshān Lù, 鸡山路). The three most magnificent gates may well be:

Sea & Sky Palace (Háitiān Lǒu, 海天堂) #38 Fujian Rd.

Golden Melon Mansion (Jīnguā Lǒu, 金瓜楼) #99 Quanzhou Rd.

Foreign Mother-in-law Bldg.(Fānpó Lǒu, 番婆楼) #35 Anhai Rd.

Gate at #38 Fujian Rd.

Many gates once bore inscriptions with construction date and family name, but most were chiselled off during the Cultural Revolution and replaced with hastily scrawled, "Long live Chairman Mao." Some are still faintly visible (below the lions at #14 Yongchun Rd.).

The lights on the less ostentatious gate in front of the former Electric Light Company (电灯公司) on Fujian Road (福建路) supposedly resemble those in such classical French films as Camille (茶花女). I also enjoy the humbler Chinese gates still to be seen here and there (try Fuxing Road or Haitan Road).

Lin Qingquan Villa

Amoy Deco Columns Amoy architects had a fetish about columns, using not only traditional Doric, Ionic and Corinthian styles but also a few of their own. Classic Greek columns are adorned with carved Chinese unicorns and phoenixes, or Taoist "taiji" diagrams. One single column may have Doric, Ionic and Corinthian, with Chinese ceramic trim.

For amateur architecture buffs like myself, who confuse "roof" with "ceiling," herein is a brief description of columns you'll encounter.

Corinthian columns, most decorative of Greek columns, are most popular in the West, and employ entasis (columns bulge slightly) so they appear straight, even though they are not. Classic Corinthians have fluted shafts (carved vertical lines) and flowers and leaves on the capitals (Chinese columns have Taoist diagrams and auspicious Chinese animals). Corinthian columns are also different from Ionic or Doric in that the cornices are flat, rather than slanted.

Doric columns, like those of Athens' Parthenon, are plain but powerful, with no bases and unfluted 20-sided shafts.

Ionic columns, Gulangyu's most common style, appear taller than Dorics because they are slenderer and, like Corinthians, employ entasis to avoid appearing smaller at the top. Large bases resemble stacked rings, and capitals are a scroll above a fluted shaft. Like Corinthians, Doric friezes are unadorned.

Tuscan columns are plain, with unadorned shafts and simple capitals, bases and friezes.

Composite columns are a combination of Ionic and Corinthian.

"As eyes are windows on the soul, so windows illuminate a building's soul."
Professor Gongjie (龚洁教授)

Amoy Deco Windows Gulangyu's endlessly varied windows can be European, American, Colonial, Chinese, Gothic, Art Deco, Art Nouveau, etc. And some buildings, like Fujian Road's Huang Rongyuan Villa (黄荣远堂) have 3 or four styles and shapes of windows on the very same wall.

Gulangyu windows are every shape, size, color, and material. They are wood, stone, concrete, or brick; single or double; wide or narrow; shuttered or unshuttered; steeply arched, or semi-circular. Some are plain and others are heavily ornamented with Eastern or Western designs (or both). Many have small balconies and rows of potted plants reminiscent of German country homes. The sheer variety is beyond my ability to describe, so you must settle for the photos below, but you can see some of my favorite windows at these four homes:

Scenic View Building (观彩楼), #6 Bishan Rd. I love this Dutch home's Disneyesque dormers. It looks like something Pluto would live in.
#21 Zhonghua Road These are "iron anchor and owl" windows.
Yang Family Home (杨家园忠权楼) Flanking "bottleneck" designs.
Lin's Octagonal Tower (林氏府八角楼）

My Favorite Gulangyu Architecture at a Glance

Longtou Road (龙头路) Straight ahead of the ferry, Longtou's Tourist Info Center is your first stop; its endless shops are your money's last stop

Lujiao Road (鹿礁路) Turn left at the ferry: Bo'ai Hospital; Seashore Inn; Octagon Building; Earlier British Consulate; Former Japanese Consulate

Fujian Road (福建路) Somc of the best architecture: Yi Garden, Huang Rongyuan Mansion; Catholic Church; Sea & Sky Mansion; Cat King's Villa

Zhangzhou Road The most "Garden-like Road": Bright Moon Garden; Koxinga Statue; Former British Consulate; John Ma's Former Residence; Lin Yutang's Former Residence; Xiamen Music Academy

Fuxing Road (复兴路) Fuxing Church; Dr. Clarence Holleman's Former Home; Dr. Lin Qiaozhi Memorial; Li Qingquan Villa on nearby Flag Hill

Quanzhou Road (泉州路) Lin House; Golden Melon Bldg; Qiu Jin's Former Residence; Former Inquest Law Court (later moved to Brush Hill Rd.)

Guxin Road (鼓新路)—Former Taihe Company Bldg; 8 Diagrams Bldg. (Xiamen Museum & Organ Museum); Maritime Affairs Residence; Hope Hospital (note the John Otte Memorial, circa 1910, in 4 languages).

Tianwei Road (田尾路) International Club (1920s); Danish Telegraph Office; Seaview Villa; former Dutch Consulate

Anhai Road (安海路) Trinity Church; Yang Villa; Foreign Lady Villa (best gate); Pleasant Garden (Yiyuan Villa)

Zhonghua Road (中华路) Former Dutch Consulate; Dafudi (200-year-old Chinese residences; David Abeel lived here); "Strange World" Museum

Yongchun Road （永春路）Koxinga Memorial Hall; Kanqing Villa

Huangyan Road (晃岩路) Gulangyu Music Hall (former Foreign Cemetery); Dr. Lin Qiaozhi's childhood home; Huang Family Gardens, Gospel Hall, Sunlight Rock Temple.

Chicken Hill Road (Jīshān Lù, 鸡山路) Yin Family Home (1st family of music); Anxian Hall; Pastors' homes; Chinese Christian cemetery

Brush Mountain Road (Bǐshān Lù, 笔山路) Former Residence of Lin Wenqing (former Xiamen University President); Scenic View Bldg; Yizu Villa; Chuncao Palace;

Sanming Road (三明路）Former U.S. Consulate (now a hotel)

Drumbeat Road (Gǔushēng Lù, 鼓声路) Drumbeat Rock; Hero Hill; Wave Listening Bluff (Tingtao Ya); Aviary and Cable Car to Sunlight Rock; Liaoxian Villa; Overseas Chinese Subtropical Plant Introduction Garden

Chapter 6

Parks and Gardens

Our "Garden Island" has hundreds of city, district and community gardens. My favorites include the Botanical Garden, Yundang Lake (the city's cultural center) the 31km. Island Ring Road with its Music Square, Boardwalk, and beach attractions, and the new "Railroad Park"—a beautiful landscaped 4 km. garden path along the old train track from harbor to train station.

The 5,000+ mango trees lining many Xiàmén streets not only provide shade but help finance the maintenance of our parks. (Locals claim mango strips dipped in soybean oil taste like crab)

Bǎilùzhōu Park 白鹭洲公园 This 59,000 m^2 park on Yuándāng Lake consists of Western Park and Central Park, which has Xiàmén's landmark, the 13.6m Egret goddess (Bǎilù Nǚshén, 白鹭女神). The goddess is often accompanied by many of the 400 doves imported from Holland (so why not a dove goddess?). The doves are fed twice daily, but are happy to receive handouts from tourists as well.

The 10,000m^2 square Western Park is known for its astrological columns, 1200m^2 dancing fountain, and kids pestering you to buy flowers for your girl.

Bǎilùzhōu also has one of Xiàmén's best antique markets, as well as a great supplier of cats, dogs and other creatures on one of the roofs (no, it's not a Cantonese restaurant; it's a pet supply).

Night Cruise Take a romantic cruise along the bay at night and enjoy the lights of Gǔlàngyǔ on one side and the Bund (Lùjiāng Rd) on the other. Some ships offer dinner, or traditional art performances—puppets, opera, etc.

15 Minutes or 5?

In the Livcom competition in Stuttgart in 2002, I'd planned to say, "In Xiàmén you are never more than a 15 minute walk from a park. But the night before my presentation, the Mayor of Stuttgart said in a speech, "In Stuttgart, we are never more than a 5 minute walk from a park."

Someone said, "He sure stole your thunder!" But I stole it back. The next morning I said, "In Xiàmén we are never more than 15 minutes' walk from a park." As some of the audience snickered I added, "Of course, I know Stuttgart's mayor said you are never more than 5 minutes walk from a park, but life in Xiamen is easier, so we don't have to walk so fast."

Some Key Xiàmén Parks

Sīmíng District Parks

Name	Hectares	Class	Purpose
Botanical Garden (Zhíwùyuán)植物园	227.2 ha	1st	Research
Bǎilù Park 白鹭公园	20 ha	1st	Multi-Purpose
Bǎilùzhōu Park 白鹭洲公园	10.5 ha	1st	City Park
South Lake (Nánhú) Park 南湖公园	16.7 ha	1st	Multipurpose
Zhōnglún Park 忠仑公园		1st	Multipurpose
E. Bǎilùzhōu Park 白鹭洲东公园	15 ha	1st	City Park
Sunlight (Rìguāng) Rock 日光岩	5.4 ha	2nd	Scenic, Historic
Shúzhuāng Garden, Gǔlàngyǔ 菽庄花园	4.43 ha	2nd	Scenic, Cultural
Bright Moon (Hàoyuè), Gǔlàngyǔ 皓月园	3 ha	2nd	Scenic, Cultural
Huáqiáo Tropical Garden 华侨亚热带	8.9 ha	2nd	Research Center
Zhōngshān Park 中山公园	11.09 ha	1st	Scenic, Historic
Jīnbǎng Park 金榜公园	48.16 ha	1st	Scenic, Historic
Goose (Hóngshān) Mtn. Park 鸿山公园	17 ha	1st	Scenic
Liánhuā Park 莲花公园	2.2 ha	2nd	Community Park
Jiāhé Park 嘉禾公园	1.8 ha	3rd	District Park
Seaside (Hǎibīn) Park 海滨公园	4 ha	2nd	On Island Ring Rd
Foxtail (Húwěi) Mtn. Park 狐尾山公园	70.63 ha	1st	City Park
Jǐngzhōu Amusement 景州乐园	30.84 ha	1st	Fun, Culture
Sōngbǎi Park 松柏公园	7.22 ha	2nd	Community Park
Húlǐ District Parks			
Húlǐ Park 湖里公园	11.76 ha	1st	City Park
Xiānyuè Park 仙岳公园	227 ha	1st	City Park
Oxhead (Niútóu) Mtn. 牛头山	6.49 ha	2nd	Scenic
Jiāngtóu Park 江头公园	6.02 ha	2nd	Community Park
Jīměi District Parks			
Xìngdōng Park 杏东公园	3.03 ha	2nd	District Park
Rìdōng Park 日东公园	10.78 ha	1st	District Park
Jìngxián park 敬贤公园	4.74 ha	2nd	District Park
S. Dike (Nándī) Park 南堤公园	2.1 ha	2nd	Seaside Park
Tan Kah Kee Park 嘉庚公园	6.65 ha	2nd	Historical Garden
Tóng'ān Parks			
Shuāngqī Park 双溪公园	1.43 ha	3rd	District Park
Dōngqī Park 东溪公园	3.38 ha	2nd	Riverside Park
Dàlún Mtn. Park 大轮山公园	20.85 ha	1st	District Park
Hǎicāng Parks			
Tianzhu Mountain National Forest	31 km^2		Bio Preserve
Fire Island Refuge (Huǒshāoyǔ)火烧屿科技	27 ha	1st	Bio Preserve
Hǎicāng Wildlife Park 海沧野生	18 ha	1st	Wildlife
Xiángwú Park 祥吴公园	4 ha	2nd	District Park
Xiǎopíng Forest 小坪森林公园	1600 ha	1st	Outside City

Island Ring Road (Huándǎolù（环岛路）
Xiàmén's 31km Park

Flowing Sea Dragon

"Flowing Sea Dragon" Nothing else in China (or back on earth either) is like our 31km. Island Ring Rd. Dubbed "Flowing Sea Dragon," it begins near Gulangyu Ferry as an elegant elevated expanse arching over the sea for several kilometers before descending to the beach by Xiàmén Univ. It offers a stunning view of Gǔlàngyǔ and the sea by day, and by night the bridge itself is a beauty to behold, aglow with subtle indirect lighting, like an army of fireflies on parade along the coast.

From Xiàmén Univ., the six-lane road to the airport varies from 44 to 60 meters wide and is bordered by miles of beaches, parks, gardens, green belts and tracks for hikers, bikers and roller bladers.

Swords to Roads

Back in 1988, Amoy's perimeter was studded with granite tank traps and concrete bunkers, but Xiàmén has turned her swords into plows—or roads. The dusty path snaking between military camps was replaced by endless gardens between the hills and shore.

Roughing it on the Island Ring Road!

Three Guinness World Records are along the route: the longest music sculpture ("Song of Gulangyu," outside XMU on the grassy median), world's largest coastal cannon (in Huli Fort), and the most marathon statues (99 of them, near the exhibition center). Enjoy the beaches and parks, rent tandem bikes, sailboats, or pedal-boats, try your hand at parasailing, go roller blading. Have a picnic, or dine at one of the beachside restaurants, where you can rent beach umbrellas, floats, mats, rubber boats… After your swim, get high legally—on a rental hot air balloon or motorized glider.

Or just relax with a good book and some Anxi tea. Enjoy the sand and surf against the backdrop of semi-tropical islands, and watch the city-sized freighters and majestic two-masted mahogany Chinese junks glide by, and fishermen's sampans bob like corks in a giant basin. If you're lucky, you might even catch a glimpse of the rare white dolphins that frequently frolic in our bay.

Song of Gŭlàngyŭ Ring Road sites include Húlĭ Hill Fort, the Music Square, parks, gardens and sculptures, and the International Exhibition Center.

The Ring Road has at least 200 works of art, by my count. One of the most *note* worthy is right outside XMU—the 247 m sculpture of musical notes depicting the "Song of Gŭlàngyŭ". It was created in 1998, and in 2001 Guinness recognized it as the world's longest music sculpture. I can't imagine keeping the grass trimmed. They must have a large staff (a score of workers, perhaps?)

China's Southern Doorstep—Huli Hill Fort (Húlĭshān Pàotái, 湖里山炮台), on the beach by XMU, has long been called Xiamen's gateway. Given that Xiamen is "China's Southern Gateway," this makes the fort S. China's doorstep.

Húlĭ Fort was started in 1891 on a bluff 25 meters above sea level. It took five years to construct the 70,000 m^2 fort of sand, clay, camphor tree juice, lime and glutinous rice. So not only was it virtually impregnable but during a prolonged siege defenders could eat their fort.

World's Largest Cannon (in Guinness) is Húlĭ Fort's claim to fame. The German 280mm Krupp coastal defense gun, installed by some big shot back in 1896, weighs 60 tons, is 13.96 meters long, and cost 60,000 taels of silver. Two 120 mm auxiliary cannons and 12 smaller steel cannons were also made in Germany.

The Fort once had two Krupp cannon, but one was destroyed in the 1950s. The Krupp had a range of 16,000 meters, and it was recorded that it was so loud that nearby houses collapsed and frightened cows jumped one meter high (probably the origin of milk shakes).

The cannon did see some action, most notably on September 3rd, 1937, when three Japanese warships entered Xiàmén port and shelled Băishí Fortress and Húlĭ Fort. The cannon sunk the Japanese destroyer "Wakatake Maru," and two others beat a hasty retreat under the cover of Japanese bombers.

A Tale of Taels and Mus

An English guidebook said the cannon cost 60,000 taels of silver. Big help! Even if you know that a tael was about an ounce, what was silver worth in 1896?

China's English guidebooks also wield *mu* on us. A Xiàmén park, for example, has 1,400 *mu*. The only entry in an English dictionary for Mu is, "The 12th letter of the Greek Alphabet." Maybe the park has 1,400 cows crying moo?

The Xiàmén #1 Dept. Store spent a pretty penny on a beautiful new English sign that boasted, "Xiàmén 1st Yibai Store." They either thought Yìbái was English, or were claiming Chinese invented E-bay. Or are they deliberately befuddling us barbarians? Well… back to my *gushi* (tale…)

Róngguāng Cultural Relics and Treasures Exhibition (荣光宝藏展览馆). Built on the site of Huli Fort's barracks, this is a joint venture between Xiàmén government and Singapore's Yizhao Gem Company (新加坡亿兆宝石私人有限公司). Mr. Zhāng Róngguāng (张荣光), a 7th generation collector, provided the five exhibits' displays, including 455 guns, swords, and cannon.

World's Ancient Cannons (Shìjiè Gǔdài Zhànpào Chénlièguǎn, 世界古代战炮陈列馆) Includes a 12th century cannon said to be the world's oldest.

World's Ancient Firelocks (Shìjie Gǔdài Huǒqiāng Chénliè Guǎn, 世界古代火枪陈列馆 (Chinese also invented firelocks)

World's Ancient Swords (Shìjiè Gǔdài Bǎojiàn Chénlià Guǎn, 世界古代宝剑陈列馆) (Chinese swords did have an edge)

Open-Air Petrified Tree Exhibit (Gǔshù Huàshí Zhǎnshì, 古树化石展示)

World's Exotic Stones (Shìjiè Qíshí Chénliè Guǎn, 世界奇石陈列馆). Includes 3,850 exotic stones, including Emperor Qianlong's "pet rock," and an 8m^2 chunk of yellow jade from Burma (a favorite stone of Emperor Kangxi). A stone from France looks just like a piece of bacon. There was another "bacon rock," eight times larger, but Chiang Kai Shek absconded with it to Táiwān. Perhaps his wife thought it was high time he started bringing home the bacon).

Add: #2 Zēng Cuò'ān Lù (Outside XMU) Tel: 2084184, 2099603
E-mail:hlspt@163.com www.hlspt.cn

Advance to Amoy Boardwalk! One of my favorite childhood pastimes was playing the real estate trading game "Monopoly" and getting the card "Advance token to Boardwalk"—the most expensive and profitable property, based on Atlantic City, NJ's boardwalk. Of course, I usually ended up paying exorbitant rent, not receiving it. Opened June 26, 1870, the world's first boardwalk is still the most famous, with 7.5km. of casinos, restaurants, stores and amusements. But while boardwalks seem to be springing up all over the planet (see Amoymagic.com for more), the most beautiful boardwalk on the planet, and one of the longest, is in Xiamen.

The 31km Island Ring Road was almost too big to enjoy except from afar, by bus or car (which as Chinese say is akin to "viewing flowers from horseback" (走马看花). But our new boardwalk lets us appreciate our home's unique beauty up close and personal.[①]

①Chinese proverb: It is hard to dismount a tiger.

The 5.9 km. Boardwalk extends from XMU beach past Huli Fort, Music Square, and several kilometers of beaches, parks, and restaurants. Eventually it will terminate at the International Exhibition Center, over 10km away.

Some areas evoke images of the Mediterranean, with sprawling white villas fronting blue sea. J. Fischer claims one section reminds him of Monterey, California, as it rises on a steel frame over the sea to skirt wind-lashed trees clinging precariously to rocks. Some sections are distinctly Chinese, with colorful S. Fújiàn fishing boats anchored offshore, and open-air traditional opera theaters.

Xiamen boardwalk has quickly become our favorite escape. My wife and I walk it most mornings and many evenings as well, stopping only to rest at the small wooden pavilions, or to view the sculptures.

Eventually, most of the walk will be lit up at night, but even now the ambient light is enough for strolls on a moonless night.

Egrets & Oars Sculptures The egret represent the sculptor's longing for his home of Xiàmén; the 12 oars symbolize the closeness of Táiwān-controlled Jīnmén. Fishermen say it takes only 4000 oar strokes to reach Little Jīnmén, which is close enough you can use binoculars to watch patrolling KMT soldiers.①

Táiwān Cultural Village (Táiwān Mínsú Cūn Jǐngzhōu Lèyuán, 台湾民俗村景州乐园) Built by Mr. Huáng Jīnshān to help promote cross-straits exchanges and portray life in Táiwān. (See Sports & Recreation Chapter")

The Golden Key is CIFIT's highly symbolic emblem. CIFIT is the key to successful investment anywhere in China (see the Business chapter), and the key is made of the numerals "8" and "9" because it is held on the 8th day of the 9th month.

① Chinese proverb: No wind, no waves.

Coconut Wind Fort (Yēfēng Zhài, 黄厝环岛路椰风寨) This place has a restaurant, coffee shop, teahouse, swimming area, barbecue facilities, swim equipment rental, and children's play area. Disembark the bus in front of the building that looks like Garfield (thanks to Prof. Vladimir Mylnikov for pointing that out).

Sea Rhyme Recreation & Amusement Scenic Area (HǎiyùnXiūxián Yóulè Jǐngqū 海韵休闲游乐景区) Sea Rhyme has anything you could want and if they don't they'll tell you they do and then have you wait while they search the island for it (Just kidding!). They have swim & shower facilities, (Yóuyǒng Chōnglìn, 游泳冲淋), seafood (Hǎixiān Dàpáidāng, 海鲜大排档), barbeque (Yěwēi Shāokǎo, 野味烧烤), beach volleyball (Shātān Páiqiú, 沙滩排球), beach soccer (Shātān Zúqiú,沙滩足球), travel merchandise, travel services, electric tour carts (Diànpíngchē,电瓶车), etc.

Tel: 2566766

A Tidy Suggestion

The water is cleanest just before high tide. To calculate high tide, find the lunar date from a Chinese calendar or Xiamen Daily and multiply it times 0.8. After the 15th of the month, subtract 15 from the date, and multiply it by 0.8. Example: 1st = 1 x 0.8, or .8 (about 00:50 a.m. 12:50 p.m.). The 15th = 15 x 0.8, or 120 (12:00 midnight and 12:00 noon). The 18th = 18-15 x 0.8, or 2.40 (roughly 2:25 a.m. & p.m.). If too confusing, ask any Chinese 7-year-old to calculate it for you.

Xiamen Music Square – Chopin was Chinese? This delightful outdoor musical museum has dozens of sculptures of famous composers, with bilingual inscriptions. But note the eyes! Even the Western composers have Chinese eyes!

As you explore the garden, solve the "Music Square Challenge" (which sculptures show the wrong date of birth or death?).

You can also enjoy live music in the square by the Xiamen Philharmonic Orchestra and others.

Chopan's Chinese eyes

Dragon-Tiger Hill Rd (Lōnghǔshān, Lù, 龙虎山路)—country roads without even leaving the island! This is the road off the Island Ring Road that leads past the Yìyuán Hotel to Shànglǐ（上李） and over the pass. Note the many sculptures along this beautiful mountain pass, and the gardens not only on either side but also in the sunken median, with winding paths and quaint arched bridges across the small creek. It's a classic Chinese miniature landscape but big enough to play in—and it leads right to Spook Hill.

Spook Hill (Guàipō,怪坡) Day and night, cars line up to coast ***up*** the hill to "Mid-Slope Temple (半岭宫)! It does look uphill, Even in photos. Is it a gravitational anomaly or optical illusion? Read on; the answer is elsewhere in this book.

Shànglǐ Reservoir (Shànglǐ Shuǐkù, 上李水库)—near Spook Hill.

Xiamen Garden (Xiàménshì Huāyuán, 厦门市花园) The narrow paved road to the left of the snails sculpture winds for miles through mountains that feel as remote as any place in the province, and just when you think you're beyond the reaches of civilization, you come to the delightful Jackstraw Farm (Dàocǎorén, 稻草人). Try their "tea, barbeque and country cooking!"

Xiamen Bougainvillea Park (near Spook Hill)

Add: Huángcuò, Shìfàn Lù Duàn Service Area 黄厝环岛路示范路段之一景点服务区（海韵台）

One Country, Two Systems, Five Hands The huge slogan reads "1 Country, 2 Systems." The statue of five hands across the road represents generations of Chinese seeking peaceful unity with Táiwān.

With good binoculars you can read the slogan that Táiwān erected on an island in the bay. It reads, "Three democratic principles ① will unite China."

On the Run Another Guinness-record site is the display of 99 strikingly life-like bronze statues of runners in the Xiàmén International Marathon, which has been held annually since 2003 on the most beautiful marathon route on the planet.

Each 2 m statue is unique in pose and features. In 1st position is an African (Africans have won every race). Last place is held by a man in a wheelchair.

Two of these statues have replicas in Lausanne's Olympic Museum.

I did 10 km. of the 2004 marathon—but jogged, not ran. Some statues were faster than I was.

99 Marathon Statues!

Which 2 of the 99 have copies in the Olympics Museum in Lausanne?

① Sun Yat-sen's "3 Democratic Principles": Government of people, by people, for people. Seems to me I've heard those before. Any case for copyright infringement there?

Exhibition Center The 99 metal Marathoners cross the finish line just before the huge International Conference and Exhibition Center. This 1.4 billion Yuan, 470,000 m^2 center is said to resemble a huge sailing ship. If so, it's a strange ship.

The five-floor center has numerous exhibition halls with capacity for 2000 cxhibition booths① and 10,000 people. In front of the center is the 4-star Seaside Mandarin. The large lawn between the Mandarin and the Ring Road is a favorite venue for kite flying and picnics. Within a few years this scenic area will also boast one of Asia's largest yacht clubs.

Getting there: take the Xiàmén Double-decker Tour Bus

Cutting Edge Technology

Two decades of peace have done a number on Táiwān-controlled Jínmén Islet's biggest industry—cutlery made of recycled mainland bomb casings. These cutlery kings now must import used bombs from the mainland to keep their competitive edge. Buy their cutlery on Dàdēng Island (see Tóng'ān chapter).

The 10,000 Rock Botanical Garden (Wànshí Zhíwùyuán, 万石植物园), has more rocks than our university cafeteria rice, and beautifully landscaped trails winding amongst 20+ nurseries with over 5,300 kinds of tropical and subtropical plants, many found nowhere else on earth (or China either).

The first of its kind in China, and China's 1st ISO-authenticated garden, this delightful botanical oasis opened in 1960 is in downtown Xiàmén and covers 2.27 km^2 (few are actually square).

Koxinga stationed troops in this area, and often came here to read. Evidently, so did other luminaries. The granite boulders throughout the garden are graced with calligraphic inscriptions (ancient graffiti sanctified by age).

① An official told me how proud Xiamen was to host so many exhibitionists. I replied that I was sure it gave the products some good exposure.

Giant boulders with names like "Laughing Rock" (Tàipíng Shíxiào, 太平石笑) are strewn across the picturesque hills. Below ground are dozens of "caves" (Chinese call any space between two rocks a cave).

Favorite sites include:

Wànshí Lake (Wànshíhú, 万石湖), a reservoir built in 1952.

Spring & Autumn Bridge (Chūnqiū Qiáo, 春秋桥) between Bamboo Path and Palm Garden.

Conifer Garden: over 80 species of pines, cypress and firs, including sequoia (found only in California and Central China) and gingko, which Chinese claim have been around 2 billion years. (They'd know, I guess).

The Bamboo Path is my favorite leading someone down the garden path (or just bamboozling them). Chinese have long said, "Better no meat than no bamboo." This giant grass has well over 1,000 uses, and China has over 200 of the world's 1000 species of bamboo. In North Fújiàn you can even find a rare square bamboo! (They should feed it to pandas; then they'd be sure of getting a square meal).

Visit the Rose Garden, Palm Garden, 1,000 m^2 Flower Exhibition Hall (over 1000 species of flowers), and Araucaria Lawn (where Dèng Xiǎopíng planted a camphor).

The Botanical Garden is free before 7 AM, making it perfect for daily morning exercises.

Xiamen University. I know, it's not a park—but it's just over the hill from the Botanical Garden, and as China's most beautiful campus, the entire school is like a park, with classic Chinese architecture, lakes, gardens, fountains. But Given the growth in tourists (thousands daily), be prepared to stand in a long line unless you have someone with a university pass to get you in. Read more in the education chapter.

Xiamen Univ. is itself one giant park

Botanical Garden Temples

Tiger Stream Temple (Hǔxī Yán Sì, 虎溪岩寺), is on the west side of Drunk Immortal Mtn. (Zuìxiān Yán, 醉仙岩), near the Botanical Garden. It's said a tiger lived in a cave, so the stone "Immortals' Bridge" (仙人桥) is also called "Cross the Tiger Bridge" (渡虎桥). The area's known for its ancient calligraphy on boulders—but what Chinese boulders *don't* have calligraphy?

Tiger Stream Night Moon (Hǔxī Yèyuè, 虎溪夜月) Locals say that on the 15th of the Lunar month, the moonlight upon the clay Buddhist figurines and the clay tiger makes them appear to come alive, and on the evening of Mid-autumn Festival, thousands of pilgrims vie to be the first to watch the moon work its magic.
Add: Húyuán Lù, near Botanical Garden. Tel: 2021732
Tiger Stream Vegetarian Restaurant (虎溪岩寺素餐馆) Tel: 2121799

Wàn Shílián Temple (Wàn Shílián Sì, 万石莲寺) in the Botanical Garden, was built in the late Ming Dynasty by General Shīlàng. The gate has a pair of antithetical couplets written by the famous Buddhist Master Hóngyī (弘一法师).

Border of Heaven Temple (Tiānjiè Sì, 天界寺), also in the Botanical Garden, is famous for its morning bell, (Tiānjiè Xiǎozhōng, 天界晓钟) which is poetically described as "Dawn Bell Ringing from Heaven's Border." Tiānjiè is also famous for the legend of Tiānjié Learner and the common Xiàmén saying, "No wife, no monkey" (see "Xiàmén Festivals and Legends chapter).

The garden's other temples include Crag in the Clouds Temple (Yúnzhōngyán Sì, 云中岩寺), Pacific Crag Temple (Tàipíngyán, Sì 太平岩寺), White Deer Cave Temple (Bǎilùdòng Sì, 白鹿洞寺), Purple Cloud Crag Temple (Zǐyúnyán Sì, 紫云岩寺), Purple Bamboo Grove Temple (Zǐzhúlín, 紫竹林寺), Immortal Crag Temple, 万寿岩寺) and Sweet Dew Temple (Gānlù Sì, 甘露寺). South Fújiàn Buddhist College Nunnery is in Purple Bamboo Grove Temple.

South Fujian Buddhist College Nunnery

Getting to Botanical Garden. The front gate is only a ten minute walk from Zhongshan Rd. (past Zhongshan Park). Also note that the Railroad Garden Path is right outside the gate, before the Martyr's Memorial (Xiàmén Lièshì Língyuán, 厦门烈士陵园) and the Wan Peony Hotel. But more adventurous souls hike over the mountains above XMU's Lover's Lake. Ascend the serpentine trail, a relic of Japanese occupation, cross the bridge and buy a pass (not cheap, but I think well worth it; I can't imagine the cost of the garden's upkeep). The trail eventually crosses the forested crest, where tigers roamed 60 years ago, and where in the 1990s folks found a 15 foot reticulated python.

But fear not! Reticulated pythons are rarer than Monty Pythons, and fear us more than we fear them. Or so I'm told.

But has anyone told the pythons?

In the 1990s, just 2 hours north in Koxinga's hometown of Nán'ān (南安), a python ate a farmer and two kids (separate sittings, of course). Well, Chinese love snake, especially stewed, so it's fair play that snakes now love Chinese—or at least have a crush on them.

But Nan'an folks probably now find the 'snakes fear us more than we fear them" claim a tad hard to swallow.

Goose Mountain Park (Hóngshān Gōngyuán, 鸿山公园) Exit a bus on S. Siming Rd. between XMU and Millennium Hotel. Hong Shan Park, which has everything from a small Buddhist temple (for small Buddhists?) to beautiful gardens, an old fashioned Carousel, and a Ferris Wheel atop a 125m. peak, where for once you'll go in circles and not mind it, while you enjoy the best panoramic view in Xiamen—with the possible exception of the summit of Sunlight Rock.

On rainy days, the peak's unique wind currents blow rain both vertically and horizontally, simultaneously, creating a unique phenomenon that locals have dubbed "knitted rain."

Hongshan Park

The 4 characters engraved on the mountainside, Jiǎo Hóng Yí, 剿红夷, mean "Attack, Annihilate, Red Barbarians." These were carved after repulsing the Dutch attackers in 1622.

Nothing personal, of course.

Tel: 2025696

Back to the Garden
True Tale of the Cultural Revolution

Zhānglì set his clay teacup on the brown plastic tray and said, "I was a Red Guard, you know, as insolent as they came. But I was given a new heart in the 10,000 Rock Garden.

"During the Cultural Revolution, public property was up for grabs by any Red Guard who wanted it. We used to seize whatever we wanted and no one dared stop us.

"One day, my friend and I decided we wanted rare and beautiful flowers for our room, so we each grabbed a sack and headed for the Botanical Garden.

"In the green house, we were overwhelmed by the variety and beauty of the tropical flowers. I was about to put a beautiful plant in my sack when I heard a noise and turned to see an old lady bent over some plants, weeding them.

"We didn't fear her, because no one dared question or hinder a Red Guard. But when she looked up at us she didn't seem fearful either, or surprised that we had barged into her greenhouse, or that we obviously planned to steal some flowers. In fact, she smiled!

"Before I could move she walked over and picked up the plant I had been eyeing and held it before my eyes. 'Isn't it beautiful?' she exclaimed. 'These are very rare and come from South America. They are difficult to grow but well worth the effort. Do you like it?'

"I was speechless! I glared at her and headed for another exotic plant, but before I could even reach for it she had set the other plant down, rushed up to my side, and asked, "Do you know what this plant is called?"

"'No,' I snarled. She was getting on my nerves.

"She smiled, and patiently explained the plant's name, origin, and how to keep it alive. She concluded, 'It is very beautiful, isn't it?'

"I stomped away, frustrated, but every time we reached for a plant she was beside us, smiling, patiently explaining the plant's origins, habitats, and needs. She never raised her voice, and when I picked up a plant anyway and started to put it in my bag, she just looked at me silently, with a little smile, but sad eyes.

"I melted. I had been so angry and bitter, and determined to take it out on society, but her gentleness and patience defused my anger, and my friend's too, and we walked out, leaving our sacks behind us, defeated—and renewed.

"We were so glad when the Cultural Revolution ended soon afterwards. It has been two decades now, and I've returned to the garden many times hoping to see the lady, to tell her how much she changed my life, but I've never seen her again. Maybe she's dead now. But I'll never forget her..."

Railroad Park (Tiélù Gōngyuán, 铁路公园)—**a family favorite** Leave it to Xiamen to transform a rusty, abandoned railroad track into one of Xiamen's most delightful new parks. From harbor to train station, the old track has been beautifully renovated as a 4km. walkway—wooden boardwalk in parts, elegantly laid baked red brick in others.

A tunnel near the Siming Rd. entrance has sculptures and photos depicting the transformation of Xiamen railroads, from the steam locomotives we saw in 1988 to the blazing bullet trains of today.

The entire route has bougainvillea (city flower) and other plants, bushes, and trees, with plenty of benches for resting, reading, or zoning out. And check out the hi-tech, clean (and free!) bathrooms!

The first time I used their Space Age W.C., I nearly went to pot when a prerecorded feminine voice explained their services. I thought for a minute I was getting more services than I'd bargained for.

The Railroad Park is delightful by day and romantic by night, with gentle illumination from old fashioned carriage-style lights on poles. It is nice to be able to walk the parks by night in safety—a luxury increasingly rare in other places.

Jīnbǎng Garden (Jīnbǎng Gōngyuán, 金榜公园), about 500 m southwest of the train station, is the birthplace of Xiàmén Culture. Visit Chén'àn's (陈黯) former residence, and enjoy tea and snacks in the tea house, which an Amoy Magic reader wrote is a "Very nice place to sit (almost like a German beer garden!)."

Jīnbǎng Garden—Birthplace of Xiàmén Culture and Home to a Celebrated Failure!

It is said that, with the exception of Neolithic settlers 3,000 years ago, Xiàmén was first inhabited on Jīnbǎng Mtn. (金榜山). During the mid 7th century, a family moved to South Fújiàn from Xī'ān, and one of that family's descendants, Chén'àn, made a name for himself on Jīnbǎng Mountain—as a highly successful failure!

Chén'àn was a prodigy, writing poetry at age 10, but then grew up to fail the imperial exam 18 times! He finally gave up at the age of 60 and lived the rest of his life as a hermit on Jīnbǎng Mountain. Ironically, "Jīnbǎng" means "Gold List of Names", or "1st rank in the exam." It was named this because of Chén'àn's intent and spirit, not his accomplishments. He taught many students and was considered one of Xiàmén's cultural pioneers.

In 1990 Xiàmén set up the 860,000 m^2 Jīnbǎng Park, which has his former residence, as well as a sculpture of Xiamen's famous failure.

Zhōngshān Park 中山公园 (built 1927). Most Chinese cities have a Zhōngshān Park, Zhōngshān Rd, etc. They are named after Sūn Zhōngshān (Sun Yat-sen, 孙中山), who sought to free China. It must have worked. Zhōngshān Park has free admittance.

Sun's statue bears his granddaughter's inscription, "The Great Democratic Revolutionary Pioneer Dr. Sun Yat-sen." She was probably biased, but so are 1.3 billion other Chinese.

Zhongshan Park, 1929

Zhōngshān Park's bumper car rink is popular, though I get enough of that driving our van, Toy Ota." in Xiàmén (see Darwinian Driving in Transportation chapter). The park also has rowboats. If you're afraid of being up a creek without a paddle, try the swan-shaped fiberglass pedal boats.

But avoid the hottest days, lest you pedal to the tune of your swan song.

Zhōngshān has numerous small gardens, a flower exhibition hall, bridges and pavilions, and a small zoo. On holidays like Lantern Festival (15th day of first lunar month), the park is packed with special performers, displays, and exhibitions from all over the country.

In the wee hours of the morning, every Chinese park teems with folk exercising their Life Force (Qì, 气) with Tàijíquán (太极拳), and petite grannies twirling swords and silks, and other forms of martial arts. (See sports chapter).

Address: Zhōngshān Lù

> **Amoy Sunsets**
> "This chapter would not be complete without a word about the glorious sunsets it is our privilege to look upon in and about Amoy. They are simply magnificent as the sun lingers for a little while behind these western hills. Such gorgeous coloring, delicate tints, glory and splendor, are not only beyond words, but not everywhere to be seen." Pitcher 1912, p.286

South Lake Park (Nánhú Gōngyuán, 南湖公园) On the North bank of Yuándāng Lake, this 16.1 ha park opened in 1995 and was one of Xiàmén's top 8 sites. All ages enjoy the 7.2 hectare lawn, the rental boats, and the egrets.

Address: Húguāng Lù (湖光路), not far from the train station.

Huli Park (Húlǐ Gōngyuán, 湖里公园) 1126 hectare park with lake, boating, bumper cars, "Flying Carpet," etc. Add: Huátài Lù 华泰路

Nánpǔtuó Temple Scenic Region (see "Religion" chapter)

Xiamen Happy Valley Water Park (Xiàměn Kuàilè Gǔ Shuǐshàng Lèyuán, 厦门快乐谷水上乐园). Ssee "Sports & Recreation Chapter".

Great Hall of the People (Rénmín Huìtǎng, 人民会堂). This is not a park, but it is surrounded by 70,000m^2 of lawns and gardens, and is well worth a visit. Opposite the city government, this is one of Xiàmen's 10 architectural landmarks. The hall has a total of 25,000m^2, including five levels above ground and one below. The largest hall holds 1500 people, and the international conference room 260 people, with facilities for simultaneous translation of four languages. And the place was built in less than a year! I remember when it was first built, Běijīng complained that it was extravagantly large, and indeed it did seem out of place. Now that the city has grown up around it, it seems rather small.

Hǎicāng Safari Park (Hǎicāng Yěshēng Dòngwùyuán, 海沧野生动物园)
This is moving to Xiang'an District (near XMU's new campus).

Gulangyu Gardens—see "Gulangyu" Chapter.

Burnt Islet (Huǒshāoyú, 火烧屿), originally called "Green Islet" (Lùdǎo, 绿岛) or Fishing Islet (Diàoyúdoǎ, 钓鱼岛), is not only *off* the beaten path but *under* it (the tiny 27-hectare islet helps support Hǎicāng Bridge).

Some say the island is named after its sedimentary rock, which includes brown sandstone and volcanic rhyolite. Others say that at the end of the Song Dynasty (960-1279 AD), villagers hid out here until they were burned out by the invading Mongols—hence the name Burnt Islet.

Xiamen reforested the islet in the 1970s, and today the island is blanketed in trees, shrubs and flowers, including the Taiwanese acacia, which is the subject of local legends (p.172).

Haicang Bridge authorities run Burnt Islet and charge an entrance fee that used to include the **Science and Technology Museum** (this has been relocated and expanded, and expat adults and children alike enjoy it).

Take a nature walk, or look for Xiamen's rare white dolphins.

The Qinqin Zoo (Qīnqīn Dòngwùyuán, 亲亲动物园), I hear has been closed, and should have been. They used to allow you to fish and eat what you caught.

I doubt they let people eat and catch the other exhibits, but one never knows.

Bottom line: the manmade attractions are not that great, but not because the government hasn't tried. They've invested a lot of time and money into this little islet but it gets far too few visitors too make a profit. Hopefully people will read this, and the website, and frequent it enough to give the government reason to develop it further.

Note: Burnt Island is closed on Mondays for maintenance. Tel: 5617771

Burnt Island Recreation! Amenities are always changing. Business is brisk in summers but boats may be unavailable in winter.

Getting to Burnt Island Take a ferry from Lùjiāng Road's Passenger Terminal（鹭江道旅游客运码头）. This is just up the road from the Lùjiāng Hotel.

Tianzhu Mountain (天竺山) **Forest Park.** If you really want to get away from it all, visit this beautiful 31 km2 natural paradise, which has attracted Chinese from all over for centuries. Tianzhu has 3 lakes, and wooden boardwalks winding through the seemingly endless ranges of lush mountains, often. You must leave cars at the gate but when visitors are enough (or if you arrange beforehand), you can use their electric transports.

Favorite sites include Tianzhu Lake, Haoyue Lake, Hundred-bamboo Garden, Longmen Temple, and Zhenji Temple.

Getting there: No. 805 bus to Tianzhushan Dongmen Station (天竺山东门站).

Jíměi（集美）Gardens

(See "Jíměi" chapter)

Sea Turtle Garden (Áoyuán, 鳌园)

Tan Kah Kee's Former Home (Chénjiāgēng gùjū, 陈嘉庚故居)

Returning Overseas Scholars Hall (Guīláitáng, 归来堂)

Tan Kah Kee Park (Jiāgēng Gōngyuán, 嘉庚公园）5,000m^2

Dragon Boat Pool (Lóngzhōuchí, 龙舟池), 100 by 800 meters.

Yanping Fort Relic (Yánpíng Gùlěi, 延平故垒） Koxinga's fort; 1660 AD.

Tiānzhú Mountain Forest Park (Xiàmén Tiānzhushān Sēnlín Gōngyuán, 厦门天竺山森林公园） This 700 million Yuan, 2651 ha park has 5 manmade lakes. Most peaks are over 700 meters, with Tiānzhú (Heavenly Pillar) Mountain (Tiānzhùshān, 天竺山）reaching 933 meters. About 36 km from downtown Xiamen or 35 km from Zhangzhou.

Wànbǎo Mountain Orchard (Wànbǎoshān Guānguǎng Guǒyuán, 万宝山观光果园）From Jīměi take the 324 Highway to the Kēngnèi crossroads (坑内路口). Take #53 bus (Sīmíng Běi Lù to Jiǎoměi, 思明北路—角美). Or take the #93 bus from Jīměi to Kēngnèi, or the Xiàmén—Zhāngzhou Mini-bus and get off at Kēngnèi. Beautiful scenery, fishing, fresh fruit year-round. Facilities include 4 suites and 8 standard rooms, meeting room, dining room, tea room.

4 Seasons of Fruit

Long'ans, (Lóngyǎn,龙眼), Litchi (Lìzhī, 荔枝), Persimmon (Shìzi, 柿子), Tangerine (Yúgān, 余柑), Olive (Gǎnlǎn, 橄榄), Philippine Mango (Fēilvbīn Mángguǒ, 菲律宾芒果), Thai Mango (Mángguǒ, 泰国芒果), American Ruby Red Grapefruit (Měiguó Hóngròu Pútáoyòu, 美国红肉葡萄柚), American Southern Peach (Měiguó Nánfāng Shuǐmìtáo, 美国南方水蜜桃), American Peach (Měiguo Yóutáo, 美国油桃), Táiwān Black Gold Pearl Wax-apple (Táiwān Hēijīnzhū Liánwù, 台湾黑金珠莲雾), Táiwān Jujube (Táiwān Mìzǎo, 台湾蜜枣), Táiwān Sweet Tangerine (Táiwān Tiántángjú, 台湾甜糖桔), Táiwān Qīnghuā Pear (Qīnghuā Lí, 台湾青花梨), Táiwān Shìjia Pineapple (Táiwān Shìjiā fènglí, 台湾释迦凤梨), Táiwān "Shùméi" (a berry? 台湾树莓), South African Grapes (Nánfēi Pútáo, 南非葡萄), Loquats (Pípá, 枇杷), Strawberries (Cǎoméi, 草莓), Malaysian Peach (Mǎláixīyà Yángtáo, 马来西亚杨桃).

Tóng'ān Parks

(See the Tóng'ān chapter for details)

Tóng'ān's Little Plain Provincial Forest Park (Xiǎopíng Sēnlín Gōngyuán, 小坪省级森林公园) 25km north of Tóngān.

Tóng'ān Film Studio (Xiàmén Tóng'ān Yǐngshì Chéng, 厦门同安影视城).

12 Vauclusian Springs [12 Dragon Springs] of North Mountain (Běishān Shíèr Lóngtán, 北山十二龙潭) In Wǔxiǎn Town (Wǔxiǎnzhèn, 五显镇).

North Mountain Scenic Area (Běichén Shān, 北辰山) 122 km^2, in Wǔxiǎnzhèn (五显镇境内) 12 km from Tóng'ān, near Film City.

Clambering thru Butterfly Valley

Tong'an Butterfly Valley (Tōng'ān Húdiégǔ, 同安蝴蝶谷) **Delightful!** Tīngxī Zhèn Rěnyú Cūn, 汀溪镇荏畲村

Tóng'ān Lotus Flower Mountain Scenic Area (Tōng'ān Liánhuā Shān Fēngjǐngqū, 同安莲花山风景区) Liánhuā Zhèn Hòupǔ Cūn (莲花镇后埔村) 10 km from Tóng'ān.

Three Hero Islands (Yīngxióng Sāndǎo, 英雄三岛) and **The Dàdèng Island Frontline Broadcast Station** (Dàdēng Dǎo Qiánxiàn Guǎngbō Zhàn, 大嶝岛前线广播站). Only 1.8 km from Táiwān-controlled Jīnmén Island.

My Own Backyard

by Patricia Puia
Principal, Xiamen International School

I find I've become a little jaded about living overseas, which is one reason I don't write as often as I used to. I keep thinking that there's nothing interesting enough to share with all of you; I have to keep reminding myself that what is commonplace to me may still be fairly exotic to someone else. The drive to get rid of that complacency, combined with the purchase of a new digital camera, has forced me to take a new look at my surroundings, and I've been pleasantly reminded that there are pleasures to be had, right here in my own backyard.

Take for example Nánpǔtuó Temple, one of the landmarks of the city. Nánpǔtuó is a Buddhist temple, still in operation, having survived both the Cultural Revolution and the growing number of Chinese young people turning their backs on tradition. The temple is actually a series of buildings and walkways designed to glorify Buddha and welcome his followers. The entrance is flanked by two enormous figures – probably 8 feet tall and brightly painted figures of a happy Buddha in ancient dynastic robes.

Outside the main building (see photo), worshippers buy incense sticks, which they hold between their hands in prayer. They take the burning incense in with them up the steep, small steps to the small enclave that houses a golden Buddha image. There they stand respectfully or kneel at small kneelers, bowing frequently and asking the Buddha for his help and guidance in matters large and small. The air around them is thick with the sickly sweet smell, and tourists step around them quietly, leaving them to their prayers. At the edge of the building, passersby strike a small gong with the palm of their hands, a gesture of good luck.

Beyond the temple, there are pathways up the hill, each with tiny enclaves for quiet reflection. A small cave hides rows and rows of Buddha figures of all descriptions. Beyond that, couples sit on a long stone bench that overlooks the main buildings. Further up, the hill overlooks the adjoining university and gives a view of the seashore, only a mile or two away. Despite a large weekend crowd, the place has an overall feeling of peace and quiet, the way it feels to walk into

Notre Dame. It's a place large enough to make one feel alone and small enough to make one feel comfortable.

Even closer to home is a small park right outside my bedroom window. I live on one of the man-made canals that cuts through the city. On a small strip of land in the center of that canal is a place I call Island Park. (I suspect it has a better name, but I don't know what it is!) On a bright, clear Saturday, I wandered through there, taking in the chrysanthemum and bonsai exhibits and snapping photos of my apartment building. It's a lovely little place, with tiny bridges and wide open spaces, and a very nice view of the ocean. Some evenings, there is music in the band shell there. I've never been able to figure out their schedule, but I have spent many nice evenings on my balcony listening to everything from Chinese music to salsa.

But the best place in town may well be Zhōngshān Park (Jhong-shan), named for Sun Yat-sen, Father of the Chinese Republic. I spent a lovely Sunday there, playing with my camera and enjoying the scenery, both human and floral. Although it's centrally located, Zhōngshān Park is not exactly Central Park, although it does try. It offers some of the same features – a small zoo, paddle boats, children's rides, and quiet spaces for people to play a little soccer.

My favorite place here is a small area under some stately banyan trees. Here, elderly Chinese come to play cards and Mahjong. It is quiet and shady, the only sound being the occasional laughter at one of the tables, or the subtle clink of dice. There are wonderful faces here – old and wizened, and vaguely suspicious of the presumptuous white woman experimenting with her new cameras. The men were willing to pose for us; the women tried to ignore us. It didn't matter either way. It was a great view of China as it must have been once, and as it remains. (See photo.)

For that is the truth of China.   But at its heart, there is still something stately and simple about this place. A walk in the park or a trip to the temple is still considered a fine way to spend a Sunday afternoon, and foreigners are still – well, foreign.

It's surprisingly nice to be part of all that, to wander the uneven pavements and lounge in the little bits of green that the city maintains. Perhaps it's not as exotic as it once was, but it is a reminder that I am still a stranger here – and not unhappy to be so.

Spook Hill Solution German engineers checked it out and said it really is a gravitational anomaly, but either they were spooking us or they got their engineering degrees from a diploma mill. Xiàmén government engineers measured the 70m spooky stretch on which a cars and bikes appear to roll "up" the 2% grade. The spoilsports discovered that, in fact, the "lower end" is 1.395 m higher than the "upper" end.

But even knowing the truth, it's still fun, and I love taking friends there, and telling them it is proof China is another planet because even gravity is reversed.

Chapter 7
Amoy Wildlife

Since the 18th century, Western naturalists have converged upon Fujian Province to explore a biological diversity that probably rivals Eden itself. Fujian is home to everything from 33-foot pythons to the "ancestor of all tigers," the Amoy Tiger. We are also home to earth's deadliest creature, the Amoy Vampire (see end of chapter).

Want to see Amoy Tigers in the flesh (or in the fur)? Visit West Fujian's Plum Mountain Nature Reserve (Méihuā Shān Zìrán Bǎohù Qū, 梅花山梅花山自然保护区), which also has nearly 1500 kinds of plants and hundreds of reptiles, birds, and animals, including 40 endangered species like leopards and black bears."

Amoy Tigers

"Tigers of enormous size constantly roam about the countryside in the interior, and keep the people in a perpetual state of terror. Not unfrequently they carry off a man, woman, or child, while at work in the fields, of whom nothing more is ever seen, excepting occasionally a few bones. However, they are in one way beneficial to the country, as they effectually prevent all robbers, and night prowlers from roving about after dark."

"Amoy General Geographical Description, &c".
China Review, Vol. 22, No.3, 1896

Hello Kitty

"Tigers possess magical qualities; their claws are talismen against devils, their bones and tendons potent medicine for healing and strength. They are sovereign because the Chinese discern the character for king on their foreheads…

"Two things in Fukien impressed Marco Polo: the beauty of the women and the size of its tigers…the Fukienese hunted tigers in the rock caves of the island's high spine. The conservative hunted in pairs; one took a flaring torch into the tiger's lair, walked on until the tiger's eyes reflected in its flame, then quickly stepped aside for his companion to spear or shoot. The modern-minded strapped electric lamps to their foreheads, and practised the hair-raising sport alone. There were still quite a lot of tigers on the island, the fishermen said, but their numbers were dwindling."

A Race of Green Ginger, by Ms. Averil Mackenzie-Grieve,
(British resident of Gulangyu in the 1920s).

Tiger Hunting in Amoy

Adapted from "Sport in Amoy," *China Review,* Vol. 22 No. 5 (1897) By H. R. Bruce

"But the crowning sport with which the name of Amoy is associated is the pursuit of that king of the jungle, the wily tiger. Tigers abound more or less all along the coast of China, and native trappers declare that they are more abundant in 'Kwang Tung' province than in Fokien.

"These trappers travel over several provinces in search of tiger lairs, and having discovered one they find that the tiger follows the same track in entering and leaving.

They survey this track, select some point where the track dips a little below the ground on one side or the other.

"On this higher ground they dig a hole like a grave and fix therein a very powerful bow with a poisoned shaft protruding through a small tunnel that connects the grave with the track. The bow is fired by a small thread fixed across the path, so as to catch a passing tiger's chest, and the poison is so effective that the wounded beast seldom gets away.

"The tiger is a valuable prize, he is good medicine from his whiskers to the tip of his tail, and all who covet strength, courage or ferocity compete for a portion of the specific. Moreover, there is no adulteration act to ensure that all that is sold as tiger, is really tiger, so that with the help of an ancient buffalo, or of a dead horse, a tiger of 300 pounds weight gives fully 1,000 pounds retail weight.

"The natives have curious ideas about tigers occupying lairs in their neighborhood. If a man has been killed they welcome the foreign sportsman most cordially, and chin-chin him as the savior of the people, but if the tiger has not been known to take human life they are disposed to propitiate him, and condemn the folly of enraging him and perhaps converting a good dispositioned beast into a maneater. Then again they will say, 'What is the use of shooting him, two new tigers will at once occupy his den.'

"Sometimes a tiger has the character of never harming the villagers who are his neighbors; although he eats up strangers and travellers by the score, the villagers are quite sure of their own safety. If one stays in the village for a few days another reason for their immunity suggests itself. Owing to their propinquity to a permanent tiger lair they have inherited habits of early hours at night, and late hours in the morning, that give the poor tiger no chance, so he has to fall back on benighted strangers with less regular habits.

"All Amoy tigers are village prowlers, and man-eaters. There is no game of any sort: goats, pigs and cows are carefully pounded at night, so that probably village dogs comprise 5/6ths of the necessary support for the tigers of this province. Their hunting ground being so much among the haunts of men, tigers, after dusk at any rate, have lost all instinctive dread of man, and the sounds and odours of humanity, and will stroll up a village street soon after bed-time, and break open a door in search of pig, or dog. It is by no means an uncommon occurrence for a tiger to take a man out of his bed, and in the hot weather many lives are lost by sleeping in the doorway, and under the eaves.

"It may be asked how it comes to pass that sportsmen bag tigers in Amoy, and not at other ports. For thirty years there have been casual hunts for tigers, but it was only some ten years ago that that indefatigable sport Mr. A. L. B. Allen succeeded in proving that patience, perseverance, lots of time, and good nerves could bring a tiger to the bag. Since then the sport has been keenly pursued, and that indomitable old shikaree Mr. Frank Leyburn heads the list with about 20 'kills.'

"There is not much jungle within 20 miles of Amoy. The tigers lie up in subterranean passages in the rocky nullahs common to every hill-side. To drive them out of these caves the native hunters fearlessly enter armed with spears, and torches fixed on long bamboos. If Mr. Stripes has a bolt-hole he will bolt and come under the guns outside; but if caught in a cul-de-sac the sportsman must crawl into the cave, wriggle past the hunters and shoot at 20 yards or less, usually a tame performance compared to an encounter in the open.

"Of course much rough work, and many discomforts attend tiger shooting, but on the other hand there are many compensations which make a trip enjoyable. If one is lucky enough to put up in one of the mountain temples, far from the madding crowd, and commanding a wide view of the neighbouring valleys, with their unrivalled agriculture feeding a thousand to the square mile, the fresh air and charming scenery are enough to live on. Again to acquire a good knowledge of the country, and to study the habits of the people is always of interest, and although one cannot hope to bag a tiger every week, when the lucky day comes, there is a decided feeling that the noble sport is well worth our most ardent devotion."

Amoy Tiger, West Fujian's Meihua Mountain Tiger Preserve, 2003

Fowl Pursuits on Amoy Back in 1860, Amoy's British Consul, Mr. Swinhoe, reported 174 kinds of birds on Amoy. Sadly, much of the wildlife vanished, but thanks to strict environmental policies, birds are now making a comeback. In 2006, my wife saw a rare black eagle right outside our kitchen window. Birdwatchers are making a comeback as well. Each march, Xiamen's Observe Birds Association (OBA) promotes "Care for Birds Week," and offers field trips for bird watchers of all ages.

Robert Swinhoe
Diplomat, Naturalist, Amoy Consul

Robert Swinhoe was born in Calcutta, India on 1 September 1836 to a family who had served British interests in India for many years. His father was a lawyer and his brother was a colonel in India.

After university in England, Swinhoe went to Hong Kong at age 18, and studied Chinese, as well as Chinese natural history. He moved to Amoy in 1855, learned the local dialect, studied the local fowl and fauna, and kept as pets a civet cat (猫香), pangolin (穿山甲), great owl, and a young falcon (猎鹰). During a trip to Taiwan, he recorded, during only two weeks 93 new birds and 17 mammals.

Swinhoe returned to Amoy, where he helped found the short-lived Literary and Scientific Society of Amoy.

At their first meeting, on 17 November 1856, Swinhoe read his first published paper, "A Few Remarks on the Fauna of Amoy." (I include an edited version of this at the end of this chapter).

Swinhoe was the first British consular official in Taiwan. He became ill and returned to England in 1862, where he set up an award-winning "Formosan Booth" at the London Exhibition, and gave lectures for many societies. Charles Darwin, in one of his writings, noted the pigeon skin specimens sent to him by Swinhoe.

Swinhoe returned to Amoy in 1866, returned to England again in 1869 on sick leave, and in 1875 had a stroke in China. He decided China was for the birds and returned to England, but died anyway in 1877 at the tender age of 41.

"A Few Remarks on the Fauna of Amoy"

Robert Swinhoe (1857)

"…Who has not wondered at the bare hills of Amoy, at the first glimpse he obtains on entering the harbor, and, seeing the great boulders of rock rise one another in endless confusion, thought to himself with a shudder, Can animal life be there? But though animal life is there to a small extent, it is to the plains, which are inhabited and cultivated with such care by the natives, that we must look for most that will interest us in our science.

"The **wily fox** is the first animal which we have to consider, for, low as he stands in the natural series of Mammals, he is here prominent as the largest of the Carnivora we possess…

"The greatest devastator among the poultry of the poor is an animal belonging to the **weasel** (鼬鼠) family (Mustelideae), and, though generally distributed, is very rarely seen. It measures about a foot and a half in length, has buff-coloured fur, with a black muzzle, and is the Hwang-shoo-lang of the Pun-ts'aou, and the Chiah-ch'oo (tawny rat) of Amoy men…

"Before leaving the Carnaria it would be as well to mention a curious animal that was brought alive to me by a native, and which I kept some months in confinement. It evidently belonged to the **civet** family (Viverridae), measured in length one foot and a half, having rather long fur of a dingy brown colour, and a black head with a white line down the snout; the tail was tipped with white. ..

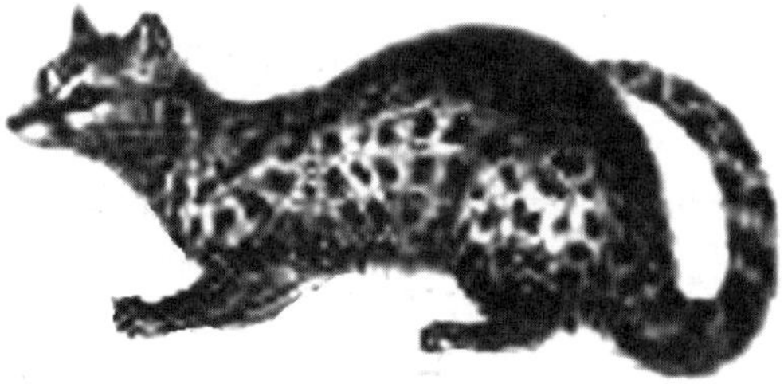

"We have also heard certain stories about the **sea-otter** that is occasionally seen prowling about on Six Islands, seeking his finny prey at the dead hour of night, and avoiding the light of day…

"…The next quadraped… is the scaly ant-eater or **pangolin** (穿山甲)…Ours is a small species (probably Manis brachyurus), measuring in toto only two feet and three inches, of the tail takes one foot. Its gait is most peculiar - with the body bent in a bow, and the head and tail downwards, as it runs along on the sides of its fore feet. ..Large prices are given by the native doctors for this animal, for its flesh and bones are employed for various medicinal purposes; and one of its scales, fastened to the end of a stick, is sold as a safe instrument to be used in scratching without fear of producing ulcers on the skin. … and also the Cetacea, the Phocaenae or porpises of which order are well known to us even in the harbour, where at times they may be seen showing their round white backs in a line, and then disappearing, to be seen again at a further distance…."

Amoy's Fowl Friends
Which can you identify?
Birdie
Peregrine Falcon
Light Vented Bulbil
Little Egret
Pintail Snipe
Eurasian Tree Sparrow
Eurasian Sparrow Hawk
Eurasian Cuckoo
Buzzard
Dusky Warbler
Mew Gull
Blue and White Flycatcher
Dalmatian Pelican
Barn Swallow
Brown Hawk Owl
Crested Myna
Common Hoopoe
Gray Heron
Blue-breasted Quail
Eurasian Marsh Hunter
Collared Crow
Chestnut-eared Bunting
Taiwan Blue Magpie
(Sue's favorite!)
Blue Whistling Thrush
Osprey
Japanese White-eye
White-throated Kingfisher
Long-tailed Shrike
Horned Grebe
Masked Laughing Thrush
Woodstockus Peanutsiensis
Spot-billed Duck
Amoy Crane
Eureka! I found him!

Swinhoe's Birds of Amoy

"… The **peregrine falcon** (Falco peregrinus) is a straggling visitor, but a pair built their eyrie last year on the high hill of Nan-tai-woo (南太武), on the summit of which stands the pagoda…. An **osprey** (Pandion) is sometimes seen even in the harbour, but little is known of him. I have seen him strike a fish close under the bows of a vessel, and bear it away in triumph. … A **sparrow owl** (Nyctipeles, Swain.), and a small tawny **Scops owl** (probably Scops rufiscens of Horsfield), are seen occasionally in winter. …

"…the **blackbird** and **rock thrush** (Petrocincla violacea) are always with us, the former enlivening our gardens by his rich full notes, and the latter enchanting the lonely wanderer among the bleak hills with his wild minstrelsy, as he sings from the summit of a monstrous boulder, or springs lightly into the air, trolling forth his merry roundelay…

"The rock thrush and blackbird are taken by the Chinese for one and the same, and called Ok`ee, though one is blue and red, and the other black. The most familiar and perhaps the best known is the magpie robin (Gryllivora), a small bird of the pied plumage of a magpie, with the habits and peculiarities of a robin. Its song, poured out at early morn or sunset from the roof-tops of our houses, is occasionally pretty, but abounding in harsh and jarring notes…

"… The most diminutive of all stands next, the little **tailor-bird** (Orthotonus), remarkable for its long pointed bill, which serves as a needle in sewing leaves together round its nest; the underside of a long leaf of the Alpinia nutans is often chosen, the edges of which are drawn together by thread made of spider's web and fibres. The prettiest construction of the kind I have seen was a nest flanked in by three orange leaves, and placed in the extremity of the boughs of an orange-tree.

"Flocks of the beautiful **white egret**, or paddy bird, as they are familiarly known to us (Herodias Garzetta), often attract our attention as they wing their way slowly through the obscure blue of a summer twilight, from the fields where they have been feeding, to their selected nest-trees, on which they settle like masses of snow among the dark green leaves. The **yellow-headed egret**, while with us in summer, is commoner, and roams about in larger flocks than the latter. A third and solitary species, **Herodias flavirostris**, is also found, and may be distinguished by its yellow bill, and the tuft of snowy feathers which surmounts the occiput. We have, besides, five or six other species of **heron**, nearly all remarkable for their elegance and beauty.

"The egret is much admired by the sentimental Chinese, and is often alluded to in poetical compositions by the style Loo-sze; and the Island of Amoy is often poetically called Loo-mun, Loo-keang, and Loo-taon, from the number of these snow-like birds that annually frequent it. Of the ninety-two species of Insessores found here, nine are British birds. Seven species of the Grallatores, and nearly all the Natatores, with the exception of the **pelicans**, **albatrosses**, and a few **gulls** and **terns**, are identical with those found in Great Britain…

" …It is unnecessary to dilate on the beauties and delights of the study of Nature: the heart of every man naturally throbs in the contemplation of the Creator's handiwork, and thrills with joy at the discovery of some new manoeuvre in the wondrous economy which so beautifully modulates and arranges all animal and vegetable life upon the globe.

"Solomon said, "There is nothing new under the sun;" so, probably, there is not; but a great deal of what passes around man is new to him, and astonishes him when brought to his notice, simply because he has not made use of those powers of observation that he has been endowed with. In conclusion, I cannot do better than quote the words that Milton puts in the mouth of the Divine Author of Nature in his address to our first parent:-- "Is not the earth With various living creatures, and the air, Replenish'd; and all these at thy command, To come and play before thee?"

Robert Swinhoe

Small Sample of Swinhoe's 174 Amoy Birds

1. **Buzzard** (Buteo vulgaris) A regular winter visitant.
2. **Osprey** (Pandion haliaet) Lives on the rocks at the mouth of the harbor and comes occasionally to Amoy, but very shy and unapproachable…
3. **Peregrine Falcon** (Falco peregrinus) Breeds in the neighbourhood and is not infrequent.
10. **Brown Hawk Owl** (Ninox scutellatus) A straggling winter visitant, common in summer at Fouchow where it breeds. The immature plumage is brown…
11. **Great Owl** (Bubo maximus) Breeds somewhere in the neighbourhood, as every early spring the young are sold in the streets…
17. **Swift** (Hirundapus nudipes) A straggler in spring during rain-storms.
18. **Barn Swallow** (Hirundo rusticas) …pretty numerous, building mud-nests shaped like a half-dish, and lined with straw and a few feathers, over the doors of Chinese huts, where they are revered as the harbingers of good luck.
19. **Red-rumped Swallow** (Hirundo daurica, alpestris) A few passing flocks spend a day or two in Amoy during winter. In Formosa it takes the place of the common species, and builds domed nests of clay and mud under the roof-tops
21. **White-throated Kingfisher** (Halcyon smyrnensis) A common resident; called "Fey-tsuy" by the Chinese, who glue the feathers, chiefly those of the wing, over ornaments worn by their women. Thus treated the lustrous blue feathers give the appearance of turquoise stone…
24. **Pied Kingfisher** (Ceryle rudis) Very common on the river; where it rises on the wing at a height above the water, and drops suddenly on its scaly prey. I have also seen it strike obliquely when flying close to the surface of the water.
27. **Prinia** (Prinia sonitans) I have named this from the crackling noise it produces when hopping or flying from twig to twig…
34. **Dusky Warbler** (Phylloscopus fuscatus) Common during winter… its most frequent note is "chick chick."
56. **Blue Whistling Thrush** (Myiophonus caeruleus) Lives among rocky caverns; not common, and very shy; native name Aw-chuy.
64. **Masked Laughing Thrush** (Garrulax perspicillatuas) Length 12 inches. Wing 4 7/10. Tail 5 2/10. Bill 9/10, to gape 1 3/10…It is a shy bird, but may be known a long way off by its loud cry of Teo-teo, uttered from time to time, or followed by a liquid guzzling low chatter.

65. **Spectacled Thrush** (Garrulax sinensis)...the Hwa-mei of the Chinese, by whom it is prized for its fine vocal powers, as well as for its pugnacious propensities.

79. **Long-tailed Shrike** (Lanius schach) Very common; has a great habit of shrieking. This is a much larger race than that found in the Indian archipelago, and is no doubt worthy of specific distinction…

82**. Collared Crow)** Corvus torquatus) Amoy's only crow.

83. **Magpie** (Pica media) Very common.

84. **Crested Myna** (Acridotheres cristatellus) A very common species from Hongkong to Shanghai; builds in holes of trees or walls, or makes large oval nests in trees; learns to speak with facility and soon becomes docile.

94. **Finch** (Ligurinus sinicus) Half goldfinch, half greenfinch; not uncommon all the year, has a pretty tinkling note; and feeds on thistle-heads as well as grain, &c.

147. **Goose** (Anser segetum) 151.**Spot-billed Duck** (Anas poecilorhyncha)

162. **Albatross** (Diomedea brachyuran) 164. **Mew Gull** (Larus canus)

168. **Loon** (Gavia Kittlitzii) 173. **Dalmatian Pelican** (Pelecanus crispus)

175. **Archaeopteryx** Extinct bird of the Jurassic period.
If you see one, you'd better lay off the rice wine!

Supplement The Discovery of the Amoy Vampire (A True Story)

I've slain more bloodsucking demons than Buffy the Vampire Slayer, but that is no great surprise because it was here in Xiamen, in the 1870s, that Dr. Patrick Manson discovered the deadliest creature on the planet. I'm speaking not of fearsome Amoy tigers, or King cobras, or even our 33-foot pythons. No, the most murderous resident of planet earth is the Amoy Vampire—a.k.a, mosquito, the Beelzebug, which even in the 21st century murders over 2 million people yearly.

On Gulangyu Islet, Dr. Manson, the "Father of Tropical Medicine," dissected these tiny denizens of the dark and discovered that they are not only a pain in the neck but deadly carriers of malaria.

I've battled these beasts for 24 years but it's a losing battle, and after one particularly bloody evening, I wrote "Amoy Vampire" (next page). This Qing Dynasty Tale, however, shows that Chinese have also battled the Amoy vampire for centuries.

"Go ahead! Make my day!"

Buddha's Bugs (Qing Dynasty Tale) A Buddhist monk vowed to offer his blood to feed other living things, but after mosquitoes had bitten him for hours the itching got to him and he began swatting them with abandon.

"What happened to your vow?" asked a bystander.

The monk sighed. "Some of them have started coming back for seconds."

Amoy Vampires

by Dr. Bill

Once upon an evening muggy, while I pondered, pestered, buggy,
Swatting quaint and curious Chinese bugs whose corpses filled the floor,
While I fretted, hands a flying, and about me bugs were dying,
Suddenly a shadow loomed upon my study's bamboo door.
"Tis some monstrous bug," I muttered, "beating at my study's door;
Only this and nothing more."

A Chinese piper's haunting tune came wafting on the scent of June,
While mashed and mangled insects writhed upon my study's earthen floor.
And then my soul began to ache and I prayed for the dawn to break,
And exorcise the terror that was beating on my study door,
And I fancied I could smell upon the winds of night a spoor,
Of bloody feasts of days of yore.

Now the beating on the screen was loud enough to burst my spleen,
It filled me with fantastic fears that I had never felt before,
How I sought to calm my terror. Surely this is but an error?
This mad creature knows not that it seeks another mortal's door?
"Tis not I you seek" I cried, "My neighbor's veins yield richer ore!
You seek them, they're right next door!"

As the darkened room grew colder, presently my soul grew bolder.
Why cringe here in mortal fear of that which lurks behind my door?
"Sir, in truth I was just eating when your wings began their beating,
Have some sweet 'n sour chicken. Beef and peppers -- nay, there's more.
Mushu pork, and Chinese dumplings, feast on this and thirst no more.
This is what you hunger for!"

Deep into the darkness staring, in my fear almost uncaring,
Listening for an answer to the plea I'd made so oft before;
But no answer did it make, and lo my heart was 'bout to break
When I detected softly on the breeze that wafted through the door
The buzz of dreams in which I'd screamed and cringed as I in fear implored,
"Chinese take-out! Nothing more."

Now I knew my doom was dawning as I saw that great mouth yawning,
And the needlelike appendage searching for my veins once more.
Now the screen was slowly breaking and my jugular was aching,
"Dracula has nothing on you, Hellish spawn of ancient lore!
Let my blood and body be, and seek elsewhere thy feast of gore.
Quoth he, buzzing, "One sip more."

Thrills of terror taunted, teased me, as the flying vampire seized me
And I swooned in senseless ecstasy upon the study floor.
Ghosts of Chinese bugs I'd splattered, laughed that nothing really mattered,
As they danced about my body, feasting on the crimson gore.
How much longer?" did I cry while rubbing on my neck the sore.
Quoth mosquito, "Evermore."

Chapter 8

Trish "Bushwalker" Boman

Trish Boman's Amoy Bushwalks

Enjoy the Old Amoy that delighted 19th century Lǎowài with bushwalks by Amoy veteran Trish Boman, of Xiàmén International School. (And check the Parks chapter for other hikes—such as our beautiful boardwalks, the Railroad Park, etc.)

Bushwalker Boman's Bio "My hometown is Brisbane, Queensland, Australia, though I was born in a smaller city, Rockhampton, beside a mountain range which inspired my first day long walk when I was about 14 (not that our mountains are anything to skite about on the world scale.)

"I am not a mountain-climber in the Everest sense, nor do I do any fancy rock-climbing, though I've abseiled and hauled myself on ropes and chains up volcanic cones, and even Uluru (Ayers Rock, in the centre of Australia).

"Brisbane is surrounded by other mountain ranges (referred to as "hills" by visitors to our fair city) variously covered with dry eucalyptus forests, or temperate rainforest. I especially love rainforest bushwalking and can deal with ticks, leeches, mud, and wait-a-while vines. I also lived in Cairns, in Queensland's far north, which has dense tropical rainforest. This really sparked off my love of bushwalking, beginning with trekking to pristine waterfalls, and swimming in fresh water creeks among the boulders and fresh-water crocodiles.

"In Xiàmén I found a like-minded person who began showing me around the Five Old Men Mountain (Wǔlǎofēng, 五老峰) behind Xiàmén University, and from then on we would choose a different hill each week and go out and find a track to climb it. In Xiàmén, many of the hills end in army bases, and have savage dogs and guards, so I've been turned away from several of them. I began to fear I'd be considered a particularly persistent spy who kept turning up in the wrong places!"

Trish Boman, the Bushwoman

Insights on "Strine" (Australian Slang)

I wrote Trish when I could not decipher her Aussie English. She replied:

> "I LOVE explaining 'Strine'…a chook is a chicken/hen, also used to fondly or cruelly chide someone: 'Silly old chook!' It is also a common nickname, mostly among men. 'Skite' is to boast and a skite is a boaster. (Both noun and verb) 'Wait-a-while vines' are rainforest vines with many barbs on long shoots that are sent out across the clearings. When you walk by, they catch on clothes, skin, hair and pull

you up to 'wait a while'. The only way to escape is to back yourself out the way you got into it. It's pretty vicious stuff. Eventually they grow up to become lawyer cane, the kind teachers used to hit kids with.

"Congratulations for including some Australian slang in Magic Xiàmén. I feel our existence is acknowledged somehow…"

Strine Struck

An angry Aussie reader wrote a scathing email to me arguing that Australians do *not* speak Strine because there is no such thing. Strange, given that the 50-year-old term is used today even by Australian government and media. I suggest the irate anti-Striners follow Trish's example and either embrace their uniqueness or go take a hike. Or bushwalk, as the case may be.

Trish Boman's Bushwalk #1

Shànglǐ 上李 Hike (Half Day)

Take the number 20 bus to the end of the line at the Railway Workers' Sanitorium (Tiělù liáoyǎngyuàn, 铁路疗养院). Walk out of the compound back across the small bridge you came over and follow the major road to the left, noting the eucalypts and sally wattles that grow on the hillsides. In the early mornings there is a strong smell of the lemon-scented gum, giving a little Australian experience for those who know it. On the right, you may catch a glimpse of the long, snake-shaped reservoir whose administration buildings you pass on the right.[1]

Path to Banling Palace

After about 1 km., with the city buildings in view ahead, there is an uphill fork on the right [this is Spook Hill; see Parks chapter]. A few hundred metres along it is a rustic stone gate on the right, with the characters: Bànlǐng gōng (半岭宫, right to left). This Daoist-style temple name ["gong" means "palace"] gives the appearance of leading to a Daoist temple above. Stone steps wind away invitingly into the greenness above.

Follow the winding stepped path, beside which are Railway Department white posts with red numbers, from about #41 up, until you reach a fair-sized Buddhist temple under construction. The only sign of the Daoist temple is a small shrine to the left, crowded with Daoist figurines, whilst above it a quite magnificent red brick Buddhist

---

① It leads eventually to downtown Xiamen, coming out at two places, either Wenzao (right fork) or Wenyuan Road (left fork) if you care to walk that far. No 83 bus will start before then and it will go to the Railway Station.

temple is being built. A magnificent view of the valley with the new road cutting through it can be enjoyed from the temple forecourt. The view extends as far as the city buildings and is filled with greenness. Military installations beam out from the opposite hill top.

Descending the steps from the temple, you can take another set of steps on the left which will lead back to the trench at a more southerly point. From here you can return to your original point and carry on to downtown Xiàmén, or you can return to Shangli the way you came.

If you still feel energetic, return to the turn-off at the end of the reservoir, mentioned above. This fork is a connecting track to the main Xiàmén Cross-Country Track (Qiánpǔ Túbùlǚxíng, 前埔徒步旅行). Along the way, you come to a rural dwelling, with chooks[①] and dogs, and the dirt track going by it on the left leads to Dōngpíng Mtn. (Dōngpíng Shān, 东坪山), a main village in the heights of Xiamen. At the T-junction, turn right to go to the back of the Taiwan Village Park (Táiwān Mínsúcūn, 台湾民俗村). At the next fork, be sure to turn left in a downhill direction, or you'll find yourself in an overgrown and fairly impassable track further on up the hill.

When you reach Táiwān Village, you will probably be stopped by workers whose job seems to be to look out for people getting in the "back door" of the Village, though if no one is around, you could try going for a little look-around. The gate-keeper will require you to exit via the nearest track which will bring you out in Huángcuò Village (黄厝村). There's a restaurant down the road to the right, (the restaurant is on your left) and it boasts some comfy upstairs rooms with air conditioning, lounges and TV which will restore lost energies.

Once restored, continue down the lovely tree-lined road towards the Island Ring Road. A bus stop just a little way to the left will return you to Xiàmén Univ. or Húlǐ Hill Cannon Fort (Húlǐshān Pàotái, 胡里山炮台) termini for your connections.

Chief Attractions

1. An excellent walkway along the creek below the new road, complete with artistic touches and cross-bridges. This keeps traffic and walkers well apart.
2. The stone stairway to the temple is green and leafy with bird song, fresh smells and rustic appearance.
3. The views from the Buddhist temple at the top of the stairs are especially expansove and green, facing down into the valley.
4. Because of links to the main Xiàmén Cross-Country track, there are possibilities for full-day walks of varying lengths.

Trish Boman's Bushwalk #2

Xiānyuè Mountain – Tiānzhú Temple (仙岳山 - 天竺岩寺)

Xiānyuè Mountain is one of Xiàmén's larger range of hills, being a barrier between downtown and the Húlǐ District. It offers a leisurely all-day, or a brisk half day outing. The use of a car to get to the temple can make the journey considerably shorter if time is limited. There are several ways to get to the temple, the easiest being up Qiáoyuè Rd

① Chooks: See Dr. Bill's A-Z Aussie Slang

(侨岳路), which is an extension of the larger Liányuè Rd. (莲岳路), which can be found at the farthest eastern point of Yúndāng Lagoon (筼筜湖), crossing Hubin North Road. Buses 13, 31 and 33 also turn the corner of Liányuè and Xiānyuè Roads. The road can be climbed on foot, but there is an off-road shortcut where the road first turns to go up the mountain. There is a "no lighting fires in the forest" sign in Chinese by a lane which is the only indicator of the entrance to the road. Once you reach the top of this shortcut, you rejoin the vehicle road just below the temple. The temple area is a busy one, with an enormous construction site begun for a major new temple. The present ones are a mixture of makeshift and elderly buildings doing a brisk trade in ancestor worship with copious amounts of holy money going up in smoke. A map and plan of the new temple are on display. Toilets are rudimentary, though there's a new one built but not open yet further up the hill.

If you want to continue on to the wonderfully constructed walk to the western end of the range, go on to the left (east) beyond the temple. There are several lookouts and trails leading off from the main track, including one which overlooks the city from an attractive pavilion. You'll also notice several "scientific experiments" among the trees, collecting insect samples and warning of poisonous contents. At the farthest point you'll come to an unsignposted collection of paths. To get down the mountain at this point, take the path on the right (Húlǐ side) and you'll eventually emerge at a staircase at the back of a residential unit. Follow the road ahead, turn left and then right at a jeep training ground, and you'll find yourself out on a bypass road that goes under the Haicang Bridge approaches. The number 15 bus calls in just to your right and will take you all the way back through Xiàmén city to Xiàmén University.

Chief Attractions

1. One of the largest downtown hills, offering excellent views of both the city and port sides of the hill. It can keep you occupied for a whole leisurely day if you take some food and drink and occupy one of the small pavilions either at the temple or along the path towards the Dongdu end of the range.
2. This is a busy temple with many devotees carrying out traditional worship activities.
3. There are several side paths that can be explored if you have time.

City Hall (Foxtail Mtn. in back)

Trish Boman's Bushwalk #3
Foxtail Mountain (Húwěi Shān, 狐尾山)

Húwěi Shān is a continuation of Xiānyuè Mn. (仙岳山) on the western side of the Hǎicāng Bridge (海沧大桥) approach. This relatively compact walk could occupy a leisurely half-day and boasts a neatly developed lookout, toilets and picnic tables with a great view of City Government buildings and beyond.

There are two main ways to this mountain: the walking path which begins from Fènghuáng Villa (凤凰, Phoenix) grounds in N. Húbīn Rd. (Húbīn Běilù, 湖滨北路) and the vehicular road that starts at Hǎishān Rd. (海山路), off Dōngdù Rd. (东渡路), a block beyond N. Húbīn Rd. T-intersection) and ends at the TV Station via the Meteorological Station on the western part of the hill. Despite being for cars, it's quite a nice walk, and a walker can link up with the forest track that links up with Fènghuáng Villa. To do this walk, catch bus 87 and exit on N. Húbīn Rd. at the Xiàmén City Administration Building stop (湖滨北路的市政府站).

If you prefer to keep off the vehicular road, then just stick to the walking path beginning from Fènghuáng Villa grounds. The gate is about half a block from the City Government office building towards Dōngdù (west). Check with the security guard and say you want to climb the mountain and it will be okay. Go straight ahead until the road curves around a couple of times and keep an eye out for the forest sign that marks an upward-leading set of stone steps. These steps will lead the vehicular road, but if you continue on across the other side, you come to a half-finished pavilion, and beyond that the road peters out at a worker's hut at the mountain top. Retrace your steps and instead of crossing the road, turn left on to it and take the stone pathway just a little way back down the road on the left. This will lead to the lookout and picnic area. The meteorological station is upwards from the picnic area while the exit is downhill. But you can return the way you came and go back to Fènghuáng Villa and avoid the traffic.

Trish Boman's Bushwalk #4
Nánpǔtuó Temple & Five Old Men Mtn. 南普陀寺和五老峰

Besides being one of Fújiàn's major temples, Nánpǔtuó Temple also backs on to a very attractive and path-riddled mountain called Five Old Men Mtn. (Wǔlǎo Fēng, 五老峰). Allow quite a lot of time for this walk, as it can also lead to treks through XMU, 10,000 Stone Botanic Garden, and link up with many other very interesting walks, probably too many for just one day. If you want to spend a half day, just stick to Nánpǔtuó's Wǔlǎo Fēng and go back down or cross the mountain to the Botanic Gardens and exit the entrance. This walk will be described first.

Catch any bus that goes to Xiàmén University (XMU), e.g., 1, 15, 71, 45, etc. Nánpǔtuó Temple is very visible as you arrive. Pay 3 Yuan to enter the main gate, and you will pass a number of very fine Meditation and Worship Halls—usually a crowded area. Keep advancing towards the rear. Don't worry which route you take because there are many, and they all lead upwards. Signboards show where you are, but just keep taking any stairs that go UP and don't stray too far to the left or right edges, unless you want to explore the many fascinating pavilions, grottoes and lookouts that abound in this marvellous place. As you get higher, there are more lookouts, including one magnificent railed platform on top of a great boulder.

Go on until after about half an hour of steady climbing on well-crafted stone steps, you reach the rest area at the top of Wǔlǎo Fēng. There is a little refreshment stall there, as well as a gate for paying your entrance fee into the Botanic Gardens. It is possible to bypass this gate by heading off to the right of the summit but the track is not well developed and there are many forks to help you get lost. Unless you have local assistance, better to pay the money. This track goes down dale and up hill, crossing a concrete road that leads to an army base nestled among the many little peaks on this rugged and complex set of hills. Keep your eye open for the Cactus Garden, housed in a glass house. To the right of this, there is a back track that goes through another mountain, offering great views and joining up with another road that meets the Botanic Garden track in a different place. When you meet any track, keep taking left turns if you want to end up in the Gardens and not in the army base or eventually, XMU, though these are well worth a visit, though perhaps on another day.

Nanputuo outing, Nov. 1925

An outing in Amoy, 1927 By Hope Hospital nurse Ms. Jean Nienhuis

Chapter 9

Sports & Recreation

Jeans, 1897

Golf in Gulangyu Graveyard, 1880s

Good Sports Chinese ruffled feathers by claiming they'd invented golf and soccer (a claim even the FIFA lent credence to). But most Chinese over the past few millennia were not into physical "sports," per se, with the exception of martial sports—archery, horsemanship, kung fu. Cultured Chinese engaged in more sedate pastimes such as painting, poetry, calligraphy and tea. Then we violent barbarians showed up with rugby, soccer, hunting, basketball and cricket (sometime before 1878).

Eric Liddell, the Scottish Olympic gold medalist who became a missionary to China, wrote that Chinese scholars insisted on wearing Confucian robes even while playing soccer—and tripped all over each other. In 1917, a young Mao Zedong's first published article was about exercise; he made some humorous observations about Chinese afraid of losing their dignity by stooping to exercise.

But it wasn't long before Chinese swapped robes for running shoes and gave the barbarians a run for their money. And in modern sports, as well as in modern education, medicine, music, arts and literature, Xiamen led the nation.

Xiamenese took to soccer soon after the Brits introduced it on the foreigners' Recreation Ground on Gŭlàngyŭ in 1898. One Chinese enthusiast was John Ma (马约翰), a 16-year-old Gulangyu schoolboy who went on to become the "Father of Modern Chinese Sports."

And ever since John Ma's day, Xiàménese have been setting world records in many sports. For example, just recently, three Xiàmén athletes shared a total of 19 world championships.

And given the popularity of tiger hunting in Old Amoy, it is not surprising that Xiamenese have set many world records in marksmanship.

This explains, perhaps, why modern Amoy has so many big shots.

Boredom is dead and buried in Xiamen. You can ice skate (2 rinks—California Mall top floor and above Carrefour near Zhongshan Rd.), windsurf, kayak, parasail, roller blade, scale rocks, fly kites, run our marathon, play tennis, badminton, basketball, and paintball—or golf a Greg Norman-designed course.

Seek something a bit more sedate? Try a stroll in our parks, or along beachfront boardwalks in Xiamen and Haicang, or the scenic Railroad Park.

Too hot to hike? Try brisk walks through air conditioned malls, or the underground plaza beneath the train station & Robinson's Mall.

After melting the calories, pile them back on with our Chinese or international cuisines, then soothe soul and sole with a Chinese foot massage.

Xiamen's 1st Sino-U.S. Match
Matt Brown and Friend, 1990

Xiàmén YMCA Leads Amoy Sports

YMCA members invented basketball, volleyball, and racquetball, coined the term "bodybuilding," and "softball," and had the first professional American football players. They also led modern sports in Xiàmén, as well as in the rest of China.

Xiàmén YMCA, one of China's first, was started in April, 1912. Our "Y" set up Amoy's first sports program, held Xiàmén's first sports meet (Yǎnwǔ Tíng, 演武亭) on Nov. 27, 1915, Xiàmén's first swim meet (on a Gǔlàngyǔ beach in 1913), and Xiàmén's first boat races (1934).

Andrew Morris wrote,

> "By 1907, staff at the Tiānjīn YMCA were rallying their Chinese charges with the cry: When will China be able to send a winning athlete to the Olympic contests? When will China be able to invite all the world to Peking for an International Olympic contest? Nearly a century later, on the eve of China's first-ever Olympic games, this innovative book shows for the first time how sporting culture and ideology played a crucial role in the making of the modern nation-state in Republican China."
>
> "Marrow of the Nation—a History of Sport and Physical Culture in Republican China."

Xiamen Fitness Centers 健身俱乐部

Island Ring Rd. Public Exercise Equipment

Hardcore about Health?① Xiàmén has dozens of modern fitness centers.

Expat salary? Exercise or swim in such starred hotels as the Millennium.

On a budget? The centers below are reasonable (phone ahead to confirm still there!)

Starving student (or teacher)? Parks and beaches have free public exercise equipment.

New Fitness 菲尼斯健身俱乐部
Add: #97 Hubin North Rd. 湖滨北路97号
Tel: 3993386/3993396 FAX: 3993576
http://www.xmfns.com.cn/y-index.htm (English; w/map)
Busses: 15, 36, 51, 72, 85, 97, 8, 12, 31, 86, 506, 812

City Trend Fitness Center, Rainbow Mall Branch 都市风健康俱乐部（天虹店）
Add: Jiāhé Lù Rainbow Mall 5/F 嘉禾路天虹商场5楼
Tel: 5080170 Busses: 311, 31, 32, 8

Bowling (Bǎolíngqiú, 保龄球)

Jīnlì Bowling Ctr. (Jīnlì Bqǒlíngqiúguǎn, 金利保龄球馆)
Add: Siming District, Huìchéng Entertainment Ctr. 6/F
思明区, 汇城娱乐中心6楼 Tel: 5125333 Buses: 6, 7, 42, 46, 79

Retirees Activity Center, Bowling Lanes (Lǎonián Huódòng Zhōngxīn, Bǎolíngqiú 老年活动中心保龄球馆). Don't let the name fool you! They sometimes even have midnight bowling—black lights and the works.
Location: opposite Botanical Garden (Wànshí Zhìwùyuán Duìmiàn 万石植物园对面).
Tel: 2123588 Buses (to Botanical Gardens): 12, 17, 87

Bowling Supplies (Bǎolíngqiú Zhuānmàidiàn, 保龄球专卖店) Also 2nd hand goods.
Add: #126 Hōu Jiāngdài Lù, Yǒngkāng Bldg. 16/F 后江埭路126号永康大厦16楼
Tel: 2222412 Website: www.kt114.cn
Buses: 10, 20, 23, 27, 30 122, 123, 136

① "Someday, there's going to be a lot of health nuts feeling pretty dumb when they're old and in the hospital dying of nothing." Red Fox, American comedian

Ice Skating (Huabing, 滑冰) The two favorite rinks seem to be:

California Mall 4/F 思明区 加州城市广场四楼
Tel: 211-5166 Buses: 11, 12, 19, 25, 101 Don't forget to try the "Taste of Greek" restaurant at the back of the "Cow Palace" right next door (to right of Calif. Mall)

China City Mall 4/F 中华城滑冰俱乐部
Add: #189 S. Siming Rd. 思明区思明南路 189 号中华城 4 楼 (above Carrefour, near Siming Rd. and Xinjie Church).
Tel: 203-1666, 203-1999 Buses: 1, 10, 11, 12, 15, 20, 21, 122

Badminton (Yǔmáoqiú 羽毛球)
Sports Arena Badminton
Address: Inside the Sports Arena, Húbīn Běi Lù #2 Tǐyù Lù (Tǐyù Zhōngxīn Nèi, 体育中心内，湖滨北路 体育路 2 号)
Tel: 506-4618, 506-2321, 539-9139 Buses: 12, 36, 58, 85, 86, 88

Longlife Badminton Courts (wànshòu yǔmáoqiú qiúguǎn, 万寿羽毛球球馆).
Address: Siming District, Wanshou Rd. # 29-31 思明区万寿路 29-31 路
Tel: 291-8118 Buses: 12, 13, 16, 17, 21, 32

Jīnbǎng Badminton Courts 金榜羽毛球馆 Beside Jīnbǎng Park 金榜公园旁
Tel: 519-0456, 826-0111 Buses: 12, 101, 109, 127\

Tennis (Wǎngqíu 网球)

Ruilong Tennis Health Club (Ruilong wangqiu jianshen julebu 瑞龙网球健身俱乐部)
Add: Huli, Dist. Dongdu Rd. 湖里区东渡路)
Tel: 220-2138 Buses: 22, 24, 43, 101, 107, 139

Songbo Tennis Courts (sōngbǒ wǎngqíucháng 松柏网球场) Siming District, Changqing Rd. 思明区长青路
Tel: 512-5609
Busses: 40, 86, 93

Boot Family's Children Prepare for Tennis Game, Gulangyu, 1920s

"Sport in Amoy in 1897"

Adapted from *China Review*, Vol. 22 No. 5 (1897)

"According to the dictionary, sport is that which diverts, and makes merry. Many men require many diversions, and what with cricket, lawn tennis, hockey, riding and shooting Amoy does its best to cater for all tastes. The public recreation ground on Kulangsoo forms the arena for games; and whether it be a tennis day graced by the patronage of many fair ladies, or a hockey day devoted to the surplus energies of boys in their teens, and of old boys in their sixties, every afternoon finds a cheerful, social, and sportive gathering on the ground.

"Riding is mostly confined to the Amoy side, where you have six miles of sand, and back again, good going, good training ground, safe, but very monotonous; however, the raw griffins down from the north often demand the whole of their riders' attention, to the entire exclusion of all thoughts of the surrounding scenery.

"Then, once a year in January, the Chinese drill ground is converted into a Race Course, and three days are devoted to the Amoy Jockey Club meeting. With eight races each day, the prizes to be won are necessarily of small value, but are none the less keenly competed for by the local sportsman. To those who are fond of ponies, the winter months' training for the races affords an excellent specific for moral, and physical health. A young man who aspired to ride successfully must adopt health habits, and cannot burn the midnight oil if he is due in the saddle at the first dawn of day for a training gallop. Racing and gambling are inseparably connected in people's minds; fortunately the machinery for gambling in Amoy, is hardly more harmful than that afforded by sixpenny points at whist

"The remaining sport is shooting, and in this, if we except tigers, Amoy figures rather badly. Pheasants, and partridges can be found in the interior, but beyond the range of a two-days' trip; and a few sportsmen care to forsake their comfortable shooting boats to share a native hovel with native creepers, on the bare chance of indifferent sport. About 4 miles up, the river expands over a large area of mud flats. Here, with the advent of winter some immense flocks of Wild Fowl, Geese, Duck, Teal &c..... Owing to the want of cover the birds are difficult of approach, and a good bag is only attainable with the help of a duck gun and punt, but cold hands, wet feet, and a bruised shoulder are part of the game, and will never deter the ardent fowler. Every species of duck common to China, is found on the flats, but the mandarin duck is rare. Pelicans, and Swans are occasional visitors, their presence indicating a cold winter. But the crowning sport with which the name of Amoy is associated is the pursuit of that king of the jungle, the wily tiger...."

R. H. Bruce

Note: see "Wildlife" chapter

Amoy Cricket! Nov. 2012, six cricket teams from Shanghai, Beijing, Nanjing and Xiamen competed in a cricket tournament on the Gulangyu sports ground, where Europeans played cricket back in the 1870s. In March, 2013, Amoy's Typhoons played Hong Kong. Want to join the fun? Read on!

Xiamen Cricket Club Charter

By Russell Woodall, December 2012

Email: typhoons.cricket@gmail.com

In the early 21st century an intrepid band of expats set out on a voyage of discovery that would take them from a small city called Xiamen, in S.E. China's Fujian province, to the fabled island of Gulangyu. Their goal was simple: to seek out the elusive sporting arena that was previously known only to the local Fujianese & some privileged foreigners to play a game of cricket.

The pioneers set out on their epic ocean voyage armed only with a bat, a ball & several Tsingtao beers. The 5 minute voyage was harrowing yet undeterred they disembarked. Wandering aimlessly through narrow cobbled streets for what seemed to be an eternity, they were running dangerously low on supplies (Tsingtao) when suddenly, up ahead in the distance, they saw a shimmering light. It was to be the sporting arena, the Mecca, the Holy Grail, the Lord's, the 'G' which is the Gulangyu Peoples Stadium. Elation filled the air as the stadium's first game of cricket was played, then & there it was decided that Xiamen needed its very own cricket club.

The rest is history.

TYPHOONS Cricket Club

Reality After a few successful cricket tournaments, including the Xiamen Halloween 666s, it was decided over several soothing beverages that what our beautiful city needed was a cricket club. Further discussions culminated in an inaugural general meeting being held at The Londoner bar where resolutions were passed and on Sunday Jan. 8th 2012 the Xiamen Typhoons Cricket Club was born, with a charter drafted focusing on having fun & community involvement.

The Aim Create a club focused on community, family & fun, & playing cricket.

Promote the sport of cricket to China, & the Chinese and foreigners, both young & old, male or female.

Provide a base where all people, members & non-members, can be involved in other activities outside cricket (Family beach parties, social events, etc)

Provide an atmosphere for members & non-members to draw on each other's experiences & expertise, share info, network business ideas, socialise & have fun.

Host cricket games & tournaments, encourage other teams to visit Xiamen.

As a club, be involved in other cities' cricket games & tournaments.

The Venue Whenever possible, cricket tournaments & games are to be held on Gulangyu Island at the Gulangyu peoples stadium. When the stadium is unavailable, alternative venues may be used such as the sports academy near Riyuegu hot springs.

Beach cricket, parties & family days are held at Haiyuntai ("beach party" beach).

Training is held at various locations such as the street out front of the Londoner bar, the park behind Yundang lake, the beach at Haiyuntai.

Equipment A complete set of genuine cricket equipment has been purchased which includes, but is not limited to; game balls, practice balls, street balls, boxes, batters' pads & gloves, wicket keepers' pads & gloves, stumps & bails and cricket bats. Thanks to the generosity of many club members the equipment list is constantly being maintained & the addition of batting helmets is on the wish list.

The purchase of a roll out pitch is high on the clubs priority list & once the logistics have been overcome this will become a reality. In the short term the club will continue to borrow a pitch from the ever accommodating Shanghai clubs.

The Uniform It was agreed that traditional long white pants & polo shirts will be the official uniform. Considering Xiamen's sub-tropical weather conditions it is likely that a resolution will be passed in the near future changing the long white pants to shorts. Each year a Halloween 666s tour shirt is produced & this is the club's uniform polo shirt for the following year.

Baggy blue (or green) hats are a likely future addition to the club uniform.

The Club To ensure that the club can operate in a conventional manner, the following items will be maintained: A written charter, a chairman, treasurer, secretary, club captain, scheduled meetings & AGMs, match calendar, members' web site, membership.

It is not a pre-requisite of membership to be proficient in playing cricket, nor to have either played or even understand the game, or have any athletic ability at all. Providing an applicant is morally sound he or she will be accepted as a member.

Annual membership fees will be kept affordable to all & discounts offered to students & unemployed; they will be paid at a time decided during the AGM.

Amoy Cricket & Homesickness (1890s)

During the winter months the play on this lawn is varied by hockey, and football, and cricket. The last named still holds its own as the prime favourite with many of the gentlemen, and is a source of attraction to the whole community....This enthusiasm is a tribute to the game itself, but it is also a powerful witness to the strong feeling that exists in every heart for the homeland, and which the long distance from it only tends to deepen and accentuate.

There is nothing that shows more distinctly how strong are the ties that bind men to their absent friends and relatives than the keenness with which anything that recalls them to their memories is appreciated. Home flowers, for example, are reared from seed and cultivated with the most loving care, whilst rare flowers, that would send people in England into raptures, are looked upon with interest, it is true, but not with the tenderness and affection that are lavished upon the more homely plants.

Macgowan, 1897

Golf (Gāoérfūqiú, 高尔夫球) – played in Xiamen since 1880s!

Orient Golf and Country Club [东方(厦门)高尔夫体育休闲中心]—China's 1st Asian PGA Tournament Venue. Selected by U.S. Golf Assoc. as one of the world's top 100 golf clubs, this 7,074-yard course hosts the annual Orient Masters Tournament.
Add: Hǎicāng Taiwanese Investment District 海沧台商投资区
Tel: 653-1316 Buses: 805, 830, 833, 854
Website: www.orientgolf.com

Kǎi Gē Golf Club (Kǎigē Gāoérfūqiú Jùlèbù, 凯歌高尔夫球俱乐部), between Jīměi and Tóngān, designed by Greg Norman.
Add: Tóng'ān, Fúzhōu—Xiàmén Highway in the area of the #415 mileage marker 福厦公路同集干道 415 公里处
Tel: 701-1678, 739-1120 Buses: 602, 603, 612, 615, 618, 627

Fùshì Golf Practice Range (Fùshì Gāoerǐfúqiú Xùnliàn, 富士高尔夫球训练)
Add: Overseas Chinese Bldg. 4/F, Huáqiáo Dàshà Sìlóu,华侨大厦四楼
Tel: 205-3881 Buses: 1, 11, 12, 15, 20, 21, 122

Bèilōng Golf Supplies (Bèilōng Gāoěrfūqiú Yòngpín Zhuānmài Diàn, 贝隆高尔夫用品专卖店)
Add: #273-12 Xiānyuè Lù 仙岳路 273-12 号
Tel: 5051216 Buses: 15, 16, 24, 25, 31, 301

Gaofeng Golf Products Club (Gāofēng Gāoérfūqiú Yòngpǐnshè, 高锋高尔夫球用品社) Add: Húlǐ, 273-1 Xiànyuè Lù, 仙岳路 273 号
Tel: 532-7826, 532-7836 Busses: 15, 16, 24, 25, 31, 301

Outdoor Recreation

Paintball, Parasailing, River Rafting, etc. Xiamen no longer has paintball, as far as I can tell, but nearby Changtai, in Zhangzhou (one hour west), is a delightful recreation center with river rafting, paintball, parasailing, military games, etc. The package ticket costs 356 Yuan, including transport, minimum of 15 people, departure from Xiamen 8:30 AM, return 7 PM. Ticketing: Xiamen Huaxia Travel Agency (Xiàmén Huáxià lvxíng shè, 厦门华夏旅行社). Address: #875 Xiehe Rd., Room 803 厦禾路 875 号 803 室

Phone first to be sure they're still in business. Tel: 18965858355, or 18965858365

Chángtài White Water Rafting Club [福建长泰马洋(厦广)漂流有限公司]
China's national kayak training center, 45 km west of Xiamen: "Xiamen's backyard"—beautiful mountains, waterfalls, valleys, trails. Also parasailing, horseback riding, hiking, a firing range (rifles, pistols), archery, etc.
Add: Changtai, 中国福建长泰十里 1 号 Tel: 0596—832-1001
Xiamen Office: #123 Yuehua Rd. Yuehua Bldg. G2 Room 501
悦华路 123 号悦华公寓 G2 501 室 Tel: 5683969 Buses: 16, 301, 523, 655

Táiwān Cultural Village (Táiwān Mínsú Cūn Jǐngzhōu Lèyuán 台湾民俗村景州乐园) Since 1995, but in a bit of disrepair. Can arrange outdoor group activities. Wood and rope obstacle courses (swinging bridges, nets, balancing bars), wild animal shows, wild Taiwan folk performances. Add: Huángcuò, Island Ring Road. 黄厝环岛路
Tel: 2560113 Buses: 948, 992, 128, 103

Aquatic Sports

Xiàmén Underwater World, Gǔlàngyǔ Islet (Xiàmén Hǎidǐ Shìjiè, 厦门海底世界) Built in 1998, it is one of China's best aquariums, with 7500m^2 of displays holding over 10,000 creatures of 350 species. See sharks up close from within the Plexiglas tunnel, and watch seal and dolphin shows.
Add: exit the blue-roofed complex to the right of Gulangyu Ferry, behind gigantic octopus sculpture. Tel: 206-7668, 206-7825 Buses: none. Ferry or swim.

Xiamen Happy Valley Water Park (Xiàměn Kuàilè Gǔ Shuǐshàng Lèyuán, 厦门快乐谷水上乐园 Xiamen Water Park—enough water slides and pools to fill a hot summer afternoon.
Add: Xiàmén, Húlǐ District, Huáróng Lù Húlǐ Park East Entrance. 厦门湖里区华荣路湖里公园东大门 Tel: 563-9972
Bus: 11, 30, 39, 80, 97, 523

Swimming Pools (Yóuyǒng Chí, 游泳池) Millennium and Marco Polo hotels have nice pools, as does Xiamen Univ. & Jimei Univ.

Yàtèlándà Water Recreation (Yàtèlándà Huóshuǐguǎn, 亚特兰大活水馆)— **a favorite with foreigners**
Add: #89 Húbīn Zhōng Lù, near Dìháo Bldg. 湖滨中路 89 号，帝豪大厦 附近
Tel: 582-3000
Website: http://www.yatelanda.com Buses: 13, 16, 17, 116, 127, 139

The People's Pool (Rénmín Yóuyǒngchí, 人民游泳池)
Add: #97 Wényuán Lù, by Xiàmén Hotel 文园路 97 号厦门宾馆对面
Tel: 202-0013

Jianjiang Swimming Pool (健将游泳池)
Add: Siming District, #61 Tiyu Rd. 思明区体育路 61 号 Nears sports stadium.
Buses: 8, 9, 86, 88, 94

Boat Rentals (Bāochuán, 包船) The Island Ring Road has rental catamarans, pedal boats, sailboats, or rent a traditional wooden Amoy boat for a day and visit outlying islands. Reasonable prices often include a beach barbeque.

We've had good service and prices with Mr. Ahbi and Mr. Chen.
Mr. Ahbi's mobile: 13003908156 Mr. Chen's mobile: 13606090373

AQUATIC SPORTS AT AMOY

"The Graphic," Nov. 3, 1883

Hot Springs (Wēnquán, 温泉)

Best Western Trithorn Hot Springs Resort: see Tong'an chapter.

Ancient Sun Moon Valley (Rìyuègǔ) Hot Springs (Rìyuègǔ Wēnquán Dùjiàcūn, 日月谷温泉度假村) Add: Hǎicāng District, Dōngfúzhèn Tāng'àn, 海沧区东孚镇汤岸 Tel: 6312222 6312345 Website: www.riyuegu.com Bus: 804

Rìyuègǔ (Sun Moon Valley) —one of Asia's best!

An airline magazine article on a trans-Pacific flight claimed one of Asia's top ten hot springs resorts is Rìyuègǔ, just 20 minutes outside of Xiàmén.

With 72 open-air pools and 35 special hot springs (milk bath, beer bath, rose bath), they'll soak you in more ways than you thought possible.

Every hot spring in China is said to cure all your ills; Riyuegu is no exception. The bubbling 82ºC waters possess traces of potassium, sodium, calcium, manganese, bromine, magnesium, etc., and frequent soaks relieve arteriosclerosis, gynecological disorders, high cholesterol, diabetes, skin diseases, insomnia, arthritis, and digestive ailments—plus encourage blood circulation and cell regeneration! Ponce De Leon sought the Fountain of Youth on the wrong side of the planet—though this place predates him by centuries.

Stories of Sun Moon Valley date back over 1000 years. And about 500 years ago, a high ranking Míng Dynasty official, Mr. Dīng Yìzhōng (丁一中), who enjoyed trekking through the mountains, heard of the springs' curative properties, and like Chinese today, could not resist either drinking it or bathing in it; sometimes both, and not always in that order. He felt such bliss that he memorializing the springs in verse as "a gift from heaven to common folk" because they were neither in city nor on mountaintop, but on a plain patch of farmland by a road, accessible to all—at least until the developers got hold of it.

An inscribed stone plaque found in the 1980s by Bǎi Yùshèng (白玉盛), a returned Indonesian Chinese who taught at Hǎicāng Dōngfú Elementary School (海沧区东孚小学), confirmed that the springs were at the site of Sun Moon Valley.

Whether the medicinal claims are true or not, it is a delightful place for a day, evening or full weekend. Try soaking in the "kissing fish" pool. They'll eat all the loose skin of your feet, legs or whatever else you dangle in the pool.

Just pray no one replaces them with piranha…

Go Fly a Kite? Offshore breezes make Xiàmén's Ring Road the perfect place for this ancient Chinese sport—or art, or science.

I marvel at adepts who with a flick of the wrist send silk dragons skywards, and then by subtly tugging on the control strings cause them to perform dizzying acrobatics, diving so close to the ground that ants and spiders duck, then soaring back into the skies. Personally, I'm happy just to get a kite up and keep it up; when my kite descends, it's not with a kiss but a crash.

Kites, like everything else, were invented by ancient Chinese. In 478 B.C., Chinese philosopher Mòzǐ (墨子) spent 3 years making a wooden hawk that actually flew.

Were Mo around today, he could just log on to www.kite-china.com and buy one of the delightful hi-tech fiber-glass spar and silk kites produced here in Xiàmén.

In 200 B.C., General Hánxìn flew a kite over a besieged city and measured the string to see how far to tunnel under the city to take them by surprise. Another general tied harps to kites, flew them over a city, and had his spies in the city spread the rumor that the waling from the heavens was angry gods who would ensure they were bitterly defeated the next day. The locals fled in terror, unaware the enemy was just stringing them along. Today, the Chinese word for kite is "wind zither" (fēngzhēng, 风筝).

Chinese armies used kites to send signals, and very large kites allowed archers to rain arrows into fortified cities. Marco Polo wrote that Chinese sea captains tied folks to a kite and sent them aloft. If they stayed up, smooth sailing was ahead. If they wobbled or crashed, it was a bad omen and the ship delayed setting out.

Polo did not say what they did with the folks who crashed with the kite.

Chinese believe that kite-flying can bring good luck—and the higher the kite, the better the luck. Personally, I'd have to be higher than a kite to believe that. But lucky or not, kite flying is fun. For me, it's like fishing with a sail instead of a hook, surfing invisible currents to catch evasive updrafts—and to avoid the deadly downdrafts.

Kite flying was banned during the Cultural Revolution (I think they should have had the Red Guards go fly a kite) but in cities like Xiàmén the beautiful sport is again catching on. I like watching the kite masters just outside the Mandarin Seaview (beside the Exhibition Center). Some of the kites soar so high they look as if they could land in Jinmen. Maybe someday Xiamen and Jinmen will have a kite flying contest, with kites meeting in the middle of the bay.

Martial Arts (Wǔshù, 武术)

Home of Southern Shaolin Kungfu

Quánzhōu South Shàolín Martial Arts School（泉州南少林武术学校）is thought by many to be the birthplace of Southern Shaolin. I asked the 29-year-old abbott why the sign at the bottom of the mountain said 600 meters when my speedometer proved it was 1.1 km. He looked at me as if wondering why my mother let me live, and replied, "The road curves a lot. It *is* 1.1 km. if you drive, but we fly to the top."

600 meters = 1.1 kilometers?

Tel: 595-226-50006, 595-226- 2075 www.qznsl.com

Eye of the tiger...

Staff meeting?

Pitchforking the foreign devil

Getting Your Kicks in Xiàmén I did kung fu in the Air Force in Taiwan (see next page). If you'd like to get your own kicks in martial arts or, more likely, just get kicked, Xìamén is a great place to start—but what style?

The Secrets of Style No matter what nook or cranny of Fujian I've visited, villagers all make the same three boasts: best cooking, prettiest girls, deadliest kung fu.

Each village has its own style, handed down only to their own clan. The carp worshippers ① of Zhōuníng, like the master in the photos to the left, teach their style only to their own village members—and only those surnamed Zheng.

Such variety of styles makes it hard to continue training if you leave China, or just move 50 miles up the road. One option is to study an international standardized style, such as Korean Tae Kwondo.

Karate Master Que Jianshēng 阙建生教练, a 7th degree black belt, was born into poverty in Zhāngzhōu in 1963. When Que was 5, his father died, and he and his mom moved to Táiwān. He studied Chinese kung fu, but fell for Karate, and now zealously promotes the Korean art in Xiamen.

Mobile: 13666080730

Xiàmén Hóngwǔ Martial Arts Club
(厦门市弘武精英武术散打俱乐部)
Add: #383 E. Liánqián Lù Rm. 506 莲前东路 383 号 506 室
Tel: 599-2652 Buses: 26, 28, 101, 126

① They *do* worship carp, and give funerals for the finned folk when they die. See "Zhouning Carp Village" in "Fujian Adventure" (out of print, but E-book available)

Feel the Force, Grasshopper!

My intro to Chinese philosophy was the '60s TV serial "Kung Fu" with David Carradine. I was 20, in Taiwan, before I learned he wasn't even Chinese. I never forgave Carradine for being Caucasian, but at least he piqued my interest in China—and martial arts.

As a young airman in Taiwan, I studied Kung Fu two hours each evening with a bunch of bald Buddhist monks. I coveted a black belt, but advances up the ranks came only by defeating students of higher levels. Not surprisingly, the only belts I ever landed were to my poor bruised body (both black and blue).

I learned that there are over 100 different styles of martial arts, using knives, spears, swords, clubs, staffs and plain old fists. After months of failure, I felt like resorting to a 45 magnum.

To complicate things, there are external styles, which stress strength, and internal kung fu, which stresses mind and life energy, or Qì (气).

In theory, as we age, we progress from movement to stillness, from firmness to softness, but as our Qi focuses it becomes more powerful than brute force. Or so said Master Li, but I was skeptical of the soft soap about soft force until he put my doubts on ice with a 200 pound block of ice.

I often chuckled—though never to his face—at Master Lin's roly-poly physique. He moonlighted as a candy maker, and it showed, but he could stand back to the wall and touch the wall above his head with his foot.

And after he demonstrated the power of Qì, I quit chuckling, even behind his back.

While his students and I watched silently, Master Lin poised one palm a couple of inches above the 200 pound chunk of ice. He concentrated. And I nearly jumped out of my skin when he slapped the ice and it shattered.

I could not have duplicated that feat with a sledge hammer.

Impressive, Master Candy Kung Fu man! But though I no longer joke about the power of Qì, I must say that I still don't think much of it as a self-defense technique. After all, what self-respecting enemy is going to lie on their back and wait half a minute while your hand hovers above their chest and charge up your Qì?

Maybe the candy making kungfu master distracted enemies like dentists distract unwary patients—getting them to let down their guard with a lollipop, and then giving the patient (not the candy) a good licking.

I think I'll market Kung Fu Kandy after I retire.

Chapter 10

Museums & Libraries

Island Ring Road Skirting Protected Ancient Tree

Xiàmén has 139 protected cultural and historical sites, 18 historical temples and churches, and dozens of museums.

Xiamen even has 533 protected ancient or famous trees, which is good for me. I was born in China's Year of the Monkey, and am often *up* a tree. It is reassuring that our trees are protected, even if I am not.

Xiamen has China's only bridge museum, its first anthropology museum, a military museum, a Sino-European art museum, weather museum and science center, and memorials to famous folk like Koxinga, Lǔxùn and Lín Yǔtáng.

Gǔlàngyǔ Islet has Asia's largest piano museum and an organ museum that is planned to be the world's largest. And Gulangyu itself is a world-class open-air museum of international architecture, with hundreds of 19th and early 20th century "Amoy Deco" mansions a vivid reminder of the "Roaring Twenties," which roared louder in "the richest square mile on earth" than anywhere on the planet.

Read more at www.Amoymagic.com or in *Discover Gǔlàngyǔ*.

Gulangyu--an Open-Air Museum of International Architecture and our Unique "Amoy Deco"

Xiàmén University (XMU) Museums[①]

Lǔxùn Memorial Hall (Lǔxùn Jìniàn Guǎn, 鲁迅纪念馆) To the right of XMU's Anthropology Museum is a statue of its founder, Lǔxùn, pen name of Zhōu Shùrén (周树人, 1881-1936). The "Father of Modern Chinese Literature," Lǔxùn broke ancient literary tradition with his first story, "Madman's Diary," in which he dared to write just as freely and informally as he spoke.

For millennia, Chinese scholars won their public offices by mastering Confucian and Taoist classics, and writing brilliant essays about brilliant essays written by forebears. Their ossified written Chinese was stylistic and terse—totally unlike oral Chinese, which lives, breathes, and changes constantly. So Luxun determined to breathe life into written Chinese.

Luxun reminds me of William Tyndale (1494-1536), who angered priests by translating the Bible from Latin into the common English of peasants. Unlike Tyndale, Lǔxùn was not burned at the stake, but his Confucian colleagues may well have wished to burn his books, if not their cantankerous author.

Lin Yutang, Luxun and Sun Fuyuan at XMU

Lǔxùn taught in XMU a few months in late 1926, but deplored the professors' constant bickering and politicking. Of course, Luxun bickered back, but in writing—endearing himself to his enemies with such cutting essays as "How to Write (怎么写)?" And having said his piece, and having shredded what little peace remained to XMU, he packed up and moved to Guǎngzhōu in January, 1927.

The Lǔxùn Memorial Hall, just inside XMU's main gate, has many mementos, including a Lǔxùn essay and postcard to his sweetheart, which XMU professor Zheng Qiwu claims has the same calligraphy as XMU's official seal of *Universatis Amoinsis*. I wouldn't be surprised. It takes a character to write a character. Or, as Confucius once said, "Different strokes for different folks."

① Refer to XMU map in the Education chapter for locations

China's 1st Anthropology Museum, Bóxué Bldg. #1 (中国第一人类学博物馆，博学一)[①] Luxun was a study in contrasts. He embraced change but also highly valued China's rich heritage. The "Father of Modern Chinese Literature was also the "father" of New China's first Anthropology Museum." In 1926, Luxun held a cultural relic exhibition at XMU, and set up a Cultural Exhibition Center in the School of Chinese Studies. Though he left soon after, he at least had got the ball rolling. In 1934, Professor Lín Huìxiáng (林惠祥) created a Director's Office for the Anthropology Museum, Xiamen, and after 1949 donated his cultural relics and books to the university.

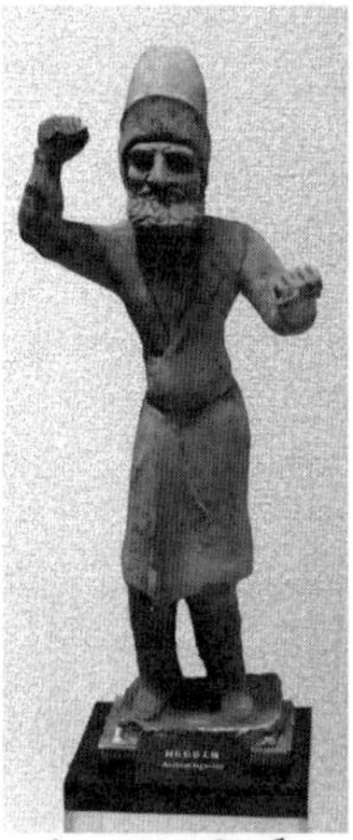

Ancient Arab of Fujian

In 1953, XMU opened China's first anthropology museum as a base for anthropological research, teaching and social education. The center has studied the New Stone Age era of Taiwan and S.E. China (mainly Fújiàn), relations between the ancient Yuè (越), Shē (畲), Gāoshān (高山), and S.E. nationalities, ancient kilns (Quanzhou's Déhuà was one of China's four ancient centers of porcelain), and ancient marine transport in S.E. Asia and China—especially Quánzhōu (start of the Maritime Silk Route; Marco Polo's port of departure, 60 km. north of Xiamen).

Nestorian Christian Angel on Headstone

The 3 main divisions—Hall of Genesis, Hall of Cultural Evolution, and Hall of National Relics from Home and Abroad—include a corridor of steles, 32 exhibition rooms, over 7000 books or journals, and 4,575 ancient and modern exhibits, including Stone Age artifacts, ancient currency, porcelain, paintings, weapons, sculptures, calligraphy, etc. The National Relics Hall has cultural relics from China, India, Australia, and South East Asian countries. Phone ahead; it is often closed.

Add: in XMU, near Luxun sculpture and Lotus Lake.

Tel: 2182474

Buses: 1, 15, 21, 45, 87, 841, 959.

Foreign Delegation Views Nestorian Christian Headstones

① Adapted from "Xiàmén University—Strength of the South"

Lín Yǔtáng Memorial Hall When Lín, one of my favorite authors, passed away in March, 1976, at the age of 80, the New York Times obituary noted,

> "Lín Yǔtáng, poet, novelist, historian and philosopher, had no peer as an interpreter to Western minds of the customs, aspirations, fears and thoughts of his people and their country, China, the great and tragic land."

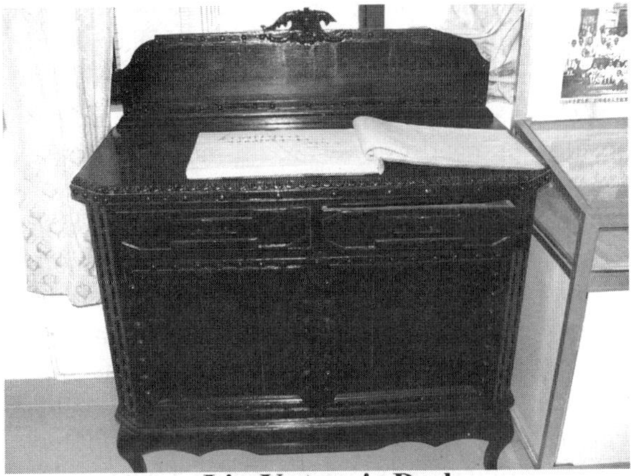

Lin Yutang's Desk

The Lín Yǔtáng Memorial hall, on XMU library's third floor, has Lín's desk and an extensive collection of his books and photos (including several of Lin and Lǔxùn together). Read more about Lín Yǔtáng in "Discover Gǔlàngyǔ," and view the couple dozen photos of him at www.amoymagic.com.

Chinese European Art Center（厦门大学艺术学院中国欧洲艺术中心）Seeing as how it was the Dutch who opened up Xiamen a few centuries ago, its apropos that they are in the forefront of opening Xiamen yet again—this time to European culture and arts.

Ms. Ineke Gudmundsson and XMU Art College opened the Center in 1999. Exhibitors have included such respected European and Chinese artists as Teun Hock, JCJ Vanderheyden, Pieter Holstein, Marcel Kalksma and Arni Gudmundson, Xie Lai, Wu Yiming and Wen Bin.

When I visited the art center, Jean Bernard Koeman was busy with a hand drill preparing his riveting exhibit, "Mental Architecture—a Travel Survival Kit." which consisted of photos and Chinese characters in oddly designed cubicles (designed, he said, to fit well in planes, and to form a sphere when stacked). It was a bit too much architecture for my mental capacities, or lack thereof, but I enjoyed the photos, and Koeman's infectious enthusiasm.

Jean Bernard Koeman

I asked why XMU doesn't have an American-Chinese Center and they said we Americans don't have any culture, but which isn't entirely true. I'm American, and I have yoghurt cultures in my refrigerator.

Exhibits change frequently; check out the latest offerings at: www.ceac99.org E-mail: info@ceac99.org

Tel: 2180850 Address: #400 S. Siming Rd., 3/F 思明南路 400 号 3 楼

Military Museum Each time I see this museum perched on the Five Old Men Mountains (Wŭlăofēng 五老峰) behind XMU, I thank Heaven that 30 years ago, when I tended missiles in nearby Táiwān, I never actually fired on what is now my home.

When you've had your fill of tanks and rockets, take the right fork, descend the hill, sip tea in the ancient tea garden, and then saunter down scenic trails through the Botanical Garden (see Parks and Gardens chapter) and past the Buddhist nunnery, which is strategically separated by an entire mountain from Nánpŭtuó, lest the wifeless monks have nun. Outside the main gate is the Railroad Park Trail and the Xiamen Martyrs Memorial (Xiàmén Lièshì Língyuán, 厦门烈士陵园). Walk straight ahead to Zhōngshān Park, and you'll eventually reach the harbor and Gŭlàngyŭ Islet. Take the ferry; otherwise it's a long swim.

And speaking of the military…

Little 8th Army Memorial (Xiăobālù, 小八路) After Chiang Kai Shek fled to Táiwān, in the 1950s he loosed hundreds of thousands of shells on Xiàmén Island and her neighbors—especially Dàdēng Island, which has a sobering museum (Tōng'ān Chapter).

When an attack upon Hécuò Village destroyed communications lines, Hécuò Primary School students rushed out and, with bare hands, held the wires together until they were repaired. The school now has a Little Heroes museum. It is probably the planet's only primary school with a military museum, and heavy artillery and machine guns on the sports grounds. A student asked me if any American primary schools had such weapons. I said, "No way. Back home, American youth would use them."

Hecuo Elementary School Playground Artillery
Home of Future Big Shots?

Overseas Chinese Museum (Huáqiáo Bówùguǎn 华侨博物馆) Given that over 2.5 million overseas Chinese in 50+ countries have roots in Fújiàn Province, mostly Southern Fújiàn, it is not surprising that the OCM's website humbly boasts they are the only comprehensive OCM in China.

Conceived by Mr. Tan Kah Kee, who gave 100,000 Yuan to start it, the 9,000m^2 museum opened in May, 1959 and has thousands of items forming three exhibitions: Overseas Chinese, Natural History, and Chinese Antiques.

1st Exhibition: Overseas Chinese

Hall 1: History of Overseas Chinese before the 1840s. Exhibits begin with the Qin Dynasty (221-207 B.C.), when China's first emperor, Qín Shǐhuáng[①] (秦始皇), sent the Taoist alchemist Xufu with 500 boys and 500 girls to find the elixir of immortality. He never returned (he supposedly found Japan instead). About 2000 years ago, the emperor sent delegations for trade and cultural exchanges to Persia and other Central Asian countries. In 399 A.D., the Buddhist monk Fǎxiǎn (法显, 337-422) traipsed over the Himalayas at age 67 and returned over 15 years later with the Buddhist scriptures, which he translated into Chinese. He also wrote a marvelous account of his travels.

Hall 2: Struggles of Overseas Chinese after the 1840s. The Míng and Qīng Dynasty emperors shut China's doors after Zhénghé, but Chinese emigration continued, and mushroomed after the 1940s, as domestic corruption and foreign invasion made life increasingly miserable.

Hall 3: From Immigrants to Citizens. Chinese abroad became citizens and made valuable contributions to their adopted homes. Although sometimes resented for dominating economies, they are also respected for giving generously, particularly in education and medicine. (See Tan Kah Kee in Jimei chapter).

The museum's "China Town" depicts the "Three Treasures:"

1. The typical Overseas Chinese community organizations

2. The Chinese schools that perpetuate Chinese language, culture and traditions (fully 90% of Philippine Chinese speak Mǐnnán Dialect, and I have visited Chinese schools there in which the entire curriculum is in Minnan).

3. The Chinese newspapers and magazines that connect those abroad with the motherland. A good example is "Tulay—Chinese-Filipino Digest," which was launched on June 12, 1988—the Philippine Independence Day.

Visit: www.kaisa.ph/tulay Bahay Tsinoy Museum: www.kaisa.ph/museum

① China's first emperor—a tyrant who burned most books and executed many scholars, but is credited with unifying China and building the precursor to the Great Wall

Hall 4: Cultural Inheritance and Integration   Chinese abroad married new ideas and old, and created a new lifestyle and ethos that made great contributions to both China and other nations (chronicled in halls 5 and 6).

2nd Exhibition: Natural Science: includes a whale skeleton and displays of many small animals.

3rd Exhibition: Chinese Antiques—Mr. Tan Kah Kee's collection of over 2,000 antiques includes pre-Qín (秦, 221-207 B.C.) bronzeware, traditional paintings, calligraphy and ancient porcelain (some European Kings bankrupted their nations in futile attempts to reproduce porcelain, including the famous *Blanc de Chine* (white from China) of Déhuà, three hours north of Xiamen.

Add: #493 S. Sīmíng Lù (near XMU, just over the hill). Tel: 2085345

Buses: 1, 2, 12, 15, 15, 20, 45, 48, 520, 659, 841, 857

They have an English website. Of course, none of the linked pages have content, but it's good finger exercise clicking them:

English website: http://www.hqbwy.org.cn/about_e.asp

Xiamen Science and Technology Museum (厦门科技馆) Interactive fun for all ages—both science center and playground. Kids love the cars, and miniature motorcycles. Driving gets a bit crazy, but just turn them loose and let them pretend they're Xiamen taxi drivers mastering "Darwinian Driving" (see Transportation chapter).

Add: Siming District, #95 Tiyu Rd. 思明区体育路 95 号文化艺术中心

Phone: 514-7666   Buses: 86, 88, 94

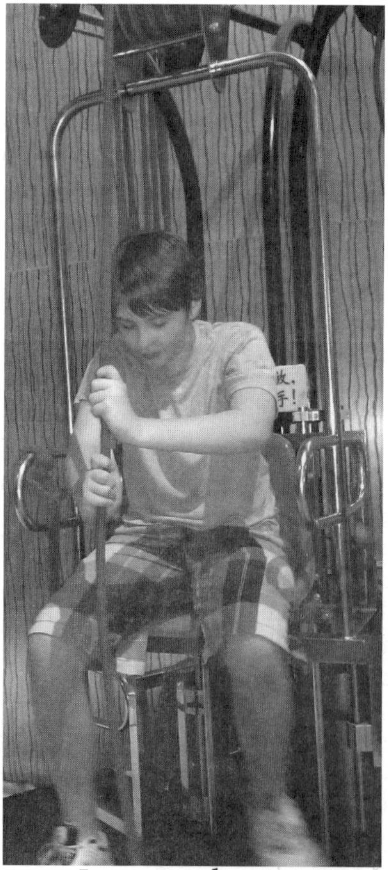

Learning the ropes?

Xiamen Youth Astronomy & Meteorology Museum (厦门市青少年天文气象馆) Don't let the name fool you. We older youth love it too.

The interactive displays helped me finally understand why weather works and weathermen don't.

The center is visible from much of Xiamen. It resembles a giant golf ball on a giant tee planted atop Foxtail Mountain, behind Xiamen Municipal Government. But though easy to see, it is not so easy to get to, especially on a hot, muggy day.

I suggest a taxi up and then hike down. Otherwise, take a bus to the nearby Zhongxin Square (Zhōngxìn Guǎngchǎng, 中信广场) and hike up.
Add: #85 Qixiang Rd. 气象路 85 号
Buses: 11, 12, 26, 31, 36, 58, 85, 88, 881

XM Weather Station (Photo by Stephen Potter)

Interactive, Educational--Fun!

Xiàmén Bridge Museum (Xiàmén Qiáoliáng Bówùguǎn, 厦门桥梁博物馆) Bridges give intriguing insights into ancient trade and travel routes, and Fújiàn has hundreds of unique bridges, both old and new. I like the elegant wooden covered bridges like the 700-year-old wonder northwest of Fúzhōu, as well as Quánzhōu's granite Ānpíng Bridge (安平桥). Built between 1138 and 1149, the 2,255m bridge was the world's longest in the Middle Ages. (See bridge photos in the Fujian Travel chapter).

Ancient Bio-engineering Quánzhōu's Luòyǎng Bridge was built 1,000 years ago of massive granite slabs—some of them ten meters long. An example of ancient biological engineering, they used secretions of live oysters to cement the granite blocks together.

Xiamen Bridge Museum exhibits also cover bridges from other provinces, such as Běijīng's Lúgōu Bridge (卢沟桥) and Sìchuān's Lúdìng Iron-chain Bridge（泸定桥）, as well as overseas marvels like the London Bridge, Normandy Suspension Bridge, and the Bridges of Madison County. Not really.

Pingnan, Fujian

The museum's three sections include the Hǎicāng Bridge's Construction, a Review of 19th Century Chinese Bridges, and Supervision Center.

The 2/F display has 5 divisions: ancient bridges; bridges from 1900 to 1949; bridges from 1950 to 1978; bridges from 1979 to 1999, and bridges to be built in the future.

Location: Below Hǎicāng Bridge. Tel:5615522 Bus: 11, 22, 26, 34, 66

Magical Bridge

China's oldest bridge, and the world's oldest open-spandrel arch bridge, is Héběi Province's 51m Zhàozhōu Bridge（赵州桥）, supposedly built between 595-605 A.D. by a magician. After he finished, a pair of gods crossed it while carrying the sun and moon in sacks on their backs. When it started sagging, the magician shouldered the burden of saving it by leaping into the river and holding it up with his shoulders. He must still be holding it up because it has survived over 1400 years of floods and earthquakes with little need for repair, other than replacing the ornamental railings every few hundred years.

Xiamen Libraries

Xiamen Library (Xiàmén Túshūguǎn, 厦门图书馆). Founded in 1919, in 2007 it moved to the sprawling new Culture and Art Center near the Sports Stadium. Check out the 2/F foreign language section, the reading rooms and gardens, and Art Gallery.

Library cards are 20 Yuan, and you must pay a deposit for books you borrow. Overdue books are punishable by deportation. Not really. I hope.

Add: #95 Tiyu Rd.（体育路 95 号）. Tel: 2031390 FAX: 2665267

Hours: 8:30 A.M. to 8:00 P.M. 7 days a week (except Friday afternoon).

Busses: either 8 and 86, or busses 13, 15 and 31 to the Sports Center.

Web: http://www.xmlib.net/index.asp e-mail: tsg9808@public.xm.fj.cnab

For English info, visit www.xiamenguide.com

Gǔlàngyǔ's Zhōngshān Branch Library This 1600 m^2 center has over 60,000 volumes and 1,000 periodicals. Take the ferry to Gǔlàngyǔ, go straight ahead on Lóngtóu Lù; turn left on Zhōnghuá Lù.

Xiàmén University Library（厦门大学图书馆）XMU library was founded in 1921 and moved to the present site in 1987. The library now has almost 4 million books (and 50,000 added each year), including half a million foreign language books. They also have over 10,000 periodicals in Chinese and foreign languages.

XMU Library

The digital library system started in 2000 offers 24 hour inter-library loans, database mirror-site services, over 100 major online databases, digital archives and libraries, and over 18,000 electronic periodicals in Chinese and foreign languages, and searches. Hours: 7 days per week, 8 AM to 10 PM.

XMU Library English website: http://210.34.4.20/english/

Gǔlàngyǔ Museums

Gǔlàngyǔ Museum of International Architecture. Location: the entire islet! See Gulangyu Architecture chapter for insights into our unique "Amoy Deco."

Xiàmén Gǔlàngyǔ Piano Museum（厦门鼓浪屿钢琴博物馆） [Adapted from *Discover Gǔlàngyǔ*《魅力鼓浪屿》] Given Gǔlàngyǔ's musical heritage, it is no surprise that Australian Overseas Chinese Mr. Hú Yǒuyì（胡友义）chose his ancestral home for Asia's largest piano museum, which has over 70 pianos from the all over the world, and over 100 priceless piano lamps.

The Gǔlàngyǔ Piano Museum's two halls are set within the tropical flowers and trees of a 2,000 square meter tract of land on the hill overlooking Shuzhuang Garden and the sea. Mr. Hú's collection includes a French street musician's barrel piano (no monkey), the Broadwood & Sons piano that won a golden medal at the Paris

International Fair, a grand piano with ivory keys from an English palace, and a piano cherished by President Lincoln.

Hall #1 has the oldest piano. Few were built by pianists, but this gem was crafted in 1801 by visionary composer Muzio Clementi (1752-1832).

Clementi crafted both uprights and grands on which to perform his more than 106 sonatas (46 were for violin, cello or flute), as well as countless smaller pieces. Clementi is also remembered for the horrifying tale in which George Grove visited Clementi's nephew, a vicar in south-east England, and found the maid lighting a fire with Clementi's manuscript! I wonder if she was fired too?

Hall #1 also has the world's tallest upright piano (an 1824 Broadwood & Sons, from London), and Hall No. 2 showcases the development of the piano with exhibits like the 1928 Haines. The most expensive of its era, the American marvel was completely automatic, able to perfectly imitate the styles of many well known pianists. It is played daily for visitors at 4pm. (Phone ahead in case the time has changed).

Add: No. Shūzhuāng Garden, #45 Huángyán Lù, Gǔlàngyǔ (鼓浪屿晃岩路 45 号) Tel: 2060238, 8882138 E-mail: glygqbwg@sina.com

Gulangyu Organ Museum① The only such museum in China and soon to be the world's largest, it is in the red-domed Bagua Building (八卦楼), and has exhibits donated by the Piano Museum's founder, Mr. Hú Yǒuyì. *Common Talk's* Vivian Zhang (张微微) quoted Hú as saying at the opening concert,

> "Pipe organs are acclaimed as the most sublime and divine musical instrument in the west. I hope one day organ lovers from all over the world will come on a music pilgrimage to my hometown, Gulangyu, to appreciate its beauty."

The organ played at the opening was a historic "Norman & Beard" made in 1909. The 6 meter high instrument has 1,350 pipes, 3 layers of keyboards and 21 organ stops, and took Ian Wakeley, an Australian organ technician, over a month to restore and tune. Ian explained why the organ was in such good shape:

> "It is made of the best materials by the best builders with the best techniques and is representative of the highest level at that time. And that is why, after nearly a century, it still remains in amazingly good condition while most other instruments of its age have long since decayed."

① Some info adapted from Vivian Zhang's "The Sound of Heaven," in "Common Talk," March 16-22, 2005 Organist Paul Carr also provided invaluable information on the organ's history, and how it was transported to Gulangyu.

This organ was formerly in England's Cradley Heath Methodist Church, where Paul Carr gave his 100th and final concert on it in June 2003. Carr is happy with its new home. He wrote, "As the organ will not be squashed into a corner, as it was at Cradley Heath, it could sound up to 50% louder!"

The church was to be razed, so organist Mark Checkley spread the word on the web that the venerable instrument needed a home. After 18 months and 250 responses, the best offer was from a local organ builder who wanted to dismantle the beauty and salvage pipes and parts for a future organ. But finally they heard that Ian Wakeley was seeking an organ for a Chinese client, and within a couple of weeks the organ was destined for Gǔlàngyǔ (it took 4 days just to dismantle and pack it). Tel: 5371607

Madame Dr. Līn Qiǎozhí Memorial Garden (Yùyuán Jǐngqū, 毓园景区) Prof. Madame Lín Qiǎozhì (林巧稚教授), Mother of Modern Chinese Gynecology, personally delivered over 50,000 babies in her lifetime, so blame her for the population problem. The memorial hall has memorabilia and photos of this selfless woman. Read "Discover Gǔlàngyǔ" for a fuller biography.
Add: from Gǔlàngyǔ's Bright Moon Park (皓月园), walk up Zhāngzhōu Lù (漳州路) or Fūxingà Lù (复兴路).

Strange World Museum (珍奇世界) A Chinese take-off of Ripley's "Believe it or Not," this had everything from the emperor's clothing and writs to a room with two headed dogs, albino reptiles—even a mummified mermaid. The mock opium den is a *high*light for some, shedding light on how folks used to get high. Others like the colonial-era antiques, or playing with the swords used to behead prisoners. You can also enjoy private puppet shows on an ornate antique stage.

Alas, Strange World shut down—believe it or not.

Old Town Cultural Arts Company (Gǔchéngfeng Yóulǎn Guǎn, 古城风游览馆) Puppet shows, tribal dances, dioramas, portraits, wax figurines of historical Chinese.
Add: #111 Lujiao Rd 鹿礁路 111 号
Tel: 2064908 E-mail: xinwān88@vip.sina.com

Remembering Old Gŭlàngyŭ Museum (Huáijiù Gŭlàngyŭ Guăn, 怀旧鼓浪屿馆) Opened by Taiwanese Mr. Hóng Míngzhāng（洪明章）, this place had over 1500 visitors within 3 days of its opening on May 1, 2006. Mr. Hóng has a collection of some 30,000 pieces, of which about 2,000 are on display.

Add: #38 Huángyán Lù, Gŭlàngyŭ (晃岩路 38 号鼓浪屿)

Gulangyu Home, 1920s

Koxinga Museum, Xīlín Villa (Xīlín Biéshù, 西林别墅，现为郑成功纪念馆). In February, 1962, Xīlín Villa opened as the Koxinga Museum on the 300th anniversary of Koxinga's liberation of Táiwān.① This elegant four-storey red-brick 2,100m^2 villa at Sunlight Rock's base was completed about 1932 by Huáng Zhōngxùn（黄仲训）. The Japanese used it as a "Rat Epidemic Disease Research Hospital"（鼠疫医院）, and Chiang Kai Shek's KMT made it a soldiers' infirmary. After Chiang Kai Shek fled to Táiwān, Xīlín Villa became a kindergarten for the "Overseas Research Information Center" (Hăijiāng Xuéshù Zīliàoguăn, 海疆学术资料馆) and the local military.

The 300+ historical relics, models, carvings, and photos are arranged in seven rooms, each room devoted to a different stage of Koxinga's career. The first hall depicts the youthful warrior's fight against the Qing, and two halls make the case for Táiwān as an age-old inalienable part of China. Another hall explains how Koxinga's son developed Táiwān, and the final hall displays famous Chinese' writings about Koxinga.

Koxinga Memorial

#73 Yongchun Rd.

Exhibits include Koxinga's apparel, such as jade belts and fragments of his robe and shoes, the silver coins Koxinga minted "Zhāngzhōu Soldier's Pay",（Zhāngzhōu Jūnxiăng, 漳州军饷）, and documents and poems written in Koxinga's own hand. The thought of a great warrior penning poetry is odd, but Chinese leaders over the ages, from the legendary Yellow Emperor to Máo Zédōng, were known for their literary, calligraphic and academic accomplishments, as well as for their military and political prowess. So I can well imagine the pirate-cum-patriot taking a break from the heat of battle to pen a poem like, "I miss you so much I can't sleep..." The entrance's characters, by the way, are by famous historian/ poet Guō Mòruò（郭沫若）.

① Oddly, In 1983, no one celebrated the 300th anniversary of Táiwān's liberation from Koxinga's grandson.

The Last Dutch Governor's Last Stand One hall of the Koxinga Memorial exhibits pages from "Neglected Táiwān" (Verwaerloosde Formosa), a fascinating and sometimes humorous account of Koxinga's conquest of Táiwān. I include juicy excerpts at the end of "Discover Gǔlàngyǔ's" chapter on Koxinga.

Xiamen Olympics Museum (厦门奥林匹克博物馆)
Tel: 400-799-7955 Add: #2017 Lvling Rd. 厦门市吕岭路 2017 号

Jimei Marine Life Museum (集美海洋动物馆)
Add: Jimei Town (across the causeway near the airport), Shigu Rd. South section (集美区石鼓路南段)
Buses: 901, 903, 921, 922, 923, 929, 959, 961
Note: see Jimei chapter for more Jimei attractions.

Tong'an District Museum (同安区博物馆) Please see Tong'an Chapter.

Quanzhou Museums (one hour north by bullet train; sure beats the 3 days it took a century ago!)

Quánzhōu's Minnan-Taiwan Relations Museum (中国闽台缘博物馆) In Quánzhōu, an hour north of Xiàmén: you could spend hours exploring this excellent museum on South Fújiàn's Táiwān links. It's just outside the North gate of the West Lake Park (西湖公园北大门外). Website: www.mty.org.cn

Quánzhōu's Maritime Museum (泉州海外交通史博物馆) I've visited this UNESCO-sponsored museum at least 30 times. The only such museum in China, it explores ancient journeys of both Chinese and foreigners, coming to and going from China. The displays include hundreds of ancient Islamic, Nestorian Christian and Franciscan tombstones, as well as Hindu and Manichean relics. Next door is a large Muslim Heritage Museum.

I like the "empty" glass case. That is—they claim it is empty. I think this is too good a museum to display an empty case. After research and deep deliberation, I'm quite certain this is a sly exhibit of an ancient stealth junk.

Refer to *Discover Quanzhou* for more about Quanzhou's museums.

Add: #425 Dōnghú Jiē 东湖街 425 号
Tel: 0595 22104255

"Stealth Junk"
Ancient hi-tech

Chapter 11

Jíměi (集美)—China's "College Town"

Note: many thanks to Prof. Huáng Shuǐkàn (黄水看), retired Prof. of Quánzhōu City Agricultural College (泉州市农校) and Jíměi School Alumni, for contributing much of this chapter's material.

Jíměi (集美) Imagine a sleepy fishing hamlet transformed into a college town with over a dozen schools and over 200,000 students from around China and the rest of the world. That's Jíměi's future, thanks to the century-old vision of Tan Kah Kee (Chén Jiāgēng, 陈嘉庚) the Henry Ford of Asia who was born and buried in Jíměi (Read about XMU's deep-pocketed benefactor at end of chapter).

Jíměi ("Gathered Beauty"), on the mainland west of Xiàmén and just across Xiàmén Bridge, has a population of about 330,000 and covers 276 km^2, with 60 km of coastline, but its fishing days are largely behind it. Government brochures claim its new 32km^2 "Jíměi Culture and Education Zone"(集美文教区)will be an important research and education center, with such esteemed centers of learning as Huáqiáo University, Xiàmén University of Technology, and Huáxià Institute of Technology. The brochure also claims Jíměi will become southeast Fújiàn's "Central Intelligence District (CID)."

I assume they're talking scholastics, not spies.

> "From now on the devious fishing village has been knolling the first sound of school bell, the Jíměi School was founded already."
>
> A Jíměi resident.

The devious fishing hamlet of Jíměi began its long journey to becoming China's College Town in 1913, when Mr. Tan established Jíměi Primary School on the site of the Jíměi Ancestral Temple (Jíměi Shè Zǔcítáng, 集美社祖祠堂).

Tan built 11 more schools, including a normal school, middle school, marine products school, agricultural and forestry school, merchants' school, etc., and funded over 70 schools in other areas of South Fújiàn, as well as many institutes around S.E. Asia. He also equipped his college town with a science center, gymnasium, library, hospital and navigation club. In Nov. 1920, Tan offered one million Yuan to establish Xiàmén University, which was opened the following year.

"The traveler will also be interested in the private school established and financed by a single Chinese gentleman…at Chin Be (Jíměi)… Mr. Tan Kak Kee established the school about ten years ago… Mr. Tan has put in about $600,000 in modern buildings, and is paying about $6,000 each month for teacher's salaries. He is planning to spend $4,000,000 in the establishment of a university in Amoy. At the present time he has the site and is getting plans from foreign architects for the buildings and equipment. This school is entirely a Chinese institution, with no foreign teachers and no foreign connections, and right out in a small Chinese village. The course of study is being made very practical, the latest thing added being a School of Fisheries. The buildings are modern in every sense, lighted with electricity, a special bath house erected, and running water in all the buildings. When we think of the future days, it is one of the most encouraging things to be seen in the whole of China."

Hutchinson 1920, p.159, 160

Mr. Tan was Chinese to the core and proud of it, but also quick to appreciate the best of the West, which he expressed in his architecture. His buildings are a marriage of Western and Chinese architecture [read about "Amoy Deco" in the Gulangyu Architecture chapter], using red brick, white stone, and glazed tiles. But the new Jíměi University makes a radical departure from the Tan tradition. This campus more resembles a posh Oriental Holiday Resort than mere hallowed halls of learning, and with its rapid expansion, seems intent on giving Xiàmén University a run for its money.

Jíměi Primary School (Jíměi Xiǎoxué, 集美小学). In 1913, Mr. Tan spent 2,000 Yuan to buy a pond, which he filled in to form part of the school grounds. He wrote that his goal was to improve the nation and society by promoting education. In 1916, he sent his younger brother, Chén Jìngxián (陈敬贤), to prepare for a normal school and middle school. The land did not come cheap, as Jìngxián had to deal with local superstition and fengshui practices.

In March, Jimei Primary School became part of Tong'an's Sixth Education District (Xiàmén was part of Tong'an at that time).

Tan started a women's primary school in February, 1917, but most families preferred their daughters stay home and work.

The normal and middle schools began in March, 1918. Tan Kah Kee and his brother wrote the motto for the schools, "Sincerity & Perseverance" (Chéng Yì, 诚毅). Mr. Tan wrote to each county government in S. Fújiàn to seek poor students, and, during the early years, the schools provided all students not only with free tuition but also, in the normal school, free bedding, mosquito nets, and school uniform. Tan also emphasized recruiting children of Overseas Chinese for the Jíměi schools to strengthen their feelings for their motherland (Jíměi schools still have a large number of overseas Chinese students).

In February, 1919, Mr. Tan started the Jimei Kindergarten (or Babyhood Normal School, as someone translated it), and in May he designated his 1.5 million square feet of shops and warehouses, and 7,000 acres of rubber trees, as a perpetual endowment for Jimei Schools. While at a Héng Měi Factory (恒美厂) banquet, Tan announced that from then on he would funnel most business profits into education in China.

Tan started the Vocational School's Aquatic Products Department in February,

1920, and the Trade Department in August, 1920. On February 23, 1921, the schools were formally named "Private Jíměi School of Fújiàn".

During the Fall of 1923, Jíměi was caught in the crossfire between the Fújiàn and Guǎngdōng Armies as they fought each other across the sea between Xiàmén and Jíměi. Jímei School appealed to both armies to consider the area as a peaceful neutral zone. Sun Yat-sen agreed, and from then on the area was known as "Jimei School Village," and considered a "Village of Perpetual Peace" (Yǒngjiǔ Hépíng Cūn, 永久和平村)

In May, 1925, the school purchased the Heavenly Horse Mtn. field (Tiānmǎshān, 天马山), on which the Agriculture and Forestry School opened in June, 1926.

By 1932, Mr. Tan was subsidizing 73 middle and primary schools in 20 counties and cities, and had helped raise the quality of teachers and curriculum throughout Southern Fújiàn.

After war broke out with Japan in July, 1937, Jíměi's schools fled the "Village of Perpetual Peace," which Japanese seemed intent on transforming into a "Village of Perpetual Pieces." The schools relocated to remote counties, and in the spring of 1938 the middle school was moved to Ānxī's Confucian Temple (listed as "Confusion Temple" on one official map). The quality of teachers and education remained high, and students were more active than ever, not only in studying but in distributing anti-Japanese leaflets throughout the countryside (the Japanese executed many Xiàménese for this).

After the war Mr. Tan sought the aid of relatives and friends in rebuilding the Jíměi Schools destroyed by the Japanese. The school reopened on November 1st, 1949—only to be bombed by Kuomintang planes from Táiwān, which damaged buildings and killed several staff and students. But Jíměi folk stuck at it and today the area is a thriving college town.

Overseas Chinese Education in Jíměi. At Mr. Tan's suggestion, Jíměi started the "Continuing Education School for Returned Jíměi Overseas Chinese" in December, 1953. Between 1957 and 1960, the school added the Jíměi Continuing Education School for Relatives of Overseas Chinese, and the Jíměi Chinese Language and Culture School was founded in September, 1982. Today, Jíměi is a favorite destination for Chinese abroad wishing to study in China.

Jíměi University After Mr. Tan died, many Jíměi educational institutions were upgraded to college level. On October 20, 1994, Jíměi University was established by merging six colleges: the Jíměi Teachers' College, Jíměi Finance and Economics

College, Xiàmén Fisheries College, Jíměi Navigation Institute, and Fújiàn Physical Education College. The School of Business Administration was founded in 1995.

The merger into one large university was a government experiment in improving education by schools sharing physical resources, reducing unnecessary overhead, and streamlining administration.

Jíměi University has 19 colleges and institutes, over 20,000 full-time students, over 5,000 adult-education students, and over 2300 faculty and staff. The campus covers 780,000 m^2, with 510,000 m^2 of developed area, includes a library with 1.5 million books.

Sea Turtle Garden (Áoyuán, 鳌园)—A Grave Undertaking I'd have thought the idea of turning an island mausoleum into a major tourist side would be dead in the water, but not so. Mr. Tan's tomb is a big draw for droves of admirers dying to learn more about the great man.

Like many tombs, Tan's tomb (and the island itself) is shaped like a turtle, because turtles symbolize longevity. But I'm not sure what the point is, given that the tombs' residents have already passed on.

Eternally dead, perhaps?

Mr. Tan knew his days were numbered but made sure his name would be remembered by spending a decade (1950 to 1960) building Sea Turtle Garden on the former site of Turtle Head Palace, a small Mazu temple destroyed by the Japanese during WW II. The ever-practical Tan chose this site because it would not waste valuable farmland. He also had a good sense of timing. He finished the turtle tomb in 1960 and passed on in 1961.

The 976m^2 garden's centrepiece is the 28-meter high Jíměi Liberation Memorial Tablet (集美解放纪念碑). The front bears a calligraphic inscription by Chairman Máo. A 78-year-old Mr. Tan spent three months in the summer of 1952 writing the inscription on the reverse side.

The eight steps of the memorial's first level represent the 8-year anti-Japanese War. The upper level's 3 steps are in memory of the 3-year Liberation War (1946-1949). In 1981, Fújiàn People's Publishing House published, *Carved Inscription & Book of Rubbings of Jíměi Áo Garden* 《集美鳌园题刻拓本》.[①]

① Pictorial compiled by Mr. Chén Lǐyì (陈礼义) and Chén Zhènqún (陈振群)

Cool Friezes On the sides of the entrance hall are carved 58 delightful Huì'ān (惠安; see Fujian Travel chapter)-style stone friezes depicting in stunning detail 58 historical scenes and personages from ancient and modern China. One carving of a political session at a round table, rather like a Socialist's Last Supper, looks so 3-dimensional and lifelike you can almost hear them debating about how to run us foreign devils off.

Flintstone Fotos The stone "photo-carvings" were created with a technique developed in the 1980s by Huì'ān artisans, who use a sharply-pointed heavy bronze stylus to make photographic-quality likenesses (variations are made by size, depth and density of tiny dots). Give your family photo to a Huì'ān artisan and within days they'll mail you a stone likeness.

The park has 653 carvings of blue stone carved by world-renowned Huì'ān craftsman①. Locals protected them from destruction by the Red Guards during the Cultural Revolution by plastering them over with mud. As a little extra insurance, they scrawled revolutionary slogans on the mud. But what Red Guards missed, the weather did not. Salt spray and wind wreaked so much havoc, especially on the earliest 292 cement sculptures, that the Jīměi School Board raised over 1 million RMB in 1992 to hire Huì'ān artists to replaced the cement sculptures with 20 shadow carvings, 42 recessed carvings and 230 relief carvings. Still, even today, Jīměi authorities are seeking better ways to preserve the artwork from the elements. Any suggestions?

Mr. Tan's tomb is behind the Liberation monument. After his death on August 12, 1961, Zhōu Ēnlǎi took charge of his funeral in Běijīng, and transported his body on a special train to be buried here in the garden.

Tan's tomb is covered with 13 pieces of green granite. It is shaped like a turtle, which symbolizes longevity and immortality; it is also said that Tan admired the turtle's earnestness and down-to-earth spirit. A small wall around his tomb has 15 carvings depicting various scenes in Tan's life.

① Huì'ān, (惠安) part of Quanzhou, is two hours up the coast. The carved tomb of Mr. Lin shows Hui'an has been into stone carving for at least 1700 years.

While in the museum, enjoy one of the performances of ancient music held every half hour with brass bells, chimes, and zither. The costumes are as intriguing as the music. The hall is air conditioned—and the show is free.

Museum gate attendants require you to exit from a gate clear on the opposite side from the entry, which forces you to wander the narrow street lined both sides with shops selling everything from fashionable clothes to DVDs, dried fruits, Chinese herbs, and sundry handicrafts. Tel: 6064884, 6101713

Returnees Hall (Guīlái Táng, 归来堂) Mr. Tan's former home is near the Jíměi Middle School on Jiāgēng Rd. It is said to be of typical South Fújiàn construction, with white walls and a green tile roof, but it doesn't look Fújiàn to me. It has a distinct foreign flair—perhaps a bit of "Amoy Deco?"

Mr. Tan lived here from 1919 to 1922 as he established Xiàmén University and expanded Jíměi School. Japanese bombers destroyed the house in 1938, but when Běijīng offered to rebuilt it after Liberation, Tan insisted that the school buildings be repaired first. His home was rebuilt in 1955 and he lived here from 1958 until he moved to Běijīng in 1960. A busy man right up until his death, he served as a Deputy to the Central Government, Chairman of the All-China Federation of Overseas Returnees, and member of the People's Congress Standing Committee (do they ever sit?).

In 1980, the home was restored to its original design, and in 1983 designated the "Returnees Hall" to commemorate Jíměi Primary School's 70th anniversary. The inner structure of the house is said to be shaped like the Chinese character Huí, 回, meaning "return."

Memorabilia include rare photos, and the battered suitcases, shoes and umbrella that Tan used for decades.

The ground floor is now a meeting place for the Jíměi School Committee; and the second floor has Mr. Tan's personal effects, as well as his drawing-room, workroom, bedroom, dining room and library. The Tan Kah Kee Exhibition Hall (Chén Jiāgēng Shēngpíng Chénlièguǎn, 陈嘉庚生平陈列馆) beside the residence has more exhibits about this amazing philanthropist.

The center of the garden has a 2.3 meter bronze state of Mr. Tan, hat and stick in hand. The folding black screen in the hall has the memorial speech from August 15, 1961. When the famous poet Mr. Guō Mòruò (郭沫若) visited Jíměi in 1962, he wrote the hall's couplet:

"鳌园博物大观百闻不如一见，
鹭江集美中学万人共仰千秋"
Áoyuán Bówù dàguān Bǎiwén bùrú yījiǎn,
Lùjiàng Jīměi Zhōngxué Wànrén Gòngyǎng Qiānqiū

Rough translation:

Àoyuán Museum's view—better to see once than to hear about 100 times;
Lù River's Middle School—respected by 10,000 people for 1,000 years."

Dragon Boat (Lóngzhōu, 龙舟) **Races** are Jimei's real drawing card. Held every fifth day of the fifth Luny month, these races have been held for at least a couple thousand years, and teams from all over the world compete in Jíměi's exciting event. (See "Chinese Festivals" chapter)

Mr. Tan made the 300x800m Dragon Boat Pond (Lóngzhōu Chí, 龙舟池) in 1952, and also constructed 10 dragon boats, each capable of holding 16 rowers. Jíměi has been famous for dragon boat races ever since.

The pond is surrounded by seven Chinese pavilions of different styles, called the "Seven Stars Fall to Earth" (qīxīngzhuìdì, 七星坠地). Mr. Tan designed the two pavilions on the lake and named them "Lonely Star Accompanies the Moon" (Gūxīng Shényuè, 孤星什月).

Yánpíng (Delayed Peace) **Old Fortress** (Yánpíng Gùléi, 延平故垒). A stone gate is all that remains of Koxinga's 17th century Yánpíng Fortress, where he trained troops to make the Ming Dynasty's last stand against the Manchu founders of the Qīng Dynasty.

A měi resident wrote of the lonely gate, "Please run your eyes bitter."

After running your eyes bitter, dry them with a hanky and note the characters, "Old Yánpíng Fortress," engraved on a rock by the gate. Mr. Tan engraved them in 1922 after building a school dorm behind the former fortress. He chose the Yánpíng Fort location to show that the ultimate revolution is education. Japanese destroyed the dorm during the war but Mr. Tan rebuilt it as a 4-storey red brick structure with green Chinese tiled roof.

In 1956, the ever pragmatic Mr. Tan also designed the 15-storey Nanxuan building, with its huge clock, and a lighthouse so fishermen could find their way home during inclement weather.

Jíxìng Causeway (Jíxìng Hǎidī, 集杏海堤) This 19-meter wide, 2.2 km 1,500,000 m^3 granite embankment's road and rail ended Xiàmén's isolation from Jíměi. Until the mid 50s, Xiàmén could reach the mainland only by a dangerous crossing on ferries, junks or small sampans. Mr. Tan suggested a causeway in 1951, and by 1955 it was in use, though the workers had to defend themselves not only from rough seas but also from up to 60 air attacks a day by Kuomintang planes from nearby Taiwan.

Xiàmén Bridge President Jiang Zemin cut the ribbon for Xiàmén Bridge's opening on December 19, 1991, and inscribed the bridge's calligraphy (and for the Haicang suspension bridge as well). This 4-lane expanse was China's first sea-spanning bridge and cost about RMB 1.5 billion. The bridge can withstand earthquakes of 8 on the Richter scale and typhoons of force 12 on the Beaufort scale. In 1995, the bridge received the Lǔbān Award[①] (鲁班奖), China's most prestigious engineering and construction award.

Jimei Marine Life Museum (集美海洋动物馆)
Add: Jimei Town (across the causeway near the airport), Shigu Rd. South section (集美区石鼓路南段) Buses: 901, 903, 921, 922, 923, 929, 959, 961

Key to the City!

Every time our son Shannon saw the bridge's gigantic golden key, he asked, "Where's the lock?" In 1999, Mayor Hong Yongshi gave me a golden key to the city (much smaller than the bridge key), and said, "This key will open doors all over Xiàmén."

"How about the Bank of China?" I asked.

"Not that door," he said.

Jíměi Gardens (See Parks & Gardens Chapter)

Supplement

Tan Kah Kee—the Henry Ford of Asia

(Adapted from *Xiamen University, Strength of the Nation*, by Dr. Bill Brown and Robin Feifei)

XMU's founder, Mr. Tan Kah Kee (Chén Jiāgēng, 1874-1961), gave about 100 million USD to education over his lifetime, but he was born into a humble family of merchants in the village of Jíměi, on the mainland across from Xiàmén Island.

Tan worked fields and fishnets until he started school at age nine, and in the fall of 1890 he moved to Singapore to help in his father's rice shop. His father's business went under in 1904, but the savvy son pulled together enough capital to buy 500 acres of forested land in Singapore and started a pineapple plantation.

A Rubber Magnate Like any good rubber magnate, Tan had a good sense of direction. He rapidly expanded into rice milling, manufacturing, sawmills, real estate, and ocean transport, but it was rubber that really stretched his fortune. He set aside a few acres of his pineapple plantation and eventually had 10,000 acres of rubber trees. His expansion to rubber manufacturing helped create the rubber industry and made him one of the four great Rubber Barons.

By the mid 1920s, the Rubber Magnate's Singapore-based empire had over 30,000 people, 150 offices on 5 continents and did business with 48 countries. But prices plummeted after 1926 and rubber never quite bounced back. Even worse, after Mr.

① Lǔbān, a legendary master craftsman, is called the father of Chinese carpentry.

Tan protested Japan's brutal "Jinan Massacre" (May 3rd, 1928), his factory was burned to the ground. Yet even as he struggled through the Great Depression he continued to finance Jímĕi School, Xiàmén University, and Chinese and English schools in Singapore—a feat he managed in part because of his frugality.

Frugal Philanthropist Philanthropists often give but a fraction of their wealth while alive but leave behind charitable foundations as a legacy. But Mr. Tan literally gave like a prince while living like a pauper, subsisting largely on rice porridge and potatoes, and using the same umbrella and battered suitcases for decades. Other rich Chinese of his day built luxurious villas on nearby Gŭlàngyú, but Mr. Tan was content with a simple home in his native Jímĕi. He wrote to a relative that as long as his hometown had great needs, "I cannot put myself before the community."

Mr. Tan's Vision for China Mr. Tan was a social and political reformer from youth. He supported Sun Yatsen, and at one point accounted for about 1/3 of the Kuomintang's finances (a feat he no doubt regretted when Chiang Kai Shek absconded to Táiwān with his money and everyone else's). But Tan's greatest hope for China was in modern education.

In 1894, at age 21, Tan began a family school in Jímĕi. In 1912, during the first year of the new Republic of China, Tan returned to China and on January 27, 1913 opened the Jímĕi Primary School. Between 1920 and 1926 he opened a school a year until Jímĕi School Village had 11 schools, including a middle school and schools in agriculture, commerce, forestry, navigation, etc. In addition, Jímĕi School Village's education promotion department donated to more than 70 middle schools and primary schools throughout Fújiàn province.

Supporting Education Abroad Tan also began or funded at least seven schools in Singapore, including Tao Nan (1907), Ai Tong (1912), Chung Fook Girls School (1915), Chung Poon (1915), the Singapore Chinese High School (1918), Nanyang Normal School (1941) and Nan Chaio Girls High School (1947). . His largesse was not limited to Chinese schools. He gave $30,000 to the Anglo-Chinese School in 1919 and in 1941 gave $10,000 to Raffles College, which later merged with the Medical College and eventually became the University of Singapore.

Daonan School (Singapore)

Xiàmén University—Apple of Tan's Eye In early November, 1920, Mr. Tan offered one million Yuan to start Xiamen University, which began with the Normal and Commerce Departments, and later expanded to five Colleges and 17 departments in Literature, Science, Law, Commerce and Education.

Mr. Tan emphasized quality education. He sent students abroad and hired teachers from other areas, purchased the latest equipment, and emphasized sports. By the spring of 1937, his financial fortunes had so suffered that he let the government take over Xiàmén University, but he continued to subsidize it. Tan wrote to the minister of education that he would "live in perpetual regret" of "a fine start and a poor finish."

That same year, Xiàmén University relocated to Chángtīng in West Fújiàn to escape destruction by the Japanese, who had occupied Xiàmén. The Japanese surrendered in August, 1945, and on October 21, 500 mass organizations in Singapore welcomed Tan's return from a decade of exile in Java. A large meeting in Chōngqīng on November 18, 1945, celebrated Mr. Tan's safety, and Chairman Mao inscribed a scroll about Tan which read, "Banner of Overseas Chinese, Glory of the Nation."

XMU returned to Xiàmén after Japan's defeat and the new president, eminent biologist, Dr. Wang Deyao, immediately set out rebuilding and expanding the campus. Tan's vision and money, and Wang's leadership, paid off. XMU was designated a key national university in 1962 and has mushroomed ever since.

On October 1, 1949, Chairman Mao invited Mr. Tan to Tiānānmén to participate in the ceremony of the founding of the People's Republic of China. Tan settled down in his homeland in 1950 and devoted the rest of his life and fortune to its reconstruction.

Tan's Final Years Mr. Tan died of cancer in 1961, and after a State Funeral in Bĕijīng, a special train transported his body to his hometown of Jímĕi. Tan left behind three million Yuan in banks, but the man who gave like a prince and lived like a pauper evidently expected his descendants to do the same—or make their own fortune.

Tan left no money to his family, but gave half a million to Jímĕi School Foundation, half a million to construct Bĕijīng's Overseas Chinese Museum, and over two million Yuan for education.

Tan's International Legacy Altogether, Mr. Tan gave an estimated 100 million USD towards education, both in China and abroad, and the Tan Kah Kee Foundation has been awarding a Postgraduate Scholarship since 1983. In 1986, Nobel Prize Laureate Prof. C.N. Yang set up the Tan Kah Kee Inventors' Award, and in 1992, Prof Yang and two other Nobel Prize Laureates, Prof Samuel C.C. Ting and Prof Li Yuan Tseh, together with Prof Chang-lin Tien, former Vice-chancellor of the University of California at Berkeley, and Prof Wang Gungwu, former President of Hong Kong University, set up the Tan Kah Kee International Society Foundation for the advancement of education and culture in the spirit of Tan Kah Kee.

In 1991, Singapore's president, Dr. Wee Kim Wee, launched the University Endowment Fund in honor of Mr. Tan, and set a goal of raising $1 billion for education.

On 11 March, 1990, the International Asteroid Center of China named Asteroid 2963 the "Tan Kah Kee Star." The naming ceremony was held at Xiàmén University.

Lastly, the School of Chemistry in my home state's University of California, Berkeley, has a "Tan Kah Kee Hall."

Tan Kah-Kee and Li Quangqian

Lĭ Guāngqián (李光前) Tan Kah Kee was a role model for many Chinese, including one of XMU's greatest benefactors, his son-in-law Lĭ Guāngqián (Lee Kong Chian, 1893-1967), who also helped fund Jímĕi schools. For more information on Lĭ, read "Xiàmén University—Strength of the Nation," or visit amoymagic.com.

Chapter 12

Tóng'ān & Jīnmén (同安和金门)

Tóng'ān is Xiàmén's remotest area—1/2 hour north of Jīměi—but well worth a tour. For most of the past 1000 years, Tóng'ān, not Xiàmén, was the area's economic, political and cultural center, as well as a wildly beautiful scenic region.

Tóng'ān was established in the Jin Dynasty, 3rd year of Emperor Taikang's reign (a barbarian-befuddling way of saying 282 A.D.) It started out as part of Nán'ān (南安), Koxinga's home), became Datong Square in 809 AD, and was renamed Tóng'ān in 933. Tóng'ān eventually became part of Quánzhōu, and Xiàmén Town was established as part of Tóng'ān in 1387 A.D.

In 1953, Tóng'ān's Jīměi became part of Xiàmén, and the rest of Tóng'ān came under Xiàmén in August 1958. Tóng'ān was returned to Jìnjiāng's（晋江）jurisdiction in Feb. 1970, and in June 1973 was put back under Xiàmén again, where it still remains—as of last week, anyway.

So why the tug of war between Jìnjiāng and Xiàmén? Tóng'ān's 1,079 km^2 not only has a rich cultural and historic heritage but also 500,000 acres of farmland (rare in mountainous Fújiàn), 400,000 acres of mudflats (though our van has had too many flats in mud), 86 km. of coastline, and 1.12 million acres of mountains. Fújiàn is almost all mountains anyway, but not like Tóng'ān's, with countless waterfalls, ancient temples atop precipitous peaks, the "Valley of Butterflies," etc. Tóng'ān is beautiful above ground and a treasure below, with ancient relics like the Tīngxī Kiln (Tīngxī Yáozhǐ, 汀溪窑址) that produced the pearlescent porcelain prized all over ancient Asia, especially in Japan

Where to start? We'll begin with Tōng'ān's favorite son, Sū Sòng（苏颂）, and then visit the ancient Confucian Temple (Kǒngmiào,孔庙), Brahma Temple (Fàntiān Sì, 梵天寺), the "12 Dragon Waterfalls"（Shí Èr Lóng Tánbàobù, 十二龙潭瀑布）of the North Mountain Scenic Region (Běichénshān Yóulǎn Qū, 北辰山游览区), and the scenic "Valley of Butterflies," (Húdiégǔ, 蝴蝶谷). Then we'll feast on the inimitable Mǐnnán cuisine of the Tóng'ān Guesthouse（Tóng'ān Bīnguǎn, 同安宾馆）.

Tóng'ān's Renaissance Man, Sū Sòng (苏颂, 1020-1101), finished the world's first astronomical clock (水运仪象台) on Jan. 16, 1089, 600 years before Europeans.

Experts claim his book on the clock was the world's first mechanical design manual, with 60 illustrations and diagrams of the 150 separate parts. The water-powered wooden tower was a bit large for the average apartment—about 10 to 12 meters high and 7 meters wide. But I suspect my Chinese grad students use Su Song's astronomical clock because they are often astronomically late to class.

The tower's upper layer was for astronomical observations, the central section demonstrated celestial phenomena, and the lower area was a chronograph with moving puppets to show time.

Sū Sòng was also an adept herbalist. In 1061 he compiled the *Illustrated Canon of Materia Medica* (Běncǎo Tújīng, 本草图经)—the definitive guide for those who think the grass is always greener on the other side. He explained, for example, when and where to find 'dragon's blood' (dracaena family), which modern Chinese claim lives for 8,000 years.

"**Dragon's blood** is from plants. The fine looking trees are dozens of feet tall. The red resin (from which it derives the name 'Dragon's Blood') oozes from the trees like glue and congeals. Harvest time varies."

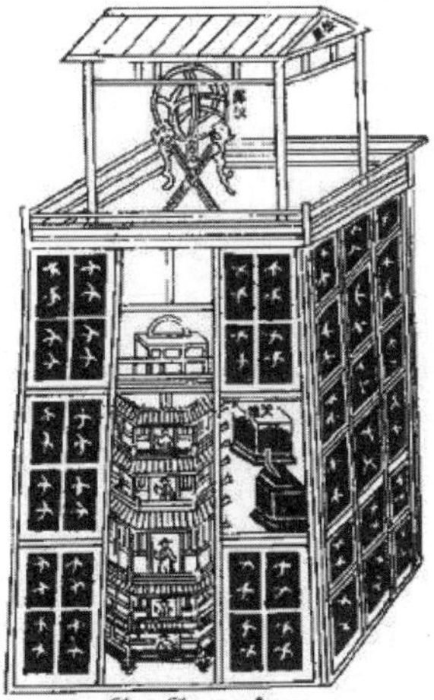
Su Song's Astronomical Clock

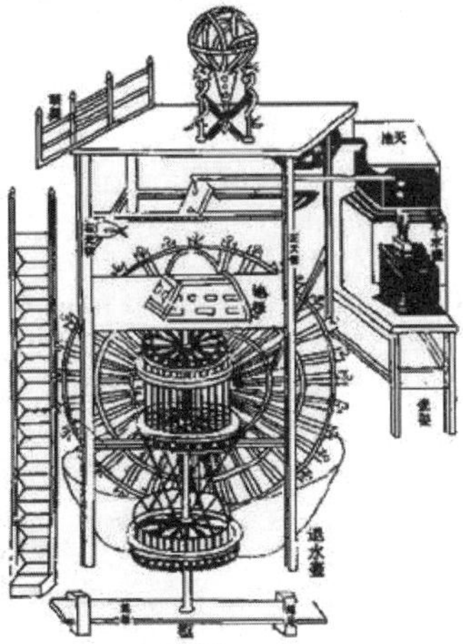
Interior

Sū Sòng's Home (Lúshān Táng Jǐngqū, Sūsòng Gùjū, 芦山堂景区, 苏颂故居). The Sū clan ancestral hall, and Sūsòng's birthplace, was built in 994 A.D. in N.W. Tóng'ān by Sū Guānghǎi (苏光海).
Add: Dàtóngzhèn Xǐhēi Chí #23 (大同镇洗墨池 23 号)
Tel: 7122883

Sū Sòng Science & Technology Hall (Sū Sòng Kējì Guǎn Jǐngqū, 苏颂科技馆景区)
Add: 大同镇城西路 80 号
Tel: 7030608

Tóng'ān Museum (Tóng'ān Bówúguǎn 同安博物馆) Opened in early 1990, this 7,000 m^2 museum is inside the Tóng'ān Confucian Temple (see Religion Chapter) and has at least a couple thousand items on display in 3 main areas: Tóng'ān historical relics, Tóng'ān historical personages, and archives.
Add: Tong'an District, Sanxiu Rd. Tel: 7022478 7317857
Buses: 615, 619, 630A, 630B About 40m from Tankou Rd. (县口路) exit.

Mǎtáng Village –Xiamen's #1 Village (厦门第一村——马塘村). About 7km east of Tóng'ān, in a remote and formerly inaccessible valley, lies the 1.8km^2 village of Mǎtáng, with 64 families and a population of about 275 people. In 1980, Mǎtáng had little arable land, bare mountains, and few resources. It was backwards and dilapidated, and had only 435 acres of cultivated land because of the lack of water. The average resident made less than 170 Yuan a month, and people in neighboring villages had a saying, "If you have money, don't loan to anyone in Mǎtáng; if you have a daughter, don't marry her into Mǎtáng" (有钱不借马塘人, 有女不嫁马塘村). So how did Mǎtáng become Xiàmén's #1 Village?

In 1985 Mǎtáng started their break from poverty with the labor-intensive Xìnghuá (兴华) canning factory. In 1990 they undertook a Sino-foreign joint venture with Xiàmén Tóngmáo Foodstuffs Canning Company, Ltd., and over the years invested 80 million Yuan improving the technology 3 times. By 1996, the village's production had reached 122.5 million Yuan, per capita income had reached 5250 Yuan (from 170 Yuan—an increase of 1071%). Workers now live in modern apartments and villas with beautiful gardens and lawns.

Xiamen's "1st Village,"— Matang, Tong'an

Visit Mǎtáng. Maybe they'll hire you!

Tóng'ān Film Studio (Xiàmén Tóng'ān Yǐngshì Chéng, 厦门同安影视城) Over 1,600 acres; includes miniature Tiān'ānmén, replica ancient town and temples, a Dinosaur World, children's park, Hall of Mental Cultivation, Hall of Supreme Harmony (for choirs?), Long Corridor of the Summer Palace, etc.
Location: Wǔxiǎn Town (Wǔxiǎnzhèn, 五显镇)
Tel: 7302870 Buses: 67, 79, 106, 617, 618, 621

A Trip to Tong An's Film City! (影视城)
By Trish Boman (Xiamen International School)

I visited Film City on a Friday morning, along with about 3,000 primary school children and their teachers. This meant that along with the Forbidden City, Summer Palace, Nine Dragon Wall, Qing-Ming Street, and other old Beijing attractions, I became an extra object of fascination, with children rushing up to surround me and shout, "Hello, how are YOOUUU!"

Unwanted celebrity status aside, it was a pleasant outing. The recreation of the Forbidden City is quite spacious and impressive, giving plenty of room to roam around and take photos in famous settings. Many buildings seem to be almost full-size - at least I couldn't tell the difference, and it's a little far to run and check. The different Halls recreated there are now inhabited by photographers with their costumes and photos-for-a-fee stalls, including sedan chairs, and for an extra payment you can even sit on the Emperor's throne.

Qing-Ming Street is complete, right down to the advertisements on the walls for insect powders and beauty products, and there are a few amusements and souvenir stalls. Behind the street, if you can find the stairs at either end, is a mini-Great Wall from which to view the entire scene. I could just imagine myself as a movie director calling the shots for the street scene of a kung-fu film, with exotic beauties flirting with the local heroes in the bustling marketplace, while in the palace forecourt, mandarins bow and scrape before Dowager-Empress Cixi.

The extensive park is big enough for hours of leisurely strolls, but there is little else to do, and refreshments are minimal. Perhaps if a film was actually being shot, it could be really exciting. But otherwise it's still a fairly peaceful interlude that lets the mind wander back to the old days of Beijing.

Tóng'ān Lotus Flower Mountain Scenic Area (Liánhuā Zhèn Hòupǔ Cūn 莲花镇后埔村 About 10 km from Tóng'ān.
Bus: Take #7 to Film City, change to #92 bus to Hòupǔ Village, and take a local motorcycle taxi about 2 to 3 km. If you survive, enjoy the ancient trees, ancient temples, and the "Holy Spring"—all the things you find on just about any mountain top that has had Chinese inhabitants for centuries.

North Mountain Scenic Area (Běichén Shān, 北辰山) This 122 km^2 attraction is in Wǔxiǎnzhèn (五显镇境内), about 12 km from Tóng'ān.
Tel: 7232018 Catch Film City bus at 9:00, 9:15, 9:45, 15:30, 15:50, 16:30

12 Vauclusian Springs [12 Dragon Falls] of North Mountain (Běishān Shíèr Lóngtán, 北山十二龙潭) I didn't know what Vauclusian was either, so I looked it up: "A spring rising up a deep, steeply-inclined, water-filled passage into a small surface pool." Located in Wǔxiǎn Town (Wǔxiǎnzhèn, 五显镇), near Film Studio, the 12 springs create a picturesque series of waterfalls 1km in length.
Tel: 7302870 Buses: 67, 79, 106, 617, 618, 621

Tóng'ān Plum Mountain Temple (Méishān Sì, 梅山寺) Very Scenic.
Add: Méishān Lù, Méishān Liánsì (梅山路梅山莲寺) Tel: 7026946

West Mountain Peak Scenic Area (Xīshānyán Jǐngqū, 西山岩景区) At 324 m above sea level, this is ***the*** escape on sizzling summer days. The peak's White Cloud Crag Temple (Báiyúnyán Miào, 白云岩庙) was built over 1100 years ago. Purple Cloud Cave (Zǐyǔn Dòng, 紫云洞) faces the temple; behind it are two "Holy Wells" said to never lack sweet water. To the left is a Míng Dynasty cliff inscription. The 18 trees represent Buddha's 18 Arhats (Luóhàn, 罗汉).
Add: Xīnmín Zhèn Yìlì Cūn (新民镇艺力村) Ten miles outside of Tóng'ān
Tel: (Mid-Mountain, 半山) : 7200516 Tel: (Peak, 山顶) 7200776

Tīngxī Reservoir (Tīngxī Shuǐkù, 汀溪水库) Built 7 km N.W. of Tōng'ān in June, 1956, the dam is 37 m high, 245 m long, and 8 m thick across the top. The reservoir holds about 48,450,000 m^3 of water.

Tīngxī Kiln Site (Tīngxī Yáozhǐ, 汀溪窑址). In 1956, workers digging a reservoir discovered one of the Sòng Dynasty's largest kilns. The site, which has shed much light on ancient Fújiàn's economy and foreign trade, has yielded kiln bricks and equipment, bowls, plates, trays, pots, daily utensils, and earthenware. This kiln was a major source of the pearlescent porcelain (Zhūguāngcí, 珠光瓷) prized in Japan.

Getting there: from Xiàmén train station, take a bus to Tóng'ān, then take a small bus or taxi to the kiln site 10 km outside of Tóng'ān, east of the reservoir.

Tong'an Butterfly Valley (Tóng'ān Húdiégǔ, 同安蝴蝶谷) This is a delightful place to spend a day—and remote, so relatively unfrequented. Mr. Yè Jīnpū (叶金铺) who runs an orchard at the base of the mountains, happened upon butterfly valley, which locals call "Stone Ship Pit" (Shíchuán Kēng, 石船坑). A few butterflies flew out of the trees about 200 meters up a narrow trail that he was exploring. The further he went, the more rugged and scenic the trail, and the more butterflies of all colors—blue, green, yellow, white, black, purple. Within 200 m he saw over 1000 butterflies of at least 10 kinds, and 10 connecting waterfalls. A short walk to the west led to 22 pools, 9 more falls (one was 60 m in height), and an 80m natural stairway. Location: Tīngxī District, Rěnyú Village (Tīngxī Zhèn Rěnshē Cūn, 汀溪镇荏畲村).

Getting there: #618 bus to Tóng'Ān, Little West Gate (Xiǎo Xīmén, 同安小西门). From there, rent a car or drive (only after reading "Darwinian Driving" in Transportation chapter).

Driving Directions: Locals say you need a guide but hcrc's how to find it on your own.From Tóng'ān City, follow the brown "SPA" signs to Trithorn Hot Springs Resort about 6 km. north. Turn left on the road just after the bridge and just before the hill (about 200 m. before Trithorn exit). After 1km., take the right fork towards Xīyuán Village (西源). Go 8.1 km to Rěnshē Village (荏畲村). Turn down the narrow concrete road to the right (just past two yellow buildings). After 0.6 km, this becomes a dirt road for 1.3 km. At the dead end, ascend the steep dirt steps to the right, turn left at the small stone canal, and follow this route until you've had enough of pools, falls, butterflies and birds (During our relatively short trek we saw some skittish yellow wagtails, red-whiskered bulbuls, and some flocks of noisy little green birds.

Tóng'ān's Little Plain Provincial Forest Park (Xiǎopíng Sēnlín Gōngyuán, 小坪省级森林公园) 25 km north of Tóngān, 45 km north of Xiàmén, covers about 400,000 acres, with facilities for tourism, aquatic sports and forestry research. Tel: 7053878 Getting there: Dàpíng mini-bus (大坪中巴) to Xiǎopíng. (小坪站下).

Tóng 'Ān Firewalkers—Soul 'n Sole Tóng'Ān was the origin of Overseas Chinese' firewalking festivals. See religion chapter for fire-walking Prof!

Three Hero Islands (Yīngxióng Sāndǎo, 英雄三岛) Only 1.8 km from Táiwān-controlled Jīnmén Island lie the "3 Hero Islands" of "Big Dèng"① (Dàdèng, 大嶝), Little Dèng (Xiǎodèng, 小嶝) and Horn Islet (Jiǎoyǔ, 角屿).

The Dàdèng Island Frontline Broadcast Station (Dàdèng Dǎo Qiánxiàn Guǎngbō Zhàn, 大嶝岛前线广播站) is a memorial to the heavy bombardment of the "3 Heroes" on August 23, 1958. A tour of the underground bomb shelter is sobering. Lights flickers; loudspeakers blare recordings of whistling bombs. Pretty unnerving—especially given that 30 years ago I was in Táiwān tending missiles destined for Xiàmén. Neither side of the Dire Straits deserves such a fate. Hopefully they'll settle future disputes more peacefully.

Dàdèng Táiwān Commodities Market's hottest item is Jīnmén cutlery crafted from recycled bomb casings, but this cutting edge industry has bombed after decades of peace. Now Jinmen must shell out cash to import old bomb casings from the mainland. Tel: 7095201 E-mail: ggy@xmeyou.com

www.xmeyou.com Buses: #56 from Harbor (Lúndù, 轮渡), #620 from Train Station (Huóchēzhàn, 火车站), #605 from Tóng'ān (同安)

① "Dèng" (嶝) means "path up a mountain")

Dictionaries Dates In 1988, I was so entranced by my Chinese-English dictionary's 'model English sentences' that I read it cover to cover twice! (Read some of them in "Mad about Mandarin" chapter). For example, how would you use the word "suppose?" The dictionary suggested, "I *suppose* she's gone to practice grenade throwing again."

Best Western Premier Trithorn Hotspring Resort Xiamen (Zuìjiā Xīfāng Xiàmén Cuìfēng Wēnquán Dùjià Jiúdiàn, 最佳西方厦门翠丰温泉度假酒店). Best Western's first 5-star resort in China, this 35,000 m^2 resort is opposite the scenic Tīngxī Reservoir (Tīngxī Shuǐkù, 汀溪水库).

This secluded resort can soak you in more ways than you thought possible, with numerous outdoor pools, unique Minnan-style hotspring villas, and private hotspring pools in each of the 198 luxurious (minimum 50 m^2) guest rooms. Trithorn has Chinese, Japanese and Western restaurants, conference and banquet facilities, bars and recreation areas, exercise facilities, massage, aromatherapy, acupressure, and traditional medicated diets which, according to the brochure:

Trithorn's Minnan-style hot springs villas

"...are on the basis of differential diagnosis and seasonal conditions, and in concert on Hotspring bath and massage. The diets are basically made of Minnan local food materials, aiming at replenishing moisture content and electrolyte. They have not only the efficiency of medicine but also the delicacy of food .and can be used to prevent and cure diseases, or for healthy people to build up their health and prolong their lives."

Sue and I made a weekend retreat of it last Valentine's Day, and visited the Tóng'ān Film City and Butterfly Valley, which are only 10 minutes away.

Jīnmén Island (金门岛)

Táiwān-controlled Jīnmén (Gold Gate) Island lies only 2,310 meters from Xiàmén. With good binoculars, you can see soldiers patrolling the coast of the 148 m^2 island, and when I was in the U.S. Air Force in Táiwān from 1976-1978, Jinmen was quite a hot spot because it lies right inside of Xiamen bay. Happily, we now have over 50,000 visitors a month taking the Xiàmén-Jīnmén ferries—but so far we Lǎowài aren't allowed to take those ferries. Swim, perhaps?

Jīnmén, population 50,000, has a fairly long history (at least by Western standards, though 1600 years is nothing for Chinese). In 803, a Tang Dynasty official, Chén Yuān (陈渊), led 12 families to settle the island. It became part of Fújiàn Province's Tóng'Ān county in 935 A.D.. Since the Míng Dynasty, the island has been called Jīnmēn, or "Golden Gate."

If we ever build a bridge to it we'll have our own "Golden Gate Bridge."

In 1914, Jīnmén came under Xiàmén's jurisdiction, and today the people share pretty much the same customs and festivals as those of Mǐnnán, particularly Zhāngzhōu and Quánzhōu. This is not surprising since, by and large, they are relatives. One particularly unique element of Jīnmén culture is their worship of lions, which are seen as the guardian angel of the island. Many village entrances have stone lions in armor, or gowns—depending, perhaps, on whether the lion's preparing for battle or for bed?

Centuries ago, Chinese gave Jīnmén such names as "Fairyland in the Sea" and "Beautiful Haven of Peace." Favorite scenic spots include Tàiwǔ Peak, Yánpíng Sword, Lying-on-Cloud Hall and Xianying Waterfall. Jīnmén also has 18 ancient buildings with the beautiful ornamentation and upturned eaves typical of Mǐnnán (S. Fújiàn) architecture.

Chapter 13

Chinese Festivals & Culture

Happy Holidays! Amoy is most magical and merry on Chinese Holidays—and we have plenty to celebrate. Chinese have so many holidays that I'm surprised they do not also celebrate the non-holidays simply because they are so rare.

In S. Fujian, we not only celebrate all traditional festivals but add our own unique twists—such as the Mid-autumn Festival mooncake games.

To add to the merry mayhem, and perhaps as an excuse to celebrate the rare non-holidays, Chinese are also adopting Western holidays.

Santa Bless You! There was not a Christmas tree in site when we came in 1988, but Chinese now seem to celebrate the Yuletide as much as we do. Even post offices have Christmas trees, and church loudspeakers broadcast traditional hymns like Silent Night, We Three Kings, Frosty the Snowman and Jingle Bells. We can even buy Christmas cards, like the classic that says, "Santa Bless You!"

Heart to Heart Chinese have also taken to Valentine's Day with a passion. A girl attendant in a remote town's sole petrol station asked me, "Did you buy your wife flowers? It's that day, you know!" Shops and stalls are full of roses. Kids sell them on street sides. And stores have Valentine's cards, and cute little sweetheart figurines.

One student said, "We Chinese learned about Valentines from the West."

I replied, "With a 1.3 billion population, I doubt it."

Chinese Valentine's Day?

As Chinese embrace Valentine's Day, some Chinese entrepreneurs are trying to tout Qīxī (七夕) Festival (or "Girl's Festival," "Double 7" Festival," etc.) as China's own Valentine's Day. Qīxī dates back to a 2519-year-old poem about a young cowherd and seamstress who are now stars separated by the Milky Way, and united once a year when magpies fly across the Milky Way, forming a bridge for them to cross.

Many protest that the festival was never intended to be a day for lovers but to celebrate a young girl's skill in weaving and sewing. Others say by mimicking Valentine's Day, it just makes Qīxī a part of pop culture, and they urge Chinese to preserve tradition.

If keeping Qīxī a holiday for seamstresses saves me from having to buy roses and chocolates twice a year, I'm all for tradition.

Sew there you have it.

Happy Couple
Xiamen, 1920s

Before you celebrate holidays with Chinese friends, bear in mind some of their unusual taboos and customs.

In China, red is a lucky color, so red paper is often placed atop a gift, wedding cars are decorated with red ribbons, and brides wear bright red, (which many Americans associate with prostitution), not white. In China, white is for funerals, because white, black and blue symbolize grief. At New Year, children are given cash-stuffed red envelopes (Hóngbāo, 红包). Some say unmarried people can receive Hóngbāos but not give them, but in Táiwān, students often give their teachers Hóngbāo. I wish my own students would adopt that custom.

Some Local Taboos

1. Never point at people with the middle finger.
2. Don't sweep in front of guests; they'll think you are shooing them out.
3. Its extremely unlucky to break a bowl or utensil at a wedding feast.
4. Never serve guests 6 dishes of cooked food. In the Qing Dynasty only death row prisoners were fed six dishes right before execution.
5. Don't place chopsticks across a bowl; fishermen's boats run aground.
6. An uneven pair of chopsticks means you'll miss a boat, plane or train.
7. Don't jam chopsticks upright in rice; it looks like sacrificial incense.
8. Dropping chopsticks always brings bad luck.
9. Crossed chopsticks bring bad luck too—except in dimsum restaurants, where waiter may cross them to show you're bill's been settled, or you may cross them to show you're ready to pay your bill.
10. Never turn a fish over to get the meat on the bottom side of the skeleton, or a fishing boat will sink. (Dr. Jan says, "Lift the skelcton out.").
11. Never pat a Chinese adult on the head.
12. Always give and receive gifts with **two hands**! When receiving business cards, don't just stuff them in your pocket. Study them 15 or 20 seconds, compliment the card's design, then set it on a table or place it carefully in your wallet.
13. Mentioning monkeys around babies may make them sick.

Monkey Business According to a Xiàmén University professor, Chinese legend has it that we Laowai are the fruit of an unseemly union between an ancient Chinese maid and a monkey. To prove his point, he pointed to my arm, smiled, and said, "See, foreigners are hairier than us Chinese!"

Tibetans, by the way, are proud of such monkey business. They boast that all Tibetans are descended from a union between the monkey God Hānǔmàn (哈努曼) and the mountain goddess who seduced him.

Darwin would be gratified.

Minnan (S. Fújiàn) Proverbs

Minnan Dialect is closest to the ancient Chinese spoken 2,000 years ago, and these colourful Minnan proverbs are a window on the wit and wisdom of those who speak it!

(Adapted from "Chinese Proverbs in the Amoy Vernacular" *China Review*, March 1887.) ***Enjoy!***

1. "Middle of the 5th month" Chhit géh poa, ah-à m chai sí. (Ducks don't know they're soon to be sacrificed to spirits). Said of wicked people who have no idea that judgment is soon upon them)
2. "Though dead, the eyes won't close" Sì liau bàk-chiu m goān khoe (The affair, though apparently forgotten, and over now, will turn up again to cause trouble)
3. "He'll let people eat the flesh but won't let them gnaw the bone" Bah, ho làng chiàh; kut, m ho lang khoè. (That man will let people speak ill of his friends, but only up to a certain extent)
4. "To spread the best shellfish on the top, and water the oysters well." Pho' biu thau, chìm chui (Tricks of the trade)
5. "A tortoise in the drain." Am-knàng-ku (A man who rarely goes out of his house, a book worm, etc.)
6. "If 3 short men enter a city, they'll surely create a disturbance." Sa oé jíp sià, bò hoán
7. "In 3 years, the child should be as big as the mother." Sa ni, chí bú tiù (The interest and principal shall be equal)
8. "A mouse transfixed on a cow's horn." Niaú chhú tèng-jíp gu-kak (In a fix)
9. "If you don't give credit, you can't do business; if you do give credit, you're ruined." Bu sia, put seng tiam: sia-liaú, tiam put seng.
10. "To take shelter under another man's umbrella." Png tang-i-hō-sòu ng (To benefit at the expense or trouble of a man)
11. "A blunt knife brings out the workman's skill." Tun to cchut tai chhiù
12. "When you're a passenger on another man's boat, you want the boat to go fast. When you're interested in any project with a partner, you want him to succeed." Che tang chun, ai tang chun chaú (Like our 'all in the same boat')
13. "To eat the bread of idleness." Chiàh eng bì
14. "There is honour amongst gamblers, but all tradesmen are rogues." Pòuh-kiaù lòng kun, boé-boē chat
15. "Too large for a beam, too small for a pillar." Boē tsún fu, boē tsún thiaú (Of a man or thing, unsuitable for our purpose)
16. "Barren land absorbs much water." Chhan yau sò chuí (A lean man eats much. Debts swallow up gains)
17. "What you earn in foreign parts you spend there." Po-thau chiu, po thau eng.
18. "To bind up a girl's feet just when she's about to be married." Beh ké, chiah pák kha (Of preparations begun late)
19. "After escaping from a highwayman, to meet with a tiger." Chán chhàtgu-tiò (Out of the frying pan and into the fire)

20. "To strike the gong after the thief has fled." Chhàt khì chiah phah lo

21. "A handsome woman isn't without some defect; an ugly one isn't so in every respect." Chhin-chí bo cháp-chung, khiap-sì bo ka-nug.

22. "To shut the stable door after the steed's been stolen." O-á-ki kek kui

23. "If you are afraid to enter the tiger's lair, how can you expect to get the cubs?" Put kám jìp hò hiát, ian-leng tek hò chù. (Nothing ventured, nothing gained)

24. "A smiling tiger." Chhió (A wolf in sheep's clothing)

25. "To hit your own head with the hoe you're carrying." Kiák pe-put, kakí kong hiàh (The engineer hoist with his own petard: caught in one's trap[①])

26. "To advance or retreat is equally difficult." Chin-thè liòng lan (On the horns of a dilemma)

27. "Fresh or salt, he eats up all indifferently." Tin kiàm Chiák bò kiam (All's fish that comes to his net)

28. "Iron strikes iron. Diamond cuts diamond." Thih kong thih.

29. "It's by drinking one little drop after another that a man at last becomes drunk." Pòh pòh chiù Chiak lang oé chuì (It's the last straw that breaks the camel's back)

30. "In one ear and out the other." Chìt ki-kang jìp chìt ki-khang chhut

31. "When waiting to eat, rice takes a long time to cook; when waiting to marry, the girl's a long time growing up." Tán bì oh noà, pán bò (A watched pot never boils)

32. "He's got ten trades, but nine of them he doesn't know." Sìp gé, kiù put seng (A jack of all trades, etc.)

33. "On sunny days, you should store up some provisions for rainy days." Chhat jìt, tiòh chek ho lai niu (Make hay while the sun shines)

34. "To hit two at one stroke." Chìt phah siang kìok (Kill 2 birds with 1 stone)

35. "The rice being brought by the chopsticks up to your lips, falls down after all." Hgeh kaù chhuí khaù, chiah ka-láh (There's many a slip between cup and lip)

36. "A man who does not know how to sail about complains of the river being narrow." Bóe hiaù sài tsun hiam khoe oéh (Bad workmen blame their tools)

37. "When you go to a country you must follow its customs; when you enter a channel you must follow its windings." Jìp hong sui siòk; Jìp kàng sui own (When in Rome, do as the Romans)

38. "To dive into the sea to feel for a needle." Hài bong chiam (To look for a needle in a haystack)

39. "Four eights are the same as thirty two." Sí poch, sa cháp jì (Six of one and a half a dozen of the other)

40. "His heart is greater than the tyrant Bong's." Sim kou khah toá ong Bòng (He out-Herods Herod).

41. "To be born in "Soochow or Hangchow, and to die in Quánzhōu, Fújiàn, is the height of good luck." Siu tì So-Hàang jí chiu. Si ti Hokkien Choan-chiu.

42. "A good man kissed [struck] by lightning." Hó sim, khit laic him. (Said of a man undeservedly injured)

43. "In buying and selling, one should be very particular; in entertaining, expense should not be thought of." Boé boé sug hun sa Chhìa bo tun.

① Petard: medieval bomb (meaning here: blown up by one's own bomb)

Chinese Holidays

Chinese New Year (Chūnjié, 春节), aka Spring Festival, is to Chinese what Christmas is to Westerners. It falls on the first day of the first month of the Luny Calendar, which is usually in January or February.

At New Year, don't even think of using public transportation. We were once stuck in Beijing two weeks because every bus, plane, truck and boat was packed with gift-laden passengers headed home for the holidays.

In the countryside, shiny new bicycles groan under the weight of parents and children returning to ancestral homes with bundles of gifts, and baskets of live ducks, geese, chickens and piglets. Even in the remotest hinterlands, mountain paths teem with families making the long but joyful trek home, possessions slung over parents' shoulders, children skipping and laughing in anticipation of grandma's cooking and grandpa's tall tales of the Japanese invasion or of the revolution.

A New Year's celebration has traditionally been a very intimate affair, family only, but either times are changing or we now have a very big family. When the MBA Center's Dean learned, to his horror, that we had not prepared our own Chinese New Year feast, he invited us to share his family's 20 course banquet. And every year since, some Chinese family has shared their intimate meal with this family of homeless Americans.

All around Xiàmén you will see traditional sayings in gold letters on red paper (some with Mickey and Minnie Mouse on them) pasted both sides of doors. They insure good luck in the New Year; a typical couplet might read:

"May there be lots of things to sell, and lots of money."
"May the marketplace be crowded, with noisy business people."

When only one character is posted, it is usually for Spring (Chūn, 春), Long Life (Chángshòu, 长寿), or Fortune (Fú, 福). Some say they are placed upside down so demons can't read them and give them the opposite, but most say it is a play on the Chinese words "fú 福" and "dǎo 倒," meaning "fortune will come."

Some folks put round mirrors above doors because demons are so ugly that their reflection frightens them away. It might work, at least on Foreign Devils. I've scared myself a few times before my morning shave.

Red paper is never used if an elderly person in the family has died in the last three years. Green paper is used for men, and yellow for women. Sayings to placate recently extinguished personages are pasted on doors. A few examples:

"Remember to be reverent for three years."
"守孝三年"

"Cherish the memory of your parents like a cloud rising to the sky."
"珍藏对父母的记忆，宛如瑞云升天"

"Wholeheartedly remember the past."
"一心一意记着往日的岁月。"

"Where did you hide the safe's key, dear departed Dad?"[1]
"你把保险柜的钥匙藏在哪里，爸爸？"

The night before New Year's Eve, families prepare sweets: cooked dates, Chinese melons, cakes and candied peanuts. In the countryside and those cities where it is not banned, people set off firecrackers to ward off demons and the dreaded people-munching Nián (年—same character as for "year") that stalks the land every New Year's Day.

Lantern Festival (Yuánxiāojié, 元宵节) falls on the 15th day of the Luny Calendar. Check out the shows at Zhōngshān Park, and buy your kids (or yourself) a battery-powered plastic lanterns and join the parades.

Traditionally, young girls prowl the night, hanging around lanterns or pulling up people's vegetables, all in the hopes of getting married.

I don't see the connection between uprooting veggies and matrimony (unless she wants a husband with a higher celery?).

Eligible lasses cast divining blocks, walk in an auspicious direction until they meet someone, and memorize the first word that person speaks. She will then seek out a fortune teller, who will tell her if the word is lucky or not, and thus whether or not she will marry that year or have to uproot more veggies the next year.

Amoy lanterns, 1920s

[1] My sons will plaster this on the doors after their dear dad departs

Dragon Boat Festival, (Lóngzhōujié, 龙舟节) The 5th day of the 5th lunar month is "Double 5th Festival" in Táiwān, and "5th Day Festival" in Xiàmén. Some people still insert Chinese mugwort (ài,艾) in doorways, poor wine on floors, and pin charms on children to ward off evil spirits. It's a great day to air out clothes and bedding, clean house, and eat zòngzis (粽子)—the pyramidal dumplings of glutinous rice and meat in bamboo leaves. The big draw is the annual International Dragon-Boat Race in Jīměi's Dragon-boat Pool. (see Jīměi chapter).

Dragon Boat Festival is one of 3 traditional days for settling accounts with both the living and the dead. Various deities are responsible for health, wealth and warfare, and with so many lakes and rivers in South China, many Southern deities live underwater. People throw rice and Zòngzis into the water to feed the hungry deities, demons, ghosts, and the chief water creature, the dragon. Tradition also says Zòngzis are thrown to an ancient poet who drowned himself.

Zòngzis supposedly originated with Qu Yuan(屈原), a Minister in the State of Chu in the 4th century B.C. He gave detailed instructions on how to wrap rice in silk with threads of five colors. They eventually came to be wrapped in leaves, in triangular shape, and bound with leaf fibers or string.

Susan Marie loves Zòngzis, and Double Fifth is the time to find them—both the sweet ones and the meaty ones. (I like the vegetarian zòngzis).

National Day (Guóqìng Jié, 国庆节). Earth's oldest nation is also one of its youngest. We celebrate *New* China's birthday on October 1st, and thanks to Běijīng's bureaucratic wizardry with weekends, we usually get a week off. This is to promote tourism, spending, and the medical profession, which rakes in the dough (or rice) treating foreigners who get ulcers queuing up for train and plane tickets. Most likely your Chinese colleagues will invite you out for a meal, and an evening of entertainment that may include fireworks, special performances of ballet or orchestras, or Mǐnnán Opera. Or you can hibernate at home and watch the gala specials on XMTV and CCTV NEWS (the English channel).

Bill's Birthday, aka Grave Sweeping Day (Qīngmíng Jié, 清明节) Millions of Chinese claim they are celebrating "Grave sweeping day" on April 5th but the evidence suggests otherwise. This is one of the few Chinese holidays that does not vary each year with the Luny calendar. It is always the 105th day after the Winter Solstice, which is almost always my birthday. Coincidence? I rest my case.

Each year on my birthday, Amoy folk tidy up the hillside tombs of extinguished ancestors' and burn billions in "Hell Money" to help the deceased pay off debts down below. With so much money burning a hole in their pockets, there must be hellish inflation down below (see "Chinese Religion Chapter").

Chinese offer a meal and 3 glasses of wine to ancestors, light candles and 3 sticks of incense, and prostrate themselves before the dead. They distract evil spirits from stealing their ancestors' sacrifices with a decoy sacrifice of Hell Money called "Outside Following Paper" (Wàisuízhǐ, 外随纸), which the dim demons scramble after.

People who can't visit their ancestors tomb can fulfil their filial duty by correspondence. They put Hell Money in large square bags, address them to the deceased, and place them and a smaller decoy package for evil demons on the bed. After lighting candles, kneeling, and worshipping, they take the parcels outside, soak them in wine, and set them afire.

So Chinese, not the U.S. Post Office, invented "dead letter mail."

On April 5th, Chinese eat 'spring cakes,' stroll in the countryside, and sweep graves, but many nowadays forego the hell money and leaves flowers at gravesides, or the cemetery of revolutionary martyrs.

For Westerners, willow is used at Easter because it is one of the first to bloom in spring. Likewise, Chinese use it for Qīngmíng Jié. Tradition has it that women must wear a sprig of willow or risk being reborn as dogs. This practice began in the Táng Dynasty when Emperor Gāo Zōng (650 to 683 A.D.) plucked sprigs of willow and ordered his retinue to wear them in their caps to protect them from scorpion stings.

Coincidentally, Qīngmíng Jié is Zhíshùjié（植树节）, or "Tree Planting Festival"; Arbor Day is April 5th in Korea, and the end of April in the U.S.

Cold Food Festival on April 4th (my mom's birthday) is a cool holiday. Chinese used to forego fire and smoke for an entire month because some official was burned to death on that day a few thousand years ago, but then they cut it back to 3 days, and now it's only one day, if even that. On Cold Food Festival, folks eat cold spring rolls, cold noodles, and cold fried chicken from KFC.

If fire's the issue, why not just use a microwave? (Speaking of which, Sue and I had one of Xiamen's first microwaves. An XMU professor actually asked how long we had to preheat it before using it).

Mid-Autumn Festival（Zhōngqiūjié, 中秋节), aka Moon Festival, on the 15th day of the 8th Luny month, is Xiàmén's most festive occasion, thanks in part to our unique Mooncake Game.

The first person on the moon was not Neil Armstrong but Chang-O, a Chinese beauty who fled earth during the Xià Dynasty (2205-1766 BC). During Moon Festival, worshippers of this Moon Goddess offer her moon-cakes, tea and fruit, and Hell money.

Before Moon Festival, people present mooncakes to family, friends, co-workers and bosses. In Táiwān's private schools, teachers give mooncakes to students, and students reciprocate with a cash-stuffed Red Envelope—a practice XMU should adopt.

Girls used to believe that the later they went to sleep on Moon Festival Eve, the longer their mother would live, so many girls stayed up all night (I think I'd start worrying if my daughter yawned and turned in early that night).

Wealthy but unmarried girls past their prime threw an embroidered ball out their window into a crowd of single men who just happened to be hanging about. She could choose whom to throw the ball to, and if he caught it he had to marry her. If he didn't live happily ever after, he at least had a ball.

In the evening, families reunite to eat mooncakes, drink wine, guess riddles, and in Southern Fújiàn and Táiwān, play the "mooncake game" that some say Koxinga invented to keep his homesick troops occupied after they kicked the Dutch out of Táiwān.

Moon-Cake Game players take turns tossing 6 mahjong dice into a bowl, taking care that none bounce out (or they lose a turn).

Prizes range from tiny cookies to medium and large mooncakes, with each representing an official position won in the ancient imperial exams. The one grand prize, Zhuàngyuán（状元）, represents #1 scholar; Duìtáng（对堂）is #2 scholar; Sānhóng (三红) is #3 scholar, etc.

The green bean and egg and fruit stuffed mooncakes are not the tastiest concoctions but they are traditional, kind of like fruitcakes back home, which are more or less edible but serve better as doorstops, paperweights and hand weapons. Nowadays, many Chinese are replacing mooncakes with fruits, food, or practical items like towels, toothpaste, and detergent. Our family wins enough toothpaste to last out the year. If we ever miss Moon Festival, our dentist will be first to know.

The mooncake game is fun, even addicting. When our sons were small, they played all year, competing for cakes they had carefully drawn and cut from cardboard.

They were probably just as tasty as the real thing.

Mooncake game rules can be confusing. For example, even if you win the Zhuàngyuán, someone else can abscond with it by throwing a higher winning combination. But not to worry. The game is really a piece of cake. Just study the rules I provide on the next page and you can learn the ropes before your Chinese hosts hang you with them.

Winter Festival（Dōngzhì, 冬至）is on the shortest day of the year, the Winter solstice, and is the best day for buying, selling, and signing contracts. Eat one bowl of Winter sweetball soup (Tāngyuán, 汤圆）this day to add one year to your life. East several bowls and it could finish you off.

Sending off the Gods Day (Sòngshén Jié, 送神节), the 24th day of the 12th Luny month, is when the gods on earth report to the heavenly emperor above who's been naughty and who's been nice. To get on their good side, people offer them sacrifices, urn hell money, and give New Year cakes to friends and family. This is also the only day they dare to clean house…

People who still follow old customs (especially in Táiwān) believe every object in a house has a resident deity, so they are very careful about house cleaning, lest they jostle and anger the deity of the couch, teapot or porta-potty. But on Sending off the Gods Day, the gods have all left to make their reports to the Emperor upstairs.

This is also a good day to marry. You don't need a fortune teller to select a propitious day because all of the trouble-making deities have skipped town.

Mooncake Game's Origin & Rules

Adapted from *Discover Gulangyu*《魅力鼓浪屿》

Mooncake Game was started about 1500 years ago by scholars craving success in imperial exams. The total of 63 prizes, based on various dice combinations, was named after imperial titles earned from the exam:

One prize for **#1 Scholar** (Zhuangyuan) The seven prize levels:

Highest 1. Zhuangyuan with Gold Flower

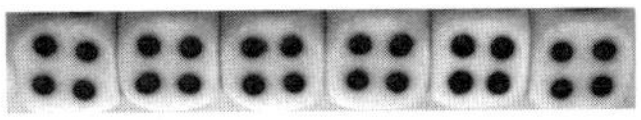

2. Hongliubo (6 fours)
3. Yaodianliubo (6 ones)
4. Heiliubo (6 of the same, except fours)
5. Wuhong (5 fours)
6. Wuzi (5 of the same, except fours)

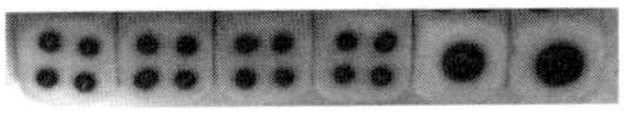

Lowest 7. Sihong (4 fours)

Two prizes for **No. 2 Scholar** (Duitang) A straight.
Four prizes for **No. 3 Scholar** (Sanhong) Throw 3 fours
Eight prizes for **No. 4 Scholar** (Sijin) Throw 4 of the same, except fours
Sixteen prizes for **No. 5 Scholar** (Erju) Throw 2 fours
Thirty two prizes for **No. 6 Scholar** (Yixiu) Throw 1 four

Rules and names of dice combos have changed little over the centuries, but chips have changed from common coins to Zhuàngyuán chips and cakes (Gǔlàngyú's are most famous). Oddly, some people in N.E. Fújiàn's Fúdǐng County (福鼎县) speak S. Fújiàn dialect, and still use "Zhuàngyuán Chips".

Legend has it that one of Koxinga's officers adapted dice game rules to create the mooncake game in order to preoccupy homesick soldiers, and according to many Qīng Dynasty writers, such as Zhèng Dàjiǔ (郑大久), in "*Taiwanese Folk Customs*" (《台湾民俗》), for centuries afterwards Táiwān folk stayed up all night shouting and tossing dice to compete for the large flour cake with a red "Yuán" character in the center.

Today the mooncake game is found not only in S. Fújiàn and Táiwān but also, it appears, wherever you find overseas Chinese of Xiàmén ancestry. A reader e-mailed me to say, "We play the Mooncake Game in the Philippines too!" Perhaps. But only in Xiàmén is the game preserved virtually unchanged. Even during the "Cultural Revolution," when all "old" thinking and practices were frowned upon, Xiamen folk tossed the dice for mooncakes—though furtively!

In 2003, Gǔlàngyú's first annual Mooncake Game Cultural Festival attracted crowds of locals, as well as domestic and overseas visitors and the media, and since then the game has become more popular than ever—though mooncakes are no longer the prize of choice (mooncakes, like fruitcake in America, are traditional but not necessarily all that tasty). Prizes today are usually more practical, like shampoo, towels, thermoses, blankets, or cutlery.

Xiamen Legends

Legend of "Longing for Brother" Rock (Wàng'gē Shí, 望哥石) The large and small rocks on the peak of Tongwen Hill, just opposite Xiàmén's Hépíng (peace) Harbor (和平码头), are said to be sisters gazing into the distance, hoping for the return of their brother—hence the name Wang Ge Rocks.

Centuries ago, an orphaned boy and his sister lived in a small village at the foot of Tóngwén Hill (同文山) and survived by fishing. While rowing home against a fierce wind, they rescued Āměi (阿美), a 13-year-old girl whom they saw flailing about in the sea. She was from a family of Táiwānese fishermen whose boat had sunk the previous day. She survived by clinging to a board, and never saw the rest of her family.

Āměi and the brother and sister lived together happily for three years, and then the villagers built a large boat to trade with Táiwān, and the brother joined the crew. When he left, he promised Āměi he would look for her parents, but the day after he left, skies darkened, seas raged, and many a boat went to a watery grave during the 3 day storm. Āměi and the sister raced to the top of Tóngwén Hill and for days neither ate nor slept, but gazed into the distance, hoping to see some sign of the brother's ship. Eventually the worried villagers ascended the hill to check on the two girls, and were shocked to find they had both turned into eastward-facing stones.

Sampan, Amoy Harbor, 1920s

From then until the end of the Qīng Dynasty, people stood on Wàng Gē Rock in hopes of a reunion with family and friends. Fújiànese have sailed abroad and not returned, so Wàng Gē Rock also came to symbolize hopes for reunification with loved ones, as well as with neighboring Táiwān.

Legend of Inverted Cauldron Rock, Seal Rock, and Sword Rock Before Koxinga left Gǔlàngyú, he burned his bridges by ordering his men to dismantle their cooking stove and toss the great iron pot into the sea, vowing that he would not return from Táiwān alive unless he succeeded in driving out the Dutch.

Koxinga hurled his mighty sword and it impaled the ground where land and sea met. He threw his personal jade seal, a gift from the king, into the waves to show that his heart, like this seal, would always remain in Xiàmén.

No sooner had Koxinga set sail than three rocks emerged from the sea where the three objects had fallen. One resembled a sword, one a seal, and the third a cauldron, and they are visible to this day.

Legend of Gǔlàngyú's Drum Rock Egrets & Goshawk Long ago, two egrets built their nest upon Drum Rock, where they passed their days contently until a lonely and jealous goshawk on nearby "Fiery Islet" (Huóshān Dǎo, 火山岛) decided to kill them.

Drum Rock

On a dark, stormy night, the goshawk attacked the happy pair and carried off the male. The female searched far and near for days, and at last the exhausted bird settled upon Sunlight Rock and died of grief. Her white feathers were borne by the wind into sea, and when seagulls saw her feathers in flight, they knew she had died, and grieved. For years, the gulls cried plaintively as they flew about the island searching for her. At last their cries moved the heart of Neptune, god of the sea. He stirred up the sea so the waves lashed upon the rock, making the sound of a drum to call the female egret. And hence the origin of the magical Drum

"Neither Wife nor Monkey" Why is a Xiàmén person with neither wife nor land said to have "Neither wife nor monkey?" Read on!

Centuries ago, the Border of Heaven Temple① (Tiānjièsì, 天界寺), near Xiàmén's Botanical Garden (Wànshíyuán, 万石园) took in a poor but handsome youth who came to be called "Tiānjiè Learner." To earn his keep he helped monks copy Buddhist scriptures, and was aided by a tame monkey that brought him books, rubbed his ink stone, and fanned him when he was hot.

A rich elderly gentleman in Xiàmén Town seeking a husband for his charming daughter heard that Tiānjiè Learner was studying hard to obtain an official post. The man thought, "It would be good to have an official for a son-in-law, no matter how poor he is. If only this youth could pass the imperial exams. I must meet him…"

A few days later the old man ascended Camel Hill to the temple and peered in the window at Tiānjiè Learner, who was absorbed in his books. "Aha!" he cried, when he saw the handsome youth. Tiānjiè Learner looked up, saw the man, and knowing he was a man of wealth at once invited him into the room. There followed an animated conversation about everything from astronomy and geography to history and poetry. The old man was delighted with the youth, invited him to his home, and mentioned that his 18-year-old daughter was beautiful and single. Tiānjiè Learner was delighted, and so was his monkey, who jumped up and down for joy and handed the gent a fan and a cup of tea.

"My, you are so upright and talented that even your monkey has learned from you!" And the man took his leave.

Tiānjiè Learner could not sleep that night, so he told the abbot what had happened. "Great for you!" cried the abbot. "But you'll need to give the man some presents, lest he think you too poor." And the kind abbot gave Tiānjiè Learner a jug of aged wine.

Tiānjiè Learner returned to his room, but tossed and turned all night. "One jug of wine is not enough. I must find something better or they will look down on me. But what can I give?"

He tossed and turned all night, and at dawn the answer hit him. "I bet the old man has never tasted monkey meat before!" When the monkey saw Tiānjiè Learner holding a piece of rope, he knew what was afoot, but knelt before his master, tears streaming down his simian cheeks. Tiānjiè Learner could barely stand the sound of the monkey's dying cries, but with visions of riches and honor, he forged ahead and killed his faithful monkey friend and servant.

---

①Read about Tiānjiè Temple in Xiàmén Parks chapter

After preparing for half a day, Tiānjiè Learner visited the old man with his gift of wine and monkey meat. The old man was glad to see Tiānjiè Learner—until he learned that the youth had killed the faithful monkey simply to gain his favor. He was speechless, and after he regained his composure he shouted, "How could I allow my daughter to marry such a cruel person as you? Get out and never come back!"

The disconsolate Tiānjiè Learner returned to the temple, and when he told the abbot what had happened, the abbot said, "From now on, you have neither wife nor monkey."

Acacia--Tree of Longing It is no wonder that locals have created a legend about the acacia. Like Xiàmén people, who have long clung to life in the face of adversity, this evergreen with fragrant white or yellow flowers survives upon little water and clings tenaciously to rocky peaks like Sunlight Rock.

And so it is said that many centuries ago, a poor husband went abroad to seek his fortune. Before he left, he planted an acacia tree beside the sea and promised to return three years later. From the day of his departure, the faithful wife stood by the tree every day, gazing upon the vast and empty sea, hoping in vain for her husband's return, but she never saw him again.

After her death, people dubbed the acacia the "Tree of Longing (xiangsi shu). The blossoms are said to represent the wife's tears, and the red dot on the flower's stamen and pistil is said to be a magical drop of the woman's blood, as her heart broke and bled for her husband.

Koxinga Legends – see *Discover Gŭlàngyŭ* 《魅力鼓浪屿》

Supplement
On Weddings & Funerals....

Weddings have been festive occasions in China since instituted almost 5,025 years ago by the legendary Emperor Fúxī（伏羲）, creator of fishing, trapping and writing. When his sister complained about the promiscuous way people were living together, Fúxī drew up marriage regulations and instituted match-making, and the redoubtable Hans have been henpecked ever since.

Early on it was ruled that people with the same surname could not marry, but given that 1.3 billion Chinese share only 400 surnames, it's fortunate that this rule was abolished, lest some bride be force to marry the Wang husband.

Traditionally, Chinese had 8 considerations in selecting a mate: 1) different surname, 2) not related, 3) rich, 4) social position, 5) behavior, 6) health, 7) appearance, 8) lucky or unlucky. I happen to be blessed with # 8, good luck: I'm lucky Sue didn't belabor the other seven.

Wedding dates are carefully chosen according to the Chinese horoscope, and presided over by seniors in both families. The day before the marriage, the bride's family sends the dowry to the groom's family and decorates the bridal chamber. Early on the wedding day, the bridegroom fetches the bride in a wedding car, and holds a banquet for guests that evening. After the feast, guests can go to the bridal chamber to joke with and tease the bride and groom.

On the third day, the bride and groom return to the bride's family, where a feast is held to celebrate their survival of the first 3 days.

But nowadays, many lovebirds forego the feasting and teasing and head straight for the honeymoon.

Wedding gifts should always be given well before the wedding day, never on or after it. But if your friend hands you a sack of sweets and says they've just been married, no gift is expected.

Wedding gifts used to be practical, like Double Happiness Brand thermoses, blankets, electric rice cookers, electric fans, děng děng. But to avoid getting five rice cookers and four fans and thirteen thermoses, many now prefer the increasingly ubiquitous cash-stuffed Hóngbāo.

Though Hell Money may be best for dearly departed newlyweds...

Till Death Do We Marry Even with divorce rates sailing past 50%, Americans still staunchly vow, "Till death do us part." But not even death unties the knot for Chinese. In fact, some don't marry until ***after*** they're dead...

In Chinese communities worldwide (though rarer in the mainland), spiritualists sometimes inform bereaved families that their dead child cannot rest until married to some other dearly departed soul. Both families then spend a small fortune to wed the dead, who attend by proxy, often in the form of engraved wooden 'spirit boards' to which sacrifices are offered.

Some girls probably end up with some real deadbeat husbands.

Speaking of dead folks... China not only has the largest population of living, but the most dying as well, so you may be invited to a funeral. Funerals, even more than weddings, have brought home to me just how alike, in the end at least, are we Lǎowài and Lǎonèi.

Filming a Buddhist Funeral At my student's request, I traipsed the village streets videotaping his father's funeral—everything from the gifts of blankets draped over bamboo poles to the rickety table covered with food offerings, and the father's photo to allow him to oversee the proceedings.

The village square facing the ancient Buddhist temple was crowded with old and young alike, as well as a few dogs and chickens. As I filmed, the crowd shouted "Lǎowài!" This shouting and pointing gets to some Lǎowài, but look at it from their point of view. We Lǎowài zip about snapping shots of old men in PJs brushing their teeth on the roadside, or of fishermen mending nets, or babies in split pants, as if they all were cultural exhibits. I'm not sure which is worse, "Laowai!" or "Flash!"

Yankee Doodle Dirge Mourners and curious onlookers watched the deceased's family bustle about preparing food for the growing crowd. Shaven headed, saffron robed Buddhist priests busily prepared for the service. And over it all, three bands played simultaneously.

Chinese funeral music emphasizes volume, not quality. Perhaps it's like the 100 million dollar hell notes, and false bottomed baskets—the dead don't know any better (their ear for music is probably dead anyway).

Amoy Funeral, 1920s

A white uniformed brass ensemble played everything from Sousa's marches to Camptown Races. A wizened trio played Chinese instruments like the suǒnà（唢呐）, a brass horn shrill enough to wake the dead or exorcise them, and the two-stringed erhu (Chinese violin), which is often high pitched and shrill but in a master's hands is as sweet as a violin. A third ensemble played Spanish flamenco on guitars. And a Chinese ghetto blaster blared a funeral dirge that cast a mournful pall that no one could bear—except, perhaps, the pallbearers.

About the time I felt like joining the mourners myself, the brass band broke into a rousing rendition of "Yankee Doodle Dandy."

Xiamen Funeral, 2012

Farewell Forever After an hour of solemnities, the relatives led a procession down the dusty path from the village to the fields, marching slowly to the three bands' merrily mournful music. The bands and ghetto blaster were followed by the pallbearers, the deceased's sons, more family, paid mourners, a solo guitarist playing Spanish music, hundreds of friends and curious onlookers, children, dogs, and one lone water buffalo, whom everyone ignored. And I ran back and forth filming the entire procession.

The sons' devastating wails reached new heights when we passed a beautiful 3-story partially completed home on the outskirts; it was to have been the father's retirement home.

After marching far out into the countryside, the mourners took a left fork in the road back to town and the male family members continued on with the coffin towards a small copse in the middle of a dusty field. We passed into the shadows of gnarled, ancient oaks, and approached a dark, musty cave piled high with moldy urns and bones, a few leg bones here, a thigh bone there, a pile of skulls on a shelf. The place had obviously seen its share of skullduggery.

I nearly dropped my camera in shock when the sons lifted the blanket to reveal not a coffin but a small porcelain urn of ashes. (I'd think a chain smoker would have preferred a lacquer ashtray to an urn).

The sons placed the 8x10 portrait and urn on a shelf dug into the damp cave wall, I shot one last scene, and we returned to the village courtyard, which was already deserted, as if the funeral had never taken place.

Life goes on.

Urns, Amoy 1920s

Supplement

Ming Dynasty Tales of Life and Death

We Laowai and Laonei really do have a lot in common—life and death, for instance, if nothing else. Chinese are certainly no strangers to suffering, and I increasingly appreciate their love of life, and even their ability to laugh at death, as in these ancient Míng Dynasty (1368-1644) tales:

Live to Tell About It On his deathbed, retired prime minister Yè Héng (叶衡) asked a visitor, "I am dying. Is death a desirable state?"

"Yes, of course it is!"

"But how do you know that?" Yè Héng asked him.

"If it were so bad," the visitor said, "they would have all come back by now, but since none have returned, they must be happy over there!"

Red Sorghum A man complained to his friend, "Your mother has just died and instead of mourning you are eating red steamed sorghum!"

The friend replied, "Then I suppose those who eat white rice every day are in mourning?"[①]

Cultural Supplement

These Are the Magi—Gift-giving in China

He who gives only when asked has waited too long.
Chinese Proverb

The Art of Chinese Gift-giving The wise men from the East who gave gifts to the Christ child could have come from China because 1) you can't get further East than China, and 2) Chinese have raised giving to an art form.[②]

Our first Christmas in China, our elderly dean gave our two sons a toy electric car that set him back at least a week's wages. Two months later, on Chinese New Year, a teacher gave each of our sons a Red Envelope stuffed with 100 RMB—half of his monthly salary. Any doubts on the importance of gifts in China vanished when I read Lesson 38 in *"Modern Chinese Beginner's Course*." The correct reply to an impromptu invitation to a Chinese friend's home was, "But we haven't brought any gift."

---

① Red symbolizes good luck, joy; white is for mourning, death

② Interestingly, 1700-yr.-old legends say there were 12 wisemen, not 3, they came from the most Eastern land, bordering the great ocean, produced silk (only China produced silk), and was named Shi (which sounds like "si," the Chinese word for silk).

Gift giving rituals vary around China. Tibetans give a white silk scarf. Hăinán Islanders place a lei of flowers over guests' shoulders. In Xiàmén, the most common gifts are bags of fruit or packages of our local Oolong tea.

Xiàmén folk avoid odd numbers of gifts. It must be two bottles of Chénggāng medicinal wine, not one or three, or 4 boxes of Tiékuānyīn tea, never three or five. And gifts must be proffered respectfully with two hands, and accepted with two hands.

Americans have no qualms in giving an inexpensive gift or card because it's the thought that counts, but not in China. Face is everything, and a small or trifling gift may be worse than no gift at all. The larger the gift, the more face for both parties. Over the years, our face has been lifted more times than Elizabeth Taylor's.

Guests have materialized on our threadbare welcome mat with 50 bananas or 30 pounds of roasted Longyan peanuts or 15 pounds of freshly caught fish or 4 dozen freshly fried home-made spring rolls. We've protested, futilely, that 50 pounds of bananas will rot before we can finish them off. In the end, we either go on banana binges or make a quick pilgrimage to a Chinese colleague's home with a second-hand gift of bananas, tea, dried mushrooms or fresh fish. They probably pass them off too, but somewhere down the line some soul has to get 50 pounds of bananas down the hatch.

Where's the Beef? We had some knotty experiences until we learned the ropes of Chinese gift giving. Shortly after we moved into Chinese professor's housing, Susan baked chocolate cake, which at that time few Xiàmén folk had tried. She gave our neighbor a couple of slices to sample, and the astonished granny thanked her profusely and shut her door slowly, politely. Next morning, bright and early, she rapped on our door, thrust a plate full of raw beef in Sue's face, said, "For you!" and beat a hasty retreat, ignoring Susan's protests.

"This is terrible, Bill," Sue said. "She should not have done that."

"This is great, Sue." I retorted. "Two pounds of beef costs a lot more than two slices of cake. We'll save a bundle on meat if we give cake to all the neighbours."

No wonder Marie Antoinette said to give everyone cake.

It is *Cheaper* to Give Than to Receive. Nowadays, we are more careful (but not paranoid!) with gift-giving, because recipients of our well-meaning largesse feel compelled to reciprocate, whether they can afford it or not. And as for receiving gifts, they sometimes have more strings than ribbons. But all things considered, I still think Chinese are the Magi—particularly where family and homeland are concerned.

Giving to the Motherland When overseas Chinese labored in abject poverty in the mines and fields of Africa and Colonial Asia, or to build American railroads, they invariably sent most of their meager earnings home to family in China. These pittances, multiplied a million fold, kept China afloat while she was bled dry through the opium trade. (See Lords of Opium chapter).

Some laborers became industrial magnates, like Tan Kak Kee, and donated millions to China. And even today, regardless of political persuasions, overseas Chinese remit millions annually not only to mainland relatives but to local governments for schools, colleges, orphanages, and roads.

Chinese, rich and poor alike, are a generous people. A lowly mason living in a shack nearby gave me 5 pounds of freshly netted fish because he heard my in-laws were visiting from America. A disabled, retired campus laborer often shares fresh greens from his garden, or new flowers for our yard. Just yesterday, an elderly neighbor gave us two papayas he'd grown. And when word got around that I needed a stone mill to grind wheat (in the days before we had Wal-marts and Metros), peasant friends headed for rural stone quarries and we soon had not one mill but three. I'll never again take wheat for granite.

These people sought nothing in return. They gave out of friendship—like the poor bicycle repairman who repeatedly insists, "It's a small thing. Pay me when you have a real problem." The man's entire world is but a tiny, dusty shop, 8 feet wide and 4 feet deep. Greased bike chains and sprockets, rims and tires and tubes, bike seats and pedals hang from nails on the walls. His only furniture is two bamboo stools, one for himself and one for customers, and a bamboo footstool that doubles as a table for his cheap tea set, which he sets up every time I stop by. He has spent more serving me tea than he will ever make from fixing my battered bicycle.

Chinese have always given sacrificially to family and immediate community, but charity beyond that was rare, for it was seen as depriving family and local community of scarce resources. But times are better now, and Běijīng is seeking to widen the scope of giving. Half a dozen programs encourage wealthier urbanites to help their less fortunate and far more numerous comrades in the countryside. "Project Hope" （希望工程） allows millions of urban Chinese to help fund poor rural children's education, and "Helping Hand" pairs up city kids and country kids, who write to each other and exchange gifts.

Get involved! Many foreigners have helped campaigns like Project Hope. To get involved, contact your Chinese colleagues or the municipal government. You can even arrange with local governments to help sponsor specific schools or poorer students. Opportunities are limited only by your imagination and your purse.

Gold Rats and Oxen – Míng Dynasty Tale (1368-1644) On his birthday, an official's subordinates chipped in to give him a life-sized solid gold rat because he was born in the year of the rat. The official thanked them, and asked, "Did you know my wife's birthday is coming up? She was born in the year of the ox."

Chapter 14

"Chinese" Religions in Xiàmén

Xiàmén's rich religious heritage includes countless Confucian, Buddhist, Taoist and Mazu temples, temples devoted to both Confucianism and Taoism (Confusionism[1]?), and the fire walking worshippers of Tóng'ān's Wú Bēn (吴夲)[2]. We have one of S.E. China's largest Buddhist temples (Nánpǔtuó Temple, 686 A.D.), China's first Protestant church (Xīnjiē Church, 1848), a Muslim mosque, and one of China's few International Christian Fellowships.

Buddhism is, of course, an "imported" religion, but for convenience I list it in this chapter, and cover Islam, Protestantism and Catholicism in the next.

Nanputuo Temple (686 A.D.)

Nánpǔtuó[3] Temple (南普陀寺) right outside XMU's old gate, sprawls across the Five Old Man Mountains like a Chinese miniature landscape on steroids, but it started out in 686 as the humble cave dwelling of one monk.

Xiàmén folk were in the throes of an unknown epidemic when Qin Hao arrived on the scene. He settled down in a cave on a hillside blessed with medicinal herbs. After his herbal brews saved the lives of many locals, they begged him not to leave, so he stayed on and taught Buddhism.

The original cave is now decorated beyond recognition, and augmented by over 20 buildings, including four halls: Heavenly Emperor Hall (Língxiāodiàn, 凌霄殿), Heroic Treasure Hall (Dàxiōngbǎodiàn, 大雄宝殿), Great Benevolence Hall (Dàbēidiàn, 大悲殿), and Buddhist Scripture Repository (Cángjīnggé, 藏经阁). Their scripture collection may be Nánpǔtuó's biggest claim to fame, with over 50,000 Buddhist scriptures—a copy of virtually every Chinese Buddhist scripture. They also have the oldest Chinese Buddhist manuscript (translated about 2000 years ago).

Nánpǔtuó is home to about 120 monks and a few hundred statues, including the Revered Three-Life-Cycle Buddha, the Four Heavenly Kings, the Eighteen Arhats, and Bodhisattva, aka the Thousand Handed Guanyin (Qiānshǒu Guānyīn, 千手观音), the patron saint of glove makers. Guānyīn started out as a man and ended up female; read about the "Guānyīn Temple later in this chapter for details.

---

① A map of Anxi, in Quanzhou, does point out a "Confusion Temple."

② Wú Ben worshippers, not Donald Trump, came up with "You're fired!"

③ Nánpǔtuó means "Putuo of the South". "Pǔtuó" mountain, in Zhèjiāng, is one of China's four sacred mountains.

Thanks to Bruce Lee (彭清洪), former Nánpǔtuó monk, for his assistance.

The Great Benevolence Hall is a 3-storey octagonal structure built by General Shīlàng（施琅）in 1684 after retaking Táiwān from Koxinga’s grandson. The Chinese Construction Ministry has taken special note of the wooden roof, which was constructed with wooden beams and brackets and has no nails. The 1,000-handed Guānyīn（观音）has a sitting Guānyīn and 3 standing Guānyīns. The standing Guānyīns have two heads, a small one over the larger one (even the Chinese think two heads are better than one). The two-faced Guānyīns face north, west and east.

Scripture Repository & Holy Buddha Beads In addition to Buddhist scriptures, the repository has former abbots’ clothing, and such treasures as a fine white porcelain Guānyīn, a Qíng Dynasty bronze bell, white Jade Buddhas presented by Burma, Thailand, Sri Lanka, Cambodia and India, and the “Lotus Scriptures”, which were written in blood by monks about 500-600 years ago. The most unusual items are the “holy cremation relics”—hard, pearl-like beads sifted from cremated saints’ ashes. The beads embody the saints’ spiritual essence, and are said to have a beneficent effect upon others. A Californian “reported feeling that his molecules were being rearranged in a more wholesome manner”).[①] But what would you expect from a Californian?

The downstairs Hall of Law is for meetings, and for disciplining monks whose molecules, apparently, have yet to rearrange. All disciplining is done before Sakyamuni’s statue to ensure fair play.

The Merit Building, just inside the gate and to the right, has wooden memorial tablets, for which relatives of the deceased pay 1000 Yuan each.

Nánpǔtuó Vegetarian Restaurant, in the Pǔzhào Bldg.（普照楼）, behind the Merit Building, has served famous veggies for a century. Read “Veggie Tails” in the Restaurant chapter to learn which dish Dèng Xiǎopíng loved so much he had his chef lug 200 pounds back to Běijīng (you’ll also learn why you should never, ever, eat taro with beef, because it is…).

Buddhist Seminary—is inside the main gate, 2nd building on the left.

Tàixū Library 太虚图书馆, completed in 1989, is behind the seminary and has over 20,000 documents. A dozen monks and lay persons run the library, which is also open to lay Buddhists who obtain permission.

South Fújiàn Buddhist College (Mǐnnán Fóxuéyuàn, 闽南佛学院) Abbot Huìquán（会泉）opened the college in 1925. It was closed after the Japanese invasion in 1937, and re-opened in 1985. The College has 4 departments: Tàixū (太虚) Library, Editing Dept., Monks’ Dept. and Nuns’ Dept. Three of these departments are at Nánpǔtuó, but the nuns’ are cloistered near the train station in Jīnbǎng Park (金榜公园). Modern monks, by the way, may leave the monastery and marry, but while at Nánpǔtuó they have ~~nun~~ none.

The college has 36 exalted-monk teachers, 110 monk students, and 6 graduate students. During the 4-year program they study Buddhist scriptures and rituals, humane studies, and Communist Party religious policies.

The nunnery at Jīnbǎng Park is considerably larger, with 40 faculty, 250 undergrad students, 8 graduate students, and 4 overseas students. According to former monk

① “Buddhist relics to arrive Friday,” by Lisa Fernandez, *Mercury News*, March 9, 2006.

Bruce Lee, the nuns study harder and write more articles than the monks, even though they adhere to the same grueling schedule:

A Monk's Schedule

04:00–04:30 Get up	05:00 Chant	06:00 Breakfast
06:30 Sweep grounds	07:30-11:00 4 Classes	11:00 Lunch
11:30 Chant	12:00-14:00 Nap	14:00—15:40 Two Classes
16:00 Chant	17:00 Supper	18:30 Two Classes
20:00 Free time	21:30 Bedtime	
22:00–04:00 Dream of Nunnery near Train Station		
04:00–22:00 Daydream of Nunnery near Train Station		

Monk Pastimes

What do monks do besides chant, study, and dream of nuns? Read on…

ē Mí Tuó Fó Monks (阿弥陀佛) The 25 ē Mí Tuó Fó monks do nothing but chant, day and night, ē Mí Tuó Fó① (Chinese for "Amitabha Buddha"). As a reward, after death they will ascend to Amitabha Buddha's kingdom, the "Western Paradise" (Vancouver?). Amitabha's kingdom is a later addition to Buddhist eschatology—a half-way house for souls until ready for Nirvana.

Meditation Monks. These 28 monks meditate (duh!) and seek to answer the question, "Who am I?" If the abbot verifies they've got it right (ID check?), they ascend to a higher level closer to Buddha and, presumably, Vancouver.

Sacrament Monks. These 8 fellows perform ceremonies for anyone willing to pay at least 3,000 Yuan; the more you pay, the more merit.

Incensed Monks. Pilgrims burn so much incense it could create a fire hazard, so these ten monks do nothing but discard used incense all day. They probably wait until the folks who paid for them have left, otherwise they'd have some incensed pilgrims.

Retreating Monks Upon request and approval monks are confined to a small house or courtyard for six months or so. They usually speak to no one. If they get sick, tough. If they die—Vancouver.

Miscellaneous Monks. About six monks sell souvenirs, ten are doorkeepers, and one handles robes and cymbals. Editing department monks handle archives, publicity, bulletin boards, and edit the "Nánpǔtuó Journal."

Merry Maitreya Pot-bellied Maitreya (Mílèfó, 弥勒佛), "god of wealth," greets Nánpǔtuó visitors. Buddhism holds that after a 10,000 year rule by Sakyamuni②, the first Buddha, international morality levels will be high enough and Buddhism will die out. Eight million years later, Maitreya will come preach. Let's hope his sermons are shorter than his prelude.

Maitreya last incarnated 1,000 years ago as the Linen-Bag Monk (Bùdài Héshàng, 布袋和尚) of Zhèjiāng Province (浙江). He traveled about free from cares, always smiling, and preaching nonstop. He thought he was Maitreya incarnate, and after he died so did everyone else.

---

① (Nánpǔtuó's vegetarian chefs probably chant Yùmǐ Dòufu (玉米豆腐) "corn and tofu"

② Sakyamuni, or Siddhartha Gautama (563-485 B.C.); 释迦牟尼 (Shìjiāmóuní)

Behind Maitreya stands the Boddhisatva Skanda (Wéituó, 韦陀), who safeguards those two most sacred pillars of most religions: doctrine and finance. And Wĕituó's staff is why Nanputuo attracts so many pilgrims.

In temples where Wéituó staff is held horizontally, he's suggesting "Try elsewhere." But at Nánpŭtuó, Wéituó's staff is vertical, indicating the temple is wealthy and offers both room and board. Pilgrims pack in by the hundreds of thousands, and happily for this guardian of finance, they leave their millions behind because Buddhists, quite literally, have money to burn…

Paper Hell Air Conditioners

Money to Burn If Chinese had not invented paper, their extinguished ancestors wouldn't have a chance in hell—literally. Paper simulations, once burned, become the real thing in the afterlife. They burn paper houses, paper furniture, paper cars, paper microwaves—even paper air conditioners.

Leave it to Chinese to install A/C in hell.

Demons, deities and dead people can't tell real money from fake, so for a few Yuán you can buy a stack of million dollar "Hell Notes" printed on cheap paper (rather like recycled TP) and give your dearly departed more money than Bill Gates.

Inflation must be hell down there.

Departed souls also get the short end of the stick with food offerings, because a 15" basket may have only 3" of sacrificial fruit over a 12" false bottom; folks down below can't tell the difference.

With nonstop burnt offerings, Nánpŭtuó is forever smoke filled, but its fitting. After all, China has 300 million smokers. Maybe in hell they're smoking paper tobacco?

But given that Buddhism has 84,136 hells, I'm not sure if folks down there are smoking or being smoked. Nánpŭtuó's studious monks aren't so sure either. I asked one monk, "Who goes to Buddhism's 84,136 hells?"

He said, "Whoever does anything wrong." He pondered this a bit, and added with a wry smile, "Everyone?"

"Is there a Buddhist heaven?" I asked.

"Of course," he said.

"Who goes there?" I asked.

The monk thought a bit, and said, "Just a minute." He pushed his Gandhi spectacles back up on his nose, flipped through the pages of a massive, musty volume, and eventually said, "No one has ever asked me that. I'll have to get back to you."

Devilish Deductions Gift shops offer Nánpŭtuó knickknacks like chant cassettes, glow-in-the-dark plastic Buddhas, and wood or stone rosaries. But don't try to pay with Hell Money or there really will be hell to pay. And unlike American religious merchandising, there's no "Suggested love offering", or tax deductible receipt. But given the state of Buddhist hells' economic affairs, you can probably just add a few zeros to your receipt and make an outlandish deduction after you die.

The Infernal Revenue Service will never know the difference.

Moneychangers in the Temple Nánpǔtuó's real excitement is outside the massive gates, where street vendors cry, "Candied crab apples on a stick!" and "Fresh sliced pineapple!" and "Tea eggs 3 mao (cents) each or 2.50 a jin" (a jin is about 1.1 pounds). Shoe repair persons from far off Sìchuān resurrect weary pilgrims' soles with glue and thread, and Tóng'ān peasants puff rice with a coal-fired cast iron contraption that goes off like a cannon every few minutes. The liveliest trade, of course, is in Buddhist paraphernalia—incense sticks, candles, "Hell Bank Notes." And until recently there was another trade that struck me as a bit fishy...

Freeing Captive Fish Pond Buddhists are vegetarians, in theory, and opposed to taking any kind of life—though enterprising peasants may enjoy beef 'n peppers, guilt-free, after arranging for a calf to strangle itself on a short leash.

If there is merit in not taking life, there is even greater merit in saving it, so pious pilgrims used to buy live fish from markets and free the finned folk from their dire fate by dumping them into the 1000m^2 Captive Fish Pond.

Given that this went on day and night for decades, I wondered how one pond could hold so many fish. Perhaps the monks could afford their Nokia cell phones by recycling the fish, which probably had more lives than my cats. [Fish freeing has ceased at Nánpǔtuó but continues at most temples big enough to have a pond. In 2012, Nanputuo monks decided to use the 50,000 Yuan they had spent annually on saving animals by promoting vegetarianism, and opened a veggie buffet behind the XMU post office, just to the right of iRock music store]

Add: Just outside XMU Old Gate Tel: 5855113 www.nanputuo.com

A Bang *and* a Whimper Nánpǔtuó's endless emancipation of captive carp went on largely in silence, but not so the other activities. Monks drive off devils, both domestic and foreign, by banging drums and cymbals day and night. And before Xiàmén banned fireworks, the temple grounds emanated an eternal cacophony of firecrackers that reverberated off the adjoining XMU Foreign Expert's Guesthouse walls, and the denizen's pounding craniums.

Chinese have been enamored of fireworks since before the dawn of recorded time 5,025 years ago. They shooed demons by burning bamboo stems, which explode when air heats up in the hollows between the joints. Somewhere down the line, an enterprising soul stuffed the bamboo with gunpowder, and eventually someone replaced the bamboo with rolls of heavy paper, giving us the modern fireworks we hear today—or used to hear.

During the mid 1990s, a stroke of the pen banned this perennial pastime in many major cities. Now Chinese shoot off their fireworks in the countryside and small towns, or pop strings of balloons, or play tape recordings of firecrackers over massive sound systems. The ambiance just ain't the same.

Hóngshān Temple (Hóngshān Sì, 鸿山寺) In front of Hóngshān Park (see Parks chapter). Add: #515 Sīmíng Nánlù Tel: 2034694

Guānyīn Temple (Guānyīn Sì, 观音寺) This gigantic complex boasts Xiàmén's highest tower and was built in the perfect location, on the 212m high Xiānyuè Hill (仙岳山), opposite SM Mall and the Wal-Mart Supercenter (Chinese religion on one side, American on the other!).

An interesting note: this "goddess of mercy" began as a male deity in India, and was gradually transformed into a female by Chinese women who felt male gods did not have proper compassion for the woes of the so-called weaker sex. She/he/it would probably go over big in California.

Add: #1279 Xiānyuè Lù (仙岳路) 1279 号 Tel: 5101176

Path to Banling Palace

Mid-mountain Palace (Bànlǐng Gōng, 半岭宫)."Bànlǐng" means "mid-mountain" and it is particularly appropriate for this temple. It's also midway between beliefs, with both Buddhist and Taoist statues. To get there, take Wéncéng Lù (文曾路) to gravity-defying "Spook Hill" (Guàipò, 怪坡), which ascends Dōngpíng Mtn. (东坪山). Bànlǐng Palace is off the picturesque path on the right. [See Parks & Gardens chapter].

Botanical Garden Temples – read the "Parks and Gardens" chapter for info on its dozen temples. Read the "Xiamen Festivals and Legends" chapter for the story behind the saying, "Neither wife nor monkey".

Folk Religions in Xiàmén Observe rural religious practices without even leaving the island! Just visit Zēngcuò'ān Village (曾厝垵), on the Island Ring Road just past the Yìyuán Hotel (驿缘酒店). This one little village has temples to the neighborhood gods, the sea god, the god of fortune, the god of seafood (just kidding—I think). Zēngcuò'ān's temples include:

Sacred Mother Palace (Shèngmǔ Gōng, 圣母宫)
Sea God Palace (Fúhǎi Gōng, 福海宫)
Mother of Mercy Temple (Wáng Mǔ Shèngdiàn, 王母圣殿)
Lake God Palace （Yōnghú Gōng, 拥湖宫）
Taoist Temple (Tàiqīng Gōng, 太清宫)
Qǐming Temple (Qǐmíng Sì, 启明寺)

Zēngcuò'ān is always having some festival or other, but for certain you can catch a ceremony on the 3rd, 13th and 23rd days of the Lunar calendar, when hundreds flock to the Qǐmíng Temple ceremonies.

Gǔlàngyǔ's Sunlight Rock Temple (Rìguāngyán Sì, 日光岩寺)

Adapted from *Discover Gǔlàngyǔ* 《魅力鼓浪屿》

One of Xiàmén's four most important temples during the Míng and Qīng Dynasties, it was built between 1506 and 1521 and called Lotus Temple (Liánhuā'Ān, 莲花庵). It was rebuilt in 1596 and renamed Sunlight Rock Temple, and is now used for worshipping Guānyīn (观音), goddess of mercy. It is nicknamed "One Tile Roof" (Yìpiān Wǎ, 一片瓦) because it is partially within a cave and a large rock forms part of the roof. It is also called "Pocket Temple" because it covers only 2,856m^2. Its location, scrunched up within a rock, prevents it from sprawling like other temples, but it makes up for size by its exquisite setting, with uniquely Chinese eaves, arches, columns, and glazed colored tiles. The neighboring European architecture only reinforces this pocket temple's essential Chineseness.

I was told this is China's only temple in which the Buddha Hall (Dàxióng Bǎodiàn, 大雄宝殿) and Maitreya (Mílèfó, 弥勒佛) Hall are face to face. There was also a Xù Pavilion (Xùtíng, 旭亭), built between 1723 and 1735, but all that remains is a cliff inscription.

Confucian Temple (Tong 'An)

Tóng'ān Confucian Temple (Tóng'ān Kǒngmiào, 同安孔庙) was first built during the Five Dynasties (907-960 AD), rebuilt in 1768 AD, and renovated in 1987. The 1050m^2 temple houses the Tóng'ān Museum and memorials for such Sòng Dynasty luminaries as Zhūxī (朱熹) and Sū Sòng.

Confusionist Temples on Dàdèng Islet (大嶝). These unusual Mǐnnán temples are devoted to both Buddhism and Taoism. "Tao" (Dào 道) means "The Way" (early Christianity was also called "The Way"), but with a mix of Buddhism and Taoism, I'm not sure *which* way they're going.

Brahma Temple (Fàntiānsì, 梵天寺) First called Meditation temple (Chánsì, 禅寺) when built in 581 AD, it was renamed Brahma Meditation Temple (Fàntiàn Chánsì, 梵天禅寺) in 1069 A.D. Tóng'ān claims this is South Fújiàn's oldest temple, but I don't see how. Yánfú Temple (Yánfú Sì, 延福寺) at the base of Nán'ān's Jiuri Mtn. (九日山), was built almost 300 years earlier, in 288 A.D. Brahma Temple was rebuilt in 1996. Location: Dàtóngzhèn, Lúnshān Lù (大同镇轮山路)
Tel: 7225879 Website: http://7225879.d592.com/

Tóng 'ān Firewalkers—Soul 'n Sole Practitioners claim modern firewalking in Overseas Chinese communities began right here in Tóng 'Ān, where it's practiced on the 15th day of the 3rd Luny month—the birthday of Tóng 'Ān's "God who protects life" (Bǎoshēng Dàdì, 保生大帝).

Bǎoshēng Dàdì (or, Wú Ben, 吴本) was born in 979 A.D. in Tóng 'Ān. As a youth, Ben read voraciously, and could recite long passages after reading them but once. He served as an Imperial Censor and then became a hermit in the mountains. During the great famine of 1032, he had rice sent to the starving peoples of Quánzhōu and Zhāngzhōu, and miraculously cured a great epidemic the following year. Alas, Ben laden with cares, died four years later at age 58; probably a victim of burnout.

Ben's village erected the "Temple of Wú" (Wúmiào, 吴庙) for this "True Man", a Taoist "perfected person" (Zhēnrén, 真人). Almost 400 years later, gentle Ben showed up in disguise and cured Emperor Yǒng Lè's (永乐) mother of an incurable illness. The grateful Emperor enlarged Ben's temple to palatial proportions, and gave him the humble title of "Palace Censor who Ascended to Heaven, True Lord of the Miraculous Way of Compassionate Salvation, and Eternal and Unlimited Lord who Preserves Life."① Today, Wú's temples are all over the mainland and Taiwan. "Bǎo'ān Gong Preservation of Peace Palace", first built in 1805, is one of Táiběi's three greatest temples.

Fire Walking On Wú Ben's birthday, hundreds of pounds of charcoal are burned for an hour or so, and then leveled off to form a path about six feet wide and thirty feet long. A Taoist priest purifies himself, and the fire walking area, and then a procession of men in white, bearing the deity in his palanquin, parade around the fire's perimeter. The priest then kneels at the south end of the fire, wearing only black shorts, and wielding his divine sword. He performs esoteric gestures, and then shovels rock salt onto the hissing coals.

After the priest sprints across the coals, villagers walk across the coals bearing a heavy palanquin within which they have placed idols. They are very careful that the idol is secure physically and spiritually, for were the little guy to get heated up over anything, the firewalkers might get the hot foot as well.

① Imagine having to put *that* title on your business card.

Firewalkers earn much merit, but not always without a few blisters and burns. Unlike other firewalkers, Tong 'an firewalkers are not in trances, and attribute their success to the Taoist priest's preparations, strict diet, and purity. So they either toe the line or toast their tootsies. After the ceremony, onlookers scoop up the coals and take them home for good luck.

Nowadays, even Westerners are on fire about fire walking's benefits for sole and soul, with fire walking schools claiming to cure stress and burnout. But I suspect this fire walking fad will fizzle out eventually. Or maybe not.

Physics Professor Walks on Fire①②

(Adapted with permission, Prof. Willey, and LiveScience, Aug. 14, 2006)

"Professor David Willey doesn't use chalk and formulas to spark his students' interest in thermodynamics. He walks on fire.

"'Nothing gets a student's attention like the possibility that I might kill myself,' said Willey, this year's winner of the President's Award for Excellence in Teaching at the University of Pittsburgh at Johnstown.

"The ritual of walking on fire has existed for thousands of years...

"Around the world, from Greece to China, cultures set trails ablaze for rites of healing, initiation, and faith.

"In the United States, fire-walking has become popular as a team spirit-building business for corporations as well as a so-called alternative health remedy...

"While no one should try to do this without proper training from an experienced fire-walker, any healthy person can walk on fire, as long as it's not too hot, according to Willey. It's a matter of stepping up to the start line with courage and training your brain to get your foot to take the first step.

"'You could keep on going forever and ever,' Willey told *LiveScience*. 'It's just a question of how much wood you want to cut.'"

① Thanks to Robert Roy Britt, Managing Editor, *LiveScience*, for permission to adapt Corey Binn's Aug. 14, 2006 article. www.livescience.com

② Thanks to Prof. Willey for providing this photograph.

Hǎicāng's Qīngjiāo① Cījì Palace (Hǎicāng Qīngjiāo Cījì Gōng, 海沧青礁慈济宫) For a different perspective on Xiàmén religion and Wúben, father of fire walking, head across the Hǎicāng Suspension bridge, hang a left, and visit the mother of all S.E. Asian Cījì Temples in Hǎicāng Township.

Cījì temples honor Sòng Dynasty medicine man, Wútao②, who spent his life treating people for free and gained, according to a local guidebook, "a world-wide reputation" (probably over the internet). He even cured the mother of Emperor Sòng Rénzōng（宋仁宗）, whose life was hanging by a thread—literally!

Physicians were mere commoners, and forbidden to touch royalty, so Dr. Wú diagnosed her disease by feeling her pulse through one end of a silk thread tied to her wrist. Chinese doctors claim to be able to feel 18 different pulses. I'm not sure if he could really feel her pulse through the thread or if he was just at the end of his rope, but in any event he discovered she had a breast disease (good thing he didn't tie a string to that!), she lived, and Dr. Wú was a hero.

In 1033, Wu fell off a cliff while gathering herbs for a cure for the plague. After his death, villagers honored Dr. Wu with the title of "Medical Saint" (Yīlíng Zhēnrén, 医灵真人), and pooled their funds to build a hall and statue in his memory. In 1161, the emperor granted the hall the title of Cíjì Temple (Cíjì Miào, 慈济庙), and in 1241 it was renamed Cíjì Palace (Cíjì Gōng, 慈济宫).

In 1999 the palace was restored to its original design, and today, thousands of pilgrims make the trek to pay homage to him.

Note: the Medical Chapter has a few delightful ancient Chinese doctor jokes.

① Qingjiao: "Green (black, blue) Reef" Ciji: "Benevolent Aid"
② Wutao and Wuben have so many similarities that they seem to be the same people, but sources conflict—so I give both stories.

Chapter 15

Birthplace of Chinese Protestantism

Xinjie Church, China's Oldest Protestant Church

1000+ Years of Christianity During the centuries preceding the 1841 Opium War, merchants and missionaries worked with Chinese in other Asian countries, and since most of those Chinese were from the Xiamen area, the foreigners learned Amoy dialect. Quite naturally, after the war forced China open, both missionaries and businessmen converged upon the one place in China that they already knew the language—Xiamen.

Today, Xiamen is known as the "Birthplace of Chinese Protestantism," with 40+ churches, including China's oldest church (Xinjie, -), but Christians were in the Xiamen area over 1,000 years ago—as were Jews, Hindus, Manicheans, Muslims...

Muslim Mosque (Qīngzhēnsì, 清真寺) A Míng Dynasty granite stele in the Fúzhōu mosque's courtyard claims that of four disciples Mohammed sent to China, two came to Quánzhōu, start of the Maritime Silk Route. Xiàmén was part of Quánzhōu, and had its best port, so Muslims probably arrived at least 1000 years ago. Records claim Muslim traders sailed into Xiàmén during Koxinga's day and built a mosque here. An elegant white mosque was built on Zhōngshān Lù in the 1840s. The present mosque is on the 4th floor of #27 Gōngyuán Nán Lù. In 2006, the Xiàmen government announced a 7 million Yuan project to help minorities, which included renovation of the mosque and construction of a Muslim cemetery in Tóng'ān (穆斯林公墓).

Xiàmén Islamic Assoc. (Xiàmén Yīsīlánjiào Xiéhuì, 厦门市伊斯兰教协会)

Add: #27 Gōngyuán Nán Lù 4/F Tel: 2034471

Nestorians & Franciscans A Xī'ān museum has a stele① dating to Jan. 7, 781 A.D., which celebrates the arrival in China of Nestorian Christianity (Luminous Religion, Jǐngjiào, 景教) in 635 A.D. The stele lists the names of 70 Assyrian missionaries. Nestorians probably also arrived in South Fújiàn about the same time as the Muslims.

In the 1300s, Marco Polo reported that Fúzhōu had a large group of Christians with roots going back hundreds of years. By the early 1300s,

① 大秦景教流行中国碑: "Stele about Spread of Persian Nestorianism in China"

Quánzhōu had 3 Franciscan cathedrals, as well as a Jewish community. And given that Xiàmén had the best port, it is not surprising that it was frequented by Muslims, Manicheans, Nestorians, Franciscans, or Sòng Dynasty Scientologists.

Gǔlàngyǔ's foreign cemetery, with its tombs dating back to the 1600s, was destroyed in the 1950s in protest of Britain's invasion of Egypt. The only surviving foreign tombstone is of a man from Bombay. Fortunately, Giles' *A Short History of Koolangsu* (1878) has a few inscriptions:

> "The following inscriptions will be found quite close to the residence of Dr. Manson:—"

Here lieth the body of
Capt. Stepn. Baker who was late
Commandr. of ye SUCCESS who
Departed this life
Octob. Ye 18, Ann. Dom.
1700. Aged 49 years.

Here lieth the body of John Duffield
Son of Henry
Duffield, Comr.
of ye TRUMBULL
Ob. Sep. 6 Anno
Et. XIIL annos Dom. 1698

Sepultura
De Domingo
FANGII INAN
Y otros dos Indios de
Philipinas que falleeie-
Ron en Oct. ano de 1759

Sacred to the memory of
Augustus Percival Greene, F.R.A.S.
Lieut. Of H.M.S. *"Plover"*
Who died on board that
Vessel on Dec. 2, 1844.
Aged 26 years 9 months 3 days

This Monument was erected
In memory of those who perished
in the British schooner Pearl
in the Typhoon off Chapel Island
On the night of the 12th June 1866.

In memory of Richard A. Breck
Late master in the U.S. navy
Who on Sep. 22, 1874
Was drowned while bathing
Aged 26. Erected by his brother Officers
of the U.S.S. "Yantic"

> "David Abeel began working out of his Gulangyu home in 1842, and in 1844 rented rooms in Amoy. On April 5th, 1846, Fujian's first Chinese Protestants, Oug-Hok-kui (father of Rev. Ong Ki-siong), aged 71, and Lau Un-sia aged 68, were baptized."
> *In and About Amoy*, by Rev. Pitcher, 1912, p.232

1st Church of China (Xīnjiē, Sin Khoe A, 新街礼拜堂) Every two-horse-town in America has a First Baptist or a First Methodist, but there is only one First Church of China—right here in Xiàmén. China's first Protestant church was built in 1848 for the princely sum of $3000. Today the church has services and programs every day of the week. Sunday services are in Mǐnnán dialect and Mandarin. Tel: 2072383.
Add: Add: #29 Táiguāng Jiē(台光街 29 号) Corner of Zhōngshān (中山路)& Sīmīng (思明路) roads, behind Carrefour.

Zhūshù Church (Bamboo Church, Zhūshùtáng, 竹树堂), Xiamen's second oldest church (1849), its leadership worked with Xīnjiē, even sharing elders and deacons.

Zhūshù's first service was Sunday afternoon, Aug. 19th, 1847, in the Bamboo House (竹树脚民房). They added an upper room with capacity of 100 worshippers in July, 1850. The church burned down in 1903, was rebuilt with American donations in 1904, and the present church was built in 1935 under the guidance of a Chinese member who had graduated from engineering school in the U.S. Church membership fell during the Japanese occupation but by the mid 1940s over 600. Services were suspended from 1966 until Dec. 20th, 1981.

Amoy's "Bamboo Church", 1921 J. Nienhuis

By 1983, attendance was up to 700. Zhūshù now has 3 pastors, 24 elders and deacons, attendance of 3,000, and programs most days of the week.

The 391.5m^2 red and white brick church is on a 2,751m^2 lot on the small market road just off Xiàhé Lù (厦禾路) near the harbor. Tel: 2987381 (2)

Add: #129 Kāihé Lù, 开禾路 129 号 Website: www.zhushu.org/

Some of Xiamen's 40 Registered Churches

Xìnglín Gāopǔ Church 基督教高浦堂

Add: Xìnglín District, Gāopǔ Village, 高浦村 Tel: 2065512

Hǎicāng Church 基督教海沧堂

Add: Xìnglín District, Hǎicāng Jiē, 杏林区海沧街 Tel: 6082672

Jīměi Hòuxī Church 基督教后溪堂

Add: Jīměi District, Hòuxī Jiē, 集美区后溪街路 Tel: 6260580

Jīměi Church 基督教集美堂

Add: Jīměi District, Xūnjiāng Lù, 集美区浔江路 Tel: 6065636

Xiáxī Church 基督教霞溪堂

Add: #24 Xiáxī Lù, 霞溪路 24 号 Tel: 2072591

Zhàishàng Church 基督教寨上堂

Add: Húlǐ, Héshānzhēng Gāodiàn Cūn, 湖里区禾山征高殿村 Tel: 6035540

Xiàmén Christian Council (Xiàmén Shì Jīdūjiào sānzì Àiguó Yùndòngwěiyuánhuì, 厦门市基督教三自爱国运动委员会) Tel: 2025281 Add: #86 Zhōngshān Lù 中山路 86 号

Xiàmén International Christian Fellowship meets on Sunday from 10:30 to 12:00 at the 7th Day Adventist Church, which is down the small road from the Public Security Bureau at the end of Zhongshan Rd. (the end opposite the Gulangyu Ferry end of Zhongshan Rd.). It works well. 7th Day folks don't worship on Sunday (though in China, Sunday is the 7th day), so we Laowai rent their church on Sundays.

XICF has Awana and adult Sunday school programs and special interest groups such as Photo Club.

7th Day Adventist Church (Site of XICF Int'l Fellowship)

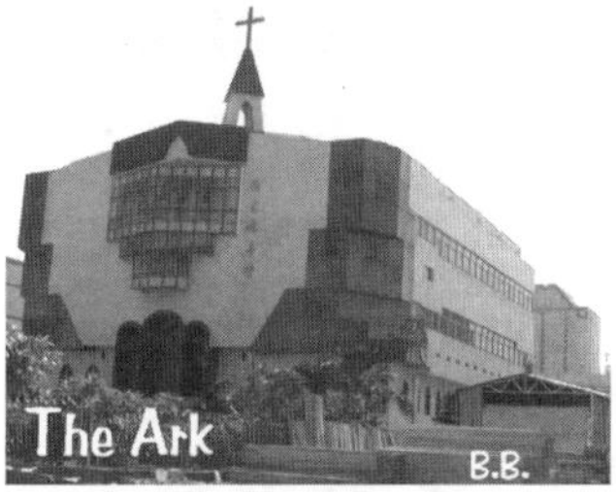

Noah's Ark Discovered! Xiàmén's largest church is the Jiāngtóu New District Church（江头新区福音堂）, just past the SM Mall. This 10 million Yuan edifice looks like Frank Lloyd Wright's version of Noah's Ark, but this ark appears to have been sinking. It once stood proud and tall in an empty field, but now is slowly sinking beneath a sea of skyscrapers. Taller cross, perhaps?

With 3,000 on Sundays, it's almost standing room only, so get there early.

Add: Jiāngtóu Jiē(湖里区江头街), Tel: 5511667

Near SM Mall, opposite to Lùzhōu Bldg.（江头绿州商厦对面）

Church Renovated for a Song

In 2006, Mayor Zhāng Chàngpíng（张昌平）helped cover the costs of some church renovations as they prepared to give 6 concerts during the 4th World Choir Games, which hosted over 20,000 singers in 400 choirs from 80 countries. His altruism had a goal, of course. He hoped the concerts would help foreigners and Chinese better understand the situation with Chinese churches—so both church and government benefited.

YMCA 厦门基督教青年会
YMCA OF XIAMEN
www.ymca-xm.org

Xiàmén YMCA (Jīdūjiào Qīngniánhuì, 厦门基督教青年会) In May, 2010, Xiamen YMCA will celebrate its centennial. Like just about everything else in China, the YMCA and YWCA (started in 1929) were shut down during the Great Proletariat Cultural Revolution, but in 1979 Běijīng reinstated the Ys in Xiàmén and 9 other cities. In 1984, Xiàmén government promulgated a couple of edicts that helped get the ball rolling, and the Y's facilities were returned.

Give them a call; their activities are expanding rapidly and they **volunteers.**

Add: #64 W. Sīmíng Rd.（思明西路 64 号）

Tel: 2113664 2102362 FAX: 2114016

E-mail: office@ymca-xm.org www.ymca-xm.org

Gŭlàngyŭ Islet Churches

Note: China's first Protestant missionaries started their work in missions, medicine and education on Gŭlàngyŭ. See *Discover Gŭlàngyŭ.*

Trinity Church (Sānyī Táng, 三一堂) China's first Protestant church was Xīnjiē, but most foreigners lived on Gŭlàngyŭ, and the bay crossing was dangerous during inclement weather. In 1927, the foreigners bought a potato field and built Trinity, which is Fújiàn's (perhaps China's) most beautiful Protestant Church.

Add: #71 Ānhăi Lù（安海路 71 号）. Tel: 2068127 www.3in1.org

Catholic Church (Tiānzhŭjiào Táng, 天主教堂) This neo-Gothic picture of Old World Beauty was built between 1912 and 1917. Today, the "Vicariate Apostolic of Amoy" (Xiàmén Tiānzhŭ Jiàohuì, 厦门天主教会) has over 80 churches in Amoy, Zhangzhou (漳州), Quanzhou（泉州）, and Putian (莆田).

With its garden setting, Gŭlàngyŭ Catholic Church has been the setting for many movies, including a Japanese film in which I was a Holy Father and Sue was a Mother Superior. Sue has claimed to be a superior mother ever since.

Add: #34 Lùjiāo Lù（鹿礁路，34 号）.

Tel: 2066150 www.cncatholic.org

Gulangyu Catholic Church

The Gospel Hall (Fúyīn Táng, 福音堂) Designed by an Englishman and built in 1905; now a Xiàmén Christian Council's retiree's center

Add: #40 Sunlight Rock Rd (Rìguāngyán Lù, 日光岩路 40 号)

Fùxīng Church (Fùxìng Táng, 复兴堂) is in the garden-like triangular plot between Fùxìng and Lùjiāo（鹿礁路）roads. This church is of Watchman Nee's (Ní Tuòshēng 倪柝声) "Little Flock" sect (Xiăoqún Jiàohuì, 小群教会).

Gulangyu's Union Church (协和礼拜堂) Gulangyu's earliest church was built in 1863 to spare Gulangyu foreigners the tiring and, in inclement weather, perilous one hour ferry trip to Xiamen's Xinjie Church.

Three denominations, the American Reformed Church, London Missionary

Society, and English Presbyterian Mission, contributed to its construction, hence the name "Union Church." It was rebuilt in its original style in 1911.

Union Church (Restored in 2010)

Union Church was beside the Catholic church and former Japanese consulate, but obscured on all sides by hospital buildings.

The Gulangyu government spent millions of Yuan removing those buildings and landscaping the grounds, and Rosanna (蔡德晔), a Xiamen businesswoman, spent millions renovating the church, which is now used for weddings, performances, etc., including Sunday Christian concerts from 15:00-16:00.
Hrs: 9:30-11:30, 14:30-16:30, Tue-Sat.

Gulangyu Union Church Described in 1897
(MacGowan, *Pictures of Southern China*, p. 151)

The public buildings on Kulangsu are few. Union Church is an unpretentious but an exceedingly useful and comfortable place of worship. The architect who designed it had evidently the comfort both of the preacher and of the congregation in view rather than an architectural style that might have been more rigidly ecclesiastical, but that would not have conduced to the pleasure of religious worship. It is light and airy, with large windows guarded by Venetians on the outside. The pews consist of five sittings, each on in the form of an arm-chair, in which the worshipper can sit with the greatest comfort' for he is not only protected against any crowding by his neighbours, but he is also secured a position of perfect ease, for the backs of these chairs have been made at the precise angle that secured absolute rest to the person who occupies them. The services are conducted by the resident missionaries, one Sunday the Episcopal service being used, and the next the Nonconformist, so as to meet the wishes of the different sections of the community.

Xiàmén's Lost Catholic Church (and school, orphanage, hospital…)

The Amoy Vicariate Apostolic was responsible for Mǐnnán (S. Fújiàn), as well as Yǒngchūn, Lóngyán, Pǔtián, Jīnmén and Táiwān. In 1860, an Italian began building the 413 m^2 Amoy Catholic church at #15 Xí'ān Lù (溪岸). An historian told me it was built in a "Roman Gothic" style supposedly reminiscent of Notre Dame cathedral.

The church built a rectory in 1873. At 1,076 m^2 it was over twice the size of the church, but from 1916 until Liberation it was also used as an activity center for Dominicans from Spain.

The Catholic Benevolent Hall was built in 1877, and between 1877 and 1951 the church adopted 5,543 orphans. Since 1952 the hall has been used by the Kāihé Elementary School (Kāihé Xiǎoxué, 开禾小学).

The Upright Friendship Elementary School (Zhèngyī Xiǎoxué, 正谊小学) was opened in 1921 at #17 Kāihé Rd , with another building in front of what is now #10-26 Diǎnbǎo Rd (典宝路). The school added another 213.91m^2 building in 1936, but shut down completely in 1937 because of the Japanese invasion. In 1938 they built a 613.97 m^2 2 storey building, and organized the Xiānshān Tavern (Xiāngshān Kèzhàn, 香山客栈) which brought in an annual income of 1200 catties① of rice.

In 1943, the church built the Ruòsè Hospital (Ruòsè Yīyuàn, 若瑟医院) at #15 Cí'ān Rd The head was an Englishman. In 1958 it merged with Kāiyuán District People's Hospital (Kāiyuán Qū Rénmín Yīyuàn, 开元区人民医院).

Today, most of the church's structures are still identifiable, though the roof is changed beyond recognition. Few now know of this Catholic churches' diverse contributions to Xiàmén—not just a church but a school, an orphanage, a hospital, an inn, etc. Rumor has it the church will be rebuilt.

THE FIRST SOUTH FUKIEN SYNOD, AMOY, APRIL 1894
Senior Chinese Minister is Rev. Iap Han-chiong, front row centre
E.P. and A.R. Missionaries include Revs. Wm. McGregor, G. M. Wales, C. Campbell Brown

The Amoy People (1880s) In August 1889, the missionary John Macgowan published *The Story of the Amoy Mission* in London. He wrote frankly of the poverty, and the problems between Lǎowài and Lǎonèi, but he also brought to life the Amoy people's passion and drive and, above all, their "English sense of fair play." Here is a passage from *The Story of the Amoy Mission*:

> Chinese stare at the foreigner, sometimes with skepticism or even thinly veiled contempt, but once they know you, "The crowd becomes sympathetic. The sneer dies out of their faces. There is nothing that touches the Chinese heart so mightily as practical benevolence. It is a virtue they highly appreciate. Their stolid, emotionless features begin to light up with genuine feeling, and the eyes of some are twinkling and flashing as their hearts are moved…[what] has just happened has been a mighty revelation. It has brought you closer to the Chinese heart than you were before, and it has revealed to you the wondrous possibilities of the future…"

① Cattie: usually 1 jīn (斤), about 0.5 kg (1.1 lbs). Catties were smaller than doggies.

Supplement
Pew Perils

Russian Orthodox Congregation, Amoy

On Easter and Christmas, even Buddhists pack the pews to enjoy Xiàmén church choirs, so get there early. While you wait they will play recordings of traditional Christmas hymns such as Silent Night, The First Noel, Frosty the Snowman and Jingle Bells. (These fit right in with the popular "Santa Bless You" Christmas cards).

Churches fill quickly, so *do* get there early! Otherwise, Lǎowài-loving ushers will oust some 90-year-old granny from her front row pew so the foreign friend can better see the service and so everyone else can better see the foreign friend. Of course, once you gallantly refuse the granny's seat and pick a pew, you're a sitting duck for a member of that Chinese sect that believes 'speaking in tongues' means mastering English. They'll plop down beside you and spend the entire hour practicing English nonstop. I really have had prayers go like this:

"Our Father who art in –"
"—What country are you from?"
"Thy kingdom come, thy will be –"
"—Where do you work?"
"Give us this day our –"
"—How much money do you make?"
"And lead us not into temptation—*like murder....*"

Chinese Communion—Breaking Wet Noodles For 2000 years, Christians have "broken bread" together during Communion (Shèngcān, 圣餐). But what about Christians who don't have bread to break?

Until the mid 1990s, Xīnjiē Church celebrated communion not with bread but little squares of noodles. Personally, I liked the chewy texture, and the Chinese wine packed more punch than the grape juice, though I quickly realized why communion cups are so tiny; it's to make sure folks were in the Spirit and not in the spirits.

Alas, Xiàmén churches have modernized. Now they use the round, flat imported bona fide communion wafers that look and taste like Styrofoam. Granted, they look nice, with that little cross stamped on them. It would have been tough stamping those crosses on wet noodles. But I kind of miss the noodles.

The wine's still good, though.

Chapter 16

Explore Fújiàn Province—Overview

Off to Anxi (1920s); Getting a bit carried away?

Amoy has more than enough to keep boredom at bay, but if you get island fever, explore the rest of fascinating Fújiàn.

I have more books about Fujian (e-books online in 2013) and 500 pages of informations and photos on amoymagic.com, but in the next few chapters I'll give a very brief overview of my favorite destinations in South Fujian (to add northern and western Fujian would need another 1000 pages).

Mĭnnán Golden Triangle

1. Xiàmén: Spring Festival, 2011, #1 destination in China (Beijing #2); top draw is Gulangyu.
2. Quánzhōu: Marco Polo's fabled "Zaytun"; tea, porcelain, home of marionettes, rich history
3. Zhāngzhōu: Dōngshān Island (Fujian's 'Hawaii'), Chángtài, Nanjing roundhouses

And the rest of Fujian…

4. Wŭyí Mountain: nature, culture, history, tea
5. Yŏngdìng: Hakka Roundhouses
6. Níngdé: Tàimŭ Mtn, Zhōunīng, etc.
7. Yŏngtài: beautiful scenery
8. Sānmíng: nature, culture, food
9. Chángtīng: Hakkas; Lil Red Shànghăi
10. Lóngyán: Amoy Tigers, Guānzai Mtn.

Quánzhōu (泉州)—Marco Polo's Fabled Zaytun

UNESCO "World Museum of Religions" 联合国"世界宗教博物馆"
The "Marionette Capital of China" 中国的木偶之都
Chóngwǔ Walled City 崇武古城 (1 hr. north of Quánzhōu)
 Stonemasons, Hui'an Maidens 惠安石雕与惠安女
 Chóngwǔ's Forest of Statues 崇武的石雕园

Quánzhōu City:
 Maritime Museum (China's best!) 海上交通史博物馆
 Ashab Mosque (1009 A.D.) 清净寺
 Kāiyuán Temple & Twin Pagodas 开元寺, 双塔
 Qīngyuán Mountain 清源山
  China's Largest Taoist Statue 老君岩, 宋代道教石刻
 Spirit Hill—Muslim Tombs, Wind Stone 灵山-伊斯兰教圣墓和风动石

Jìnjiāng—Home of Philippine Hero Jose Rizal 晋江黎刹纪念广场
 Earth's Last Manichaean Temple 摩尼教草庵 (1/2 hr. south of Quānzhōu)

Nán'ān—Hometown of Koxinga 南安—郑成功的故乡
 Jiǔrì Hill, Maritime Silk Route 九日山, 海上丝绸之路的"官方"起点
 Mǐnnán Village Cultural Landmark 蔡资深建筑群

Déhuà Town—Ancient Porcelain Capital 瓷都德化 (2 hrs. N.W.)
 Qūdòugōng Ancient Kiln 屈斗宫古窑址
 Déhuà Pottery Museum 陶瓷博物馆

Ānxī—China's Tea Capital 茶都安溪 (1 hr. west)
 Ānxī's Potala Palace (Qīngshuǐ Temple) 清水岩—安溪的布达拉宫
 Ānxī Confucian Temple (1000-yr-old) 安溪文庙
 Hútóu, Ancient Home of Prime
  Minister Lǐ Guāngdì 湖头, 李光地故居

Not this year, Dear... Ancient Huì'ān custom dictates that, until a child is born, newlyweds may sleep together only on 3 nights a year①: Spring Festival, Grave Sweeping Day, and Mid-Autumn Festival. Until a child is born, if they meet one another on the street, they must act as if they don't even know each other.

They must really make hay on the holidays!

"Not this year, dear. I have a headache."

① This custom is slowly dying out—as is the custom of wearing the unique Huì'ān costumes. Go see them while you still can.

Zhāngzhōu (漳州) "Land of Plenty"

"100 Flower Village" 百花村
Lónghái Volcano Beach 龙海古火山口
Zhào Family Palace 赵家堡
Chángtài (长泰), Xiàmén's Backyard
Mǎyángxī Kayak Center 马洋溪皮划艇训练中心
Líndūn Ancient Walled Village 林敦古城墙
Opium Baron's Manor 鸦片大王的房子
Dōngshān Island – Fújiàn's Hawaii 东山岛, 福建的夏威夷
Widow's Museum 寡妇村博物馆
Tēnfú Tea Museum (World's Largest) 天福茶庄，世界上最大的茶博物馆

Níngdé (宁德) —Birthplace of Southern Chinese Civilization

Tàimǔ Mtn. Nature & Religion 太姥山：自然美景与宗教文化
36 Temples, 36 Scenic Spots 36 座寺庙, 36 处景点
Xiápǔ—Japanese Holy Place 圣地霞浦
Yǎngjiāxī Bamboo Raft Ride 杨家溪竹筏
Sāndǔ'ào World's Deepest Ice-free Harbor
三都澳—世界上最深的不冻港
Zhōuníng—Natural A/C City 天然空调城周宁
Lǐyú Village Carp Worshippers 鲤鱼村
Kung Fu Fighters 武术世家
9 Dragon Falls (九龙漈瀑布), China's Largest falls Complex
Bǎishuǐyáng (白水洋)—Walk on Water!

Big Foot meets Bound Foot!

Fúzhōu (福州)—Banyan City

Mǎwěi—Cradle of Chinese Maritime 马尾——中国船舶驾驶技术的摇篮
Mǎjiāng River Naval Battle Memorial Hall 马江海战纪念馆

Fúzhōu City
3 Lanes, 7 Alleys Sānfāng Qīxiàng 三坊七巷
Fúzhōu City Museum 福州市博物馆
Fújiàn Prov. Sci-Tech Hall 福建省科技馆外
Nántái Island (南台岛) colonial architecture
Stone Church (石头教堂)
Buddha Jumps the Wall (Soup) 佛跳墙
Drum Mountain Gǔshān 鼓山 (30 min. east)

Yǒngtài—Scenic Wonderland 永泰的迷人风光 (I hr. west)

Pǔtián (莆田) –City of Lychee

Měizhōu Island—Home of Sea Goddess Mazu 湄洲岛，海上女神妈祖的发源地
Potala Palace on the Sea 海上布达拉宫
Southern Shàolín Kung Fu Temple 南少林庙
Sakya Buddhist Pagoda 释迦文佛塔
Mùlán Dam 木兰陂
Guǎnghuà Temple 广化寺
Hánjiāng—Venice of China 涵江——中国水上城市威尼斯
Xiānyóu (仙游)—9 Carp Falls and Dream Praying
Xiānyóu Woodcarvers 仙游工艺美术城

Wǔyí Mountain (武夷山) –Fújiàn's Eden

Yùlíntíng Sòng Dynasty Dragon Kiln 遇林亭宋代龙窑
9-Bend Bamboo Rafting 九曲溪风景区
"Tour of Heaven" Peak 天游峰
Wǔyí Wildlife Preserve 武夷山自然保护区
Ancient Mín King's Palace 闽越王国宫殿遗址
Ancient Town, Mín Relic 汉城，闽越发源地
Mínyuè Kingdom Museum 闽越王国博物馆
Big Red Robe (most expensive tea) 大红袍茶

Lóngyán (龙岩) – Hakka Homeland

Hakka Roundhouses 客家土楼
Liánchéng's Guānzai Mtn. 连城冠山风景区
Yǒngfù Flower Village 永福花乡
Chángtīng –Hakka Homeland 长汀客家首府
- Little Red Shànghǎi 红色小上海
- Hakka Museum 客家博物馆
- Woodcarving 长汀的木雕
- Táng Dynasty Sānyuán Gate 唐代的三元阁城楼
- Túfáng Hakka Village 长汀，涂坊客家村落

Meihuā Mtn.'s Amoy Tigers 梅花山自然保护区，华南虎
Sìbǎo (1 of China's 4 Ancient Printing Centers). 四堡印刷

Scenic Sānmíng (三明)

Shāxiàn 沙县访古
- Largest Sleeping Buddha, 中国最大的卧佛
- Shāxiàn Shoulder Opera 沙县的肩膀戏
- Fújiàn's Gourmet Town 沙县福建美食城

Míngxī—Gem Capital 宝石之都明溪县

Shíbì—Hakka homeland 客家祖地宁化石壁
Yùhuá Caverns 玉华洞
Tàiníng—Míng Dynasty Home, Gold Lake 泰宁，尚书第、大金湖
Wànshòu Crag Stone-Age Culture & Geshikao 万寿岩文化和格氏栲森林

Fújiàn Bridges I could write a book on just Fújiàn's delightful wooden covered bridges (木质廊桥), (some of them 3 stories high), the ancient stone bridges, and modern wonders like Xiàmén's Hǎicāng suspension bridge (visit Xiamen's bridge museum).

Fújiàn Bridges

"The bridges of China are wonders! On some of them people build their temples and houses and shops--where they live and carry on their business. There are at least two bridges of this kind in the Amoy district, each having a population of from fifty to one hundred inhabitants--perhaps more. These bridges are generally of wonderful construction. How the largest of them were built must always remain a matter of pure conjecture.

"Twenty-five miles west of Amoy there is a famous bridge...There are natives who will tell you that man could not have lifted, by any imaginable machinery, to their present position those immense stones of which it is made. The only conclusion they can come to is, the gods must have done the work.

"The bridge is called 'The Po-lam Bridge'--a place much frequented by foreigners residing in Amoy. It is 200 yards or more long, built upon solid stone piers each about twelve feet high. Some of the stones laid on these piers are of great length and weight. One of them is seventy feet long, five feet thick and four feet wide, weighing something like 107 tons. It always has been a question: How were they put in place?"

Pitcher, *In and About Amoy*, 1912, p.297-8

Hakka Roundhouses (Kèjiā Tǔlóu, 客家土楼) I've visited these earthen castles over 30 times. Reagan and the CIA believed they were missile silos, **Best route:** Xiàmén freeway towards Lóngyán, exit at Nánjìng exit just after Zhāngzhou. Follow beautiful road along river and over the mountains to Nánjìng earthen houses. Then continue west to Yǒngdìng's excellent exhibits and museums (English guides). Have some country cookin,' spend the night, return via Lóngyán and freeway.

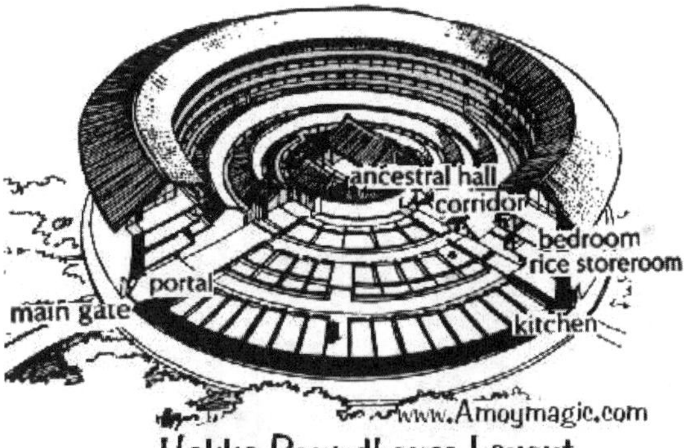

Hakka Roundhouse Layout

Have fun in Fujian!
Brushed lately?
(Photos from "Magic Fujian")
Cuddle with planet's longest snakes (10 meter pythons)
Meet Koxinga--last defender of the Ming
Learn how China's largest Taoist statue can help you live to be 120!
Get a kick out of S. Shaolin Kung Fu
Stay overnight in a well-rounded Hakka earthen castle
Give traditional Zhangzhou handpuppets a hand
Discover why Hui'an Maidens' bare their bellies!
MFJ
FJTV
Play with Fujian kitty cats! (Meihua Mtn's Amoy Tigers)

(from "*Magic Fujian*")

Make a pilgrimage to Ninghua (Home of the Hakka)

Marvel at ancient biological engineering on the world's longest bridge of the Middle Ages!

Visit the Planet's last temple to the Persian Prophet Mani

Explore 2000-year-old ruins of the Min Kingdom (Wuyi)

Enjoy ancient wooden covered bridges

Frolic in China's largest waterfalls complex (9 Dragon Falls)

More Fun in Fujian!

(from "*Magic Fujian*")

Visit Mawei--Cradle of Chinese (Since 200 B.C.!)

Visit the *real* "Water World!"

Tour Gulangyu Islet's international architecture

Smell the roses in Zhangzhou "City of Flowers"

Delight in China's largest piano museum (Gulangyu "Isle of Music")

Discover why the Buddha jumps the wall!

(from "*Magic Fujian*")

Visit start of "Long March" (and "Short April")

Let Wuyi's Wu Guangmin enlighten you on Big Red Robe-- (world's most expensive tea at over 34,000 USD per ounce!)

Visit the Carp Cemetery (locals have worshipped carp 800 years!)

Ascend a Stone-age escalator?

Zhouning Highland Tea

Or... enjoy an elegant Minnan Tea Ceremony (and fine Anxi tea, which even we mortals can afford!)

(from "*Magic Fujian*")

Visit China's 1st Protestant Church (1848, in Xiamen)

Study Chinese in Xiamen Univ. China's most beautiful campus!

Learn about famous scholars like Zhuxi-- founder of neoConfucianism

Seek your fortune in Mingxi--China's 4th largest gem bed.

Try to rouse China's largest sleeping Buddha! (Sanming's "god of xiuxi?")

Feast on Shaxian cuisine Famous throughout S.E. Asia

(from "*Magic Fujian*")

Find out who is pulling strings in Quanzhou--home of Chinese Marionettes

Learn how egrets battled snakes for Xiamen!

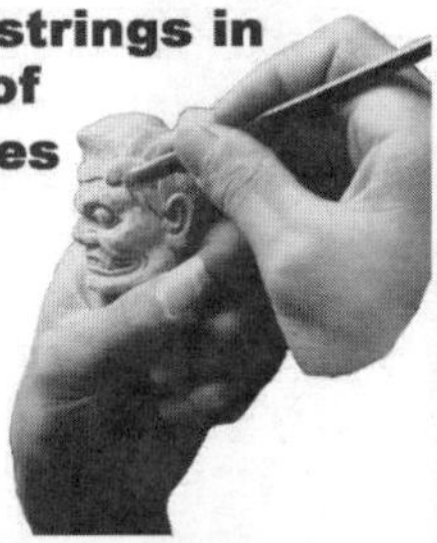

Try to find your way in Chongwu--one of China's few remaining walled cities

Spend all your money saving money in Dehua--one of China's 4 ancient porcelain capitals

Discover that Chinese *do* use forks!

Learn to walk on water! (Baishuiyang)

(from "*Magic Fujian*")

Visit "Potala Palace on the Sea"

Discover how little Miss Mo became the sea goddess

Anxi has a "Potala Palace" as well

Learn how a Fujianese lady built ancient Mulan Dam

Ponder the purposes of the "Stone Bamboo Shoot" (fertility totem)

(from "*Magic Fujian*")

Visit Putian's famous S. Shaolin Kung Fu temple

Raft down 9-Bend Stream in Wuyi (UNESCO World-Heritage Site)

Savor surrealistic scenery (Mt. Taimu)

Bed down in the Xianyou temple where "Dream Praying" began

Would Pandas get a square meal from Wuyi's famous "square bamboo"?

Supplement

Fujian Specialties (Fújiàn Tèchǎn, 福建特产)

Fújiàn was long famous not only for China's famous teas, silks, porcelains and papers, but for many other arts, crafts and traditions. So take some money when you explore our province.

Wood carvings (Mùdiāo, 木雕). Fúzhōu (福州) and Xiānyóu（仙游).

Folding Chinese fans (Zhéshān, 折扇) Gǔlàngyǔ has best prices and selection.

Fúzhōu paper parasols (Zhǐsǎn, 纸伞) Origin of Japan's exquisite parasols.

Fúzhou bodiless lacquerware (Fúzhōu Tuōtái Qīqì, 脱胎漆器). One of China's national treasures (no, I don't mean Shànghǎi fashion shows' bodiless models).

Fúzhōu Shoushan stone carvings (Shòushān Shídiāo, 寿山石雕) Add: #42 Wǔyī Běi Lù 五一北路 42 号 Tel: 0591754-5205.

Fúzhou cork carvings (Ruǎnmùhuà, 软木画) Delightfully intricate carved landscapes under glass.

Xiānyóu's ersatz antique mahogany furniture (Fǎngǔ Táohuāxīnmù Jiājú, 仿古桃花心木家具）

Huì'ān stone carvings (Huì'ān Shídiāo, 惠安石雕) Over 1700 years of stone carving here; take some home in your carry-on; you won't take them for granite.

Pearls (Zhēnzhū, 珍珠) Try Pearl World, #115 Lóngtóu Lù, Gǔlàngyǔ .（茜茜珍珠专卖店, 龙头路 115 号）
Tel: 2063620

Porcelain: Déhuà (Déhuà Táocí, 德化陶瓷) One of China's 4 ancient porcelain centers.

Ānxī tea: (Ānxī Cháyè , 安溪茶叶) Sparked Boston Tea Party, saved U.S. judges from white wigs.

Wǔyí Tea (Wǔyú Cháyè , 武夷茶叶). For connoisseurs

Mǐnnán tea sets (Mǐnnán Chájù, 闽南茶具) Try Gǔlàngyǔ; priced from pennies to thousands of Yuan.

Quánzhōu marionette heads (Mùǒutóu, 木偶头)—whether exquisite handcarved camphor or cheap resin, get at the factory. Call David Feng. Tel: 0595-22989432 Mobile: 13799503010
E-mail: aghzeng@hotmail.com www.jinshow.com

Quánzhōu miniature landscapes (Pénjǐng, 盆景) Famous for 1,000 years. Also try Zhāngzhōu, for centuries famous as the "City of Flowers." (漳州花卉市场). Literally miles of shops along the highway.

Wicker (Ténzhì Jiājù 藤制家具) and **bamboo furniture** (Zhúzhì Jiājù, 竹制家具 W. Fújiàn's Liánchéng（连城）.
Root sculptures (Gēndiāo, 根雕) Sold everywhere; cheapest in West Fújiàn.
Xuān paper (Xuānzhǐ, 宣纸)：Liánchéng. One of China's 4 ancient printing centers, and famous for handmade papers.
Baskets (Lánzi, 篮子) Xiàmén sells hand woven baskets in every shape and size.
Kites (Fēngzhēng, 风筝) If someone tells you to go fly a kite you're in luck. Fújiàn has long been known for them, and the 8km. stretch between the Asia Gulf Hotel and the Convention Center is a favorite with Chinese and foreign kite enthusiasts.
Xiàmén Míngjiàn Sport Equipment Co.（明鉴工艺品厂）in Qiánpǔ, makes all kinds of kites. Their excellent site even shows how to make your own. (See end of Chapter 8, Sports and Recreation). Tel: 5927465 www.kite-china.com
Chinese Chops (Yìnzhāng, 印章) Yogi, on Gǔlàngyǔ, will translate your name into Chinese for your own personal "chop." www.yogiart.com Tel: 2060978

Flowers and potted plants: "Landscape Mall" on Xiàmén's Liánqián Lù. (莲 前 路), or neighboring Zhāngzhōu City (漳州市), ancient "City of Flowers"
Paper Cuttings (Jiǎnzhǐ, 剪纸) Handmade in many towns; try Sānmíng City's Shāxian town (also famous for cuisine).
Forklift to carry it all home. Linde of Xiàmén.

Specialty Foods

Try Lóngyán peanuts（龙岩的花生）, Chángtīng dried tofu（长汀豆腐干）and dried sweet potato（地瓜干）, Xiānyóu's mushrooms（仙游的蘑菇）, Ānxī Hútóu's rice noodles（湖头米粉）, and Wǔpíng County's famous dried pig gallbladder (武平著名的猪胆干). Yum. Also savor Hétian2 Chicken（河田鸡）, Shāxiān "snacks" (沙县小吃), and the deep fried tea leaves in Wǔyī. But I don't recommend bringing live critters like piglets back in the car

Peanuts and Piglets

I used to take a dozen students at a time on trips to the countryside in our 15-passenger van and I liked everything about those trips except the shopping. My students invariably packed Toy Ota with local specialties that, because of poor roads and distribution back then, were not often outside of their town of origin.

I didn't mind foodstuffs that sat still—like Lóngyán peanuts, Chángtīng tofu, or Hútóu rice noodles. But I tried to draw the line, futilely, at live chickens, ducks, rabbits, and even piglets. "No problem, Prof. Bill," they'd reassure me. We'll clean the car afterwards." Whether they helped wash it or not, it still smelled like a barn for weeks afterwards.

"What's the point?" I complained. "Peanuts are peanuts; tofu is tofu."

But after 18 years in Xiàmén, I've come to appreciate the unique flavors (and bargains) in every corner of the province, and I too load Toy Ota down with foodstuffs—but not foodstuffs that are still eating or excreting.

Chapter 17

Zhangzhou 漳州– Land of Plenty

Zhangzhou, on the "9 Dragon River"

"Chiang-chiu is a large city of 200,000 inhabitants, situated on a wide river, 30 miles west of Amoy... The scenery, it seemed to me, was the most beautiful I had ever witnessed. Within the circle of our vision lay that immense city with its extensive walls, its temples and pagoda, its river, bridges and boats, its gardens, its trees and shrubbery, and its densely crowded streets... Still further on, in every direction, our view was bounded by lofty hills whose cloud capped tops seemed as pillars on which the heavens rested. Nature had done her best to make this region a terrestrial paradise... Through the centre of this scene may be traced the course of the river with its numberless canals, like the Nile of Egypt, giving fertility wherever nature or the art of man conducts its waters...

"The same good feeling towards foreigners seems to extend far into the interior. At least we go from, village to village wherever we please without hindrance, and are always treated with kindness."

Diary of Rev. Talmage (Sept. 23, 1847)

"The city itself, when viewed from the walls, was one of the most beautiful that I have ever seen in China. Looking over it, it seemed like a huge forest. The Chinese have a passionate love for trees and flowers, and consequently every householder had planted some kind of a tree in his courtyard. These, during years of undisturbed prosperity, had grown large and spreading, until at length the city seemed to lie beneath the shadow of a mighty forest. Lines of streets could here and there be distinguished through the foliage, but it was difficult to realize that down below, a hundred thousand people lived, that great busy streets, crowded with buyers and sellers, stretched far away into the distance, or that the river beyond was lined with craft of all kinds, in which thousands of people passed their lives, and had no home besides them.

..."The people of Chiang-Chiu were proud and haughty. They were prosperous and well-to-to... They were proud, too, because of the exquisite silks and satin stuffs they could produce. Their looms were famous, and their designs were rare, and beautifully executed."

Rev. Macgowan, *The Story of the Amoy Mission*, 1889

Home of Narcissus Zhangzhou was the home of flower children centuries before Bob Dylan was blowing in the wind. Settled by the ancient Minyue people over 5,000 years ago, Zhangzhou prefecture was established in 686. Today, Zhangzhou administers nine counties and a district, with a population of almost 5 million spread out over 12,888 km^2.

Officially, Zhangzhou has 33 scenic spots. I'd pass on some, but I highly recommend the ancient Song Dynasty fortress, Xiangcheng (the city of flowers and fruits"), delightful Dongshan Island, the beautiful beaches of Longhai Crater, China's kayaking capital, Changtai, and the "100 Flower Village," where residents have more plants than the FBI.

For centuries, Zhangzhou people have grown an unimaginable variety of potted flowers, plants, and miniature Chinese landscapes (which go for as little as $10 or so). A brochure claims that "100 Flower Village" boasts 20,000 flowers species and over 10,000 potted flowers and miniature trees—at least until my wife shopped there.

Zhangzhou is most famous for Narcissus, which Chinese call "Water Sprite Flower." Secrets for its cultivation have been handed down from one generation to the next for centuries.

Zhangzhou had such a glorious past that many scholars argue Zhangzhou, and not Quanzhou, was Marco Polo's ancient Zaytun. I doubt it, but in its day it was a major international port of call. And as Rev. Macgowan noted, Zhangzhou was famous for its quality silk (and Rev. Macgowan should know: he was a 'man of the cloth'). Zhangzhou silk is sold even today in Hong Kong for over $100 USD per yard.

Zhangzhou's "33 famous sites at home and abroad" include:

Zhangzhou's Hongjian Village, 1 km. from Ciji Palace, is the ancestral home of Corazon Aquino, former Philippine president. Her great-grandfather, Xu Yuhuan, and other villagers sailed to the Philippines over a century ago. Corazon visited here in 1988, and donated money to rebuild their ancestral hall. Zhangzhou is also the ancestral home of Singapore's Prime Minister, Lee Kuan Yew, and Taiwan's Lee Teng-hui.

The Zhao Family Palace (赵家堡) was built in 1279 by a Song imperial family member who fled invading troops from the north. Earthen Outer Walls were built on a stone base, and is 6 meters high, 2 meters thick, and 1,200 meters in circumference.

An imitation of a Song dynasty imperial palace, the Outer City has five rows of houses and over 150 rooms, linked by walled courtyards.

The Inner City resembles the square Hakka structures in western Fujian, and is protected by a 20 meter high rammed earth wall. The complex boasts a flagstone courtyard and a lake with pavilions and arched bridges (including the excellent Bianpai Bridge), a primary school, stores to cater to the 500 resident families, a tourist museum, Jufo Pagoda, and Yu's granite stele recounting Da Yu's achievements in river control, Jufo Pagoda, deng deng.

Zhangzhou's Nanshan Temple (南山寺) Originally the home of Chen Yong, a Tang Dynasty (713-741) bigwig. It was so grandiose that he was accused of upsetting the social order and putting on imperial airs. Chen's quick-witted daughter immediately became a nun and her father made it a temple.

Since ancient times, worshippers have flocked to pay homage to the 62 meter high stone Buddha, and in the rear Scripture Hall, the unique 2 meter, 2,000 kilogram white jade Buddha impresses even the most jaded tourist.

LongHai Old Crater (龙海古火山口) lies on the shore of Niutou Mountain. A guidebook claims, "According to scientific records, its last eruption dates back to more than 22 million years ago." Only Chinese would keep records for 22 million years.

Better than the crater is **White Sand Beach** (龙海白滩), one of the few places near Xiamen with waves strong enough to beach your boogie board.

Changtai (长泰), **home of China kayak team**. The Mayang River Kayak Center hosts domestic and international rafting and kayaking events. A brochure boasts of the 8 km course, "rip currents with blustering surges account for more than 50%. Soul-stirring, exciting and without danger, the place is the paradise for the braves." If ***you*** are a "brave" and want your soul stirred, phone: (596) 832-1001 or 136 0507-0871.

Take a hike! Changtai is hiker heaven. Endless trails wind through deep, verdant valleys, with pristine rivers foaming over polished granite boulders. There's also a lot of wildlife, like 100+-year-old giant tortoises, and pangolins. Until just a few decades ago, Amoy Tigers also roamed the hillsides. Today about all you'll see, if you're lucky, are wolves, wild boar, and mountain goats. And if you pay attention you might see snakes, but you have to keep a look out, as they fear us far more than we fear them. I took some Chinese friends on a hike and they walked right past a 1 m. green bamboo viper blended right in with the leaves. I took a photo, then called my friends back to show them what they'd missed (photo to the right). They nearly fainted.

Fortunately, we didn't run across any of Fujian's 33 foot reticulated pythons (better yet, they didn't run across us).

While in the area, visit the beautiful, 70 m high Baizhangya Falls—but phone ahead to make sure its turned on! Neighboring Anxi county diverted the water for a power plant, so most of the time the Falls trickles like a Fujian mountain monkey with prostate problems.

Balancing Growing & Greening Apart from debacles like Baizhangya Falls, this area is something of a small development miracle. It is hard to believe that just a decade ago, "Xiamen's Backyard" was an environmental nightmare.

A decade ago, I spent an entire day hiking along the riverbank with county officials and investors for the proposed water rafting resort. The pristine river foamed over rocks and boulders flung across it like polished granitegems. But only 3 years earlier, that river had been a black, stygian stream of noxious industrial effluents that vomited forth to poison the valley. It's resurrection was due primarily to a visionary young

county magistrate, Yang Ming-yuan, who told me, "It is pointless to prosper by destroying our environment. It is also senseless to go overboard environmentally and starve. So we emphasize both economic development and environmental protection."

One way that Changtai minimizes pollution and waste is with its closed cycle. The manure from Changtai's 30,000 cows fertilizes the grass they feed on, and tens of thousands of fruit trees, and over 2 million square meters of mushrooms (and the mushroom soil, after harvest, is also used for fertilizer). They've even found a use for the dairies' prodigious production of cow urine: it is converted into methane for cooking and lighting.

Changtai's environmental restrictions on have cost them tens of millions of dearly needed revenue, but the leadership is confident their policies will eventually attract both tourism developers and green industrialists. Magistrate Yang said, "We need to have a clean environment. We also need to eat!" I hope Changtai can do both.

Lindun Village Wall (Changtai)

Lindun Town I visited Changtai's Lindun Town half a dozen times without realizing that many of its ancient walls still stood. The walled city was built over 400 years ago to keep out the invading Japanese pirates, who for centuries pillaged and raped and wreaked havoc on even these remote valleys. Chinese called them wokou (a disparaging term meaning "midget barbarians").

Lindun was unique in that it had a wall down the middle of town, as well as around it. I was told the village had two factions who fought each other constantly—except when united against the midget barbarians.

Opium Baron's Manor

The Opium Baron's manor was built over 150 years ago by a Xiamen tobacco king—and built to last! One granite slab is 10 m. long.

Before you leave Lindun, sample the local mountain delicacies—rare wild veggies and critters. A restaurant with hot springs attached is run by Mr. Lin, which is no surprise, since virtually every one in Lindun is surnamed Lin.

Liudoushan Tropical Rainforest, only 75 km from Zhangzhou city, is the perfect place for a wet walk (average annual rainfall is 2 m.). This virgin rain forest has some of the planet's rarest creatures and plant life, including over 700 "rare medicinal herbs". This is not surprising; for Chinese, everything seems to be medicinal.

Tenfu Tea Depot and Museum Tenfu Tea Depot has one of the best tea shops in the province—and the largest tea museum (and tea pot) on the planet.

The 8000m^2 museum is divided into four areas: Main Exhibition Hall, Tea Ceremony Classroom, Tianfu Painting and Calligraphy Hall, and Japanese Tea

Ceremony Hall. The site also includes, I am told, ten major scenic spots, including "drinking vessels flowing on winding crook." You figure that one out.

Address: Tianfu Museum Co. Ltd. Zhangzhou City, Zhangpu Industrial Dist. (天福茶博物院有限公司, 漳州市漳浦县盘陀工业区) Tel: (0596) 288-2305

Dongshan Island is Fujian's Hawaii, with miles of beautiful beaches, and some of Fujian's best and cheapest seafood. It also has a rich history.

Supposedly, the last Ming emperor had a palace just offshore, and when he was killed by the Mongols on Hainan Island (the southernmost part of China, near Vietnam), the palace mysteriously sunk into the sea. Tongshan town has a large statue of the last Prime Minister of the Ming Dynasty. He was so mischievous as a child that his father put him on an island just offshore, where he lived and studied in a cave. It must have worked. I'm considering trying the same thing with my two sons.

Copper Mountain Castle (铜山古城) and Guandian Temple are Dongshan's big attractions. I especially enjoyed the big crack in a rock, with an inscription below that proclaimed, "On May 31st, 1992, at 3:32 p.m., the rock cracked, smoke poured forth like a stone monkey, and an 80-pound python emerged."

Stone monkey of smoke? Sounds like someone was stoned on some funny smoke!

There was also a Wind Rocking Stone, but we couldn't budge it even when we lay on our backs and pushed with our feet. Perhaps we could have used a few strong German sailors (Xiamen had a fine wind rocking stone until 1908, when German sailors teamed up and pushed it down the mountain).

Supplement
Fujian's Famed Silk Industry

> "Zhangzhou in the Middle Ages was the seat of a great silk manufacture and the production of its looms, such as gauzes, satins, and velvets, were said to exceed in beauty those of Soochow and Hangchow."
>
> George Philip, British Consul at Amoy, 1889

A century ago, villagers near Minhou (outside Fuzhou) were well known for raising silkworms for Fujian's once legendary silk industry. Fujian is no longer famed for silk, but it should be. Fujian has the climate, and the three kinds of mulberry trees that are useful for commercial raising of silkworms.

To appreciate the silk industry, I offer you quotes from Claude R. Kellogg's monograph①, "The Silk Industry in Fukien" (presented to Fuzhou's Anti-Cobweb Society on May 22nd, 1931).

> "One of the oldest and most fascinating industries, no matter from what angle it may be studied, is that of the production of silk. Ancient Chinese writings, themselves yellow with age, tell of an industry already well developed, with its beginnings some 5000 years ago. Four priceless scrolls, depicting the production

① Monograph: scholarly essay on a specific subject

of silk in detail, were for generations in the possession of the royal families of China but were so carefully guarded that no knowledge of the industry reached the outside world until the secret was stolen by some monks early in the sixth century…

"In the first century A.D. great caravans of snarling camels, laden with bales of silk stuffs, crept ceaselessly over the frozen wastes of the Pamirs so that the pampered aristocrats of the luxurious Roman court might be clothed in fine raiment. Some two thousand camels per day, on the average, were needed to carry the great bales of silk cloth to the borderland of China, from where it was transported by nomad merchants to the Roman Empire…

"It is also interesting to note that no raw silk was sold to the western peoples. All silk was taken through Constantinople to the Island of Cos, in the Mediterranean Sea, in the form of woven fabrics and there unwoven, as this was the only way in which the Romans could get silk thread from which to reweave the costumes so desired by the few who could afford them. Silk at that time was worth its weight in gold. Until 550 A.D. no outsiders knew from what silk was procured.

"…Reports on Fujian silks made by the International Testing House, in Shanghai, showed that Fujian silk, if properly handled, would equal in quality that produced elsewhere. Any differences, then, would be due, not to the inherent quality of the silk itself, but to the methods used in its production.

"…The climate, though not of the best, offers no insurmountable difficulties, the mulberry trees of the necessary varieties grow readily and the land upon which they can be successfully grown is all about us, some of it not even being put to any use at the present time. Representatives of the American Silk Association, while in Foochow predicted that Fujian was capable of producing from 15 to 20 millions of dollars (Mex.) worth of silk per year. The pity of it is that not only are we not producing the silk as we should but we are even importing it from other parts of China. All that is needed is a careful painstaking following of the most approved modern methods of rearing silkworms and Fujian, who once sent out silks equal to the very best from any part of China, will again be enabled to export silks of the very highest quality, this time produced from silkworms reared on her own soil.

"…The Fujian silkworm (monovoltine) increases in weight 5,000 times, and 20 times in length. It then spins its cocoon, which is placed in hot water to kill the pupa and dissolve the cement holding the silk strands together. The cocoon is unwound, and the hapless pupa is dried, fried in peanut oil, and served up as snacks."

Chapter 18

Quanzhou 泉州– Port of Marco Polo & Sinbad

Melting Pot of Asia Quanzhou, not New York City, was our planet's first great melting pot (probably stirred by our Tong 'An firewalkers).

Quanzhou opened to the world as never before or since. Laowai became Chinese citizens, intermarried, and held even provincial level leadership positions—to China's great benefit. The Arab who managed China's trade at one point brought in ¼ of China's entire revenue.

The government appreciated and honored its foreign experts, and Laowai and Laonei mixed freely, trading commodities, culture—even religions.

The Emperor actually financed foreign missionaries, helping them to build Muslim mosques and Franciscan Catholic cathedrals. Andrew of Perugia, the Franciscan Bishop of Quanzhou, wrote that the Emperor's budget for these 'cultural activities' exceeded the entire annual budget of some European countries.

Start of the Maritime Silk Route China's first major international port was Guangzhou, to the south of Amoy, but merchants soon had enough of the corruption and wars, and moved to the more stable Quanzhou, which Arabs and Marco Polo called **Zayton**, and from which we get our word "satin."

Zayton boasted several natural harbors, including Amoy, one of the world's top ten natural deep harbors. Better yet, Zayton was closer to Hangzhou, the silk capital of China--though early 20th century foreign experts claimed that Quanzhou's silk was superior to the fabled cloth of Hangzhou.

Over 1,000 years before Christ, the West valued Chinese silk more highly than gold. The poet Horace wrote of the silks from the legendary land of Seres (the Roman name for China), and the poet Lucan wrote of Cleopatra's "white breasts… revealed by the fabric … close-woven by the shuttle of the Seres."

After Romans and Greeks got a glimpse of Cleopatra's undies, silk demand mushroomed, and so did silk supply, thanks to Quanzhou, the starting point of the Maritime Silk Road. One ship carried as much silk as 700 cantankerous camels on the not-so-silky Silk Road of the Desert.

By the mid 1300s, Quanzhou had 500,000 people of every race, creed and color. Historians wrote that "100 large ships and numerous small ones" anchored in the harbour. Marco Polo, who sailed for home from Quanzhou, claimed it rivaled Alexandria Egypt as the planet's largest and busiest port.

Magnetic compasses, which helped Chinese sail the seven seas, eventually attracted the attention of Europeans, but sea captains often banned the eating of onions, which they feared could interfere with miraculous devices' properties. Their understanding of magnetism was poles apart from that of the Chinese.

"A gift for European traders!"

Chinese merchants brought home ivory, pearls, hawksbill turtles and rhinoceros horns, and sold satin, tea, iron wares, and other Chinese treasures in great demand throughout the known world. Quanzhou's Dehua "blanc de chine" porcelain was prized highly, and the Mogadisu and Kilindini in East Africa almost worshipped blue and white porcelain. But the broadest demand was for Chinese silk (Quanzhou and Zhangzhou silk were legendary). Damask and red and green silk went to Vietnam; printed silks to Thailand; colored satin to Malaysia; floral designed silk to Indonesia; brocade to Burma; colored brocade and white silk to India; green brocade to Iran; colored thin silk to Kenya; and colored brocade to Iraq, Egypt, Morocco, and Saudi Arabia.

For a good feel of what it was like to sail the seven seas in a Chinese junk, visit the recently excavated Song Dynasty vessel displayed in a museum beside the famous 1,000 year-old Kaiyuan Buddhist temple. The ship, which lay at the bottom of Quanzhou bay for 700 years, was 24 meters long and 9 meters wide, had 13 cabins, and boasted a 200 ton capacity.

Excavated Song Dynasty Ship (24m x 9m)
Quanzhou

Quanzhou Maritime Museum has a world-class display of exhibits on China's marine developments and explorations, as well as the astonishing history behind this ancient port. The museum displays hundreds of religious artefacts, including Islamic, Catholic and Nestorian tombstones, Hindu statues, and Manichaean pieces. After reading so much about the Bishop of Quanzhou, Andrew of Perugia, I was excited to see his headstone on display! Though I do wonder where the Bishop now rests his head.

Quanzhou Maritime Museum

"World Museum of Religion" is what UNESCO named Quanzhou in '91, and with good reason. Over 1000 years ago, all world religions prized this "Jerusalem of Asia" because it was rich, had the greatest market of souls, and was easily accessible through unparalleled trade networks on land and sea. Even Mohammed himself set his sites on China – particularly Quanzhou.

When Mohammed's beliefs were outlawed at home, he exported, and the biggest market was China. Between 618 and 626, the persecuted prophet sent one missionary to Guangzhou, one to Yangzhou, and two to Quanzhou. You can pay them a visit in the Sacred Tombs of Islam (Ling Mountain, outside Quanzhou's East Gate). For 1300 years, the tombs have been well-kept by faithful members of Quanzhou's 40,000 strong Muslim community – many of whom frequent the oldest mosque in Southeast Asia.

Tomb of Muslim Saints B.B.

Tushan Street's imposing mosque was constructed of blue and white granite in the year 1004 (400 by the Muslim calendar). It imitated a Damascus mosque and included the Fengtian Altar, Mingshan Chamber, and Prayer Hall. The dome collapsed during a 1607 earthquake, but the 20m. high vaulted entrance and four walls remain, and a new mosque has been built beside it.

Nestorian Christians made their China debut about the same time as the Muslims, and both had their work cut out for them competing with Taoism, Hinduism, Buddhism, and the proponents of esoteric Manichaeism—as well Tibetan Lamaism, Jainism, Confucianism...

B.B.

Tombstone inscribed in both Chinese and Arabic

Star of David? A stone with what resembled a Star of David was unearthed in 2001, and excited those seeking the first archaeological proof of the city's ancient Jewish community. An excavated synagogue in Roman era Capernaum had a "Star of David" architectural motif, so it is intriguing. But the 6-pointed star has been used the world over. The Hindu Satkona Yantra, for example, is a 6-pointed star with the Tamil "Om" in the center.

Workers have also found over 300 Hindu fragments, many near the Tonghuai Gate, suggesting Quanzhou had a Hindu temple. There are also Hindu motifs in some Buddhist temples.

The elephant in the photo is offering flowers to Shiva's lingam (stone phallus). Given the population problem, I'd think Indians would do well to worship another area of the anatomy.

Break the Pots, Scuttle the Boats… is how Laonei say "burn one's bridges." And that's exactly what happened to Quanzhou …

While strolling down Jubao (Treasure Trove) Street, it is hard to believe that at one time this was our planet's center of international trade in jewels, pearls and gold. But

Quanzhou's fame and prosperity came to an end and the fabled port of Zayton so completely disappeared from maps that, by the 19th century, some foreigners argued that Zayton had been in Zhangzhou, not Quanzhou.

Quanzhou's demise was due, in some part, to foreigners' squabbles.

For at least three centuries, a mix of merchants, emissaries, missionaries and sailors lived in the Fanfang (Foreigners Living Area), which was an eclectic hodgepodge of architecture - temples, mosques, churches, houses. A raucous community of Arabs, Persians, Indians and other Southeast Asian Laowai mixed freely with the Chinese. In fact, foreigners actually ruled. The ruling Mongolians were too much in the minority to control Quanzhou's Han Chinese, so they passed the reins to Quanzhou's Chinese Arabs—and this proved to be their downfall.

Arab troops mutinied during the early Ming Dynasty, and when imperial troops attempted to suppress them, disgruntled Han Chinese seized the opportunity for revenge. The Ming then made a fatal move – attacking the Arab's religion.

Quanzhou descended into chaos as inter-racial feuding escalated. The Ming Emperor responded by breaking the pots and scuttling the boats – literally. Like rulers before and since, he valued stability above all else. He burned and sank the world's greatest fleet of merchant ships and forbade foreign trade, and Alexandria's glorious Asian rival began her long slide into anonymity.

Quanzhou never recovered. Neither did China. While the world moved on, China closed herself off from the barbarians outside. And from that time on, Chinese have feared (with reason, sadly to say) foreign influence in her affairs.

Happily, Quanzhou's glorious past remains alive yet today – in her people. Many Quanzhou citizens are direct descendants of mixed marriages between Chinese and Arabs, who once lived together in peace. But faced with increasingly xenophobic Chinese neighbors, many Laowai adopted Laonei names to avoid trouble. Even their Arabic writing took on a Chinese slant. Islamic tombstones scattered about Quanzhou are engraved with fanke mu – "foreign guest's tomb." The words are written in an Arabic script that strangely resembles Chinese characters.

The Arabs are still here today, in a way. Quanzhou's Baiqi Island has over 10,000 descendants of Arabs, though you'd never know it from their surname of Guo. The Ding clan in Chendai village are also of Arab descent. Their ancestral hall is built in southern Fujian architectural style, but the decorations are Islamic.

Some Quanzhou residents had no idea they were of Arab descent until historians told them. Only recently, the Bu and Huang people of Yunlu Village were informed that their common ancestor was none other than Pu Shougeng, an Arab in charge of foreign trade during the Song and Yuan Dynasty, and eventually the assistant to the Fujian governor.

Quanzhou's 2,000 Sites Quanzhou's official tourist brochure spreads it a little thick with its boast, "2,000 tourist sites famous at home and abroad." Still, there is definitely enough to keep you busy a few days. Main attractions include:

Kaiyuan Temple & Mulberry-Lotus Tree Zhou Enlai ordered the Cultural Revolution's zealous Red Guards to spare both Kaiyuan Temple and its famed Mulberry-Lotus tree.

Legend has it that a monk asked the owner of a mulberry garden to donate his land for a temple. The rich man said, "I'll donate the land if this mulberry tree sprouts lotus flowers within 3 days." To his dismay, it did, so he coughed up the land for Kaiyuan Temple.

Multiculturalism inevitably bred syncretism, traces of which can still be found in Kaiyuan Temple's Mahavira Hall, where two carved stone poles bear carvings of Hinduism's Shiva the Destroyer. The poles were transported to Quanzhou from a collapsed Indian temple.

Mahavira Hall has 24 bat-winged flying apsaras, arms outstretched and holding not harps but Nanyin musical instruments. These Oriental angels (from Batman heaven?) have bat wings because bats, according to legend, bring good fortune.

The East and West Pagodas flanking KaiYuan Temple were originally built of wood and stone, then brick, and later stone. Thanks to 22 years of Song Dynasty reconstruction, they have withstood 1,000 years of earthquakes and tourists, and are China's best preserved stone pagodas.

The East pagoda is named Zhenguo ("nation-protecting") and the West is Renshou ("merit and longevity"). Both of the five story octagonal structures are carved top to bottom with vivid relief sculptures, and warriors are carved into the niches of each story.

The stone carvings are an unusual combination of Chinese and Indian styles-not only because China's contacts with India were frequent, but also because the Chinese monk supervising reconstruction died when only four stories had been completed, and a monk from India took charge.

I particularly like the Monkey King carvings. "Journey to the West," which originated the Monkey King tale, was not written until the 16th century, so some argue that the legend of the Monkey King originated right here in Fujian. (More likely, he was borrowed from the monkey-god Hanuman in the Indian epic, Ramayana).

Weasel the attendants into unlocking the pagoda gates and enjoy a marvelous view of the city from the top – and a view of Spirit Mountain to the north.

Spirit Mountain, aka "Fujian's Fairy Land," is an enchanting park of winding paths, pagodas, temples, and 36 caves dug into precipitous hillsides. Before the Red Guards got to them, pilgrims used to worship the hundreds of statues in the 36 caves. Now they worship empty caves. (Because they're holey?)

Old Stone Saint, near Spirit Mountain, is a granite statue of a Song Dynasty Taoist saint (some claim he is Lao Tzu, Taoism's founder). The fellow is 5.5 m. high and 7.3 m. wide. Legend has it that if you rub his nose you'll live 120 years; rub his eye and you'll reach 160.

They also used to say you'd die early if you rubbed his mouth, but this didn't go over well with tourists so now they've changed it to "Rub mouth, get good luck." But 1,000 years of rubbing Lao Tzu the wrong way was rubbing his nose away, so a few years back they fenced him off and hired a guard (though if you rub his palm with a few Yuan, you can still rub noses with the Old Stone Saint). Try it, and you'll never again take life for granite.

There seems to be a lot of rubbing going on all over China. In a narrow defile of Yunnan Province's Stone Forest, a guide told me, "Don't touch either side and you'll live to 100."

I brushed the left face, and he said, "No problem. You'll reach 95."

Then I lightly rubbed against the right side. My imperturbable guide assured me, "Now you'll at least live to 90." I guess he didn't want to rub me the wrong way.

The Little People Spirit mountain may well be "Fujian's Fairy land" because I've seen real fairies in Quanzhou.

As a child, I firmly believed in "little people"—like leprechauns, fairies, brownies, elves, civil service workers, husbands). I still believe they exist, especially after visiting Quanzhou, which has long been the marionette capital of China and has more puppets than Parliament.

Be sure to take in a puppet show, where Chinese puppeteers perform miracles with hand-painted wooden puppets, which strut and fret and dance across the stage with more abandon than Macbeth. (They use from 16 to over 30 strings!).

And visit a puppet factory (around the corner from the Overseas Chinese Hotel, on a small lane behind the KFC) and watch the uncannily lifelike woocden heads take shape, or girls embroidering the intricate costumes.

Also visit the Chen family's Puppet Museum (behind Ashab Mosque).

Zaytun Night Life Early travellers claimed that Zaytun was intoxicating, and no wonder, with travellers from all over the known world converging on this port city. You wanted it, Quanzhou had it. Marco Polo even said it was China's tattoo capital.

Quanzhou still comes to life at night, though I'm sure it's a lot tamer. Bright lights are strung through the trees, and across buildings and pagodas. And every night the city has traditional artists performing music or drama on stages at major intersections. We enjoy the streetside artists painting, or sketching caricatures in charcoal, or transforming names into beautiful works of calligraphy. Vendors offer snacks, both traditional and modern—everything from Xinjiang raisings and chestnuts to popcorn and cotton candy, and barbeque chicken.

And Quanzhou night markets are a shopper's paradise (and perhaps her husband's nightmare!). The city is also a haven for fortune tellers—once the lowest rung of Chinese society, right next to barbers. Some of them look pretty down on their luck; maybe they're not allowed to tell their own fortunes?

Water World (Shuíshàng Lèyuán, 水上乐园) in Quanzhou is a real hit with our family. You won't find Kevin Costner here, but you will find the wee folk—and the big ones too. Our family spent 11 hours one summer day on water slides, and paddling boats, and playing in the tidal pool (though I've had bigger waves in our bathtub). Water World's sole drawback is that there is neither escape nor respite from the nonstop Chinese pop music played at 200 decibels from speakers strung up every ten feet. Earplugs, perhaps?

After a nice wet day, head home on the new Quanzhou-Xiamen Toll-way to recover from your sunburn. Or else head north to Luoyang Bridge…

Luoyang Bridge, just north of Quanzhou, was the first stone beam bridge in China. This 1,000-yr.-old 1.2 km. bridge may be one of the oldest examples of biological engineering: they wedged live oysters between the granite blocks to cement them with their secretions.

I asked how they trained the oysters to do that but they clammed up on me.

Legend has it that Cai Xiang tried ten times to lay the foundation, but each time it was swept away by the powerful tides. In frustration, he sent an officer to find the Sea God and ask advice. The officer returned from who knows where with a one word suggestion, "Venigar." Cai Xiang took it to mean, "Lay the foundation on the 21st." He did, and was successful, and ever since Chinese have said, "You may not believe a gentleman but you may well have belief in the Venigar."

Personally, I'd watch my purse with either one.

Not far way is the Five-Mile Bridge, a similar structure but longer - the longest in the world, in fact, during the Middle Ages. And it too has tales, but I'll cross that bridge if we ever get to it.

Sisters-in-Law Tower South of Quanzhou is Shíshī (石狮, Stone Lion) City, a modern center of commerce and industry and the garment capital of Fujian. A few kilometers south of Shishi, in Yakou, is one of the finest stretches of sand in China. After a day of sun and surf, visit the Sisters-in-Law Tower.

Legend has it that way back in the Song Dynasty (when Dehua pottery went for a Song and a dance), a man sailed forth to Southeast Asia to seek his fortune and promised to return in 3 years. His wife and sister missed him so badly that they piled up stones by the river and watched for him, year after year, but he never returned. The two girls died of grief, and the sympathetic villagers called the rock pile "Sisters-in-Law Tower." And somewhere along the line, the rock pile metamorphosed into a 4-story pagoda that is a landmark even today.

Anhai Manichaean Temple Near the Sisters-in-Law Tower is one of the world's last bastions of the Persian religion Manichaeism, "The Religion of Light"—an esoteric mix of Gnosticism, Zoroastrianism and Christianity.

Long before George Lucas wrote, "Use the Force, Luke!", the Persian founder Mani (216-276 A.D.) taught that existence is but the eternal battle between the two sides of good and evil, light and dark. He adopted elements of many religions, reasoning that each contained at least a grain of truth. Mani's malleable metaphysics appealed to St. Augustine, who followed the religion for a decade until his conversion to Christianity.

St. Augustine, as a youth, knew too well the eternal battle between good and evil. The intellectual genius partied by night and prayed by day, "God, grant me chastity—but not yet!" After his illegitimate teen-age son died, he entered the clergy, denounced Mani, and then became a bishop and a saint, though it is not clear whether he ever achieved chastity.

St. Augustine

The "Religion of Light" found increasing acceptance around Quanzhou for 600 years – until an Emperor snuffed the light out. Emperor Taizu, who ruled from 1368-1398, banned the Religion of Light because "ming"(明), the Chinese word for "light," also happened to be the name of the Ming Dynasty, and in one of the earliest arguments for intellectual property rights, the emperor decreed that only he could use the name. Thus was the world's very last stronghold of Mani's light extinquished, though locals continue even today to worship the Manichaeist deity in the Cao'an 'Thatched Nunnery' (which some take to be the popular Goddess of Mercy). This temple also boasts the last Manichaeist carving in China - of two angels holding lotus flowers and a cross (a combination of Greek, Persian and Chinese mythology).

It appears that the Persian's followers made their way into China in the late seventh century, at the same time as their arch rivals, the Moslems and the Nestorian Christians. The Manichaean Temple was built in 1339, after villagers had spent 26 years carving statues of Mani all over the cliffs of Huabiao Mountain. Evidently the artists didn't have a photo to go by, because Mani bears a striking resemblance to the standard issue Chinese deities found elsewhere - except that he sports four braided dreadlocks. Still, the statues are unlike any others in China.

Yang Amiao's Former Home (杨阿苗故居) **Avoid it!** Pascoe Trott, Chief Rep for Oxford Instruments up in Beijing, visited the place and received the rudest welcome imaginable from the man and woman out front playing mahjong. They said, "We did not invite you, and did not put the sign up. Get out!" When Pascoe tried photographing the house from the public highway, with a telephoto lens, the man ran after him, ready to "come to blows."

Quanzhou's city grandfathers should strike Mr. Yang's house from Quanzhou's "2,000 sites famous at home and abroad." But the indefatigable Mr. Trott said a sight not to be missed is the beautifully preserved Minnan Village just down the road. I've visited several times, and heartily concur.

Minnan Village Cultural Landmark (蔡资深建筑群) is just before Guanqiao, and 2 km west of the 324 highway. Pascoe Trott writes,

> "It consists of a small village of beautifully preserved 100 year old "Minnan" houses. They were all built at the same time with money from Mr Cai Zishen who had made it big in the Philippines. I heard about this place from an article in a Chinese travel magazine. I would say that it was well worth a visit. The curator / caretaker was very friendly and knowledgeable, and a 5th generation Cai himself. There are still about 200 people living in this tidily laid out settlement but of course many others have moved out to the city or newer homes. There are many beautifully preserved stone and wood carvings both inside and around the doorways…"

Nan'An Mayor and MBA Dean Wu Shi Nong enjoy local music

Just a few months back I visited the village with MBA Dean Wu Shi Nong (a Quanzhou native) and the Mayor of Nan'An. It was delightful. No wonder Minnan folk have a saying, "You can have lots of money but still not have a house like Mr. Cai." The sprawling complex is one vast museum of intricate carvings in stone, wood and tile. We toured the rooms, enjoyed Minnan tea, and then listened to some elderly musicians as they gave an impromptu performance.

Taoist-Confucian Temple Given that Taoism and Confucianism are poles apart in philosophy, it's surprising that DaDeng Island has a temple where pilgrims manage to worship both! Confusionism, perhaps? (Amusingly, a Quanzhou map actually shows a "Confusion Temple" in Anxi).

Unlike Confucianism, which emphasizes education to preserve absolute obedience, conformity, and standards, Taoism is the Montessori approach to enlightenment. Taoism means "The Way" (as New Testament Christianity was called "The Way"), and is based on the teachings of Lao Tzu in 6th Century B.C. China. Unlike rigid Confucianism, Taoism's Way is relative; there is no absolute right or wrong, no standards for behavior. The emphasis is individual freedom, loose government, and mystical experience.

Not surprisingly, the powers that be preferred Confucius to Lao Tzu—though not in Confucius' own lifetime:

> **Confucius** spent his youth mastering poetry and history classics, and the six arts (ritual, music, archery, charioteering, calligraphy and arithmetic). Then in his 30s, he became a teacher and devoted his life to insuring that Chinese for the next 3000 years followed suit.
>
> Confucius humbly claimed that he was an ordinary man of ordinary intellect, so all people could follow his lead in seeking perfection through study and conformity to society. The problem was that no one wanted to follow his lead because he was usually jobless, homeless, and half-starved.

Confucius' failures often ate at him. He once said, "It is these things that cause me concern: failure to cultivate virtue, failure to explore in depth what I have learned, inability to do what I know is right, and inability to reform myself when I have defects."

I think what really ate at him was his wife, because she too was usually homeless and half-starved – not exactly choice ingredients in the immortal's elixir of marital bliss.

While claiming to be just one of the boys, the unemployed Confucius also said he was unstoppable and immortal until his heavenly mandate was completed. "If Heaven does not intend this culture to be destroyed, then what can the men of K'uang do to me?"

Not much, except to keep him unemployed. So at age 56 he left the inhospitable leaders of Lu, who still weren't hiring, and spent the next 12 years traveling about with a slowly growing following. He returned home at age 67 and died 6 years later, leaving behind 3,000 disciples who were usually jobless, homeless and half-starved. But they kept alive the teachings dear to 2400 years of imperial hearts.

Confucians taught that moral community begins by cleaning up one's own backyard (and ignoring the emperor's). The foundation of society is filial piety. Obedience to father and elders and magistrates and emperor guarantees social order, stability, and peace; deviations of any kind insure anarchy.

They learned that lesson only too well.

A few centuries back, a young man saw a girl drowning in a river. He debated whether to save her, because society forbade young men, under penalty of death, from touching young women. In the end he leaped into the raging torrent, rescued her, and was promptly arrested. The magistrate said, "Saving life is good, but arbitrarily disobeying society's rules is not. You will not be killed, but for your dangerous precedent, you are banished for life."

Not much of a concession; for Chinese, banishment is worse than death.

Emperors have always loved Confucius's emphasis on obedience, but his warning that revolution would topple unjust governments never went over well. In 231 B.C., the emperor tried to eliminate Confucius' influence by destroying every book in China, but evidently he missed a few. Confucians crawled back out of the woodwork, regained the upper hand, and have been stacking China's deck ever since (while being careful to remove all the wild cards).

Jiuri Mountain (九日山) Starting point of the Maritime Silk Route, Jiuri (9th Day) Mtn in Nan'An is just west of Quanzhou City. Yanfu Temple, at the base, is Fujian's oldest Buddhist Temple, built during the 9th year of the Taikang of the Jin Dynasty (the barbarian-befuddling way of saying 288 A.D.).

My Chinese guide boasted, "Every meter of this cliff has ancient calligraphy!"

"We have the same thing in New York City subways," I said.

And to add to it, in 1991 a UNESCO Maritime Silk Road Expedition visited Jiuri Mtn. and left an English inscription, with signatures in many Western languages.

The Stone Buddha (石佛) is 300 years older than the Old

Stone Saint in Quanzhou. His head was destroyed during the Great Proletariat Cultural Revolution, but Hui'an artists replaced it with a cement head. I'm not sure why they didn't use stone, given that Hui'an artisans are masters of granite sculpting. Maybe they thought this material would help cement relationships. Or maybe they wanted the Stone Buddha to have more concrete ideas. Whatever the case, this is certainly one Buddha who won't take getting a head for granite.

Hui'an "…an out-of-the-way village, in the county of Hui'an, or Gracious Peace. The situation of this village is a most picturesque and beautiful one. Just outside of it, Toa-bu, or the "Great Mother" rises abruptly from the plain, and towers up amidst the peaks and mountain-tops that range themselves around it… In front of it there flows a stream that comes out of the heart of the mountain, its waters pure and sparkling, and as yet undefiled by their touch with the outer world. It never dries up, for its fountains repose deep in the bosom of those everlasting hills; and no summer's drought, nor fiery-faced sun can penetrate to where they lie. Its music, too, never dies out, for jutting rocks, and stones worn smooth, and curves and winding passages, and miniature falls make it sing an endless song."

MacGowan, *The Story of the Amoy Mission*, (1889, p.127)

Walled City of Chongwu

Hui'An（惠安）Beauties 'n Beaches Two hours north of Xiamen is the coastal village of Chongwu Town (崇武), one of only two ancient Chinese village walls still completely intact.

Ancient Chongwu, on the horn-shaped Chongwu Peninsula, was originally an easily defended sentry post prized by famous heroes like Koxinga. The first Ming emperor, Zhu Yuanzhang, changed the name to Chongwu, which means "advocation of arms" (the Emperor was a Republican?).

Although the typical concrete, glass and bathroom tile high rises are springing up outside the 1,000 year old battlements, within the walls the old town remains a maze of winding, narrow roads, less than 8 feet wide at points, apparently laid out to confuse enemy troops and foreign tourists.

The 2.4 km. Chongwu wall has 1,300 battlements, averages 7 meters in height, and has a 3.5 meter deep granite foundation. It is China's best preserved Ming Dynasty wall and made entirely of Hui'an's greatest natural resource: granite.

Day and night, throughout Hui' An, young and old chip away with stone and chisel to create everything from intricate temple dogs and garden lanterns to Mickey Mouse statues. They also build their homes of granite. I know for a fact they're cold in the winter—and the poor men have no one to snuggle up too, as you're about to learn...

Tougher than Hui'an Granite are Hui'an's hardworking women, who fascinate Chinese as much as they do foreigners. Because of Chongwu's isolated position, the ancient Baiyue inhabitants never quite assimilated into the Han culture, and much of their unique culture and dress still survives today. Many a Chinese social scientist has camped out in Chongwu, studying their unique fashions and strange marriage customs.

The women's colorful jackets are tight and short, leaving bare bellies above skintight black hip huggers that flare out baggily on the legs. While bellies are bare, heads are almost completely covered by colorful kerchiefs and yellow bamboo hats that are often decorated with emblems resembling the butterflies that their ancestors once worshipped.

Chinese call this bare belly/covered head custom "democratic bellies and feudalistic heads." I think it's just a tantalizing "revenge."

Legend has it that long ago, a young girl refused to marry a wealthy man so he bound her and married her anyway. (Now that's how to tie the knot!) ①. Today, the designs around shirts' sleeves and waists remind girls of their tragic ancestor's bonds, and their wedding traditions (once common throughout China but disappearing elsewhere) are a form of eternal revenge upon all men.

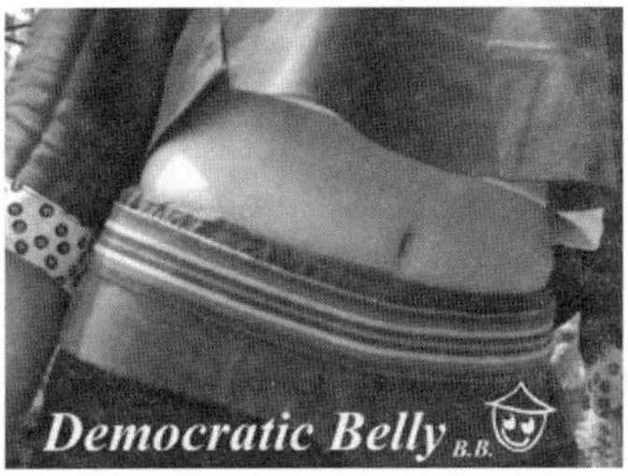
Democratic Belly B.B.

According to ancient custom, bride and groom may not stay together on their wedding night. The groom stays in a friend's house. On day two, the bride pays respects to the groom's family and gives gifts to the elders. On day three, the groom's sister leads the bride to the communal well to draw two buckets of water. After five days of obeying various customs, she returns to her parents' home. Bride and groom are not allowed to live together until she bears a child. But I conceive a problem: when could she conceive?

Until she has a child, she is neither allowed to stay with her husband nor even to talk with him. If she meets him on the street she must treat him like a stranger, and if her husband visits her home, she must avoid him, waiting in back until he leaves.

The newlyweds are allowed to stay together only 3 times a year: Spring Festival, Grave Sweeping Day, and Mid-Autumn Festival.

I bet they really make hay on the holidays.

Hui'an lassies may be bothersome brides but they are also indefatigable laborers. They clean house by night and by day lug ponderous loads of rock or grain on baskets slung over their deceptively petite shoulders. Meanwhile, the men fish, or chisel stone in quarries, or hawk victims for their motorcycle taxis, or hang out in tea shops moaning because their bride just told them, "Not this year, dear. I have a headache."

And there are other restrictions on marriage that apply not just to Chongwu folk but to everyone in China. Just inside one of the ancient city gates is a blue enamel sign with row upon row of tiny, white Chinese characters explaining in detail the rules governing marriage and child-bearing. Girls must be at least 20 years old to marry, and boys must be 22. To bear children, girls must be at least 20 years and 10 months, and boys must be at least 22 years and 10 months.

I'd have never imagined that boys bear babies at any age. This may explain China's burgeoning population, or how Chongwu couples have children when they don't sleep together. Men just grin and *bear* it.

---

① Tie the knot: euphemism for "get married" (another is 'get hitched')

Religion is a big part of Chongwu life, and with wives like theirs, I see why. On festivals, Chongwu people light candles and incense and offer sacrifices in the Temple of the 12th Lord, but nowadays, many also attend the newly renovated and expanded Protestant church, which was first built in the 1880s. As late as 1995, members sat on pews made of tree trunks split in half, but now the church has been rebuilt and expanded, and equipped with genuine pews, much to my derriere's delight.

Hui'an Art Hui'an folk have been stone masons for at least 1700 years, when they carved a local granite tombstone for a Mr. Lin. And folks have long come from all over Asia to buy stone carvings, furniture, art.

Take a nice statue home in your carry on.

Shadow Carving is a recently developed Hui'an stone technique. They can reproduce virtually any painting or photograph on a smoothly polished marble slab by tapping out the design, dot by dot, and then coloring it in. The carvings of Michael Jordan look like they could pop right off the stone!

Give them a family photo and they'll copy it for you, and mail it to your home! Try the little green souvenir shop just to the right of the stone gate with the elephants in front. An 8 × 10 will run about 200 to 300, depending on the quality desired. But make sure the photo is top notch, or they can't reproduce it.

Walled City Most Chinese tourists come for 'official' tourist stuff, like the 500 new statues portraying events in Chinese history and literature. But I think the best part of the walled city is… the Walled City.

Enter the gate nearest the church (the original built in the 1880s). Hang a right at the "T" intersection and go all the way to the temple at the end. Note the tailor you pass on the left. He uses a 100-year-old Min River sewing machine—much the same as the Butterfly Brand made today. But why reinvent the wheel?

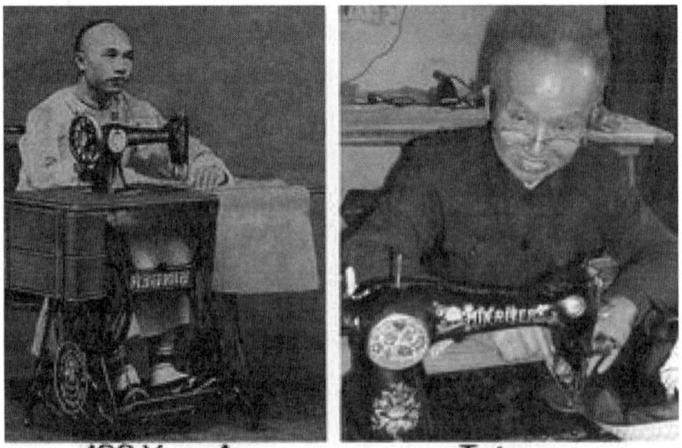

100 Years Ago Today

They work (though he said the news one have cheap plastic parts that break, whereas his is a real workhorse).

Ascend the wall, and head left to the lighthouse, from which you get a great view of the walled city, and of the large crescent of a beach, with its fine white sand (Hui'an has miles of beautiful beaches). Then either return the way you came, or walk along the top of the wall.

As you explore the city, you'll pass unique old architecture—homes that are hundreds of years old new. Though the people live much like their forebears, folks like Granny Chen also have the most up-to-date kitchens to engage in that most Chinese of all endeavours—cooking, and eating! And indeed, the Chens have long been making and selling Chongwu's famous fish rolls; buy a few *jin* (1.1 lbs.), take them home, slice them thin, fry them, and enjoy.

Dehua (德化) **Porcelain Paradise,** in the mountains northwest of Quanzhou, was one of ancient China's 4 great porcelain , and home of the famous Blanc d' Chin (white porcelain). Since 1949, archeologists have found over 180 ancient porcelain kilns, dating from the ancient Song Dynasty to the recent Qing. These massive kilns have fired the imagination of guidebook authors like the man who wrote of the 17 chamber Qudougong Kiln, "Such a large-scale kiln of ancient times looks like a dragon crouching on a hill, magnificently."

That dragon went to pot, but modern Dehua still offer every porcelain product imaginable if you have a limited imagination: fine dishes, statues of deities and demons, and vases big enough to hide in.

Some factories will give tours, even souvenirs.

The drive is as interesting as the destination. The nicely paved concrete road snakes through valleys and past unique villages. One village is dusted in crimson, as if the Red Tide had become a red snowfall. They make incense (I'd be incensed[①] if I had to live with that; at the very least I'd see red[②]).

I also enjoy watching the folks in the kilns making bricks—endless rows of them, formed by hand in wooden molds.

Robert H. Blumenfield, an American collector of Dehua's blanc de Chine, wrote "Blanc de Chine—the Great Porcelain of Dehua." Amazon has it for $52.50 (compared with the $75 retail price).

Supplement
Philippine Chinese Hero from Quanzhou

Jose Rizal was born June 19th in Calamba, Phlippines, and died December 30th, 1896, in Manila. This patriot, physician and intellectual was an inspiration to many generations of Filipinos.

Rizal was the son of a wealthy landowner on the island of Luzon, and his mother was one of the most educated Filipino women at that time. Rizal studied medicine in the University of Madrid and became leader of the Filipino students in Spain. He pursued reform of Spanish rule in the Philippines, though he

① Incensed: angry, furious
② See red: angry, furious (as in, "The bull saw red.")

stopped short of demanding Filipino independence of Spain. In Rizal's eyes, the Philippine's primary enemy was not Spain, which was undergoing dramatic reform, but the Catholic faction that clung to power in Spain's impoverished colony.

Rizal continued his medical studies in Paris and Heidelberg, and in 1886 he published his first novel, in Spanish. "Noli e Tangere" exposed the evils' of the Catholic friars' ruleli much as Uncle Tom's Cabin brought to light the evils of America's slavery.

Rizal returned to the Philippines in 1892 to found a nonviolent reform society, La Liga Filipina, in Manila, but was deported to northwest to Mindanao, where during his four years of exile he continued scientific research and founded a school and hospital.

A nationalist secret society, the Katipunan, launched a revolt against Spain in 1896. Though Rizal had absolutely no connections with Katipunan, he was arrested, found guilty of sedition, and executed before a firing squad in Manila. i The evening before he was executed, he wrote the Spanish masterpiece, "Mi Ultimo Adios" (My Last Farewell"), which helped Filipinos realize that there was no alternative to independence from Spain.

Rizal International Shrine in Jinjiang In 2002, Jinjiang (a suburb of Quanzhou) invested 10 million Yuan to create the 5-hectare Rizal Memorial Park, with its 18.61 meter high statue of Rizal (much higher than the 12-meter statue of Rizal in Manial). Filipino business leaders invested an additional 2 million Yuan. Filipino House Speaker Jose de Venecia said that China's park was a "great symbol of the 1,000-year-old friendship between our two nations," and, "This Rizal Park in China helps elevate the status of our Philippine national hero Dr. Jose Rizal as a hero for the whole Asian region."

The park will become a must-see for Filipino-Chinese, 80% of whom, like Rizal himself, trace their roots to Southern Fujian.

Quanzhou Specialties

Hui'an Stone carvings and Shadow Carvings. Family portrait?

Puppet Heads. The hand carved camphor wood heads are rapidly giving way to mass produced plastic puppets, so buy them while you can (and while you can afford them).

From block of camphor to puppet head

Silk Flower Lanterns. Quanzhou Silk Lanterns are legendary. Visit the city on Lantern Festival (15th day of the Chinese New Year).

Dehua Porcelain—a limitless variety of fine China, as well as the ivory white porcelain figurines.

Anxi Rattan and Bamboo—several factories produce quality baskets, shelving and furniture, even made to order. Check the internet for sites.

Edible Specialties

As in most of China, most specialties are edible.
Those that are not edible are called medicine and ingested anyway

Old Fan Zhi Magic Lees—a concoction of corn, beans, and over 50 Chinese herbs, it is said to cure everything from stomach and spleen ailments to indigestion deng deng and perhaps dung dung.

Qingyuan Tea Cake , made from herbs and tea, has for a century been reputed to increase appetite, strengthen the spleen, (Chinese seem to have a thing about spleens), aid digestion, etc.

Anxi Oolong Tea—the tea that sparked the American Revolution—we threw it overboard during the Boston Tea Party. I can see why that would have tea'd the British off; I'd have been madder than the hatter myself.

Yongchun Preserved Vinegar, a black vinegar reputed to be one of China's "Four Famous Vinegars," has been a Quanzhou staple since the Song Dynasty. But I'd be careful with vinegar. "Drink vinegar" is a Chinese euphemism for "jealousy" and infers one's spouses is unfaithful.

Shishi Sweet Rice Cakes Dating from the Ming Dynasty, these are said to be some of the best rice cakes, but I wouldn't know.

I prefer German chocolate cakes myself.

Dehua Famous Alcohol—brewed with herbs, it is "pure, mellow, fragrant, and "curative effect is prominent." Drink enough and you won't care if you're cured or not.

Hui'an Beer – a favorite with seafood

Chapter 19

Earthen Hakka Fortresses (Round Houses)

I have visited the down-to-earth, well-rounded folks in the earthen round houses at least two dozen times. I prefer castles that Hakka still dwell in, but official tourist traps also have their advantages. English speaking guides can explain the unique architecture, customs, history, etc. You can also spend the night in a roundhouse, and enjoy the local cuisine.

My favorite itinerary is the mountain road to Nanjing's roundhouses, then over the mountains to Yongding's tourist area, and returning on the Longyan-Xiamen highway. It can be done in one killer day, but best to spend the night in a roundhouse, or nearby guesthouse.

A Hakka elder told me the houses were round to keep out bandits and warlords (and probably traveling salesmen). I replied, "No, it was so your wives could not catch you in a corner!"He grinned and said, "Makes sense!" His wife did not smile, so it may have been no joke.

Nowadays, only about 360 earthen houses are round; about 4,000 are square. Some square dwellings in Northern Fujian are over 1,000 years old, but don't look a day over 980.

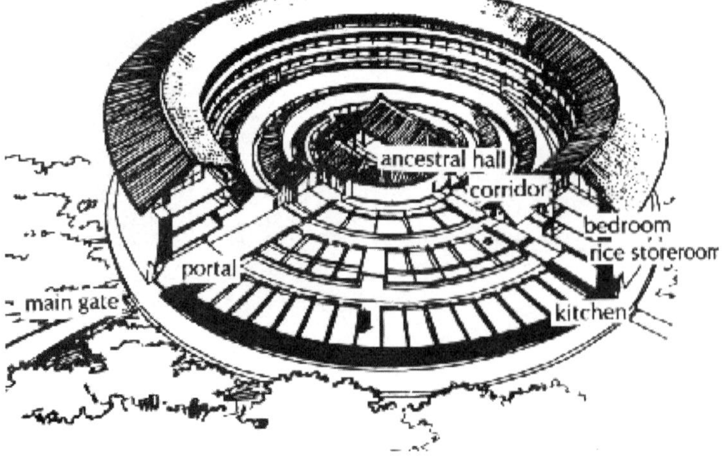

Earthen fortresses house extended Hakka families numbering 300 and 400. These massive structures are rammed into shape layer by layer, using an esoteric mixture of raw earth, sand, lime, glutinous rice and brown sugar, all reinforced by "bones" of wood and bamboo.

Roundhouses are generally 3 story affairs, with first floor for cooking, second for storing grains and grannies and grandpas, and third floor living quarters for the spryer younger folk.

As added protection, only the third floor has external windows.

Roundhouses boast central courtyards in which families socialize, work, or eat. They usually have a well. A basketball court would help.

Archaeologists the world over have studied this unique Hakka architecture, and the culture behind it. Earthen architecture is relatively inexpensive, very durable, low maintenance, ecologically clean, aesthetically pleasing, and acoustically and thermally insulated. It is no wonder Hobbits like to live in holes in the ground.

The Pentagon folks were shocked when roundhouses showed up on satellite photographs! From space, they looked like missile silos.

I asked one roundhouse dweller if the satellite dish on the roof was for their missile guidance system. He was shocked. "No! It's for television! We don't—"

"—I'm just joking!"

I guess that joke bombed.

Prosperity Castle (Fǘxìng Lǒu,福兴楼), my favorite, was built in 1963 by the Xiao (肖) Clan. I asked them what it cost to build this magnificent three story castle and they said "Nothing! The earth and wood were all local. It just took a lot of labor." A lot of love, too, I could tell, judging from the care that had been spent on the fine wood doors, windows, and railings.

Prosperity Castle is a "real" roundhouse, lived in by an extended family that greets eve unexpected foreign devils with a hearty laugh and, "Have some tea!"

I've packed Toy Ota with my MBA students and visited Prosperity Castle at least a dozen times, and even filmed two documentaries of the place. Most Chinese have never seen them and are as fascinated as we are.

If you too visit the Xiao Clan, take a generous bag of sweets for the beautiful children! They'll of course politely refuse, so give it to the granny, who will pocket a bit to gum to death later, and distribute the rest to the kids.

Hanker for more Hakka lore? Then make your way west to Changting, the "Little Red Shanghai," and to Shibi Village near the Jiangxi border, but before you do, pick up a copy of my "Fujian Adventure," still available at less discerning bookstores everywhere!

And now... on to Longyan and the X-rated mountains of Liancheng.

Chapter 20

Longyan 龙岩– Dragon Crag

Longyan, in S.W. Fujian, is where Mao began his Long March (just before the Short April?). This enchanting 19,000 km^2 area, home to 2.5 million people, and ancestral home of over 200,000 Overseas Chinese, boasts primordial mountains and forests, and rivers cascading through lush valleys.

Amoy Tiger, Longyan, Dec. 2003

Amoy Tigers vanished from Amoy, but you can still find them in the Meihua Nature Preserve—a biological wonderland with over 1500 kinds of plants, hundreds of insects, and a Noah's ark variety of animals, including leopards, black bears, and of course, thanks to a USD 17.6 million project, the magnificent Amoy Tiger (these kitties can weigh up to 390 pounds). In addition to breeding the few protected tigers, the project has "rewilded" tigers that were born in China and grew up in South Africa, where they were taught to hunt in the wild. To learn more, or to make contributions, visit, **http://www.savechinastigers.org/sct-adopt.htm**

Longyan is also a geological gold mine, boasting South China's largest deposit of iron, as well as gold, manganese, tungsten, etc. In addition to mining and agriculture (tobacco is the biggest crop), West Fujian is into electronics, metallurgy, machinery, forestry, building materials, chemicals, textiles, food, and light industries. The area exports handmade paper, rabbit fur, pepper, dried mushrooms, smoked plums, and peanuts. But the big claim to fame is Wuping County's dried pig gallbladder. The brochure claims,

> "Dried pig gallbladder contains various carbohydrates and vitamins, especially it is the best gift and delicious dish to be given or to entertain guests and friends with."

It would take a lot of gall, and guts, to dish that out to friends.

The **Chengang Wine (沉缸酒) Factory,** established in 1957 in Longyan, just off the 319 Highway, is well worth a visit. I've toured the place thrice, and while the speeches can be murder by monologue, the factory tour is fascinating. The Apostle Paul may have meant Chengang Wine when he urged young Timothy to no longer drink water but take a little wine for his stomach's sake. The 200-year-old recipe for Chengang Wine has 31 Chinese medicines that cure anything that ails you, and a few things that don't.

The 500 employees and 96 technicians put out 10,000 tons of the sweet yellow wine each year.

Add: #78 Shuangquan Rd. Xinluo District, Longyan. Tel: (0597)221-1222.

Gutian (古田), just north of Longyan city, is where Mao held his 1929 congress in a small school (hence the Mao "school of thought"). Dress in a PLA uniform and have your photo taken by Mao's old table-cum-desk and the ancient tattered posters of Lenin and Marx. It was in this general area that Mao wrote, "A single spark can start a prairie fire."

This begs the questions, if one spark can ignite a prairie fire, why does it take an entire box of matches to light a campfire?

To really get into the spirit of things, read this pulse-pounding paragraph from the official Gutian brochure:

> "Nowadays, step into Minxi this sacred land, tracing the footprint of revolution herald, and we still can feel the warm of kindling which set the prairie of ablaze and touch the pulse of revolution struggle which was blistering the heaven, boiling the mountains, and shaking heaven and earth and taste indeed that the revolution leader and the herald they rushed around, searched about and conquered numerous difficulties and endured all kinds of hardships and die for nations and natives with a generosity."

Well, I'm sold.

Yongfu Village of Flowers (永福) in **Zhangping (漳平) County**, elevation 755 meters, is *the* place to feast your eyes on exotic orchids and your nose on camellia, and tantalize your taste buds with local teas and samples of the excellent pears, oranges, kumquats and tangerines. Visit during the annual Flower Fair (6th day of the 1st month of the Chinese New Year).

Also check out their bamboo hats, rattan furniture, and unique paper cuts, and historical sites like Liuxiu Tower and Changqing Castle.

Liancheng （连城） resembles North Fujian's whimsical Wuyi Mountain, but it is much closer to Xiamen - a mere hour north of Longyan (though with Fujian's new roads, even Wuyi is no longer that far away—a 7 hour drive today, compared to 35 hours in 1993!).

I thought ancient Chinese artists were high or drunk when they painted surrealistic mountains amidst seas of mist, but not so. Liancheng really looks like the paintings, with absolutely breathtaking mountains, lakes and falls.

Roots 'n Doors of Life Rental boats touring the 5 km Shimen Lake below Mount Lianfeng (Lotus Peak) cruise past strange jutting peaks and narrow clefts that bear an uncanny resemblance to various private parts of the human anatomy. Locals, of course, caught on quick, and gave them names that leave little to the imagination. For example, the brochure for "Root of life" peak, and the tall narrow cave, "Door of life," relates:

> "Root of life (生命之根) about 60m high… and Life's Door (生命之门) of Shimen Lake are standing and facing each other, which can be rated as superb scenes of Guanzai scenic spot."

I suggest a **Liancheng Birds'n Bees Exhibit**. Better yet, isolate the sensual scenery until China's population problem is resolved.

Sibao Printing. Liancheng was one of ancient China's four great printing centers, thanks to forests of camphor (to carve the printing blocks), pine (burned to produce soot for the ink), wild animal fur for brushes, and bamboo to produce the fine snow-white paper for which the area is still famous even today.

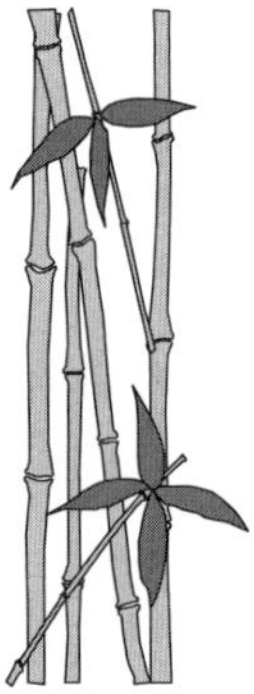

Bamboo Fujian's famous Anxi tea has figured in everything from the Mad Hatter's Tea Party to that even madder Tea Party in Boston, but Fujian's biggest money maker has been not tea but humble bamboo.

Bamboo is not a tree but a species of gigantic and graceful grass, and is so indispensable that Chinese artists portray it more frequently than anything else. As an ancient Chinese poet opined, "Better to live without meat than without bamboo."

Chinese ascribe to bamboo the attributes of a superman—chastity, honesty, gentleness, humbleness. The bamboo is strong, yet hollow and empty, even as "a humble man is not filled with his own importance."

Chinese claimed that bamboo is used to make a thousand products, and I believe it. A brief list includes: shirts, shoes, chairs, tables, dishes, shelves, scaffolds, bridge piers, houses, pens, hats, rakes, chairs, tables, stools, beds, musical instruments, dippers, pipes to blow the fire, strainers, steamers, chopsticks, kettle cleaners, dust pans, brooms, drain pipes, handles, smoking pipes, back scratchers (which Chinese aptly dub, "not call man"), pig baskets, cradles, toys, fences, gates, rope, screens, flour mills, hen coops, bird cages, tally sticks, lanterns, knitting needles, curtains, and umbrellas. To top it off, bamboo shoots, whether stir-fried or pickled, are delicacies of the first order. And finally, no plant panders to a panda's palate better than bamboo. (Try saying that last line 3 times fast).

Bamboo Paper… is treasured by artists because it is soft, absorbent, and snow white. The bamboo is felled in August and chopped into small chunks, and workers sing while rhythmically pounding it to pieces. They soak the pieces in a lime pond for half a month before removing and cleaning them, and boiling them for a week. Then more pounding and singing, after which the fibers are washed, and stirred to a pulp.

The most exacting of the 72 steps in bamboo papermaking is scooping the pulp onto a bamboo screen held by two people, who swing carefully, expertly, to spread the pulp out evenly. When the pulp has dried, they cut it into squares of smooth, white paper—provided that no one has cursed it with a slip of the tongue.

There are many superstitious customs associated with papermaking. Workers are fed white tofu so the paper will also be white. It is forbidden to speak the word 'black' or 'protrusion,' lest the paper become spotted, or not be smooth. And papermakers cover their bases by worshipping Cai Lun, the legendary creator of paper and tutelary god of papermakers. Before Cai Lun came along, scholars wrote on tortoise shells, bones and metal, and later moved on to bamboo slips and wooden tablets. Silk was also used, but it was too dear for any but the Emperor. Eventually, Cai Lun discovered how to make paper from a pulp of hemp, bits of rope, rags and old fishing nets, and he has been worshipped ever since by papermakers and the bureaucratic devotees of the cult of triplication.

If you're sold on paper, buy some in Liancheng. This city's Xuan paper is, according to their report, "the best paper for calligraphy and drawing and it is an elegant gift for noted public figures."

Enchanting Changting – Little Red Shanghai

"China's two most beautiful small cities are Fenghuang in Henan and Changting in Fujian."
Rewi Alley

I did not even mention Changting in the first issues of Amoy Magic, but once I'd visited the place a few times, I gave this delightful little mountain town 25 pages in "The Fujian Adventure."

An hour northwest of Longyan, on the Jiangxi Province border, Changting straddles the Ting River, mother river of the Hakka people. "Hakka" means "Guest People." Over 1,000 years ago they fled to Southern China from the central plains and settled down as "guests," and they still call themselves guests 1,000 years later.

Hakka (architects of the earthen round houses), are a unique and headstrong people, but quick to point out that they are not a minority but bona fide Han Chinese. They take great pains to trace their ancestry back dozens of generations, and in the town of Shibi (just north of Changting, in Sanming), the Hakka Ancestral Temple has thousands of records of lineages. When I visited Shibi, one fellow excitedly pointed out the ancestral records for my adopted name of Pan. He was shocked when the tour guide explained to him that I was a foreigner, not a real Pan (though he reluctantly admitted that my blond hair and blue eyes had aroused his suspicions).

Changting's attraction is three-fold: people, places, and fine Hakka Cuisine. All Chinese are hospitable, greeting you with "You're here! Come in, have some tea," but Changting folk bend over backwards to make you feel at home.

Babushka and Family

My host, the award-winning photographer Hu Xiaogang (胡晓钢, nicknamed "Babushka" because he came from N.E. China and was blond as a child), led me right into people's homes without so much as a knock or how do you do. Babushka said, "They don't mind. Their doors are open."

I learned this was true in every sense of the word.

They served us tea, and showed us about the centuries old homes. It seemed every family had a side business—making matches, or candles, or miniature paper umbrellas, or wooden handled brushes. No wonder their overseas Hakka relatives are so successful. They are entrepreneurs of the first order.

They are also fine cooks! Hakka food is some of the best I've had, and Changting's cuisine has won many a national award. There is even a Chinese cookbook devoted entirely to Changting specialties, which include the mouth watering Hetian chicken. I've had so-called Hetian chicken in many other places, but never anything to match what they serve up in Changting.

Changting's sites range from the natural beauty at the mouth of the Ting River to delightful walled Hakka villages like Tufang. Here are some favorites:

Tingzhou Hakka Museum (汀州客家博物馆) has Hakka exhibits in the left hall and revolutionary exhibits in the right hall. The building behind the garden is the former revolutionary headquarters. All fascinating, but no Chinese subtitles below displays, so you'll need a guide, like the lovely Miss Hong who led me about. Changting people (like everyone else in Fujian) boast the prettiest girls in the province, and the museum's Miss Hong was a runner up in a national beauty contest.

The two trees in the central courtyard, by the way, are 1,000 years old, and said to be male and female lovers.

South Avenue (南大街) is a delightful old street with ancient homes, and a restored Tang Dynasty gate and pavilion (Sānyuán Gě, 三元阁). For a great look at yesteryear, check out the home at #105 South Street (and have them show you the loft where beautiful young Hakka maids were kept until they were married).

Carpenter Alley （唐宋古街） When I was in the U.S. Air Force in Taiwan, a favorite pastimes was visiting the woodcarving village. I spent a small fortune on furniture and carvings, most of which I sent home to my parents and sister. Alas, it is not so easy, for some reason, to find such bargains in the mainland, but I was happy to learn that Changting (and Xianyou, near Putian on the coast) has plenty of woodcarvers. As I talked to one craftsman, I learned why they are hard to find. The work is hard, the pay is relatively poor. He told me that he enjoyed the art, that it was more like a hobby than a job—but his son had already left home to find better employ in Guangdong province, leaving his father behind to lumber along in the wood business.

Hakka Mother (客家母亲) Carpenter Alley ends near the river; the statue in a small park across the river is the Hakka Mother, erected in 1995. Hakka never adopted foot binding, preferring instead the strong robust women who were as capable in the fields as in the home. It was the strength of Hakka women that made it possible for so many of the men to seek, and find, their fortunes abroad, and today, Hakka from all over the world return to West Fujian every October 28th to pay homage to the Hakka Mother.

Southern Meditation Temple (Nánchán Si, 南禅寺) Local Buddhists leveled an entire mountain to prepare the perfect fengshui for this mammoth temple complex. When completed in 2,010, this 50 million Yuan complex will be the largest in Jiangxi, Fujian and Guangdong provinces.

Three temples, on three different levels, each have their own idol, including a large Buddha carved from pure white jade. (We foreigners usually think of jade as green, but in fact it comes in many colors).

The Buddhist Abbess asked me if Xiamen University had a religion department, and if I had interest in helping to start one. Given that Xiamen has China's oldest Protestant Church, and that Quanzhou is UNESCO's World Museum of Religion—maybe I should pass the plate for a collection.

Changting has a Confucian temple that, according to locals, has been miraculously free of cobwebs since built in 1133 A.D. And though landlocked, Changting also has a massive temple complex for sea goddess Mazu, the rationale being that until this century, the Ting River was the only means of transportation.

Church of the Revolution The London Missionary Society opened the Gospel Hospital (福音医院) on East Gate St. (Dōngmén Jiē, 东门街) in 1908. In 1925 it became the Red Army hospital, and a foreign missionary doctor became a local hero because of his support of the Communist party—and became he delivered one Mao's sons. The church was, for a short period, Revolutionary headquarters, and Zhou Enlai had his office and bedroom in a small room upstairs in back. It's quite sobering to walk through the old rooms, which are now warehouses, and realize the historical of the meetings held in this little church 70 years ago. The elderly ladies who live in an apartment to the left of the church are delighted to have visitors and will happily show you around.

Hakka Hamlet of TuFang (涂坊) I was delighted to learn that the model of a Hakka walled village in the Hakka Museum was based on a real village only an hour's drive East of Changting, so Babushka and I saddled up Toy Ota and we headed to Tufang village. I felt like I was blazing new trails for Laowai until Tufang's headman told me that an American businessman had opened a factory there. It turned out to be Bill Job—resident of Xiamen since 1987! (Ironically, Bill had invited me to visit his factory that day, but I had planned a trip to Changting, and so declined).

Changting is more isolated and less populated than Yongding so Hakka did not need to build three story fortresses; many are only one story high, and some are only partially enclosed (giving rise to the name "cow horn village").

I was surprised when Babushka had me stop at the Chuanxinzou Stables farmstead, (穿心走马楼) in Yang KengCun Hamlet (洋坑村). The photographer had discovered, only recently, that the walls inside the deserted buildings were covered with revolutionary slogans and political cartoons from the 20s or 30s. "These should be in museums!" he complained. "Vandals are destroying them and soon they'll be gone."

I tried to take photos, but it was too dim and I had no flash. I hope they're still there next time I visit. Or maybe I can get Bill Job to take photos, provided he knows how to use a camera. He and his wife Kitty are from Tennessee, so you never know.... (That's why he went into business instead of teaching at Xiamen University. Just imagine Chinese students trying to speak English like they do in Tennessee!).

Other Changting Sites

Xiamen University's Former Campus (厦门大学校本部旧址) When the Sino-Japanese war during the 30s and 40s, Xiamen University hid out in Changting for 8 years. (Which is when the lady at the Protestant church moved to Changting).

Tingzhou Hakka Research Institute (Zhōngguó Tīngzhōu Kèjiā Yánjīu Zhōngxīn, 中国汀州客家研究中心)

Tingzhou Ancient City Wall (Tīngzhōu Gǔchéng Qíang, 汀州古城墙)
Tang Dynasty, at least 1200 years old.

Zhongshan Park and the Qiu Bai Pavilion (Qīubái Tīng, 秋白亭).

Every two-ox town in China has a Zhongshan Park (named after Sun Yat-sen, but called Lenin Park during the Soviet Chinese days). The Qiu Bai Pavilion is named after Qiu Bai, the young revolutionary martyr. To the rear of the Hakka Museum you can see where he was imprisoned, and where he was shot.

Hakka Girls. Everywhere—but I didn't look ***that*** closely, Susan Marie.

Ancient Well (Lǎo Gǔjǐng, 老古井) Changting's oldest well, considered a miracle because it never dries up, whatever the conditions. On top of that, while Mao ZeDong lived in Changting, every morning he used the well to wash his face, brush his teeth, and clean his clothes (not necessarily in that order). And to make the well healthier, he brought in a well specialist, which I thought was a well-meaning gesture.

Chaodou Rock's Shuiyun Temple. The Buddha is said to have his back to tourists because he's piqued that so few people repent and begin life anew.

And enjoy the rest of fascinating Fujian!

A few years ago, I wrote and filmed a 62-part Fujian TV series about my favorite places in Fujian—and had we not been limited by time and money, I probably could have written 100 more. With its unique history and culture, and enchanting mountains and valleys, Fujian should easily be the most interesting province for any foreigner who really understood what it has to offer.

Visit Putian and its ancient Shaolin monastery, or Fuzhou, the 2200 year old birthplace of Chinese maritime shipbuilding. Or visit Ningde and the otherworldly Taimu Mountains, with a 1000-year-old Manichean shrine perched on top. You can literally walk on water in Baishuiyang, then visit the carp-worshippers of Zhouning—and Wuyi mountain is a wonderful of historic and geographic treasures, and a biological diversity that attracted French naturalists over 200 years ago. And of course there's Sanming, with China's largest reclining Buddha, the famous Shaxian foods, beautiful underground caverns, a Stone Forest, etc.

But there is far too much too include in this book. Check our websites or other books for more information.

Sanming's magnificent "Anzhen Castle." By Zhu Qingfu

Chapter 21

Intro to Chinese Cuisine & Tea

One should eat to live, not live to eat.
Molière (1622—1673)

Molière never had Chinese food.
Bill Brown (1956—?)

An earnest Běijīng reporter asked me, "Why'd you move to China?"

I earnestly responded, "Because Chinese food is too expensive in America." It wasn't entirely a jest.

People the world over love Chinese food, and where better to get it than China, where 1.3 billion people are living proof that Eve was not Chinese (for had Eve been Chinese, she'd have tossed the apple and eaten the snake①).

Chinese greet one another not with, "How are you?" but with, "Have you eaten yet?" Americans may eat to live, but Chinese live to eat, and if we summed up China in a nutshell, we could engrave the nut with "Food"—provided we got to the nut before some Chinese gastronome stir-fried and ate it.

China has always had a love affair with food, but only recently have peasants even in remote villages begun to share the Horn 'O Relative Plenty. A few years back, I visited a remote mountain hamlet, which I reached after a rocky boat crossing, a torturous bus ride, a jaunt on a 3-wheel tractor, and a two-mile hike. Villagers who had never seen a foreigner kept their aplomb and greeted me with their cheery, "You've come!" A farmer invited me in, and apologized for an impromptu lunch that included fresh fish, duck, pork, tofu, stir-fried rice noodles, and various vegetables. Their 'simple' fare would have set me back a small fortune in Los Angeles' Chinatown.

The Evolution of Chinese Cuisines

Food has been China's avocation ever since the first mythical hero, hunter/fisherman Fúxī（伏羲）, invented the kitchen and cooking. At least 3,019 years before Christ, Chinese in Xī'ān's Bànpō Village（西安半坡）feasted on steamed chicken, carp and elephant. And in 700 B.C., Chinese chefs wowed emperors with exotic bitter melon soup, and lamb stewed with sugar cane.

① A Philippine Chinese said that I was not entirely correct; if Eve had been Chinese, she'd have eaten the snake and ***sold*** the apple!

The Hàn Dynasty (Hàncháo, 汉朝, 206 B.C.-220 A.D.) gave China flourmills, noodles and tofu, and the Tángcháo Dynasty (唐朝, 618-907 AD) saw the advent of the wok and stir-frying. But it was an overabundance of food during the Song Dynasty (Sòngcháo, 宋朝, 960-1279 AD) that fuelled the explosion of culinary innovation.

Even Lǎowài influenced Chinese cuisine. The Manchus left behind the winter hot pot now popular throughout China, but adapted in Xiàmén to feature seafood instead of mutton. And chili peppers introduced through Portuguese Macao helped ignite Sìchuān's fiery fare.

A few millennia of culinary evolution has given Chinese cuisine a diversity unimaginable for simple American souls such as myself, for whom variety is baked potato instead of mashed, or a side of canned peas – never such common but delectable Chinese delicacies as pea plant leaves or spinach roots. But for all its infinite diversity, most Chinese food fits roughly in five (some say "eight") basic schools: Běijīng, Sìchuān, Shànghǎi, Fújiàn and Guǎngdōng (most popular abroad).

There are also hundreds of local styles. Fújiàn cuisine is sweeter in the south, saltier in the north, and heavy on sweet potato, rice flour noodles, taro and peanuts in the west. (**Warning:** never eat taro with beef. It's taro-bull).

Běijīng Cuisine (Běijīng Cài, 北京菜) Tofu and wheat, rather than rice, are staples in Běijīng, where vendors sell steamed breads, buns stuffed with pork and vegetables, and Chinese dumplings stuffed with garlic, cabbage, pork, onions and MSG. One popular Northern dish is "Beggar's Chicken" (Jiàohuā Jī, 叫花鸡). The hallowed recipe begins, "First, steal a chicken."

The famous "Winter Hotpot" (Huǒguō, 火锅) helps benumbed Běijīngers survive frigid winter evenings, but they feast on Běijīng Duck year round.

Běijīng Duck (Běijīng kǎoyā, 北京烤鸭) Diners adopt a live duck for life by painting a number on its side. But it's a very short life. The hapless duck is promptly murdered, stripped to its skivvies, and sewn up tightly to hold the boiling water that ensures the roasted carcass will be succulent and savory inside. The first course is the crisp skin, basted with sweet Hoisin sauce (Miànjiàng, 面酱) and served with scallions wrapped in small, thin pancakes. For the second course, the leavings are cooked and served with bean sprouts or slices of bamboo. Nothing is wasted. Even the bones are crushed and cooked with water, ginger and onion, and then boiled with cabbage and sugar to make soup.

Běijīng Duck is served in many fine Xiàmén restaurants. Try Marco Polo's 2/F Chinese restaurant (it's Cantonese style Běijīng Duck, but tasty!).

Sìchuān Cuisine (Chuāncài, 川菜) Sìchuān's fiery fare is the perfect antidote to the sultry summers of this remote but most populous province. Chefs combine ginger, red peppers, onions and soy sauce to create dishes that will ream your sinuses. But not all Sìchuān food is hot; they also serve up sweet, sour, salty, fragrant, and bitter in every combination possible and some that are not possible but come off anyway.

Shànghǎi Cuisine (Shànghǎi Cài, 上海菜) In coastal Shànghǎi, crowds throng about vendors hawking rolls stuffed with pork and beef, and gourmands from all over Asia fly in to sample Shànghǎi hairy crabs, four-gill carp, and meats spiced with Shàoxīng wine (Shàojiǔ 绍酒), often arranged in beautiful floral designs on delicate china. But where's the beef? With grazing land at a premium in this populous nation, beef is still rare, in Shànghǎi and elsewhere. Besides, peasants see it as poor form to reward an ox's faithful service by eating him. So the pig remains the perennial king with Chinese chefs, who use everything from offal to oink.

You have eaten Shanghai Cuisine. The foreigners' perennial favorite, Sweet 'n Sour① Pork (Tángcù Ròu 糖醋肉) is not Cantonese, as some think, but Shanghai.

Cantonese Cuisine (Guǎngdōng Cài, 广东菜)

Question: What's the difference between Cantonese zoos and restaurants?
Answer: not much...

The Venetian vagabond Marco Polo wrote of his Chinese hosts, "They eat all sorts of flesh, including that of dogs and other brute beasts and animals of every kind which Christians would not touch for anything in the world."

Evidently, Lǎonèi still don't touch them. A Chinese restaurateur complained of meat and potato Canadians, "They don't want real Cantonese cuisine. It's always sweet 'n sour pork, lemon chicken, beef and green peppers, fried rice, spring rolls, and Chinese fortune cookies" (which originated not in China but California).

While Lǎowài may prefer frozen fish sticks over fricasseed fish lips, Chinese still devour anything that won't eat them first. If they can't eat it, they call it medicine and ingest it anyway. But Cantonese take the tofu. Even other Chinese say of them, "They eat anything that flies but planes, and anything with four legs but the table and chairs."

Cantonese menus include live monkey brains, sparrows, wild ducks, snails, snakes, eels, frogs, turtles, deer penis soup, and canine cuisine. (In 1990, an MBA student asked me to invest $10,000 in his scheme to export canned dog to America. I asked him if he'd ever heard of market surveys).

Cantonese restaurants abound in Xiàmén, but some of the more popular are in Bǎilù Zhōu (along the lake) and on North Húbīn Lù, past the Sports Arena. They are always packed to the gills—and fins and flippers as well.

Xiàmén Cuisine (Xiàmén Cài, 厦门菜) Canton, though renowned its seafood, comes nowhere close to Xiàmén's offerings. Off magical Amoy's contorted coastline, if it swims, crawls, wiggles, or squirms, some enterprising soul will wrest it from the sea and serve it up with Mǐnnán rice noodles, taro dishes and five-spice meat rolls, salty and peppery roast chicken, abalone, duck webs with glutinous rice, scented pork kidney, stuffed cucumbers, braised frogs, shark, crab, mussels and oysters (stir-fried with eggs), sea urchins, mineral-rich seaweed, and sea cucumber. And of course there's Xiàmén's #1 specialty – boiled seaworm embedded in cold jellyfish (Tǔsǔndòng,土笋冻).

For authentic Xiàmén cuisine (a cross between Cantonese and Fúzhōu styles, with a little Táiwān thrown in), try Xiàmén City Hotel, near Zhōngshān Park, or the Overseas Chinese Hotel, near the PSB on Zhongshan Rd.

① Favorite Chinese dish in Scandinavia? Swede 'n Sour

Froggy Food

Never try to catch two frogs with one hand.
Chinese Proverb

Chinese frogs clear emigration

A Chinese friend removed from his kitchen cabinet a plastic baggie of about four ounces of a grayish, stringy dried matter, rather like a finely shredded sponge. "Only 210 RMB," he said, grinning. "My brother brought it straight from the mountains!"

This expensive gray stuff was a rare Chinese medicine and cooking ingredient, second in efficacy only to bird's nests (made from dry swallow spit). It was dry frog spit. Not just any frog spit, mind. It was that of a rare mountain frog, and collected only during a very brief season in the spring.

It seemed everyone had frogs on the brain. A few nights later, halfway through a meal with some MBA students from the provincial government, the waitress set in front of me a shot glass full of a bright, evil looking ruby liquid. It was redder than the inside lining of Dracula's cape, and shimmered with a life of its own. I suspected it wasn't V-8 Juice.

"What is this?" I asked.

"Oh, blood of a rare mountain frog, second in potency only to the blood of …"

"No thanks, I'll pass."

"But Professor Pan, you're the guest of honor!"

"I have no honor. You drink it!"

Eventually the rankest person present took the small cup in both hands, ceremonially offered it to each diner, then downed it in one gulp and smacked his lips. The waitress then handed me a cup of pale yellow liquid. "What's this?" I demanded. "Frog pee? Second only to—"

"—Of course not," she said in disgust. "It's beer."

Frog blood, beer, cobra venom—I've had it all (yes, even the venom).

I wish they'd stick to tea**…**

Tea Time

Our trouble is that we drink too much tea. I see in this the slow revenge of the Orient, which has diverted the Yellow River down our throats. J. B. Priestley

According to tradition, tea cures bad eyesight, eases rheumatism and impotence, and was an ingredient in the Taoist's elixir of immortality. It also tastes good, which is why the Portuguese, Dutch and British flooded into Xiàmén. Tea fanned the flames of independence in Boston. Tea made the Hatter Mad. And the major pastime in Xiàmén is once again becoming the Mǐnnán tea Ceremony**…**

Okakura wrote in his timeless classic, *The Book of Tea*,

"To the latter-day Chinese tea is a delicious beverage, but not an ideal. The long woes of his country have robbed him of the zest for the meaning of life. He has become modern, that is to say, old and disenchanted. He has lost that sublime faith in illusions which constitutes the eternal youth and vigour of the poets and ancients...His Leaf-tea is often wonderful with its flower-like aroma, but the romance of the Tang and Sung ceremonials are not to be found in his cup."

The problem was never ideals but economics. Until the early 1990s, even in Anxi, tea capital of the world, my tea-growing peasant friends could not afford to drink their own tea. While Anxi's Oolong (Wūlóng, 乌龙) and Tiekuanyin (Tié Guānyīn, 铁观音) graced tables from Boston to Bali, Anxi farmers brewed choice weeds and grass. But a decade of rapid economic reform has helped rekindle the romance of the Tang and Song ceremonials. Once again, the cult of Teaism (Chádào, 茶道) is flourishing.

Teashops lining Xiàmén streets purvey specialty teas from all over China, ranging in price from pennies a pound to hundreds of dollars an ounce, depending on the type and size of leaves, when and where they were picked, and how they were prepared.

Mǐnnán lasses in minty green mini-skirts lure pedestrians with samples from the Heavenly Blessing Tea Shop, and I once succumbed (to the tea, not to the minty green mini-skirts).

I squatted inside the tiny shop on a wooden stool before a thickly lacquered cross section of a tree that served as a table. A girl rinsed miniscule Mǐnnán cups, like thimbles with handles. She measured out half a swallow of Jasmine Tea (Lìhuā Chá 莉花茶) and with two hands presented the tiny cup to me.

Tea connoisseurs eye the color, sniff the bouquet, roll the tea on the tongue, swallow, and compliment the host. But I'm used to guzzling ½ liter plastic mugs of coffee from petrol stations. I downed the hatch, smacked my lips like a bona fide barbarian, and said, "Good stuff. How much?"

In truth, it was marvelous tea—nothing like the black brew back home we make palatable only with shovels of sugar and cream – a sacrilege to Chinese who add naught but pure water. Though Chinese were not always such purists. 1500 years ago they poured on not just cream and sugar but rice, ginger, salt, orange peel, spices, and even onions. They eventually abandoned most of these. Salt was the last to go, during the Sòng Dynasty, but Tibetans still consume copious amounts of salted tea flavored with rancid yak butter. Yum. (Northern Fújiàn's pounded tea still has many of the old ingredients; it's so thick you can literally eat it).

A few sips of pure, Chinese red tea (Hóngchá 红茶; what we call "black tea") is enough to help even American coffee fiends to appreciate why ancient Chinese raised Teaism to cult status – and why Japanese still worship what are essentially just glorified Camellia leaves. But as Solomon said, there's a time for everything. I concur with Wendell Holmes, Sr[①], who wrote,

① Oliver Wendell Holmes: 温德尔·霍姆斯

"The morning cup of coffee has an exhilaration about it which the cheering influence of the afternoon or evening cup of tea cannot be expected to reproduce."

We Told You So… Chinese, you will learn, are indefatigable proselytizers, especially of Chinese medicine and tea. Every single one of my friends has argued, "Coffee's bad, tea is healthy."

How I hate a smug, "I told you so" – especially 1.3 billion of them.

On September 11, 1997, the University of Kansas issued a news release, "More Proof that Green Tea May Postpone Cancer, Heart Disease." The study claimed green tea was twice as effective as red wine, 35 times more effective than vitamin E, and 100 times more effective than vitamin C at protecting cells and their DNA.

Ok, so tea's healthy. But as a wise man (Redd Fox) once said, "Someday all those health nuts are going to feel pretty stupid lying in hospitals dying of nothing."

The Book of Tea

Kakuzo Okakura's *The Book of Tea* offers marvelous insights into the influence of tea on Asian culture, and also highlights the differences between East and West, and why we should try to narrow them:

"[Teaism influences] our home and habits, costume and cuisine, porcelain, lacquer, painting—our very literature…the initiated may touch the sweet reticence of Confucius (Kǒngzi, 孔子), the piquancy of Laotse (Lǎozǐ, 老子) and the ethereal aroma of Sakyamuni (Shìjiāmóuní, 释迦牟尼) himself."

"The average Westerner, in his sleek complacency, will see in the tea ceremony but another instance of the thousand and one oddities which constitute the quaintness and childishness of the East to him…. When will the West understand, or try to understand, the East? We Asiatics are often appalled by the curious web of facts and fancies which has been woven concerning us. We are pictured as living on the perfume of the lotus, if not on mice and cockroaches. It is either impotent fanaticism or else abject voluptuousness. Indian spirituality has been derided as ignorance, Chinese sobriety as stupidity, Japanese patriotism as the result of fatalism. It has been said that we are less sensible to pain and wounds on account of the callousness of our nervous organization!"

"Why not amuse yourselves at our expense? Asia returns the compliment. There would be further food for merriment if you were to know all that we have imagined and written about you. All the glamour of the perspective is there, all the unconscious homage of wonder, all the silent resentment of the new and undefined. You have been loaded with virtues too refined to be envied, and accused of crimes too picturesque to be condemned. Our writers in the past—the wise men who knew—informed us that you had bushy tails somewhere hidden in your garments, and often dined off a fricassee of newborn babes! Nay, we had something worse against you: we used to think you the most impracticable people on the earth, for you were said to preach what you never practiced.

Such misconceptions are fast vanishing amongst us. Commerce has forced the European tones on many an Eastern port. Asiatic youths are flocking to Western colleges for the equipment of modern education. Our insight does not penetrate your culture deeply, but at least we are willing to learn. Some of my compatriots have

> adopted too much of your customs and too much of your etiquette, in the delusion that the acquisition of stiff collars and tall silk hats comprised the attainment of your civilization. Pathetic and deplorable as such affectations are, they evince our willingness to approach the West on our knees. Unfortunately the Western attitude is unfavorable to the understanding of the East."
>
> "Perhaps I betray my own ignorance of the Tea Cult by being so outspoken. Its very spirit of politeness exacts that you say what you are expected to say, and no more. But I am not to be a polite Teaist. So much harm has been done already by the mutual misunderstanding of the New World and the Old, that one need not apologise for contributing his tithe to the furtherance of a better understanding. "
>
> "Let us stop the continents from hurling epigrams at each other, and be sadder if not wiser by the mutual gain of half a hemisphere. We have developed along different lines, but there is no reason why one should not supplement the other."

Perhaps the supplementing has begun with McChina™ …

McChina（麦中国）In the late '90s we used to take the bus clear across town to the newly opened Xiàmén Plaza (Xiàmén Dōngnányà Jiúdiàn, 厦门东南亚大酒店) just because it was the only place in town that served ice water. Now that Xiàmén has a dozen McDonalds, 17 KFCs, 4 Pizza Huts, and hundreds of fine restaurants, it's hard to imagine how excited Xiàmén's cheese-less Lǎowài were to hear that Uncle Ronald was coming to Xiàmén during the Mid-Autumn Festival.

But the grand opening was postponed until Christmas, then New Year, then Chinese New Year. We finally figured it was like the Second Coming—no man knows the day or the hour. Though local bigwigs must have known both. On the long awaited day, we raced to the Zhōngshān Lù McDonalds, but two guards stopped us and said, "Invitation only."

Forget McDonalds! But two weeks later, Sue and I were strolling down Zhōngshān Lù on our weekly date, and it was hard to ignore the bright paper posters and menus plastered on the giant plate glass windows. We succumbed, ordered burgers and fries, and were told, "Electricity's out. Nothing but drinks"—to the vast delight of Muslim barbeque vendors who had planted their charcoal braziers right on McDonald's doorstep.

Sue ordered a coke and I a coffee, and I contemplated devouring the paper placemat's color photo of a cheeseburger.

After our liquid feast I sought out the bathroom, which as expected was spotless. Or I think it was. With no lights, windows, or power, it was pitch dark. I hope that was the urinal and not the sink.

We finally landed our burgers a week later. I still prefer Lin Duck House's cheap pork rice special (Páigǔfàn, 排骨饭), but McDs is a nice break from routine, and has the hottest (and cheapest) coffee in town.

Cheeseburger, Hold the Cheese Better than ***eating*** burgers is ***watching*** others eat them. I've seen folks use soda straws as makeshift chopsticks to eat burgers piece by piece. Speaking of grasping at straws, I cringe at the memory of the granny in

McDonalds who let out a blood curdling scream after sipping her scalding tea through a plastic straw.

I'm sure that was the last straw. Had she been in America, she could have sued McDonald's and retired her entire extended family for life, and soda straws, which are too small for warnings, would now come equipped with instruction manuals. But not in China.

I once fell flat on my back on a soapy McDonald's floor. Instead of apologizing they looked at me as if I were an idiot and said to be more careful on slippery floors.

Fast Food Wars Thanks to street-side Ronald McDonald performances and weekly offerings of "Collect Them All!" plastic burger men, fry folk, and plastic Snoopy dolls, Xiàmén may become like Japan, where children think Big Macs are as indigenous as sushi. But Ronald McDonald is not the only player on the field. At Xiàmén University the demilitarized zone between McDonalds and KFC is less than 100 meters. Several times I've seen the Chinese Ronald McDonald, who looks more like a Japanese Opera star, wooing kiddies away from KFC's magician.

Burgers, pizza and fried chicken may be okay for a break, but one of the nicest aspects of life in China is **Chinese** food. For ½ the price of a Big Mac, I can have Lin Duck's Pork Special. But mom and pop shops are having a tough time holding out against Uncle Ronald. With golden arches around every corner, the day may come when Xiàmén tourists can find nothing but burgers and chicken McNuggets, or perhaps McSweet 'n Sour™, McFried Rice™ and McLemon Chicken Nuggets™. So get those seaworms and jellyfish while you can!

KF China Matt has lived in China since he was six months old, so we have to make allowances for some of his questions. When we drove around America in 1995, the six-year-old asked, "Dad, do they have Kentucky Fried Chicken in America?"

1988—Xiàmén 1st "Cheeseburger"

In November, 1988, we were thrilled to learn that the Overseas Chinese Hotel (Huáqiáo Dàshà, 厦门华侨大厦) had started serving cheeseburgers. We made a dash for the OC Hotel, ordered our cheeseburgers, and about half an hour later were given sweet Chinese buns the size of small dinner rolls, inside of which were small lumps of meat marginally larger than my thumb. And no cheese.

"Where's the cheese?" I asked? "The menu says 'cheeseburgers.'"

"There's no cheese," the waiter said. "That's just the name."

"Then its just a hamburger, not a cheeseburger," I protested.

"Hamburgers don't have ham," the waiter said. And then he stormed out. He returned about five minutes later, plunked a tiny can of Parmesan on the table, and said, "Here. Cheese."

Chapter 22

English/Chinese Menu

"It is a sad truth, but we have lost the faculty of giving lovely names to things. Names are everything. I never quarrel with actions. My one quarrel is with words. . . . The man who could call a spade a spade should be compelled to use one. It is the only thing he is fit for."

Oscar Wilde

Getting a Handle on Chinese Food

Chinese prefer strange and exotic foods, but failing that, they give common foods strange and exotic names. They pass off plain chicken as "Phoenix Breast," or duck eggs as "Lotus Eggs." And the famous "Monk Climbing the Wall" soup has neither monk nor wall. I hope.

The playwright who quarreled with words would have appreciated these offerings from Chinese menus:

Silver Fish Wrapped in Snow, from Beijing, is neither winter precipitation nor the ornery bugs that ate holes in my wool Scottish tie. It is simply cooked macaroni fried in whipped egg white.

Chicken in a Lantern, also from Beijing, is cooked chicken and vegetables wrapped in clear cellophane and tied with a ribbon.

Phoenix Breast, from Sichuan, is not the legendary Egyptian fowl but plain old cheap chicken breast.

Lotus Eggs have a fowl source; they're simply chicken eggs.

Dragon and Phoenix Ham, from Sichuan, is naught but duck, pork, water chestnuts, chicken wing bones, ham and white bread – mixed and fried.

Steamed Dragon's Eye rolls, from Sichuan, are strips of pork rolled around red bean paste, topped with a cherry, and served on glutinous rice.

By the time I've worked my way to a menu's soup section and come across, "Bright Moon in a River" and "Buddha Leaps the Wall," I'm ready to climb the wall myself. But it's worth the climb. China's elegantly named dishes are invariably just as elegantly prepared and served, and well worth the wait.

To make life easier, I've compiled this handy dandy Magic Xiamen Menu in English, Chinese, and Pinyin—and added tone marks. If you don't understand tones, turn to "Mad About Mandarin" chapter for tips on mangling Chinese tones.

If you still can't say it—**just point!**

Magic Xiamen Menu

CHICKEN 鸡类 Jī

* Stir Fried Diced Chicken and Peanuts 果仁鸡丁 Guǒrén Jīdīng
* Chicken & Peanuts (spicy) 宫保鸡丁 Gōngbǎo Jīdīng
* Cashew Chicken 腰果鸡丁 Yāoguǒ Jīdīng
* Lemon Chicken 柠檬鸡片 Níngméng Jīpiàn
* Sizzling Chicken (iron skillet) 铁板鸡肉 Tiébǎn Jīròu
Stir Fried Chicken & Green Peppers 青椒鸡丁 Qīngjiāo Jīdīng
Chicken in Ginger Sauce 姜汁热味鸡 Jiāngzhī Rè Wēijī
Fried Breaded Chicken Nuggets 软炸鸡片 Ruǎnzhá Jīpiàn
Fried Chicken Slices 炒鸡片 Chǎo Jīpiàn
Stir Fried Chicken & Bamboo Shoots 冬笋鸡片 Dōngsǔn Jīpiàn
Sweet 'n Sour Chicken Strips 糖醋鸡条 Tángcù Jītiáo
Chicken with Mushrooms & Bamboo Shoots 双冬鸡条 Shuāngdōng Jītiáo
Stewed Chicken and Chestnuts 栗子鸡 Lìzi Jī
Stewed Chicken with Tofu 油豆腐鸡 Yóu Dòufu Jī

Crispy Fried Chicken 油酥鸡 Yóusū Jī
Shredded Chicken in Oyster Sauce 蚝油手撕鸡 Háoyóu Shǒusī Jī
Fried Chicken 炸鸡 Zhájī
Paper Wrapped Fried Chicken 炸纸包鸡 Zhá Zhǐbāo Jī
Fried Chicken Shish-ka-bob 炸鸡肉串 Zhá Jīròu Chuàn
Roast Chicken 烤鸡 Kǎojī
Stewed Gizzards & Bamboo Shoots 冬笋焖胗 Dōngsǔn Ménzhēn
Steamed Chicken & Straw Mushrooms 草菇蒸鸡 Cǎogū Zhēngjī
Lotus-wrapped Chicken & Chestnuts 荷包栗子鸡 Hébāo Lìzi Jī
Sesame Chicken 芝麻鸡 Zhīma Jī
Curried Chicken 咖喱鸡 Gālí Jī
Braised Chicken Wings with Brown Sauce 红烧鸡翼 Hóngshāo Jīyì

DUCK & OTHER FOWL PLAY 鸭类，鸡类，等等

Spicy Sparrow & Walnuts 核桃禾花雀 Hétao Héhuā Què
Baked Stuffed Sparrow 烤酿禾花雀 Kǎoniàng Héhuā Què
Fried Minced Pigeon Meat 炒鸽松 Chǎo Gēsōng
Braised Swallow's Nest, Minced Chicken 鸡茸燕窝 Jīróng Yànwō
Beijing Duck 北京烤鸭 Běijīng Kǎoyā
Braised Duck with Oyster Sauce 蚝油扒鸭 Háoyóu Bāyā
Whole Braised Duck 'n Soy Sauce 红烧全鸭 Hóngshāo Quányā

EGG DISHES 蛋类 Dàn

Egg & Bitter Melon Casserole 苦瓜烘蛋 kǔguā hōngdàn

Fried Pigeon Egg, Minced Meat 炸象眼鸽蛋 Zháxiàng Yǎn Gēdàn
Steamed Ham and Eggs 火腿蒸蛋 Huǒtuǐ Zhēngdàn
Minced Pork Omelette 肉末鸡蛋 Ròumò Jīdàn

PORK 猪肉类 Zhūròu

* Sweet & Sour Pork (Boneless) 糖醋里脊 Tángcù Lǐjǐ
* Pineapple, Green Pepper & Pork Strips 菠萝咕唠肉 Bōluó Gǔláoròu
Sweet & Sour Pork Rib 糖醋排骨 Tángcù Páigǔ
Deep Fried Sweet & Sour Pork 锅包肉 Guōbāoròu
Sizzling Pork (iron skillet) 铁板里脊 Tiébǎn Lǐjī
Breaded Pork Strips 软炸猪排 Ruǎnzhá Lǐpiàn
* Stir Fried Pork & Veggies on Sizzling Rice 锅巴肉片 Guōbā Ròupiàn
* Fried Pork Balls 炸丸子 Zhá Wánzi
Stir Fried Pork & Green Peppers 青椒肉丁 Qīngjiāo Ròudīng
Chicken Fried Pork Strips 包肉丝 Bāoròusī
Sesame Pork 芝麻里脊 Zhīma Lǐjī
Beggar's Ribs (fried) 叫花排骨 Jiàohuā Páigǔ
Green Peppers Stuffed with Pork 青椒塞肉 Qīngjiāo SāiRòu
Stir Fried Pork Slices 炒肉片 Chǎo Ròupiàn
Stir Fried Pork Slices & Eggs 木须肉 MùxūRòu
Braised Pork with Brown Sauce 红烧猪肉 Hóngshāo Zhūròu
Braised Pork with Chestnuts 栗子红烧肉 Lìzi Hóngshāo Ròu
Stir Fried Pork & Bamboo Shoots 冬笋肉丝 Dōngsǔn Ròusī

BEEF 牛肉类 Niúròu

* Sizzling Beef, Onions, Peppers 铁板牛柳 Tiébǎn Niúliǔ
* Beef Curry 咖喱牛肉 Gālí Niúròu

Garlic Beef 黑蒜子牛肉 Hēi Suànzi Niúròu
* Beef with Broccoli 西兰花菜牛肉 Xīlánhuācài Niúròu
Stir-fried Sliced Beef 炒牛肉片 Chǎo Niúròu Piàn
Beef & Potato Stew 土豆炖肉 Túdòu Dùnròu
Twice-Fried Beef 回锅牛肉 Huíguō Niūròu
Beef Wrapped in Rice Paper 纸包牛肉 Zhǐbāo Niúròu
Braised beef in Soy Sauce 红焖牛肉 Hóngmèn Niúròu
Braised Beef in Oyster Sauce 蚝油牛肉 Háoyóu Niúròu
Braised Beef Tenderloin in Soy Sauce 红烧牛腩 Hóngshāo Niúnǎn
Beef & Green Peppers 青椒牛肉 Qīngjiāo Niúròu

SEAFOOD 鱼 Yú

* Steamed Mandarin Fish 清蒸桂花鱼 Qīngzhēng Guìhuāyú
* Sweet and Sour Fish 糖醋鱼片 Tángcù Yúpiàn

* Sweet 'n Sour Garoupa 糖醋石斑鱼 Tángcù Shíbānyú
* Deep-Fried Mandarin Fish 炸桂鱼 Zhá Guìyú
** Whole Fish with Apple & Tomatoes 鲜果松鼠鱼 Xiānguǒ Sōngshǔyú
* Steamed Fresh Fish 蒸鲜鱼 Zhēng Xiān Yú
* Crispy Fried Garoupa Slices 酥炸鱼条 Sūzhá Yútiáo
Stir-Fried Fish Strips 炒鱼片 Chǎo Yúpiàn

Deep Fried Fish Strips 炸鱼条 Zhá Yútiáo
Braised Fish in Soy Sauce 红烧鱼 Hóngshāo Yú
Braised Eel in Soy Sauce 红烧鳗鱼 Hóngshāo Mányú
Braised Carp in Soy Sauce 红烧鲤鱼 Hóngshāo Lǐyú
Braised Turtle in Clear Broth 清炖甲鱼 Qīngdùn Jiǎyú
Stir-Fried Squid 炒鱿鱼 Chǎo Yóuyú
**Deep-Fried Squid (family favourite!) 炸鱿鱼 Zhá Yóuyú
Braised Fish Lips in Oyster Sauce 蚝油鱼唇 Háoyóu Yúchún

SHRIMP 虾 Xiā & **CRAB** 蟹 Xiè

Boiled Shrimp 盐水虾 Yánshuǐ Xiā
Stir-fried Shelled Shrimp 清炒虾仁 Qīngchǎo Xiārén

Deep-Fried Shrimp Balls 油炸虾丸 Yóuzhá Xiāwán
Shrimp & Cashews 腰果虾仁 Yāoguǒ Xiārén
Sizzling Shrimp & Onions (iron skillet) 铁板虾仁 Tiébǎn Xiārén

Braised Prawns in Brown Sauce 红烧大虾 Hóngshāo Dàxiā
Deep-fried Prawns 炸大虾 Zhá Dàxiā
Fried Prawn Shish-ka-bob 炸虾串 Zhá Xiā Chuàn
Fried Prawn Cakes 炸虾饼 Zhá Xiābǐng
Fried King Prawns in Soy & Ginger 煎酿大明虾 Jiànniàng Dàmíng Xiā
Crispy Fried Prawns & Bamboo Shoots 炸竹笋脆虾 Zhá Zhúsǔn Cuì Xiā
Fried Prawn Balls 炸虾球 Zhá Xiāqiú
Steamed Crab 蒸螃蟹 Zhēng Pángxiè

Stir-Fried Crab Meat 炒蟹肉 Cháo Xièròu
Stir-Fried Crab Meat in Cream Sauce 奶汁蟹肉 Nǎizhī Xièròu

OTHER SEA CREATURES

Braised Sea Cucumbers in Brown Sauce 红烧海参 Hóngsháo Hǎishēn
Stewed Sea Cucumbers with Shrimp 虾仁海参 Xiārén Hǎishēn

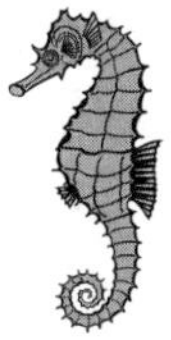

Fried Dried Scallops with Vegetables 油爆干贝 Yóubào Gānbèi
Stewed Dried Scallops in White Sauce 白汁干贝 Báizhī Gānbèi
Fried Oysters 面拖牡蛎 Miàntuō Mǔlì
Stewed Abalone in Oyster Sauce 蚝油焖鲍鱼 Háoyóu Mèn Bàoyú
Braised Abalone in Brown Sauce 红烧鲍鱼 Hóngshāo Bàoyú
Braised Abalone & Black Mushrooms 冬菇鲍鱼 Dōnggū Bàoyú

Fried Razor Clam 清炒蛏子 Qīngchǎo Chēngzi

VEGGIES 蔬菜 Shūcài

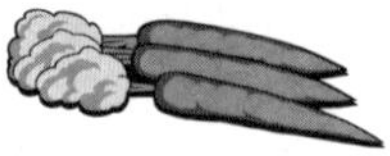

Stir Fried Mixed Vegetables 炒素菜 Chǎo Sùcài
Fried Eggplant Stuffed with Pork 炸茄盒肉 Zhá Qiéhé Ròu
Batter Fried Eggplant in Sauce 鱼香茄子煲 Yúxiāng Qiézi Bǎo
Eggplant in Brown Sauce 红烧茄子 Hóngshāo Qiézi
Sautéed Chinese Cabbage 醋熘白菜 Cùliū Bǎicài
Stir Fried Cabbage with Meat 小白菜 炒肉 Xiǎobáicài Chǎoròu
Sweet and Sour Cabbage 糖醋莲白 Tángcù Liánbǎi
* Stir Fried Spinach & Mashed Garlic 蒜泥菠菜 Suàn ní Bōcài
Stir Fried Spinach 炒菠菜 Chǎo Bōcài
Braised Bamboo Shoots 油焖笋 Yóumèn Sǔn
Stir Fried Bamboo Shoots 炒青笋条 Chǎo Qīngsǔntiáo
Stir Fried Mushrooms & Bamboo Shoots 炒香菇笋片 Chǎo Xiānggū Sǔnpiàn
Stir Fried Vegetables & Mushrooms 菜心扒鲜菇 Càixīn Bā Xiāngū
Stewed Fresh Mushrooms & Veggies 烩鲜菇蔬菜 Huì Xiāngū Shūcài
Stir Fried Heart of Greens 清炒空心菜 Qīngchǎo Kōngxīncài
Stir Fried Onions and Carrots 洋葱炒胡萝卜 Yángcōng Chǎo Húluóbo
Stir Fried Broccoli 清炒 西兰花菜 Qīngchǎo Xīlánhuācài
Stir Fried Snow Peas 清炒荷兰豆 Qīngchǎo Hélándòu
Soybeans and Ground Pork 青豆焖肉 Qīngdòu Mènròu
Quick Fried Rapeseed Leaves & Stems 呛油菜苔 Qiāng Yóucài Tāi
Romaine Lettuce in Oyster Sauce 蚝油生菜 Háoyóu Shēngcài
Corn with Pine Nuts 松子玉米 Sōngzǐ Yùmǐ
Scrambled Eggs and Tomatoes 西红柿炒鸡蛋 Xīhóngshì Chǎojīdàn
Teriyaki Cauliflower & Egg 酱油炒蛋花菜 Jiàngyóu Chǎodàn Huācài
Green Beans with Shredded Pork (Spicy) 干煸四季豆 Gānbiān Sìjìdòu
Stir Fried Sliced Lotus Root 炒藕片 Chǎo Ǒupiàn
"Tiger Skin" Cooked Whole Green Peppers 虎皮青椒 Hǔpí Qīngjiāo
Shoestring Potatoes 干煸土豆丝 Gānbiān Túdòusī
French Fries 油炸土豆条 Yóuzhá Túdòu Tiáo
Spicy Potato Pie 土豆饼 Túdòu Bǐng
Mashed Potatoes 土豆泥 Túdòu Ní
Pickled Vegetables (cold) 泡菜 Pàocài
7-Flavor Chinese Cabbage (cold) 七味白菜 Qīwèi Báicài

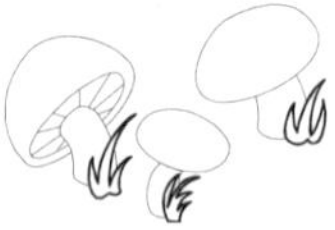

MISC CARCASSES & CRITTERS

(Lassie, Bambi, Kermit, Thumper, Winnie…)
or… "How to Wok Your Dog"

Twice—Boiled Dog's Weenie (Chinese hot dog?) & Herbs

过江龙牛七炖狗鞭 Guòjiāng Lóngniú Qídùn Gǒubiān

Stir Fried Bunny Rabbit 炒兔片 Chǎo Tùpiàn

Braised Bambi in Brown Sauce 红烧鹿肉 Hóngshāo Lùròu

Braised Bear Paw in Soy Sauce 红烧熊掌 (Hóngshāo Xióngzhǎng

Fried Frog Legs 炸田鸡腿 Zhá Tiánjī Tuǐ

(For broader selection, visit the zoo after hours)

TOFU 豆腐 Dòufu

* Home-style Tofu 家常豆腐 Jiācháng Dòufu

* Tofu Cubes in Spicy Sauce (hot!) 麻婆豆腐 Mápó Dòufu

* Braised Tofu in Brown Sauce 红烧豆腐 Hóngshāo Dòufu

Stir-Fried Tofu 炒豆腐 Chǎo Dòufu

Deep-Fried Tofu 炸豆腐 Zhá Dòufu

Japanese Tofu with Shrimp & Cashews 日本豆腐 Rìběn Dòufu

Stinky Tofu (and it really does!) 臭豆腐 Chòu Dòufu

Bear Paw Tofu (fried, spicy) 熊掌豆腐 xióngzhǎng Dòufu

Braised Tofu with Mixed Vegetables 素什锦豆腐 Sùshíjǐn Dòufu

Braised Tofu, Shrimp, Meat 红烧什肉虾仁豆腐
Hóngshāo Shíròu Xiārén Dòufu

Soft Tofu and Beef Slices 牛柳豆腐 Niúliǔ Dòuhuā

Tofu Stuffed with Minced Fish 鱼脊肉酿豆腐 YúJǐ Ròuniàng Dòufu

Tofu Stuffed with Minced Pork 猪肉酿豆腐 Zhūròuniàng Dòufu

Tofu in Oyster Sauce 蚝油豆腐 Háoyóu Dòufu

SOUPS 汤 Tāng

Chicken Corn Soup 鸡茸玉米汤 (Jīrǒng Yùmǐ Tāng

Beef Soup 牛肉汤 Niúròu Tāng

Duck Soup 鸭汤 Yā Tāng

Fish, Shrimp & Pork Ball Soup 三鲜汤 Sānxiān Tāng

Abalone & Chicken Soup 鲍鱼鸡片汤 Bàoyú Jīpiàn Tāng

Hot & Sour Soup 酸辣汤 Suānlà Tāng

Bird's Nest Soup 燕窝汤 Yànwō Tāng

Tofu Soup 豆腐汤 Dòufu Tāng

Tofu & Egg Flower Soup 蛋豆腐汤 Dàn Dòufu Tāng

Egg Drop Soup 鸡蛋汤 Jīdàn Tāng

Mushroom & Crispy Rice Soup 锅巴口蘑汤 Guōbā Kǒumó Tāng

Dried Scallop Soup 干贝汤 Gānbèi Tāng

MUTTON 羊肉类 Yángròu

Braised Beef with Soy Sauce 红烧羊肉 Hóngshāo Yángròu

Roast Mutton 烤羊肉 Kǎo Yángròu

Stir Fried Lamb and Onions 葱煲羊肉 Cōngbāo Yángròu
Roast Mutton Chops 烤羊排 Kǎo Yángpái
Fried Mutton with Sesame 芝麻羊肉 Zhīma Yángròu

WHEAT, RICE (Dumplings, Rolls, etc.) 面,米 Miàn, Mǐ……

Steamed Bun 馒头 Mántou
Steamed Bun Stuffed with Veggies 素菜包子 Sùcài Bāozi
Steamed Bun Stuffed with Pork 肉包子 (ROU BAO ZI)
Boiled Chinese Dumpling 饺子 or 水饺 Jiǎozi or Shuǐjiǎo
Steamed Chinese Dumpling (Jiaozi) 蒸饺 Zhēngjiǎo
Steamed Seafood Jiaozi 三鲜蒸饺 Sānxiān Zhēngjiǎo
Lightly Fried Jiaozi 锅贴 Guōtiē
Mini Dumplings in Bamboo Steamer 小笼包 Xiǎolóngbāo
Deep Fried Spring Roll 春卷 Chūnjuǎn
Pancake with Green Chinese Onion 葱花饼 Cōnghuābǐng
Fried Meat Pie 肉饼 Ròubǐng
Baked Sesame-Seed Cake 烧饼 Shāobǐng
Steamed Rice Cake 米糕 Mǐgāo
Deep-Fried Dough Sticks (breakfast food) 油条 Yóutiáo

NOODLES 面条 Miàntiáo

Hand Pulled Noodles (usually Muslim) 拉面 Lāmiàn
Pulled Noodles with Beef 牛肉拉面 Niúròu Lāmiàn
Noodles with Pork Rib 排骨面 Páigǔmiàn
Fried Noodles 炒面 Chǎomiàn
Beef Fried Noodles 牛肉炒面 Niúròu Chǎomiàn
Shrimp Fried Noodles 虾炒面 Xiā Chǎomiàn
Seafood Fried Noodles 海鲜炒面 Hǎixiān Chǎomiàn
Fried Noodles and Vegetables 蔬菜炒面 Shūcài Chǎomiàn
Instant Noodles 方便面 Fāngbiàn Miàn
Rice-Flour Noodles 米粉条 Mǐfěntiáo
Noodles with Shredded Pork 肉丝拌面 Ròusī Bànmiàn
Noodle Soup 汤面 Tāngmiàn
Seafood Noodle Soup 三鲜汤面 Sānxiān Tāngmiàn

FRIED RICE 炒饭 Chǎofàn

White Rice 白米饭 Báimǐfàn
* Yangzhou-style Fried Rice 扬州炒饭 Yángzhōu Chǎofàn
Egg Fried Rice 蛋炒饭 Dàn Chǎofàn
Fried rice with shrimp, mushroom & chicken 什锦炒饭 Shíjǐn Chǎofàn
Pork Fried Rice 猪肉炒饭 Zhūròu Chǎofàn

Beef Fried Rice 牛肉炒饭 Niúròu Chǎofàn
Chicken Fried Rice 鸡炒饭 Jī Chǎofàn
Vegetable Fried Rice 蔬菜炒饭 Shūcài Chǎofàn
Mushroom Fried Rice 蘑菇炒饭 Mógu Chǎofàn

DESSERTS 饭后甜食 Fànhòu Tiánshí

* Apple Fritters 拔丝苹果 Básī Píngguǒ
* Banana Fritters 拔丝香蕉 Básī Xiāngjiāo
Sweet Almond Paste 核桃酪 Hétao Lào

DRINKS 饮料 Yǐnliào

Coca Cola 可口可乐 kěkǒu Kělè
Sprite 雪碧 Xuěbì
Pepsi 百事可乐 Bǎishì Kělè
Tea 茶 Chá
Bottled Water 矿泉水 Kuàngquánshuǐ
Coffee 咖啡 Kāfēi

MISC. SURVIVAL 杂项 Záxiàng

NO MSG, Please! 请不要味精 Qǐng Búyào Wèijīng
Menu 菜单 Càidān
Bill 账单 Zhàngdān
I'm out of money! 我没有钱! Wǒ méiyǒu Qián
Where's the back door? 后门在哪里? Hòumén zài nǎlǐ
Etcetera… 等等 Děngděng
Where's our Consulate? 领事馆在哪里? Wǒmen Lǐnshìguǎn zài nǎlǐ?
How do I get back to planet earth? "Wǒ zěnme huídào shìjiè ne? 我怎么回到世界呢?
Will this chapter ever end?

Pappy's Pizza & Pies—Chinese *and* Foreign Foods

If you still can't figure out the menu, Alex (Pappy), a Hungarian-Australian married to a Chinese, now has two restaurants, and both have Chinese/English menus with color photos, and a broad range of both Western and Chinese foods. Delicious, healthy—and state-of-the-art, spotlessly clean kitchens.

See Chapter 24 for more information of their
Website: www.xmadk.com/en/index_ms.php

Note: I receive no income or even discount for any referrals in this book. They are all simply the best and most reliable that we or our friends have found.

Chapter 23

Chinese Dining in Amoy

In the early 90s we had few quality Chinese restaurants and zero foreign fare. But nowadays we're spoiled with every cuisine you'd want and some you would not want. Of course, my own tastes are simple (Sue says I have no taste at all), and I could live happily on the simplest 6 yuan special for years—but now I eat the same thing daily out of choice, not necessity.

We have thousands of Chinese restaurants of all styles, but also hundreds of foreign restaurants. We have Spanish, Italian (over 40 places), Mongolian, Korean, Thai, Brazilian—you want it, we've got it—everything, that is, except really authentic Mexican. Heavy sigh. But like shops, Xiamen restaurants pop up like mushrooms overnight, and fail just as quickly.

So this issue of Magic Xiamen, to minimize reader complaints, I've curtailed this chapter. Please check the Amoy Magic website, which I can update more easily—and ***please phone ahead*** to make sure they are still there!

Water on the Rocks

Jesus must have been talking about China when he said, "Those who give even a cup of cold water in my name will receive their reward," because Chinese don't drink cold water. They drink boiling water, which they say is better on the stomach (I'm in enough hot water without drinking it too).

Until the early 90s, the only place in Xiamen that served ice water was Xiàmén Plaza (Xiàmén Dōngnányà DàJiǔdiàn, 厦门东南亚大酒店). And we found out even the 5-star places in Běijīng served only hot water!

In 1993, the waiters in Běijīng's finest hotel insisted they had nothing but boiling water, even though they did have buckets of ice for wine and soft drinks. I suggested pouring hot water into the ice bucket and they said, "Won't work. Hot water melts ice."

On the third day I barged into the 5-star kitchen, poured boiling water in a bucket of ice, and proved that some ice could survive a boiling baptism, yet next meal we were again told, "No ice water." I repeated this demonstration 4 times over the next two days, and only on our day of departure were we finally served lukecool water.

Before I checked out, I dropped by the kitchen and presented the staff with a neatly printed recipe for ice water.

Ironically, after 20 years in Xiàmén, I now prefer to drink hot water…

Dining Survival Tips

Phone Ahead! ***Again***—Xiàmén establishments are like mushrooms; they spring up overnight and vanish just as quickly. Phone ahead to make sure they're still there, and double check the websites: www.amoymagic.mts.cn & www.xiamenguide.com

Famished at the Feast. While many foreigners like eating rice with their meat and vegetables, Chinese eating out often don't want rice at all. They order only what they don't get at home—like jellyfish and seaworms, pickled piggy toes, and stewed duck webs. These exotic delicacies may well tantalize the taste buds but they don't stick to the ribs, and you can easily find yourself famished at the end of a 20 course feast unless you can top it off with a plate or two of rice or noodles. And herein lays the problem.

Unless you hound the waitresses, they won't serve the rice until the very end, and plain, white rice is not the most appealing way to top off a meal (except for our youngest son Matthew, who has been in China since he was six months old and therefore has taken leave of some critical faculties).

You must beg the waiter, "Please bring the rice first!" (Qǐng Bǎ Mǐfàn Xiān Shàng! 请把米饭先上!). They will happily reply, "Hǎole! Hǎole!" (好了,好了! Okay!), but their brains in no way hear what their lips are saying. Chinese don't order rice and so they cannot believe you would either, so you must hound them for it, and even then you'll probably still end up getting rice only as your just desserts.

A waitress in Xiàmén's finest foreign-run hotel (you guess which one) agreed three times to bring the rice and we still did not get it until after we'd paid. Then she had the nerve to suggest a doggy bag for the rice.

We've begged the Xiàmén University restaurant waitresses, several times a week, for years, to bring the rice first. Only in the last few months have they given in. In fact, now they often plop bowls of white rice in front of us even before they take our order—and then we get to stare at white rice until the entrees arrive half an hour later. But cold rice is better than no rice.

MSG. If you're one of the 10% of Americans allergic to MSG, you should see Gǔlàngyǔ's Catholic priest about last rites.

You can beg the waitress all you want, "Please—no MSG" (Qǐng Búfàng Wèijīng, 请不放味精), but when your tongue tingles and your face flushes you'll know your cook was of that sect who adds MSG with a shovel and believes no creature could live without this all-purpose culinary chemical. But check out American cookbooks from the 1950s; they called for MSG, which they called Accent," in everything from meats and veggies to desserts! Fortunately, some restaurants now advertise "No MSG!"

The best way to avoid MSG is to cook Chinese food at home… so in the next chapter I share recipes for some Xiàmén favorites.

South Fújiàn Cuisine (Mǐn Cài, 闽菜)

Hǎoqīngxiāng Restaurant has delighted gastronomes from all over South-east Asia since 1940 with its Southern Fújiàn snacks, including my wife's favorite Zòngzi's (粽子, the pyramidal bamboo wrapped glutinous rice and meat dumplings), as well as garlic cake and meat onion dumplings, taro cake, and jelly fish (no peanut butter fish yet). Menu favorites include "High quality chicken stewed with Ginseng," or "Low quality chicken boiled with dandelions?" (for those on a budget?) Also try, "Braised squid and straw mushrooms," "Lucky and sweet dew prawn ball," "Glutinous rice porridge with sea crab," "Deep-fried five-flavor rolls" (one of Xiàmén's most famous delicacies), "Steamed crayfish," "Deep-fried fish in squirrel shape" (I'm nuts about that one), "Deviled lion's head" (Chinese meatball – excellent!), and "Deviled duck in dipper shape." Tel: 2219778

1st Location: #59 Húbīn Zhōng Lù (湖滨中路 59 号)
Near Zhōngshān Hospital (中山医院)

2nd Location: #1 Zhōngshān Lù Dōnghǎi Hotel 6/F (中山路 1 号东海酒店 6 楼)
Near the harbor facing Gulangyu (Lúndù, 轮渡) Tel. 2988578

Lùjiāng Hotel (鹭江宾馆)—on the harbor facing the Gulangyu Ferry Terminal. Lùjiāng's Mǐnnán cuisine and "herbal" recipes have even been featured on American television. Also try their dimsum. Rooftop dining offers great view of Gǔlàngyǔ.
Add: #54 Lùjiāng Lù (鹭江道 54 号)
Tel: 2022922

> **Dim Sums** I think the word "Dimsum" has more to do with accounting than Diǎnxīn (点心). You choose delightful treats like chicken feet, dumplings, meats and veggies, rice congees, piggy toes and pickled peppers from carts laden with trays and little bamboo steamers. Then the server stamps cryptic runes on what resembles a Chinese Bingo card. If you ask for prices they'll give you a dim sum, figuring Lǎowài are too dim to sum it.
>
> But seriously, Xiàmén has great dimsum—and for a fraction of what I'd pay back in California.

Xīnqiáo Hotel (Xīnqiáo Jiúdiàn, 新侨酒店) The brochure says,

> "To welcome all people at home and abroad, "Chun Hui Yuan" Chinese Restaurant would like to recommend you 'Xin Qiao' delicacies – Cold Spicy Pork Intestines, Iced Crab Meat in Chicken Soup, Drunk Pigeon w/Bear, Egg Roll in Laver, Jellyfish Salad w/Minced Chicken, together with dishes of Guang Dong typical, South China typical and hundreds of Xin Qiao morning teas."

Yum. But these are delightful: "Shrimp w/Minced Taro," "Wrapped Thin Pancake," "Two flavor lobster," "Dumpling stuffed with prawn."

Add: No. 444 Zhōngshān Lù, (中山路 444 号) Tel: 2038883

City Hotel, Xiàmén (厦门宾馆), near Zhōngshān Park, is famous for such local dishes as "Monk Climbing the Wall" (Fótiào Qiáng, 佛跳墙), a combination of carefully cooked carcasses of exotic land and sea creatures. Also try, "Sun rises from east mountain" (Ríchū Dōngshān, 日出东山) or "Eastern Ocean Lobster," (Dōnghǎi Lóngxiā, 东海龙虾).
Add: Xiàmén Bīnguǎn, Húyuán Lù, # 16 (厦门市虎园路 16 号)
Tel: 2053333 Website: www.cityhotelxm.com

Overseas Chinese Hotel (Huáqiáo Dàshà, 华侨大厦) Famous for its Mǐnnán cuisine; try the "Beancurd braised with cucumber," "Crescent crisp fragrant-flowered garlic cake," "Xiàmén pancakes," or "Chicken roll in lotus shape."
Add: 70-74 Xīnhuá Lù (新华路 70-74 号) Off Zhōngshān Lù by the PSB.
Tel: 2660888 www.xmhqhotel.com.cn

Xiàmén Mandarin (Yuèhuá Jiúdiàn, 悦华酒店) back in 1988 won its way into Lǎowài hearts and wallets with its Western Café's macaroni 'n cheese—Xiàmén's first western food. Now you can find just about any kind of cuisine in Xiamen, but its still hard to beat the Mandarin's Chinese cuisine, ambience, or prices. Try "Dragon attending banquet" (fried lobster), "Deep-fried Crab Legs," "Monk Jumps the Wall", "Coin-shaped Crab Cake," "Abalone Embellished with Radish Ball," "Flock of Birds (prawn) Exposing to the Sun" (fowl exhibitionists?), and "Deviled Roast Eel." Open 24 hrs.
Add: Hǔlǐ District, #101 Yuèhuá Lù (湖里区悦华路 101 号)
Tel: 6023333 Website: www.xmmandarin.com

Mandarin Seaview, adjacent to the Exhibition Center, offers an extensive breakfast, lunch and dinner buffet. Check out some of their special promotions, like the recent Hakka Cuisine Festival.

Shūyǒu Seafood Restaurants (Shūyǒu Hǎixián Jiǔlóu, 舒友海鲜酒楼), perhaps Xiamen's finest, is a marriage of Sea World and Red Lobster. Select your favorite eel, fish, octopussies, squid, seaworms, sea urchins, shellfish, deng deng, from rows of fish tanks on the first floor, then ascend to the second floor dining rooms and wait for your victims to be served. Top quality food (top prices too).
Website: www.shuyou.com

Shūyǒu Seafood Restaurant, Bīnběi Branch (湖滨北路)
Add: Bank of China Building 1-4/F (湖滨北路中行大厦裙楼 1-4 楼) Tel: 5098888 5095588

Nine Dragon Pool (Jiǔlóng Táng Shífǔ, 九龙塘食府) Delightful seaside dining in cabins converted from ship containers! Mǐnnán, Cantonese and seafood.
Add: #49 Island Ring Road (Huándǎolù, 环岛路 49 号).
It's behind Húli Hill Fort (胡里山炮台后面) Tel: 2515335

South Seas Fishing Village (Nánhái Yúcūn, 南海渔村), with several Xiàmén locations, serves S. Fújiàn (Mǐnnán) and Cantonese cuisines, as well as more sea creatures than Sea World.

Their aquariums are chock full of live creatures crawling, slithering and sliding in and out of basins, aquariums and woks (probably dinner plates as well). I saw a small army of savory scorpions scaling a plastic bucket, and high tailed it before *I* kicked the bucket. Choose indoor or outdoor seating, then choose your victims.

Exhibition Center Branch (Huìzhǎn Diàn, 会展店)
Add: Island Ring Road, Facing Exhibition Ctr. (会展中心对面环岛路旁） Tel: 5023188

Bāshǔ Sìchuān Cuisine (Bāshǔ Chuáncài, 巴蜀川菜）Sìchuān, but also good Mǐnnán (try spicy prawns)
Add: Liánhuā Intersection, opposite Xiāngjiāng Park（莲花路口, 香江花园正对面）
Tel: 5136617

North Fújiàn Cuisine (Mǐnběi Cài, 闽北菜)

Wǔyí Mtn. Country Kitchen (Wǔyí Nóngjiā, 武夷农家）Natural foods, natural freshwater fish, wild vegetables; country-brewed rice wine.
Add: Siming District, Xiàhé Lù #881 11-14 Qiānxǐ Park
（思明区厦禾路千禧园 881 号 11-14）Tel: 5814111, 5814222

Northeast Fújiàn Cuisine (Mǐndōng Cài, 闽东菜)

Mǐndōng Tàilǎo Restaurant（闽东太姥酒楼）
Add: 323-17 Xiàhé Commercial Center; opposite #6 middle school（厦禾商厦 323 之 17 六中对面）Tel: 2284615

Cantonese Cuisine (Yuè Cài, 粤菜)

Guǎngdōng (Cantonese) folk are said to eat anything with four legs except the table and chairs, and anything with wings but an airplane. All of the really funky dishes you hear about, such as live monkey brains and raw rat babies, are Guangdong (Cantonese) style dishes. If you have a hankering for such dishes, find them yourself.

Lucky Full City (Cháofú Chéng, 潮福城)
Add: No.28 Húbīn Běi Lù, Jiànyè Bldg. by Bank of China (湖滨北路 28 号，建业大厦裙楼，中行对面） Tel: 5058688

Fortune Seafood (Fúmǎn Lóu, 福满楼） Tel: 2682188 2682388
Add: #189 Xiàhé Lù 6/F Bank Center（厦禾路银行中心 6 楼）

Bìgōng Hotel (Bìgōng Jiúdiàn, 碧宫酒店) offers excellent Guangdong cuisine, prepared by well known chefs under the guidance of Chinese dieticians. Try their morning tea (dimsum), and such items as "Green & gold crab in lotus shape," "Wild chicken in Phoenix-tail shape," and "Lobster flakes in lamp shape." 24 hour service.
Add: Húbīn Zhōng Lù, Tobacco Bldg (湖滨中路烟草大厦). Tel: 5854828

Sichuan Cuisine (Chuān Cài, 川菜)

Sìchuān, one of the most popular, is everywhere. Look for the characters (川菜) (Chuān Cài) Also see "Hotpot" section

Bāshǔ Sìchuān Cuisine (Bāshǔ Chuáncài, 巴蜀川菜)
Sìchuān; also Mǐnnán; try the spicy prawns Tel: 5136617
Add: Liánhuā Intersection, by Xiāngjiāng Park (莲花路口， 香江花园正对面)

Shǔdū Sìchuān (蜀都川菜) Near Chángshēng Hotel (长升大酒店站)
Add: #161 Chángqīng Lù (长青路 161 号) Tel: 5087736

Chóngqìng Shùnfā Sìchuān (重庆顺发川菜)
Add: Húlǐ, #47-2 Jiāyuán Lù (湖里区， 嘉园路 47 之 2) Tel: 5659437

Hùhuá Sìchuān (沪华川菜)
Add: #25 Fùshān Huāyuán (富山花园 25 号) Opposite Dàzhōu Market (大洲菜市场对面) Near World Trade Ctr. (在国贸站) Tel: 5052197

Ānhuī Cuisine (Ānhuī Cài, 徽菜)

Xiāoyáo Jīn Anhui Restaurant (逍遥津徽菜馆)
Add: #6-16 Dǐngwò Zi 顶沃仔 6 号之一 (Near XMU West Gate) Tel: 2196983

Hotpot (Huǒguō, 火锅)

(warming in the winter)

Xiāngāo Lóu 3 Flavor Hotpot (Xiāngāo Lóu Sānwèi, 鲜羔楼三味火锅)
Add: 425-3 Xiānyuè Lù (仙岳路 452 号之 3)
Tel: 5106761)

Júdì Smokeless Barbeque and Hotpot (Júdì Wúyān Shāokǎo, 桔地无烟烧烤与火锅) Korean and Japanese influence
Add: #78 Héxiāng Xī èr Lù (禾祥西二路 79 号)
End of Héxiāng Xī Lù , near harbor.
Tel: 5041177, 5369922

Old #6 Lee Hot Pot City, Huming Branch (Lǐ Lǎoliù Huǒguō Chéng, Húmíng Diàn (李老六火锅城， 湖明店) Good Chunking-style hotpot (Chóngchìng wei, 重庆味) 3858788 Near World Trade Ctr (国贸大厦)

Uncle Walt goes to hotpot

Cháozhōu Cuisine (Cháozhōu Cài, 潮州菜)

(Great seafood)

Hǎifú Fāng Xiūxián Huì Restaurant (海福坊休闲会馆)
Add: Liánhuā Hǎishān Intersection #2 Jiāliánlǐ Villa (莲花海山路口嘉莲里 2 号别墅)
Tel: 5215888 Fax: 5258777

Lion King Chinese Restaurant (Shīwáng Fǔ Zhōngcāntīng, 狮王府中餐厅)
Also Dōngběi Cuisine.
Add: Shàngli, Wéncéng Lù Beside Railworkers Sanitarium, Shànglǐ（上李文曾路铁路疗养院旁） Tel: Tel2562835

Shànghǎi Cuisine (Shànghǎi Cài, 上海菜)

Xiàmén "Drunk With Love" Restaurant! (Xiàmén Zuìài, 厦门醉爱)
Shànghǎi, Cháozhōu, Mǐnnán and Táiwān Cuisines; highly rated.
Add: #91-1 Héxiáng Xī Lù 2nd Street, Overseas Chinese Seaview City（禾祥西二路华侨海景城 91 之 1） At the end of Héxiáng Xī Lù, near harbor. Tel: 2683131

Lùfā Gourmet Restaurant Húlǐ Branch (Lùfā Měishí Húlǐ Diàn, 鹭发美食湖里店)
Their specialty is Taiwanese, Mǐnnán and Guǎngdōng cuisines, and Australian and South African abalone (which Lu Fa claims cures virtually everything).

> "Abalone has a function of nourishing yin, balancing blood pressure and tonifying the skin. Chinese traditional medicine believes that abalone can replenish vital essence and relieve dryness, improve the function of liver and eyes and can cure the deficiency of vital essence of the liver and kidney, consumptive fever, deficiency of blood of the liver and blur sight.
>
> "Modern medicine considers abalone full of nourishments with plenty of protein, fat, iodine, calcium, phosphor and vitamin A and a very good tonic. Cooked in clay pot in an ancient way abalone is the best dish for diners."

Add: #22 Hǎitiān Lù, Húlǐ（湖里区海天路 22 号）
Near Huli Construction Bank（湖里建行站） Tel: 5658888

Northeastern Cuisine (Dōngběi Cài, 东北菜)

When I'm feeling down in the dumplings, I need a treat—like some Dōngběi ravioli-like Chinese dumpling (Jiǎozi, 饺子), which are stuffed with pork, beef, lamb, seafood, tofu; spinach, carrots, leeks, garlic, onions—you name it, they'll stuff it. Dōngběi dishes are often heavy on meat , thick sauces, vinegar, and garlic, and have more wheat than rice. Enjoy the noodles, stuffed buns, fried meat dumplings, and steamed breads.

Dōngběi King of Chinese Dumpling, Liánqián Branch (Dōngběi Jiǎozi Wáng, 东北饺子王) Add: #18 1-4 Liánqián Xī Lù (莲前西路 18 号之 1-4） Tel:: 5521132

Lǎozhīqīng Dumpling Shop Jiǎozi (老知青) My wife's favorite; 5 Stars. Broad selection, great prices—especially if you buy the discount coupons. Try the meat and veggie wrapped in tofu skins (a Beijing duck sort of effect).
Add: #98 Húbīn Nán Lù (湖滨南路 80 号) Tel: 2202855

Lǎozhīqīng Dumpling Shop, Fùshān Branch (Lǎozhīqīng Jiǎozi Guǎn, 老知青饺子馆富山店) Add: facing Jiāhé Lù Holiday Shopping Ctr. (嘉禾路假日商城对面) Tel: 5169699

Húnán Cuisine (Xiāng Cài, 湘菜)

"Xiāng Cài" is known especially for its aromatic smoked vinegar and liberal application of pungent peppers. Máo Zédōng (毛泽东), a Húnán native, even had peppers baked into his bread.

Xiāoxiāng Qínghuái Hunan Restaurant (Xiāoxiāng Qínghuái Xiāng Cài Guǎn, 潇湘情怀湘菜馆) Add: Jīnbǎng Lù Dōngfāng Bālí Qún Lóu (金榜路东方巴黎裙楼) Near Jīnbǎng Park (金榜公园站下车) Tel: 5825929

Jùdé Pavilion Hunan Restaurant (Jù Dé Xuān Xiāng Cài Guǎng, 聚德轩湘菜馆) Add: #91 Héxiáng Xī Lù 2nd Rd , Overseas Chinese Seaview Village G2-G3 禾祥西路二路 91 号华侨海景城 G2-G3 Tel: 2387137

Central Hunan Restaurant (Xiāngzhōng Xiāngcài Guǎn, 湘中湘菜馆) Add: #18-19 Yǒngtóng Chāng Jǐnxiù Plaza, (永同昌锦绣广场 243 号) Tel: 5203538

Hangzhou Cuisine (Hángzhōu Cài, 杭州菜)

Chamber of the Jade Unicorn (Yùlíngé, 玉麟阁) Add: 2/F Húbīn Nán Lù SOHO Building 湖滨南路 SOHO 二楼 Tel: 5333366

Hángzhōu Dinner Guest (Hángzhōu Shìkè, 杭州食客) Tel: 5825957 Add: Train station area; behind Galaxy Building (火车站附近银河大厦)

Hángzhōu Xiǎolóng Tāngbāo (杭州小笼汤包) Snacks Add: #48 Xīnhuá Lù Near Cultural Palace (新华路 48 号) Tel: 399 6586

Hakka Cuisine (Kèjiā Cài, 客家菜)

"Never eaten Hétián (河田鸡) chicken? You've never been to Chángtīng"—or so goes the Hakka saying[①]. Authentic Hakka cooking is simple but heavenly. Hakka cuisine outside of Hakkaland is not always the Real McCoy, but even the knockoffs are worth a try. Check out these places:

1st House of Hakka, Cultural Palace Branch (Kèjiā Dìyī Fǔ-Wénhuàgōng Diàn, [客家第一府（文化宫店）] Tel: 3996995

4-Corner Well Hakka Kitchen, Húlǐ (Sìjiǎo Jǐng Kèjiā Cài, 四角井客家菜) Add: #126 Jiāyuán Lù (嘉园路 126 号) Tel: 6030092

Famous Hakka House (Míng Kèjī Shífǔ, 名客家食府) Tel: 5036816 Add: Húbīn Zhōng Lù , beside Bǎilùzhōu Main Gate (湖滨中路白鹭洲正大门旁)

---

① "没吃河田鸡，不算到长汀" Méi Chī Hétiánjī, Búsuàn Dào Chángtīng"

Veggie Tails

For over a century folks have feasted on Nánpǔtuó Temple's（南普陀）vegetarian fare—a feast for both eyes and stomach (as Japanese say, "The eyes eat, as well as the stomach"). Dèng Xiǎopíng liked their taro so much his chef took 200 pounds back to Běijīng. But take heed: never eat taro with beef, because it is taro-bull.

Veggie Ribs 'n Rice!

The restaurant is inside Nánpǔtuó Temple (through gate nearest XMU, straight back under arch). Website: www.nptveg.com

Tel: 5855113

7th Day Adventist Sanatorium, Gǔlàngyǔ (Měihuá Lǎorén Liáoyǎng Yuàn, 美华老人疗养院）—excellent vegetarian, inexpensive. Phone a day ahead for reservation. They bake whole grain breads, make homemade noodles, and are happy to sell organic grains. Have a meal, or spend a few days in this healthy hilltop retreat center. Getting There: take the ferry to the **Gǔlàng Villa Hotel** (Gǔlàngyǔ Biéshù Jiúdiàn, 鼓浪别墅酒店) , on the back of the islet. From the ferry, turn right, walk up the coast a bit, ascend the narrow granite path behind the bust of the man who invented Pinyin, take the left fork. It is just past the cemetery on the hilltop. Tel: 2066517

Dàfāng Vegetarian (Sùshí Guǎn, 大方素食馆) **Family favorite**, just outside Xiamen Univ. to the left of McDonalds (what isn't nowadays?), facing Nánpǔtuó temple. I love their vegetarian sweet 'n sour ribs—veggie bones and all!—or veggie fish (replete with head, scales and veggie tails! And try their vegetarian Jiǎozi.

Add: #412-9 S. Sīmíng Lù (思明南路 412 之 9 号)

Tel: 2093236

Northwestern Noodles (Xīběi Lāmiàn, 西北拉面）

N.W. Noodle Shops You'll never pig out here because cow is king in shops run by Muslims from N.W. China's Xīnjiāng (新疆). Just look for the swarthy fellows sporting white linen beanies.

They make hand-pulled or knife-shaved noodles on the spot. Try beef soup and beef Jiǎozi, or hand-drawn noodles and beef. Cheap and filling, but they can be salty. They will cut back on oil, salt or hot peppers, but it is easy to miscommunicate, so use your noodle…

Use Your Noodle

Northwest China's Muslim's murder Mandarin's tones as badly as we Lǎowài! Long-term Xiàmén resident Bill Job asked for hand-pulled (Lā, 拉) noodles without hot peppers (Là, 辣). Bill correctly used the 1st tone for "pull" and 4th tone for "pepper," but the tone-deaf Xin1jiang1 fellow exclaimed, "How can I make hand-pulled noodles without pulling them!"

Xīnjiāng Āh Fántí Restaurant (新疆阿凡提饭馆) ***my favorite!*** A Middle-Eastern oasis in downtown Xiàmén! Great ambience, fine food, good prices.
Add: #170-15 Héxiāng Dōng Lù, near train station, opposite petrol station. (禾祥东路 170-15 号，加油站对面，火车站附近)
Tel: 5819220

Húyīdāo, XMU—our sons' favorite (胡一刀厦大店)
Add: XMU W. Village, facing Post Office (厦大西村顶澳仔邮局斜对面) Tel: 2573858

N.W. Noodles, XMU (Xīběi Lāmiàn Xiàdà 西北拉面，厦大)
Add: #101 XMU Street, Qúnyì Bldg., facing Nánpǔtuó (厦大一条街群益楼 101 号)
Tel: 2574381

N.W. Noodles, Jiāngtóu (Xīběi Lāmiàn Guǎn Jiāngtóu, 西北拉面馆江头)
Add: #66 W. Jiāngtóu Lù (江头西路 66 号) By Jiāngtóu Veggie Market (江头菜市场站) Tel: 5567322

Old Xinjiang Saying

"Eat stewed lamb and grandpas become just like lads,
grannies become just like lasses."
"Qīngdùn Yángròutāng, "Lǎotóu Chīle Xiàng Xiǎohuǒzi Yíyàng,
Lǎotàitài Chīle Xiàng Dà Gūniang Yíyàng"
"清炖羊肉汤"老头吃了像小伙子一样，老太太吃了像大姑娘一样"

Qingzhen #1 House of N.W. Noodles (Qīngzhēn Xīběi Dìyī Jiā Lāmiàn, 清真西北第一家拉面) Add: Húbīn Běi Lù , by Special Trade Bldg. (特贸湖滨北路特贸大厦旁)
Tel: 5334591

Qīngzhēn N.W. Noodle House (Qīngzhen Xīběi Lāmiàn Guǎn, 清真西北拉面馆)
Add: #20 Jiāyuán Lù (嘉园路 20 号) Tel: 5753791

Beef Noodles(牛肉面)

(Try S. Fújiàn's famous Quánzhōu Beef)

Dr. Soup's Chinese/Western Beef Noodle Soup Kitchen (Tāng Bóshì Niúròumiàn Zhōngxī Cāntīng, 汤博士牛肉面中西餐厅)
Add: #117 Sīmíng Nán Lù (思明南路 117 号) Tel: 2134879

Quánzhōu Beef Shop, Jiāngtóu (Quánzhōu Niúròu Diàn, 江头泉州牛肉店)
Add: #344 Jiāhé Lù , Jiāngtóu (江头嘉禾路 344 号) Tel: 5529096

Zhēngzōng Quánzhōu Beef Shop (Zhēngzōng Quánzhōu Niúròu Diàn, 正宗泉州牛肉店) Add: #31 Yǔhòu Nán Lù (屿后南里 31 号) Near Sōngbǎi Park (松柏公园站) Tel: 5071929

Ahféi Táiwān-Style Braised Beef Noodles (Afféi Táishì Hóngshāo Niúròumiàn, 阿肥台式红烧牛肉面)
Add: Beside Huáchāng District Govt. Bldg. (华昌路区政府旁) Tel: 5748553

Knife-Shaved Noodles Watch them deftly shave strips of dough and flip them into a boiling wok. Fresh noodles are fried with meat, veggies, seasonings. You won't find fresher noodles anywhere, and just a few Yuan a bowl.

Mongolian Cuisine (Měng Cài, 蒙菜)

Prairie Town (Cǎoyuán Chéng, 草原城) near the Philippine Consulate in Liánhuā, has lassies in Mongol garb serving up Mongolian munchies as if you were the Khan himself. Try the Fēibǐng cakes (飞饼), and roast leg of lamb wrapped in thin pancakes with scallions and plum sauce (like Běijīng Duck without the duck).

If you're not sheepish, order a whole roasted sheep. Two girls bear a large wooden platter with the charred creature standing upright, jaw grimacing, bandaged eyes staring straight at you. Very appetizing; not.

Jared had a little lamb. Yum.

Phone ahead 24 hours for the whole roasted lamb.
Tel: 555-3318.
Add: Jiāliánlǐ Jiālǐ Huāyuán, (嘉莲里嘉莲花园 3 号)Near Philippine Consulate. (Fēilùbīn Lǐngshìguǎn Fùjìn, 菲律宾领事馆附近)

Canine Cuisine (Gǒuròu, 狗肉)

My two sons, who grew up in Xiamen, have eaten dog, though I've ***never*** touched it. But I used to eat pigs, which are smarter than dogs, so…[①]

Chinese Hot Dog?

Bǎntóu Dogmeat Restaurant, **Jīměi** (Bǎntóu Gǒuròu Diàn, 坂头狗肉店)
Add: Jīměi Qū, 324 Nat'l Highway & Bǎntóu Lù Intersection (集美区 324 国道坂头路口)
Tel: 6261005

Yuèyuán Hotel Lùyàn Restaurant (Yuèyuán Jiúdiàn Lùyàn Cāntīng, 悦园酒店鹿宴餐厅) Add: #203 Húbīn Nán Lù (湖滨南路 203 号悦园酒店) Tel: 2217808

① Oldest son Shannon is now vegetarian, like his dad, though Joshua Kellard, our resident Englishman, says he's vegetarian too because the animals he eats eat grass.

Chinese Fast Food

You deserve a break today...from burgers & fries.

Wúzàitiān Snacks (吴再添小吃店) This is the locals' idea of McDonalds. The place boasts 300 seats, usually packed to the gills with guests feasting on such Xiamen delicacies as "Scallion cake," "Taro cake," "Fried onion dough," "Zongzis," "Noodles with prawn," "Deviled noodles," "Jelly fish," "Octopus," (my favorite), and "Braised pig's feet and trotter in soy sauce" (after trying trotters, I was trotting too).
Add: #25-7 Hexiang W. Rd. 禾祥西路美湖路 25 号之 7 号 Tel: 2057789

Huángzéhé Peanut Soup Shop (Huángzéhé Huāshēngtāng Diàn, 黄则和花生汤店), founded the same month as New China (October, 1949), would thrill Jimmy Carter with its 20+ kinds of snacks and drinks made from peanuts. And the prices are peanuts. Feast on "Fried dough with egg and sesame seeds," "Peanut soup," "Dumpling soup," "Deep-fried jujube," "Seasoned millet mush," "Deep fried glutinous rice," and for a real breath of fresh air, try "Deep-fried garlic." Locations all over Xiàmén, but the main shop is on Zhongshan Rd. near the Gulangyu Ferry.
Add: #22-24 Zhōngshān Lù (中山路 22-24 号) Tel: 2024670

A fowl way to get a head in life...

World Trade Center Mall Rooftop Food Court (beside train station). Pretty, costumed lasses serve a broad array of ethnic cuisines from all over China, as well as planet earth: Yunnan yummies, Japanese sushi, Chinese dumplings—even burgers.

Duōduō Love [DDL] (Tiāntiān Duōduō Lè, 天天多多乐) Korean, Japanese & Táiwān styles. Branches in Lianhua, Wenyuan, Jinbang, etc. Check our website's dining pages for locations.

"No Name Cafeterias" (Wú Míngzi, 无名子) Scattered throughout Xiamen—Huli, Dihao Bldg. Powerlong, etc.

Again, locations are listed on the website's food pages.

Nothing beats these fried starfish, seahorse and scorpion on a stick—except, perhaps, raw rice beetles, chocolate-covered ants, 1,000-year eggs...

Chapter 24

International Cuisine in Amoy

Xiamen has virtually every kind of international cuisine you could hope to find—with the exception of good Mexican food. Heavy sigh.

We also have many Western fast foods, including half a dozen Pizza Huts, dozens of McDonalds and KFCs, several Burger Kings and Subways, and a few Starbucks—including the largest Starbucks in the world (four stories, facing Gulangyu).

You really haven't lived until you've had authentic Chinese-style Western food.

And you may not live *after* you've had it. This may explain the sign on a Gulangyu hotel/restaurant that reads, "Stop here if you aren't living."

Caution! As with Chinese restaurants, Western establishments pop up overnight, and no sooner have I recommended them than they either fold or else they start cutting corners, the quality deteriorates, and I am on the butt end of angry phone calls and emails. Quite frustrating, especially given that I cannot update this book until the publisher has sold out its stock and wants to reprint. I therefore am cutting this chapter short, introducing only my absolute favorites—and request that you check the restaurant section of the Amoy Magic website for the latest recommendations.

And, as always—***phone ahead*** to make sure they are still there!

Xiamen's First Cheeseburger, October 1988. I love Chinese food, but when we first arrived in 1988, I craved Western food, so was delighted to hear the Overseas Chinese hotel was advertising Xiamen's first cheeseburger!

We rushed to the place—only to be served a tiny bit of meat the size of my thumb stuck between the halves of a dinner roll—and no cheese!

"A cheeseburger must have cheese!" I complained.

"Why?" asked the waiter. "Hamburgers don't have ham." After arguing, he left in a huff and returned ten minutes later with a small green can of grated Parmesan cheese, which he slammed on the table. "Cheese!" he said, and stalked off triumphantly, never to be seen again.

Note: I am not compensated for any recommendations in this book. I base them on the quality of food and service and length of time in business. Hopefully they will still be around when you read this—and the quality will hold up! I had to delete an entire page of favorites from the last edition.

Pappy's Pizza and Pie. Formerly AFD Western Bakery and Restaurant, foreigners and Chinese alike love Pappy's because of its variety of both Western and Chinese foods, its quality (Alex, a Hungarian Australian, is an expert on healthful diet and cooking), and cleanliness (the upstairs kitchen is a beautiful, spotless, space-age work of art).

We love the "Shannon Salad"—a mountainous pile of veggies, fruits and cashew cream named after our oldest son, who is Vegan; it serves two or three people).

I also love the Mexican Pizza, the German potato salad, the vegetarian dishes (burgers, steaks, etc.)—and of course, the meat and vegetable pies, which even our XMU Management College Cafe now supply hungry professors. Try the chicken mushroom, curry chicken, or curry beef.

Lastly—try the broccoli. Every place serves broccoli, but none like Alex. Cooked to perfection, and with such a delicate taste than I can (and do!) eat it as dessert. (Granted, I'm mostly vegetarian, so have strange view on desserts; Susan Marie says I'm liable to get my just desserts).

Website: www.xmadk.com/en/index_ms.php

Tel: 597 8927 Add: 918-16 Eastern Lian Qian Rd. (莲前东路 918-16 号)

Millennium Harbourview Hotel, Zhenhai Rd. Yes, I know this is a hotel, not a restaurant—but Xiamen's first and still best international hotel has four of our favorite restaurants.

Harbourview Cafe (Millennium) has a great buffet (phone to inquire which international cuisine is being served that evening). I especially love their breakfast buffet.

Portofino (Millennium) Of Xiamen's 40+ Italian restaurants, I prefer Chef Pippo's creations—especially the extensive menu with its flexible mix and match pastas and sauces. Not on the menu? He can probably make anything you can think of.

Loong Yuen (Millennium Hotel)—okay, I know this is not Western but Cantonese, but what a treat watching Pasta Master Dai Fankai whirl his dough into noodles—thick Japanese soba, triangular or square, or angel hair quite literally thin enough to thread a needle. He could be a Las Vegas act—swirl and serve.

And, of course—they taste great.

Sakura Japanese Restaurant—an old standby.
Millennium's Add: #12-8 Zhenhai Rd. (12-8 Zhēnhǎi Lù, 镇海路 12-8 号) www.millenniumxiamen.com

Open 6PM – 10PM. Reservations: 2023333 or 2026616.

Bamboo House & Red Armadillo (Zeng Cuo'an Fishing Village).

Only 3 years ago the Zeng Cuo'an fishing village was a nondescript little out of the way place with 2 and 3 story fishermen's homes. Now, dozens have been remodeled into cute and inexpensive bed & breakfasts. The place is bustling at night, with dozens of Chinese and foreign restaurants. Our favorites include Red Armadillo (probably the oldest foreign-run establishment—try their mammoth burgers and chili fries) and Bamboo House.

We love the ambience of both the Red Armadillo and the Bamboo House, sitting outside under trees lit with soft lights strung through the branches, surrounded by the bamboo fence that helps you forget you're sitting in the middle of a bustling tourist village. Try Bamboo House pizzas—some of the best in town, and very modest prices.

Bamboo House Add: #378 Zeng Cuo'an Rd.(曾厝垵 378 号曾氏祠堂侧)
Tel: 251 8366
Red Armadillo Add: #235 Zeng Cuo'an Rd.(曾厝垵 378 号) Tel: 2087377
Website: http://www.theredarmadillo.com/cindex.asp

Japanese Cuisine (Rìběn Cài, 日本菜)

Tokyoto (Dōngjīngdōu, 东京都)

Add: #16 Húbīn Běilù, Block A, Newport Square (Xīngǎng Guǎngchǎng) (湖滨北路 16 号新港广场 A 座) Tel: 5314688

Momotaro Japanese Restaurant (Táotài Láng Rìběn Měishí Guǎngchǎng (桃太郎日本美食广场)

Add:#805 Héxiāng Xī Lù World Trade Square 2/F (禾祥西路 805 号国贸广场 2 楼) Tel: 2214545 www.momotaro.com.cn

Dosun Japanese Restaurant, SM (Duōsāng Rìběn Liàolǐ, 多桑日本料理)
Add: 2/F SM City Plaza (SM 城市广场 2 楼) Tel: 5528181

> **Why Japanese *Really* Eat Raw Fish** Pity the poor Japanese, who after decades of phenomenal economic growth still can't afford fuel to cook their fish, or even chairs to go with their tables. Of course, face is everything for Japanese, so they claim it is culture, but we know better.
>
> Still, these folks' fishy fare must have something going for it because Japanese live longer than anyone on the planet.
>
> Japanese food is low in cholesterol, fat and calories, high in fiber, and pleasing to both eyes (Japanese say, "The eyes eat, as well as the stomach").
>
> So pass the sushi...

Korean Cuisine (Hánguó Liàolǐ, 韩国料理)

Given that Korea is a peninsula thrust into the Pacific, it's no surprise Koreans love seafood. As in Japan, fish, pickles and rice are mainstays. Unlike the Japanese, Koreans can afford to cook their fish, but evidently they still can't afford chairs.

Koreans also eat meat—more pork in the north, and beef in the south.

Korean cuisine includes flavorful casseroles and stews, soups, grilled or stir-fried entrée, and of course the infamous "Kimchi" (pickles, which can be made of just about anything that will sit still long enough to be in a pickle).

Meals are spiced up with pungent fermented chili pastes and soybean pastes. Korean Airlines hands them out in little toothpaste tubes; I always take a couple home to liven up my lunches. I've also left them in the bathroom in the hopes that someone would mistake it for toothpaste.

No takers so far.

Friendship Korean Cuisine (Yǒuqíng Hánguó Liàolǐ, 友情韩国料理)
Add: Beside XMU Oceanographic Institute (厦门大学海洋三所旁)
Tel: 2573114

Arirang Korean Restaurant (Ah1lǐláng Hánguó Liàolǐ, 阿里郎韩国料理)
Add: # 820 Xiàhé Lù Dìháo Bldg. 1/F (厦禾路 820 号帝豪大厦 1 楼)
Tel: 2960722

Gāolìyǎ Korean Restaurant, SM Mall (Gāolìyǎ Hánguǒ Liàolǐ, 高丽雅韩国料理) Add:#384-385 SM Mall 3/F (SM 商业城 3 楼 384-385) Tel: 5595245

Korean Supermarket (Hànfǔ Bǎihuò Hánguǒ Shíshàng Diàn, (汉釜百货韩国时尚店) Add: Húbīn Nán Lù Wànhé Square 2/F #3 (湖滨南路万禾广场二楼 3 号店)
Tel: 5076098 Near Fùshān Trust-Mart Square (富山诚达购物广场)

Thai Cuisine (Tàiguó Cài, 泰国菜)

Spicy Thai pleases palates and sears sinuses. Our favorites include:

Golden Elephant Bay (Jīnxiàngwān Tàiguó Cāntīng, 金象湾泰国餐厅)

Add: Manila Bldg., Héxiāng Xī Lù, Overseas Chinese Seaview City (Héxiāng Xī Lù Huáqiáo Hǎijǐngchéng Mǎnílā Lóu, (禾祥西路华侨海景城马尼拉楼) Tel: 2387999

Brazilian Barbecue (Bāxī Kǎoròu, 巴西烤肉)

Brazilian barbecue, cooked on skewers over an open fire, is big in Xiàmén but the portions are tiny. We were shocked at the tiny sliver of roast beef they sliced off for us—but had no idea they would reappear every few minutes with lamb kebabs, chicken legs, sausages, prime rib, steak. I had my fill all too quickly (just the buffet and salad bar were enough for me).

Wànlóng Brazilian Barbecue (Wànlóng Bāxī Kǎoròu, 万隆巴西烤肉)

Add: #55-57 Húbín Běi Lù 1/F Zhōngxìn Huìxiáng Guǎngchǎng [Square] . (湖滨北路中信惠祥广场) Tel: 5369223

Yàmǎxùn Brazilian Barbecue (Yàmǎxùn Bāxī Kǎoròu, 亚马迅巴西烤肉)

Add: #8 Lújiāng Dào Int'l Bank Bldg. 3/F (鹭江道 8 号国际银行大厦 3 楼)

Tel: 2078810 E-mail: xmyamaxun@hotmail.com

French Cuisine (Fǎshì Cài, 法式菜)

Red Rock French Restaurant, Quánzhōu City (Hóngshí Fǎshì Cāntīng, 泉州市红石法式餐厅)

Add: Quánzhōu City, Lǚyóu Wénhuà Jiē Bǎiyuán Lù (泉州市后城旅游文化街百源路) Tel: 0595 22187273

About a 90 minute bus ride.

Indian Cuisine (Yìndù Cài, 印度菜)

Indiano Johns SAMRAT (Yìndù Fēng, 印度风). Good ambience; pricey. In Kāimíng Theater Complex (Kāimíng Diànyǐng Chéng, 开明电影城) Add: #69 Jiāngtóu Běi Lù (江头北路 69 号) Tel: 5557699

Latin Cuisine (Gǔbā Cài, 古巴菜)

Havana (Hāwǎnà, 哈瓦那) near the Philippine Consulate in Liánhuā McDonalds serves up tapas and barbeque in a rustic décor reminiscent of Mexico—wood, wrought iron, everything but the black velvet Elvis. Don't miss this place!

Add: #88 Língxiāng Lǐ (凌香里 88 号) Tel: 5536005

Hollywood Cuisine (Haǒláiwù Cài, 好莱坞菜)

The House (Lǎobiéshù Xīcāntīng, 老别墅西餐厅) The head chef and GM of "208 Rodeo", an exclusive Beverly Hills restaurant, helped his friend Arik start The House in an elegant, secluded villa near Zhōngshān Park. (中山公园附近) Add: 10-1 Bǎihé Lù (白鹤路 10-1 号) Tel: 2044358

Cafés (Kāfēi Tīng, 咖啡厅)

Xiamen now has literally hundreds of excellent little cafes scattered around the island. Try the area on Yundang Lake, by Marco Polo Hotel (马可勃罗酒店).

Relax Café (Měilì Shíguāng, 美丽时光) Just outside XMU, across from Xiamen University hospital, this is a favorite with Lǎowài. Rustic wood décor, comfy couches and chairs for dining, reading (nice library) or surfing the net with their WIFI. Nice homemade breads.
Add: #23 University Rd. (Dàxué Lù #23, 大学路 23 号) Tel: 2191687

Sun Dance Café (Rìwǔ Kāfēiwū, 日舞咖啡屋) Live music most weekends; good food, vast CD library of music from all over the planet (some not even from this planet). Try the roast lamb & veggies (3-hours advance notice). Awesome; be sure Michael makes the yeast rolls too. Also visit his "Brown Sugar" Café near XMU. Add: #252 Lùjiāng Dào, Guómào Hǎijǐng Bldg. (鹭江道 252 号国贸海景) Tel: 2390538

Brown Sugar (Hēitáng Kāfēi 黑糖咖啡) Favorite for foreigners; great yeast rolls.
Add: #19 Ding'ao Zai 2/F (顶澳仔 19 号) Near XMU (厦大附近) Tel: 2198726

Bars & Nightlife (Jiǔbā, 酒吧)

My family is my nightlife (daylife too) so I'm not the expert. But favorites seem to include the Hollywood Bar at the Millennium Hotel, Mask, ELITE, etc.

Mask （面具酒吧） Add: #15 Hubin Bei Lu Foreign Trade Building 2/F (湖滨北路 15 号外贸大厦 2F) Tel: 2388886

ELITE Bar 酒吧 Add: #14 Jianye Rd. Chaoyang Bldg. (厦门建业路 14 号阳明楼)

KFC (Kěndéjī, 肯德基) & McDonalds (Màidānglǎo, 麦当劳)

No point in giving addresses for KFCs and McDonalds because they are everywhere. Check their websites for addresses and phone numbers (many are all night, and some have free Wifi).

Both KFC and McDonalds offer free delivery, and both have drive-thru locations (in Lianhua, near California Mall).

KFC China Website: www.kfc.com.cn
McDonalds China Website: www.mcdonalds.com.cn

For a treat, try the KFC down the road from SM Mall, which was opened in a converted temple. It is an appropriate combination, given that Chinese worship food—though there is some debate as to whether American fast food is, strictly speaking, actually food.

Chapter 25

Home Cooking in Amoy

Stewed Turkey Feet For Thanksgiving. Yum!

Dining out in China is fun and cheap, but home cooking is also fun because Amoy is the cornucopia that suckled Zeus himself, with an astonishing variety of veggies, fruits, fish, fowl and fungi. You name it, Xiàmén has it, and fresher and cheaper than back home.

We've put most of our "E-Z Laowai Survival Recipes" on our website, but recipes for S. Fújiàn (Mǐnnán) cuisine are still hard to find, so here are recipes for some Mǐnnán favorites—minus the MSG (wèijīng, 味精) used in everything.

We also include favorite recipes for those most versatile and healthy of staples—oatmeal and tofu.

> **Bring From Home…**
>
> Rubber spatula, serrated bread knife, cheeses, liquid smoke, maple flavoring, almond flavoring, peppermint extract, lemon juice, bay leaves, rosemary, pumpkin pie spice, allspice, sage, thyme, marjoram, summer savory (the latter four make good sausage), coriander leaves, paprika, mace, celery seed, mustard, bacon bits, parsley, dill weed, wax paper, angel food cake pan, pie plates, AK-47 assault rifle (just checking to see if anyone really reads this). Metro, near the airport, has a great selection of spices.

Xiàmén (Mǐnnán) Specialties

Spicy Fried Rolls (wǔxiāng, 五香)Wrap dried tofu sheet around a mixture of cubed pork, fish meat, onions, water chestnuts, soy sauce, five spices, and sweet potato starch. Deep fry, cut in slices, serve.

Spring Rolls (chūnjuǎn, 春卷) These "Mǐnnán burritos" use spring roll wrappers (sold in markets) instead of tortillas, and a filling of: shredded carrots and bamboo shoots, green peas, shredded meats and shrimp, tofu, and anything else that strikes your fancy or wanders in off the street. Cook filling well, add salt and soy sauce, wrap in spring roll wrappers, serve with mustard, chili sauce, plum sauce, scrambled eggs, leeks, and Chinese parsley (coriander). Heavenly!

Oil-Scallion Cake (cōngyóubǐng, 葱油饼) Add fish to diced pork and water chestnuts; add scallions, and dashes of sweet potato starch, Five Spice, sugar and salt. Form into balls, coat with rice starch in bowls, and steam. Let cool. Sprinkle with your favourite condiments, such as chili paste, pickled radish…

Seaworms and Jellyfish? Yum!

"100 Year Egg?" Double Yum!

Twice-boiled fish stomach soup?

Jelly Fish and Sea Worms (túsǔndòng, 土笋冻) Xiàmén folks' favourite delicacy, these are dug from the mud on the beach. Enough said.

Wash jelly fish, stew over low heat until gelatine dissolves. Pour soup into cups, add seaworms, let cool into jello-like substance. They go down better with Chinese chili sauce, wasabi and vinegar.

Fried Squid (zhàyóuyú, 炸鱿鱼) Lin Duck House (林家鸭庄), opposite Nánpǔtuó, serves my favourite, but here's how to make your own. Clean squid well, soak in clear water for a couple of hours. Cut thin slices and score with intersecting diagonal cuts. Fry squid with bamboo shoots, scallions, tomato, sugar and vinegar until they roll up into a tube shape. (Don't overcook or they'll have the texture of rubber grapes).

Fried oyster-egg cake (hǎilìjiān, 海蛎煎) Dip oysters in sweet potato starch, add soy sauce, fry. Pour beaten eggs on mixture and continue to fry until done. Add Chinese parsley (coriander); eat with mustard or chili sauce.

Stir-Fried Rice Noodles (chǎomǐfěn, 炒米粉) Deep fry rice noodles until golden, then rinse in boiled water to remove grease. Stir-fry shredded pork, fish, mushrooms and bamboo shoots in peanut oil and add chicken bouillon, Shaoxing wine, and salt. Add the noodles and serve hot. Awesome.

Zongzi (zòngzi, 粽子) Sue's favorite: pyramid-shaped dumplings of glutinous rice and other stuff wrapped in bamboo leaves. Originally served on the Dragon Boat Festival, but now year round. Make your own by stir frying glutinous rice, pork, chestnuts, mushrooms and shrimp (or some use red beans), and wrap them with bamboo leaves into a pyramid shape, and tie them, then braise them in a soup until well done.

Western Cooking in Amoy

Chinese food is fresh, varied, and healthy, and eating out is both fun and relatively cheap, but when a bout of homesickness lays you low, and you tire of dried mushrooms and fricasseed fish lips, some home-cooking is in order. Fortunately, Xiàmén now has virtually everything needed to cook any kind of cuisine. We list our favorite recipes and tips on the following pages—with special attention to breakfast, which has been my most persistent challenge in China.

Surviving Breakfast I love Chinese food—but not three times a day, seven days a week. When I hit the day—or it hits me—I prefer something familiar...

Breakfast options. Xiàmén has oatmeal (Màipiàn 麦片) from England, Australia and the U.S., but Chinese oatmeal, much of it from the steppes of Mongolia, is adequate, and up to ½ the price.

Oatmeal makes great porridge, muesli/granola, muffins, or pancakes (use local yogurt in batter, add sliced bananas). For a real treat, slice and toast Chinese steamed buns (Mántou, 馒头). Very much like English muffins! As for cereals, they go for $7 or $8 a box, so try making your own.

Oatmeal muesli/granola is fun to make, healthy, and cheap, thanks to the wide variety of dried fruits and nuts, and quality Mongolian *rolled* oats.

Barbarians and Breakfast

Adapted from *"Discover Quanzhou"*

If the way to a man's heart is through his stomach, Chinese have certainly won my heart—except with breakfast. By noon, I can stomach the salted minnows, pork fat, deep fried fish lips and sea worms in jellyfish mold, but first thing out of bed I crave familiarity and simplicity—such as coffee, eggs, and toast.

My hotel's breakfast buffet offered over 60 hot and cold items, but they were the same foods served at noon and night. But I was immune to the allure of those gastronomic delights, opting for humble coffee, toast, and eggs—though I fought daily, for two weeks, to keep the chef from baptizing the eggs in soy sauce

My culinary callousness bewildered my Chinese hosts, for whom all meals must be at least ten courses, half of which are critters seen only on National Geographic, and the other half strange veggies harvested from mountains or scavenged from cracks between sidewalks.

After an especially long day with little lunch and no supper at all, I went to bed hungry but happy, knowing that in a few hours my hotel would serve me, albeit begrudgingly, my coffee, toast and eggs.

Next morning, my hosts banged upon my door and announced, "None of that common buffet today, Professor. We've something special!"

"Don't let me trouble you!" I pled. "Common is fine! I'm a common man. Let's save time and money and just—"

—But my arguing was to no avail. My hosts proudly led me straight to Wenling Delicacy Street, where I was served a big bowl of steaming congealed pig blood soup. Yum.

1 Month Supply of Dr. Bill's Oatmeal Muesli

Fill a large bowl or washbasin with ***rolled oats***. Mix a spoon of salt through the dry mixture. Slowly dribble peanut oil over mixture while stirring to keep oatmeal flaky and reduce clumping; add only enough to moisten the flakes. Repeat the dribble process with a cup or two of honey. Stir in 2 spoons of vanilla and spoon of cinnamon. Add raw peanuts and other nuts. Bake in **preheated** oven at 350° for 20 to 30 minutes, stirring every ten minutes or so to avoid burning. Allow to cool, then add finely chopped dried fruits, all widely available in Xiàmén: shredded coconut, banana chips, and dried papayas, mangoes, pineapple, apple, apricots, raisins, figs…

For the ultimate in convenience, stir in a couple bags of powdered milk and store in a tightly sealed container. Then simply pour into bowl, add ice water, stir, and serve.

Oatmeal & Tofu

Both oatmeal (màipiàn, 麦片) and tofu (dòufu, 豆腐) are tasty, healthy (both help fight cancers), inexpensive, and versatile. Tofu is even a healthy and tasty substitute for cream cheese or ricotta cheese.

On the next couple pages I list my recipes for cookies, oatmeal bread, etc., as well as Susan Marie's favourite tofu recipes for entrees and desserts (they taste so good it is hard to believe they are also good for you).

A good way to spend time with friends, or make new friends, is to invite Chinese over to help you with your cooking and baking. They enjoy learning about your culture and foods. And while you're at it, have them teach you how to make some Chinese dishes. It is amazing what Chinese can whip up in minutes with nothing more than a cleaver, cutting board and wok, and a bit of veggies, meat, soy sauce and garlic.

Oatmeal Pancakes Mix 1½ Cups oatmeal with 2 Cups sour milk (add 2 Tbsp. vinegar to 2 Cups of milk). Let sit. In another bowl, stir together ½ Cup flour, 1 tsp. sugar, 1 tsp. soda (pinch with finger so no lumps), 1 tsp. salt. Add this to oatmeal mixture; stir in 2 beaten eggs. Fry in hot greased griddle until golden brown. Top with Chinese honey, sliced bananas.

Dr. Bill's Own Oatmeal Bread Combine in large bowl:

2 cups oatmeal ½ cup honey 1 Tbsp. salt 2 Tbsp. margarine

Add 2 cups boiling water.

Dissolve: 1 package (1 Tbsp.) dry yeast in ½ cup warm water.

Add yeast after batter cools, and stir in 5 to 6 cups of white flour.

Knead and add white flour until the dough is satiny and smooth.

Place in greased bowl, cover with cloth, let rise until doubled.

Punch down loaves, place in greased loaf pans, allow to double, brush with beaten egg; bake in **preheated** oven at 350° F. for 30-40 minutes.

Cool on rack, slice, and serve up with a hearty barley & cabbage soup.

Oatmeal Cookies (four dozen) Put through a sieve:

1 ½ cups white sugar	1 ½ cups brown sugar	3 cups sifted flour
2 tsp. salt	2 tsp. soda	1 tsp. baking powder.

Cut in 2 cups shortening, and add 6 cups oatmeal.

Combine mixture in bowl with 2 beaten eggs and 2 tsp. vanilla.

Drop teaspoonfuls onto greased baking sheet, flatten with fork, and bake in **preheated** oven at 350° for 12 minutes or until well browned.

Tricks & Treats with Tofu

Tofu (dòufǔ, 豆腐), or Chinese beancurd (essentially, a bean cheese), is nutritious, high in protein, helps fight cancers, and is a great substitute for cream cheese and ricotta cheese—hence Susan Marie's tofu recipes for cheesecake and lasagna. They're both tasty and healthy.

Tofu Cheesecake

E-Z 8 "pie crust: fin ely crush cream-filled cookies, like Oreos, mix in 2 Tbsp. of margarine, use large spoon to press firmly into bottom of pie pan, bake in **preheated** oven at 350° 5 or 10 ten minutes, or until brown. Cool.

Filling: 1 lb. tofu (2 cups) 2 Tbsp. lemon juice ½ cup brown sugar
¼ cup oil 1/3 cup honey 1 tsp. vanilla pinch of salt
1 Tbsp. unbleached white flour

Blend ingredients in food processor until smooth and creamy, then pour into the unbaked pie shell and bake for about 45 minutes in an oven preheated to 350° , or until cracks begin to form on the edges of the filling.

Tofu Cookie Pudding

½ lb.(1 cup) steamed tofu 1/3 cup sugar 2 Tbsp. oil 1 tsp. vanilla pinch of salt. Blend ingredients in blender or food processor until smooth and creamy, fold 8 Oreo cookies (broken into quarters) into the pudding, and chill from 2 hours to overnight.

Making Christmas Cookies with Chinese and German Friends

Two-Tofu Lasagna

Follow your favorite lasagna recipe, but substitute tofu for ricotta cheese, and use wonton wrappers (buy stacks of them in produce markets) for pasta. After you've tried wonton wrappers, try using dried tofu sheets instead (soaked until tender but don't fall apart) for a highly nutritious and exceptionally tasty lasagna. Here's Susan Marie's Lasagna Recipe:

Spaghetti Sauce 1-2 packages of tofu
1 ½ lbs. wonton wrappers ***or*** a stack of dried tofu sheets
Mozzarella and Parmesan cheeses (from Olive Oil store)

Prepare spaghetti sauce with browned ground meat. Add minced garlic (optional) and sauted minced onion cooked in chicken bouillon (the more onion the better). Put a thin layer of spaghetti sauce with meat on the bottom of a 9 x 13 inch pan. Cover with 1-2 layers of wonton wrappers (or sheets of soaked, dried tofu), spoon on stirred tofu, layer with meat sauce, parmesan cheese and mozzarella cheese. Repeat layers until pan is full. The top should just be a thin layer of meat sauce, with a little mozzarella and parmesan. Cover and bake at 350° for 45 minutes or until done.

Serves four adults or half a teenager.

Substitutions

For	Use
1 cup sour milk	1 cup milk & 1 T. vinegar or lemon juice
1 cup sweet milk	½ cup evaporated milk, ½ cup water
Ricotta cheese	soft white tofu
Philadelphia Cream Cheese	soft white tofu
Cheddar cheese*	No substitute! ☹
1 T. cornstarch	2 T. flour
1 cup honey	¾ cup sugar, ¼ cup liquid
1 pt. whipping cream	1 pt. water and 2 cups dry nonfat milk solids; add 1 T. sugar and 1 T. lemon juice before whipping
1 cup nut meats	1/3 cup butter
1 egg (for leavening)	½ tsp. baking powder
1 cup granulated sugar	1 cup honey or syrup
1 tsp. baking powder	1 tsp. cream of tartar & 1 tsp. baking soda
1 ½ cups corn syrup	1 cup sugar plus ½ cup water
1 cup canned tomatoes	1 1/3 cup chopped fresh tomatoes simmered for ten minutes
½ cup catsup or chili sauce	½ cup tomato sauce plus 2 T. sugar, 1 T. vinegar, 1/8 teaspoon cloves,
½ cup tartar sauce	6 T. mayonnaise plus 2 T chopped pickle relish
1 cup tomato juice	½ cup tomato sauce & ½ cup water
¼ cup cinnamon sugar	¼ cup granulated sugar plus 1 tsp. cinnamon
1 teaspoon allspice	½ tsp. cinnamon, 1/8 tsp. ground cloves
1 cup chicken broth	1 chicken bouillon dissolved in 1 cup boiling water

*Metro has a wide variety of cheeses, though they can be quite pricey. It is not difficult to make your own, but for convenience, purchase powdered cheddar cheese online. The two best sources, as of this writing, are www.nuts.com and www.firehousepantrystore.com Shipping to China is expensive, so order in advance and bring it with you. A five pound bag of powdered cheese goes a long way, and is great for sauces (mac and cheese, broccoli and cheese, etc.)

Supplement

Before You Come to Xiàmén…

When East Minces West If you too are enchanted enough with magical Amoy to make it your home, the best way to make yourself at home is to bring a little home with you. I've seen Lǎowài boast, "I'm going native," and I've seen them flee months later, disenchanted and tail tucked between their legs.

Although I love Amoy, the endless staring and shouts of "Lǎowài!" remind me I am not and never will be Chinese. When the pressure mounts, I retreat to familiarity. Otherwise, I take it out on family and friends—or my bewildered Chinese hosts.

So make yourself at home by lugging a bit of home in your luggage.

What to Bring from Home? Photos of family and homeland, wall hangings, favorite music CDs and DVDs, a SW radio, a board game or two. Such niceties help save your sanity, and help Chinese learn more about you and your own homeland.

Xiàmén still lacks some Lǎowài staples, so give your palate and psyche a break by bringing from home such hard to find essentials as: basil, cinnamon, nutmeg①; taco shells or tortillas and seasoning, powdered cheese (see previous page).

Mexican food goes over big with Laowai and Laonei alike (still no Mexican cuisine in Xiamen). DIY is the easiest. Lay out the tortillas and fillings (salsa, refried beans, olives, meats, corn ships—all available from Metro); let guests assemble their own burritos, tacos, etc.

Pizza is a cinch if you use Muslim flat breads for the crust. Share home-made pizza with Chinese friends and build yet another bridge between East and West!

Buy China! Wal-Mart once urged Americans to "Buy America!" Today, everything in America is made in China, so why buy imported products if we can buy domestic products that are cheaper and of equal quality? Now that we've made the transition from distribution to actual marketing, it is getting easier to buy quality Chinese products—Ma Ling Ketchup, whole Mongolian milk powder or oatmeal, boxed fruit juices from Běijīng, and fruit jams from Shànghǎi—made not with chemicals and preservatives but with real fruit. In America they'd be labeled "All Natural!" and be thrice the price. Though a warning: many products labeled "100% natural *do* have white sugar and additives (but I found the same thing in the U.S. as well).

In the same vein (or artery, if you don't watch the lard), foreign Megastores aren't the only players in town, and certainly are not the cheapest.

① Many spices and pastas now available at Metro (màidélóng，麦德龙)

Many mom and pop shops offer good selection, low prices, and service with a smile, so give them a try.

Veggie Tips Vegetables are often fertilized with nightsoil, so wash thoroughly with soap and water, and peel – or dip in boiling water for 10 seconds. Or rinse vegetables in chlorine water (1 T. to a gallon), then in boiled water.

Boil drinking water for ten minutes. (Some say babies under 3 months old should be bathed in drinking water!)

B.B. The Sweet Potato Man

In Season, & Out... One of the nicest aspects of life in China, and especially Xiamen, is our abundance of fresh fruits and vegetables. Of course, fresh fruits are seasonable, but the seasons are getting longer, thanks to more local greenhouses, as well as better roads and shipments from all over China.

And canned and dried fruits are, of course, available year round.

Fruit lovers enjoy Zhāngzhōu's mandarin oranges and bananas, Pǔtián's lichees, Chángtài's pomelos (rather like a grapefruit), Lóngyán's pears, deng deng. As broad a selection as you'll find anywhere back home, though at much better prices—when in season…

Bananas xiāngjiāo 香蕉- All year
Cantaloupe hāmìguā 哈密瓜-May & June (hami is similar to cantaloupe)
Coconut yēzi 椰子- All year
Grapes pútao 葡萄- July & August
Guavas fānshíliu 番石榴-June
Kumquat jīnjú 金橘- Dec. & Jan.
Lemon níngméng 柠檬– mainly July & August (but increasingly year round).
Loquat pípa 枇杷- March & April
Mango mángguǒ 芒果- May & June
Oranges liǔchéng 柳橙- Oct. thru Jan.
Papaya mùguā 木瓜- May & June
Pear lí 梨- August
Persimmon shìzi 柿子- Aug. & Sept.
Pineapple bōluó 菠萝- May, June
Plums lǐzi 李子– April & May
Pomelo yòuzi 柚子- Aug. thru Dec.
Star Fruit yángtáo 杨桃- March, April
Strawberries cǎoméi 草莓- April
Sugar Cane gānzhè 甘蔗- Jan. thru March
Tomatoes fānqié 番茄- All year
Watermelon xiqguā 西瓜-July, August

Chapter 26

Shopping A to Z!

Seller's Market Now that we have malls, shopping centers and international retail chains blanketing the island, it is hard to believe that in the early 90s we barely had stores. A typical shop had but a dozen or two products placed side-by-side on dusty shelves to make them look full. Every shop sold the same products at the same time—and all ran out at the same time. When we found a treasure (raisins, oatmeal, cocoa, jam) we bought cases of it because we knew we'd probably never see it again.

No Mayo, lots of Méiyǒu. In 1989 I pedaled our family 10 km. through blistering heat in our heavy wooden-bodied pedicab to Xiàmén's only store with imported foodstuffs because we'd heard it had mayonnaise and tuna fish. It did not have tuna or mayo, but did have plenty of Méiyǒu (没有, "no"; "don't have").

Xiàmén Lǎowài used to prowl Amoy's narrow alleys in search of real toothpaste, soft toilet paper, or bread that wasn't purple and stuffed with pickled eggs and green bean paste. In my first "survival guide" I gave tips on sourcing everything from milk, eggs and flour to chocolate and cheese, but nowadays you can find just about anything in our malls and department stores, so I've cut this chapter short (well, relatively short). Check the website for more suggestions.

Malls & Department Stores

SM Mall (SM 商业广场), on Jiāhé Lù (嘉禾路), 120,000 m^2, has a Wal-Mart Supercenter, Watson's, restaurants and fast food chains, Fujian's largest book store, a large furniture section, and a Cyber City with broad selection of computers, peripherals, and all manner of electronic products. Tel: 5517933

Mingfa Commercial Mall (厦门明发商业广场) one of Asia's largest, is near Liánbǎn. This multi-billion Yuán 400,000 m^2 venture includes a 164,400 m^2 Commercial plaza and below ground parking for 2000 cars. The architecture is said to incorporate a S. Fujian Hakka motif. They will have one of the world's largest Ferris wheel, an "entertainment city," canals, gondolas, and theaters.
Add: W. Liánqián Lù & Jiāhé Lù (厦门市莲前西路与嘉禾路交汇点)

World Trade Center Mall (Shìmào Shāngchéng, Huóchēzhàn, 火车站世贸商城). Nice Food Court; Xiàmen's most Lǎowài-friendly theater (many foreign movies). Add: Xiàhé Lù (厦禾路), beside train station.

Wal-Mart (Wò'ěrmǎ, 沃尔玛) We have at least half a dozen Wal-Marts, one near Zhongshan Rd., one at the train station, and even two across the street from each other at California Mall. For locations, check their website: wal-martchina.com

Metro (Màidélóng, 麦德龙). The world's 3rd largest retailer, this German firm has dozens of outlets in China. Foreigners get free membership cards by showing passports. Prices aren't all that cheap but they have imported products not found elsewhere

(cheeses, for example). It's remote, out by the airport. Take a taxi, or bus 22 or 33. Tel: 5758888 Website: www.metro.com.cn Address: 8 Chánghào Lù, Húlǐ District, (厦门市湖里区长浩路 8 号)

Carrefour (Jiālèfú,家乐福) of France. World's 2nd largest retailer; has over 70 in "Hypermarkets" in China. And we can see why they're called Hypermarkets. Carrefour is larger than Wal-mart, but also a lot noisier! Sue prefers the quieter Wal-mart (though after 18 years of Chinese restaurants you'd think the din would not bother her). Tel: 2928849
Address: 1/F Míngfā Commercial Mall (previous page)—or one near Zhongshan Rd. (莲前西路与嘉禾路交汇处明发商业广场负一楼) Website: www.carrefour.com

Huálián's Stairway to Heaven

Huálián, aka Dōnghǎi (东海), was our first real department store, and also had the first escalator. We had endless fun watching old and young alike trying to gather the courage to ascend the moving stairs.

One day, as a crowd of burly dockworkers were daring each other to jump aboard, 3-year-old Shannon and I squeezed through the crowd and stepped boldly out where no Xiàmén peasant had gone before. As they watched Shannon run and skip up the escalator, one muscled man stamped out his cigarette, rolled up his sleeves, stepped onto the escalator—and fell flat on his face. Shannon laughed, pointed, and said, "Look at the funny man, dad!"

"It's not polite to point, Shannon," I said.

"Why not?" Shannon said. "Chinese point at us all the time!"

Olive Oil Store! Xiàmén Xùlì Restaurant Supply (厦门旭立贸易有限公司) Add: #18-8 Héxiāng Dōng Lù (禾祥东路龙祥花园 18 号之八)
Tel: 5179188 Want cheese, bacon, tuna, olive oil, hot dog relish? Get it here! Called "Olive Oil Store" by loyal Lǎowài, it's a ten minute walk from the train station and has imported foods you won't find elsewhere, for great prices.

Gǔlàngyǔ (鼓浪屿), **A Tourist Shopper's Haven** For a tourist trap, Gǔlàngyǔ has surprisingly reasonable prices on everything from pearls and puppets to antiques and unique crafts like Yog's "interior paintings."

Zhōngshān Lù (中山路)
Xiamen's Mainstreet

Zhōngshān Lù, the commercial and cultural heart of Old Amoy, offers great scenery, nicely renovated colonial-era architecture, and a variety of shops, boutiques, restaurants, and fast food outlets. Zhōngshān Lù was named after Sūn Zhōngshān (Sun Yat-sen), and runs from the harbor —opposite Gǔlàngyǔ Islet to the Cultural Palace and Zhōngshān Park.

Though delightful by day, Zhōngshān really comes alive by night, when it is lit up brighter than Vega. The harbor to Sīmíng section is a "Pedestrian Walk" (bùxíngjiē 步

行街), and closed to cars. It rather reminds me of a Chinese version of Disneyland's "Main Street USA," with chic boutiques belting out Chinese pop songs, and vendors offering tea, coffee, snacks, Japanese pastries and New Zealand ice cream.

Zhōngshān Lù Main Destinations

Bank of China (Zhōngguó Yínháng, 中国银行) Add: #4-10 Zhōngshān Lù (中山路 4-10 号) Tel: 2038076 Across from the Dōnghaǐ (Huálián) Dept. store. I used to joke that it was right under the giant Ronald McDonald sign's armpits, but the city fathers disarmed me when they removed the Ronald McDonald sign.

You can have your funds wired from abroad to your RMB or foreign currency account, or just use the ATM machines. The service charge is no more than you'd pay back home, and nowadays the ATM is even open during lunch…

Long Arm of the ATM

Xiàmén's first ATM machines, in the mid-90s, were for closed during noon naps (Xiūxi 休息). I told an official, "I think Xiàmén just wants to look modern and our ATM's are fake. A little peasant hiding inside hands out money, and he goes home for lunch."

"Not true!" he protested. "These are real ATMs!"

"I was joking!" I said to the blustering banker, but he wasn't mollified. Soon afterwards they started keeping ATMs open even at lunch.

I hope I didn't cost the little guy his job.

Huángzéhé Xiàmén Specialty Snacks (Huángzéhé, 黄则和)
Add: #22-24 Zhōngshān Lù (中山店) Tel: 2024670

Liúchūn Pharmacy (Liúchūntáng Yàodiàn, 留春堂药店)
Add: #66 Zhōngshān Lù (中山路 66 号) Tel: 2101639

Printemp (Bālí Chūntiān, 巴黎春天)
Add:#76-132, Zhōngshān Lù (中山路 76-132 号) Tel: 2040018

Stamps of Approval

You'll win Chinese friends through judicious distribution of canceled stamps from back home—and consider collecting beautiful Chinese stamps.

The Post Office at the end Zhōngshān Lù, facing the Police Station, ha a great selection charges regular rates even for hard to find limited designs.

The post office used to regulate stamp sales to stop the black market, but who would bother buying black stamps when colored are prettier?

New China Bookstore (Xīnhuá Shūdiàn, 新华书店), one of Xiàmén's best.
Add: 163 Zhōngshān Lù (中山路 163 号) Tel: 202-4059.

People's Theater (Xiàmén Rénmín yǐngyuàn, 厦门人民影院)
Add: #217 Zhōngshān Lù （中山路 217 号） Tel: 2118776

Wal-Mart (facing Carrefour)
Add: #158 Sīmíng Nán Lù （思明南路 158 号）
Dìng'Ān Night Market (Dīngān Lù Yèshi chǎng, 定安路夜市场） Now indoors.

Maps: The Lost Tribes of Isareal might have wandered China for centuries (see Xiamen history chapter), but you don't have to. Excellent bilingual maps of Xiamen are sold at bookstores and by street vendors—only 6 to 10 Yuan. But it is absolutely amazing how detailed online Google maps have become. You can almost zoom right in to the street stalls—and in English!

Shopping A to Z

Please check the website for more suggestions and updates. And ***phone ahead!***

AIRLINES (See Transportation chapter)

ANTIQUES Bailuzhou (白鹭洲) shopping area on Yuándāng Lake, or numerous shops on Gǔlàngyǔ's Lóngtóu Lù (龙头路).

Antique Store (Wénwù Diàn, 厦门文物店) #36 Húbīn Běi Lù Tel: 5111349

APPLIANCES (Jiāyòng Diànqì, 家用电器). In 1988, we had no microwaves, coffeepots, toasters or large refrigerators. Now we have everything—and fast delivery and installation are usually free. Try GOME, Metro, Wal-Mart, etc.

GOME Appliances (Guóměi Jiá Diànqì, 国美电器) Excellent service, good prices
Add: #628 Xiàhé Lù, Měirén Ctr. (厦禾路 628 号美仁广场)
Tel: 2668913 Website: www.gome.com.cn

Yǒnglè Home Appliances (Yǒnglè Shēnghuó Diànqì, 永乐生活电器) Good Shànghǎi-based chain has almost 30 outlets in Fújiàn, including ten in Xiàmén. Current addresses: http://www.yongle.cn/filiale/md-dizhi.asp?itemid=5

> **In a Fix—but Fast Fix**
>
> We probably had Xiàmén first microwave. Friends marveled, and an XMU professor asked, "How long do you preheat a microwave?"
>
> We also bought Xiàmén's first imported washing machine—a Sharp.
>
> Actually, we wanted to support China and buy a domestic brand, so we asked an XMU English professor which brand had best quality. "Oh, buy XX brand!" he said. "I bought one last week, and it has great service!"
>
> "If you just bought it, how do you know it has great service?" I asked.
>
> "Well, it broke the 2nd day, but they fixed it fast!"
>
> We bought the Sharp.

APPLIANCE REPAIR (Diànqì Wéixiū, 电器维修)
Many large firms offer appliance repair, but through much trial and error—and far too much error—we've found the best service and prices (scrupulously honest) to be that

from a small family shop, Fuqun Repair (Fùqún Wěixīu Bù, 富群维修部) on South Siming Rd., right beside Hongshan Park.

This amazing little shop has repaired virtually everything—our fridge, air conditioners, televisions and DVD players—even American appliances that they've never seen before, such as our massive Kitchen Aid. For large repairs, they will come to your home. They don't speak English, but they're so accommodating you almost don't need it. For us, they've been a lifesaver—quite literally.

Add: #339 South Siming Rd. (思明南路 339 号) Tel: 2078669.

Der Bücherwurm, Carl Spitzweg, 1850

ART Have a beautiful, professional oil painting done of your family photo! Xiàmén puts out **18%** of the planet's oil paintings. One of China's top 3 centers, with over 6500 artists, we have reproductions of everything from Renoir to Van Gogh, or quality Chinese originals.

For best quality & value, try Art Forest Int'l., which offers originals, reproductions, or customized paintings—any image, any size. Have an idea? They'll create something completely new. For my birthday, my wife Sue had them paint the 1850 classic "The Bookworm" (Der Bucherwurm) by Spitzweg. Visit Art Forest website: www.oilpainting109.com Tel: +86-592-5500370

Art. Forest Int'l（艺术森林国际有限公司）
Address: No.2 Bldg., No.267 Northern Industrial Zone, Jinli Village,Haicang District, Xiamen.
（地址：厦门市海沧区锦里北片工业园 267 号 2#楼）

AUTO REPAIR **Shùnlóng Auto Center** (Shùnlóng Qìchē Wéixiū Zhōngxīn, 顺龙汽车维修中心） Another firm we could not easily live without, they not only keep our van in top shape but also handle the bureaucracy (Red China got its name from the Red Tape)—from insurance and traffic fines to taxes and annual inspections.
Add: #172 Dàxué Lù, beside XMU Hospital（大学路 172 号，厦门大学医院隔壁）.
Tel: 208-5533, 219-1393, or 13906040676

BADMINTON & SUPPLIES

Badminton & Tennis Supplies (Wēilín Tǐyù Yòngpǐn, 威林体育用品）
Address: #272-1 Húbīn Nán Lù; opposite Mǐnnán Bldg. (湖滨南路 272 之一号， 闽南大厦对面） Tel: 5804682 Buses: 10, 27, 30

BAKERIES (Miànbāodiàn, 面包店） Chinese call breads sweet (Tiánde, 甜的）or salty (Xiánde , 咸的)，but "salty" isn't really salty; it just isn't sweet. Buy "salty".

For a delightful morning treat, toast and slice Chinese steamed breads (Mántou, 馒头). Much like English muffins. Serve with quality Chinese fruit jams.

Try Metro, Wal-Mart (they do custom birthday cakes), or such bakeries as Andersen's (Āndélǔsēn, 安德鲁森), Xiàmén's first "Western" bakery, though they have some distinctly Chinese breads—like the sliced stuff with green and purple-swirls resembling toxic mold. It isn't. I hope.

Well Bread

A large glossy poster at the World Trade Center Mall's Andersen's showed 8 or 10 beautiful loaves of specialty breads. I was in hog heaven—until they told me they did not sell even one of those breads.

"What's the point of the poster?" I asked.

The girl smiled brightly and said, "Those are photos of the breads we don't have."

French Chinese English... Speaking of Carrefour—leave it to the French & Chinese together to come up with some pretty unusual English signs. Given they're French, maybe it is deliberate? My favorite Carrefour sign is this one in their men's bathroom. Quite moving—or could be, if you obeyed it.

BARBERS & BEAUTY SALONS (Měifà, 美发）Price often includes hair wash and good massage of head, back and arms (they'll even ream your ears out for you.)

XMU barbers will scalp you for only 6 Yuan, and some Cosmetology schools do it free. But you get what you pay for, and it can be a hair-razing experience.

Many older barber shops have museum-quality chairs. By the way, traditional barber poles had red stripes because barbers moonlighted as surgeons and used red to hide the blood. But Chinese barbers use green stripes. Vulcans?

BICYCLES (Zìxíngchē, 自行车） In the early 1990s Xiàmén's narrow roads were thronged with bikes, and cars were a rarity. Now bicycles are rare. It's a pity. Engineering studies of animals and people show the planet's most efficient means of transportation is the bike. They're also good exercise and non-polluting. Buy them in department stores, METRO, Wal-mart, etc.

BOOKSTORES (Shūdiàn, 书店） It is still quite difficult to find foreign language books and magazines, but I've ordered hundreds online, and rarely are any lost. We did have a child's English grammar book missing from a box. When I complained, the Chinese postal worker replied, "It wasn't us. Many U.S. postal workers are immigrants with poor English. That's why they stole the book."

Try the huge **Xiamen Int'l Book Store** (XIBS,厦门外图书城) near the Mingfa Plaza Carrefour. Add:#8 Yuehua Rd. XIBC Tower (悦华路 8 号外图物流大厦)
Tel: 5099777 www.xibc.com.cn (Has English tab—but does nothing).

How Chinese Shop

Adapted from *"A Race of Green Ginger"*
by Mrs. Averil Mackenzie-Grieve, British resident of Gulangyu, 1920s

"My Chinese women friends had taught me what to look for in embroidery: to pinch up the satin-stitched motifs which, they said, should bend smoothly and look as even as the silk itself, not showing a single loop; to look for fine tight Peking knot-stitch—the aristocrat of stitchery—and to examine the twist of the threads themselves.

"They showed me how to discover whether chopsticks were made of genuine ivory. Putting them side by side, they would lay a bamboo sliver horizontally across a drop of water placed on the sticks. If they were ivory the sliver would immediately come alive, swing round vertically and stop. On any other substance it would remain motionless. But the skill by which they could infallibly distinguish carved lacquer from veneered composition, good cloisonné from pieces lifted and assembled on modern bronzes by Japanese craftsmen, would, I knew, never be mine. It was their inheritance, compounded of discerning sight and the miraculously sensitive touch that, for them, made the incised mahjong tiles so easy to read with finger-tips alone.

"Our Chinese friends had taught us too the rudiments of judging jade. The women showed me how to look for transparency, texture, depth of colour and so brilliant a polish that the stone looked 'dipped in water'. But they themselves prized only the precious emerald jade as a jewel, while I preferred the variegated stone which lent itself so perfectly to imaginative carving."

Xiàmén Int'l Book Center (Xiàmén Duìwài Túshū Jiāoliú Zhōngxīn, 厦门对外图书交流中心) Has some foreign books and magazines. Add: #408 Sīmíng Nán Lù, near XMU (思明南路 408 号，厦门大学附近) Tel: 2195976

Jehovah Nissi Bookstore (Níxī Shūwū,尼西书屋) One of several Christian bookstores in Xiamen; offers books, gifts, and calendars (and many of my books; no accounting for taste).
Tel: 86-592-2191219 Email: nissi.cn@gmail.com
Add: S. Siming Rd. $479 (below Chenggang Ave. Overpass & tunnel)(思明南路 479 号, 成功大道下面) Website: http://www.7grace.cn/

New China Bookstore (Xīnhuá Shūdiàn, 新华书店), one of Xiàmén's best. Address: 163 Zhōngshān Lù (中山路 163 号) Tel: 202-4059.

O^2SUN Bookstores/Reading Cafes (Guānghé Zuòyòng, 光合作用) –over a dozen locations in Xiàmén, many of which have "reading cafes" serving coffee, teas, etc. Check website for locations. E-mail: service@ósun.com Website: www.ósun.com

A *MUST BUY* Book!

Oxford's Concise English-Chinese Chinese-English Dictionary*:** (Jīngxuǎn Hànyīng Yīnghàn Cídiǎn, 精选汉英英汉词典) Informed Lǎowài tote this little red volume more zealously than Red Guards wielded Mao's little red book. The ***best dictionary for daily use—small, and easy to whip out and wield on unsuspecting Lǎonèi.

Better yet—use PLECO on iPhone or Android phones

BOWLING SUPPLIES (Bǎolíngqiú Zhuānmàidiàn, 保龄球专卖店) Also has 2nd hand supplies. Address: #126 Hōu Jiāngdài Lù, Yǒngkāng Bldg. 16/F (后江埭路 126 号永康大厦 16 楼) Tel: 2222412 Website: www.kt114.cn

BUSINESS SERVICES For comprehensive business services, or Expat help with home searches, settling in, newcomers' orientations, etc. contact **OrientPlus.**
Tel: 5811891 13906028020 E-mail: Eunice.orientplus@gmail.com

BUSINESS CARDS (Míngpiàn, 名片) Quality has improved since they started using computers instead of hand-misaligned rubber blocks. Try photo developing shops or photocopy stores.

CAMERAS Try Cyber-Mart (SM Mall) or Electronic City (Diànzi Chéng, 电子城) on Húbīn Nánlù (湖滨南路).

CAMPING/EQUIPMENT (Lùtiān Sùyíngjù, 露天宿营具) SM Mall shops. See **OUTDOOR RECREATION**

CARPENTRY For 24 years, we've turned to Mr. Chén Gēngshēng (陈更生) for custom furniture, remodeling, or repairs. If you can draw it, he can make it. He also subcontracts most other services. Tel: 218-4496 13003975041

CARPETS & TAPESTRIES (Dìtǎn, 地毯) Try Orient Home, facing Metro (see "Furniture" for address)

Yellow Peril (True Story)

When preparing to come to China in 1988, Sue discarded her brightly colored dresses. "Mainland Chinese wear only dark colors—dark blue, dark green, dark black..."

"That was the Cultural Revolution!" I said. "China's changed!" Sure enough, Xiàmén girls weren't wearing blue Mao caps and coats but brightly hued dresses and mini-skirts.

"See! I told you so!" I said as I pointed to a lovely lass in a yellow mini-skirt.

"Well," Sue said, "It's a *dark* yellow!"

CARPET CLEANING Liàngjié Jiāzhèng (亮捷家政) (Also cleans air conditioners). #1-301 Húbīn Nán Lù Fùshān Míngshìyuán (湖滨南路富山名士园 1 号 301)
Tel: 5077189 E-mail: wufe1314n@sina.com

CHEESE (Gānlào, 干酪; Nǎilào, 奶酪; Rǔlào, 乳酪) The Olive Oil Store (see "Food Markets") has cheap blocks of cheddar, mozzarella and Edam. Metro has a broader assortment, but pricier. If you're up north, buy some Běijīng cheese. It's tasty and cheap; I've brought back 40 pounds at a time.

Say Cheese!

Why on earth did Chinese have 3 words for cheese when they didn't even eat the stuff until the mid 90s? I saw Chinese, in both Xiàmén and Hong Kong, order cheeseburgers and then throw away the cheese! I asked why they didn't buy a plain burger, which was cheaper. They said, "Foreigners eat cheeseburgers, so I want one too!" And tossed the cheese! Go figure.

Western doctors had theories, of course. They said Chinese were lactose intolerant. But Xiàmén now has several Pizza Huts, and locals stuff themselves with pizza, cheeseburgers, yoghurt, and wash it all down with milk. So what happened to the alleged lactose intolerance? I'll tell you. The entire Oriental Lactose Intolerance bit was just a Chinese conspiracy to torment cheese-craving Lǎowài. They loved cheese all along and just never let on. Now that I've gotten it out of my system and can survive without it, they sell it everywhere—and eat it to spite me.

CLOTHES (Yīfu, 衣服 or Fúzhuāng 服装) The Mao blue and gray of the 80s are gone. Try the chic boutiques on Zhōngshān, or the Laiya Stores, or visit a local tailor

One Size Fits All! My wife dug through a pile of sweaters in a street side stall in W. Fújiàn's Lóngyán City (龙岩市). She liked one but it was too small. "Don't worry!" (Búyàojǐn! 不要紧!) the lady said. "It stretches when you wear it!"

"I don't know," Sue said. She found another sweater she liked, but it was far too large.

"Búyàojǐn!" the lady said. "It shrinks when you wash it!"

(see FABRIC MARKET).

COMPUTERS (Diànnǎo,电脑) **Electronic City** (Diànzichéng, 电子城) has the best selection. Add: #69 Húbīn Nán Lù. (湖滨南路 69 号) Also try SM Mall **Cybermart**

COMPUTER REPAIR Try Electronic City shops, or contact:
Xiàmén PC Hospital (厦门电脑医院) Day Tel: 2293890 Night Tel: 8882513
E-mail: 86592@126.com www.xmpc120.com

CONDIMENTS Forget Heinz! Try Xiàmén's own BB Brand (no, B.B. doesn't stand for Bill Brown, or Brewed in Bathtub). Mercy Food Company, with 50+ years' experience, spent $3 million USD on Taiwanese equipment to make dozens of great sauces: hot sauce, satay sauce, sweet 'n sour sauce, Worcestershire, sesame oil, BBQ chili oil, soy sauce… Check out my webpage on the Amoy Magic site about the "Super Sisters" behind this unique company. For hard-to-find Western condiments, try Metro.
Tel: 5930227 E-mail: mercy@public.xm.fj.cn www.bbmercy.com

CRYSTALS & MINERALS I've collected minerals and crystals since I was seven, long before they became New Age cures for everything from asthma to zenophobia. Our apartment has a few hundred pounds of specimens from all over China—Mongolian amethyst, Tibetan quartz and turquoise, rubies and sapphires from Fújiàn (Míngxī, in Sānmíng, has China's 4 largest gem bed, with rubies and sapphires). Xiàmén has such gem shops as "Táorán Qíshí Xuān" (陶然奇石轩).
Add: SM Mall, Basement, Shop WS02, near Wal-Mart.
Tel: 2056760 Cell: 13950171117

DENTAL CARE (See "Healthcare Chapter")

These ladies were really egging Shannon on!

Egging Us On
Chinese swear the large, whitish duck eggs (Yādàn,鸭蛋) are healthier than smaller, brown chicken eggs (Jīdàn,鸡蛋). Some swear by quail eggs. Maybe I'm chicken, but I quail at the thought of eating those tiny things). But don't duck the issue. Whatever eggs cracks you up, be sure they're fresh, else they can get pretty fowl.

EGGS (Dàn, 蛋). Ducks eggs are larger; good for baking. In Xiamen, you can easily buy pigeon eggs, ostrich eggs, goose eggs. Try open air markets for best selection.

EXPRESS DELIVERY (Kuàidì, 快递)
DHL: (Dúnháo Kuàidì, 敦豪快递) 601-0503/4/5 Hotline: 800 8108000
Website: www.cn.dhl.com
EMS: (Zhōngguó Yóuzhèng Kuàidì, 中国邮政快递): (Chinese Post Offices)
Website: www.ems.com.cn
UPS: (Měiguó Liánhé Bāoguǒ, 美国联合包裹): Tel: 563-9828 / 2835 / 2765
Website: www.ups.com/asia/cn/chsindex.html
FedEx: (Liánbāng Kuàidì, 联邦快递): Tel: 510-1771, or 800 830-2338
Website: www.fedex.com/cn
China Air Express: (Mínháng Kuàidì, 民航快递) Tel: 5730771
E-mail: xmn@cae.com.cn Website: www.cae.com.cn

Pony Express: Just neigh**. Eggspress**: that's no poultry undertaking.

FABRIC MARKET (Bùliào Shìchǎng, 布料市场） Broad selection of fabrics, fine tailors. Add: Héxiāng Xī Lù Gǔlóng Shāngchéng (禾祥西路古龙商城). Donald Linn, of Amoy Paintings Int'l, recommends Yuling Tailor（玉玲裁缝), at # 60 Shítíng Lù（石亭路 60 号）, near City Hall at Tel: 5050211 05922669057

Man of the Cloths

In the early 90s, quality clothes were hard to find. Buttons fell off, zippers broke, seams split the first time they were worn. So I was happy to see a youth squatted on a Gǔlàngyǔ sidewalk selling quality shirts for only 15 Yuan. But no bought. They couldn't believe good shirts could go for 15 Yuan.

Finally, he upped the price from 15 Yuan to 150 Yuan—and sold every shirt.

FLOUR (Jīngfěn, 精粉）We no longer must grind our own flour on the hernia-heavy granite mill I lugged from the countryside on bike and boat. Good thing, too. My sons are bigger than me now, and would make me do it myself.

Cornmeal (Yùmǐfěn, 玉米粉）is now sold, but whole wheat is hard to find. **Tip**: substitute 1/3 oatmeal for flour in bread recipes for a hearty bread. And use "fine cake flour" (Olive Oil Store, WalMart) if you want your bread to raise any higher than saltine crackers. [①]

FLOWERS (Huā, 花）Shops behind Zhōngshān Park sell potted and cut flowers, and supplies for birds, fish, turtles. Check out the sprawling Landscape Supply Mall on Liánqián Lù（莲前路）outside the tunnel leading to the Island Ring Rd.

FOAM RUBBER (Hǎimián, 海绵）In China, you really do get "Room & Board." Chinese beds are hard—just a board pretending it's a mattress. But this Tong'an company (off-island) will deliver any shape, size or density piece of foam you want (even space-age "memory foam"). Great for mattresses, furniture, sound rooms, primal scream therapy rooms.
Tel: 579-1579 Mobile: 13328767992

FORKLIFTS: If you shop like Susan Marie, you need a forklift from the German firm Líndé (林德）Tel: 5533888. www.linde-xiamen.com

FURNITURE (Jiājù, 家具) Check the sprawling 4-story Orient Home (厦门东方家园), facing Metro. Tel: 2611111. Also try Lucky Home World (吉家家世界).
Add: Huli, Jinhu Rd. (湖里金湖路) 3837977 Website: http://www.xmjijia.com.cn/

GOLF EQUIP. (Gāoérfūqiú Yòngpǐn,高尔夫球用品）See Sports Chapter

HOME ELECTRONICS—See APPLIANCES

HOUSEKEEPER（Bǎomǔ, 保姆）A good housekeeper/cook will help you survive!

---

① Old ginger is hotter than new ginger. Chinese Proverb

Ms. Eunice Chao can help find a Baomu. E-mail: qp21@public.xm.fj.cn

ICE CREAM (Bīngqílín, 冰淇淋) In 1988, I found it hard to swallow that Chinese had invented ice cream, especially after tasting the local "White Snow" brand (better than "Yellow Snow," I guess). And Xiàmén shops sold it only in summer, claiming other seasons were too cold, though Běijīng folk ate ice cream even in winter. But foreign firms came along and it went from a seller's market to a buyer's market. Three foreign firms now dominate 30% of the market (China's per capita consumption is 2 liters a year, and expected to reach 6 liters by 2020).

Get foreign and local ice creams at Wal-Mart, Metro, Carrefour.

No Money, No Honey (Fēngmì, 蜂蜜)

I joke with students, "No money, no honey," but in the early days we lacked both. Only country doctors, 4 hours away in the mountains, sold pure honey (for medicinal purposes). Xiàmén shops always watered honey down with sugar water. "Keeps it from spoiling," they said, though in fact, pure honey keeps forever, whereas adulterated honey invariably fermented, blew out of the bottle, and stank up the kitchen.

Supermarkets now have quality honey; we even have specialty honey shops.

So now we have the honey. Still waiting for the money.

INTERNET (Shàngwǎng, 上网) How on earth (or China) did we survive without internet or e-mail? And China has some of the easiest to use internet service on the planet. Just dial 16300 from any phone to access the internet without an account (the minimal charge goes to the phone you dial from).

Call 10000 to get a DSL account (cheaper by the year) Cable TV: Phone 968810

JEWELRY (Shǒushì, 首饰) Jewelry stores are everywhere, but not all that glitters is gold; buy from reputable stores such as those on Zhōngshān Rd or Malls.

Gold Egret Jewelry (Jīnlù Shǒushì, 金鹭首饰) Reliable; been around awhile.
Add: #80 Zhōngshān Lù (中山路 80 号) Tel: 2019078

KOREAN SUPERMARKET (Hànfǔ Bǎihuò, Hánguǒ Shíshàng Diàn (汉釜百货, 韩国时尚店)
Add: Húbīn Nán Lù Wànhé Square 2/F #3 (湖滨南路万禾广场二楼 3 号店)
Near Fùshān Trust-Mart (富山诚达购物广场) Tel: 5076098

LACQUERTHREAD SCULPTURE (Wéiyì Qíxiàndiāo, 惟艺漆线雕). For 300 years a Xiàmén family has been making these exquisite crafts that are now rated as a national treasure.
Add: #42 Zhōngxìng Rd, by Zhōngshān Park (中兴路 42 号) Tel: 2023621

Mr. Cai teaches gold thread embroidery

MAPS Large bookstores sell English maps of Xiàmén for only 5 Yuan (same maps go for 15 to 20 Yuan in hotels). Street hawkers by Nánpǔtuó and Gǔlàngyǔ ferry also sell

English maps with bus routes. "Discover Gǔlàngyǔ" has a 1908 map and modern map of Gǔlàngyǔ; my book on Xiamen Univ. has a map of 103 school sites.

MARGARINE (Huángyóu, 黄油). Like bread, it comes as "salty" (Xián, 咸) or "sweet" (Tián, 甜). Get the "salty." Some is just colored lard; try Meadowgold.

MASSAGE—RUBBED THE RIGHT WAY! China has some of the planet's best therapeutic masseurs, at great prices. You might feel they're rubbing you the wrong way while they're laying hands on you harder than a televangelist, but the effects are healing and long lasting. Try full body massages, foot massages, and head massages. Ten or twelve Yuan can get you a shampoo and a head and upper body massage (try the Hair Salon in Xiamen University's Yifu Bldg.).[1]

Peony Wànpéng Hotel (Mǔdān Wànpéng Bīnguǎn, 牡丹万鹏宾馆) ***Our favorite*** foot massage. Faces Botanical Garden (Wànshíyuán, 万石园)
Add: #17-19 Húyuán Lù Xiàmén 361003 (虎园路 17-19 号) Tel: 2662888
E-mail: info@peony-hotel.com www.peony-hotel.com

BLIND BODY MASSAGE (Zhōngyī Mángrén Bǎojiàn Tuīná Zhōngxīn 中医盲人保健推拿中心). This is one of the fields in which the blind excel. Their almost preternatural sense of touch allows a skilled blind masseur to hit me right where I knead it And I feel less self-conscious knowing these folk cannot see my contours!

Gold Coast Blind Massage (Jīn Hǎiàn Mángrén Ànmó Zhōngxīn, 金海岸盲人按摩中心) Add: #99 Húbīn Nānlù, near Zhōngshān Hospital, diagonal from Xiàmén Airlines Jīnyàn Hotel [(湖滨南路 99 号, 中山医院附近, 厦门航空金雁酒店(湖滨南路斜对面)].[2] Tel: 2213393 Buses: 45, 46, 528

Míngài Blind Massage (Míngài Mángrén Ànmó Zhōngxīn, 明爱盲人按摩中心)
Add: Jīnbǎng Bldg. #1 3/F (金榜大厦 A 栋 3 楼)
Tel: 5853278 Buses: 1, 3, 21

MEAT (Ròu, 肉) Buy open air market meat early in the day because it often isn't refrigerated. Beef (Niúròu, 牛肉) is less popular than pork (Zhūròu, 猪肉), so pricier. Quality varies from imported Australian to domestic road kill. Check Olive Oil Store, Trust-mart, Wal-Mart, Metro or Carrefour for ground meats.

MILK (牛奶, Niúnǎi). Fresh milk is hard to find, though there is a dairy an hour west in Chángtài, but whole powdered milk is tasty, and good for baking. Domestic brands are cheaper but quality varies. Bagged is cheaper than canned. Buy unsweetened.

---

[1] Of the 36 strategies, running away is the best. Chinese Proverb
[2] Failure is the mother of success Chinese Proverb

MUSIC (Yīnyuè, 音乐). We love music; we have a piano, synthesizer, two sitars, a dozen guitars, several drumssets. We're like the Trapp Family; when we sing, people ask us to keep our Trapp shut.

Huáchéng Piano (Huáchéng Gāngqín（华成钢琴）Since 1932; Xiamen's oldest. Add: #123 Zhōngshān Lù. (中山路 123 号） Tel: 2055923 http://www.xmhcqh.com/

Wànjiā Piano Store (Wànjiā Qīnháng, 万佳琴行） New & used pianos; other instruments. Add: #56 Băilùzhōu Lù (白鹭洲路 56 号)
Tel: 2209456 Buses: 8, 12, 15, 26, 72, 85, 86, 87, 88, 97

> **Stringing Us Along**
> China's two-stringed èrhú （二胡）was the world's first violin! Though it can sound shrill to Western ears, in the hands of a master it can ring as sweetly as a violin, faithfully reproducing beautiful Western classics.

MUSIC PERFORMANCES Xiàmén hopes to become S.E. China's music center. Every month we have performances by visiting orchestras, ballet troupes, opera stars. Unfortunately, I've never succeeded, even after 24 years of effort, in getting the media to inform foreigners of events before they happen. As a rule, we learn of them only afterwards, when we read the glowing reports of how our cultured little island just hosted this or that.

OUTDOOR RECREATION EQUIPMENT Try SM Mall, and Molife.
Molife Outdoor Equipment (Mònài Hùwài Xiūxián Yòngpǐn, 莫耐户外休闲用品)
Add: #57 Húbīn Nán Lù, Jīnyuán Bldg.#8A(湖滨南路 57 号金源大厦 8A)
Tel: 2295600 E-mail: info@mlo.cn http://www.molife.cn

PETS (Chǒngwù, 宠物) Gone are the days when we could find dogs nowhere but in the restaurants…

LìKāng Pet Hospital (Lìkāng Chǒngwù Yīyuàn, 利康宠物医院) Everything from kitty litter to cat milk (no joke!)
1st Location: #5-8 Huáchāng Lù (华昌路 5-8 号)
Tel: 5682505
2nd Location: #194 Héxiāng Xī Lù (禾祥西路 194 号)
Tel: 2202428

Dogs and cats? The best selection, other than Cantonese restaurants, is the rooftop shop in Băilùzhōu's antique shopping area.

Matt plays with his food...

For birds and fish, and well crafted bird cages, see Mr. Băi at the #2 Shop, 3-1 Gōngyuàn Bĕi Lù. (贡院北路 3 号至 1，2 店面) By Zhongshan Park Tel: 2020797

Spread-eagled!

I'm glad we now have vets. In 1998m we had a people doctor neuter our cat. He tied the poor feline spread-eagled to a chair before emasculating him. Not pleasant to watch—or listen to.

Happily, the cat survived, and today's he a nut, even though he lacks them.

PHARMACIES (Yàodiàn, 药店) New pharmacies are opening daily in Xiàmen. (Is that good or bad?). Zhōngshān Lù and SM-Mart 1/F have pharmacies, as well as many outlets for Watsons, Hong Kong's largest pharmacy chain.

PLUMBING, HARDWARE, ELECTRICAL... (Wǔjiān Jiādiànlèi 五金家电类) For large "Home Depot style" stores, try Orient Home, opposite Metro, B&Q by Carrefour, or the row of shops by SM Mall.

REAL ESTATE (Fángdìchǎn, 房地产) We have many real estate agencies, including Century 21, but for private housing, try Xiǎo Zheng. He can help find nice places on the Island Ring Road near the beach for reasonable prices. Tel: 889-0841.

Ms. Eunice Chau (Huáng Jiālì, 黄嘉力), of Symphony Trading Co., Ltd., helps with home searches, travel arrangements, education advice, orientations, etc.
Add: Unit 1206 Hǎixiā Bldg., Húbīn Xī Lù. Tel: 581-1621 Fax: 581-1718
E-mail: qp21@public.xm.fj.cn

SECOND HAND MARKET (Xiàmén shì jiùhuò shìcháng , 厦门市旧货市场) has everything from drums to fridges & freezers. It's off Húyuán Rd. (虎园路), near the Xiàmén Hotel (厦门宾馆).

SPICES OF LIFE (Xiāngliào, 香料). Chinese eat anything edible, and if it is not edible, they call it medicine and ingest it anyway. Still, it is hard to find many spices that we take for granted. Stores will have ten shelves of white pepper and five of MSG, but no basil or oregano. Metro and the Olive Oil Store have some hard to find spices but bring hard to find ones with you (see list earlier in this chapter).

SPORTS EVENTS Xiamen folk have sporting in the blood, and not a week passes without a game or competition. Buy tickets at the Sports Arena West Gate on Húbīn Nán Lù (湖滨南路体育中心西门) Tel: 506-4618 or 506-2107

SUBSCRIPTIONS Get Chinese magazines and newspapers subscriptions at post offices or one of these service centers: #3 Zhōngshān Lù Tel: 2021662
#47 Sīmíng Nán Lù Tel: 2021227 #6 Húyuán Lù Tel: 2109988

Some of my Favorite Periodicals

Fújiàn Pictorial (Fújiàn Huàbào, 福建画报) great photos of Fújiàn places & people—like this one of Shannon and Matthew in 1991!
China Daily (Zhōngguó Rìbào,中国日报) www.chinadaily.com
Beijing Weekly (Běijīng Zhōubào, 北京周报)
China Today (Jīnrì Zhōngguó, 今日中国) www.chinatoday.com
Women of China (Zhōngguó Fùnǔ Zázhì, 中国妇女杂志) www.womenofchina.cn
World of English (Yīngyǔ Shìjiè, 英语世界)—for English learners, but good foreign articles

RICE (Mǐ 米)

Rice is a weighty topic for Chinese, who revere the grain almost as much as Cambodians (for whom it is a criminal offense to insult a rice plant).

Don't skimp on rice. Grades and prices are innumerable, but cheaper grades are prepared on roadsides and include, at no extra charge, white gravel masquerading as rice. After a few chipped teeth, I heeded my comrades' rice catechism and became a connoisseur of rice.

Locals prefer Thai rice, but I enjoy "Dōngběi" (Manchurian rice, or 东北大米), which is even cheaper than local rice.

There are dozens of ways to serve up the dozens of grades of humble rice. In Northern Fújiàn, cooked rice is so dry it rasps your throat. In the South it's almost mushy. Xiàmén folk like rice congee – a watery porridge livened up with salted and pickled vegetables, shredded pork, dried minnows (such sad little dried faces) and diced Thousand Day Old Eggs (which are purplish greenish, gelatinous, and smell of ammonia or horse pee).

For Chinese (in the South, at least), rice is life and they use it for everything – except weddings. No self-respecting Chinese would irreverently toss rice. When they hear of this, I suspect they'll seek revenge by tossing cheeseburgers at Chinese weddings.

Tip: Try Oat Rice. White rice, you may know, has been largely stripped of nutrients. Try brown rice (at Metro and Wal-Mart). Better yet—try the "Oat rice." Oat meal, of course, is quite healthy. Oat rice is oats pressed into the shape of rice. Tasty, very nutritious (we mix it with brown rice or white rice). Sold at Pappy's Pizza and Pie (see Int'l Restaurants) or Metro.

THEATERS (Yǐngjùyuàn, 影剧院)

Jīnyīng Theater, World Trade Center (Shìmāo Jīnyīng Diànyǐngyuàn, 世贸金鹰电影院 Nice Food Court, and Xiàmen's most Lǎowài-friendly theater (many foreign movies). Add: #888 Xiàhē Lù 5/F (厦禾路 888 号世贸商城五楼)
Tel: 5805408 Website: www.jyfilm.com

Sīmíng Theater (Sīmíng Diànyǐngyuàn, 思明电影院)

Add: #2-14 Sīmíng Běi Lù (思明北路 2-14 号) Tel: 2132873
E-mail: lww.928@163.com Website: www.smdyy.com

Kāimíng Theater Complex (Kāimíng Diànyǐngchéng 开明电影城)
Add: #69 Jiāngtóu Běi Lù (江头北路 69 号) Tel: 5517918
E-mail: silm@xmkming.com Website: www.xmkaiming.com

Getting Thinner

When we came to Xiàmén in 1988, it took me weeks to learn that nutmeg (ròudòukòu, 肉豆蔻) and cinnamon (ròuguì, 肉桂) were sold only in Chinese medicine stores. Better yet, vanilla (xiāngcǎojīng 香草精) was sold only in paint stores! I asked why, and was told, by many Chinese, that paint, vanilla and thinner should be sold together because they are all chemicals.

Maybe they're right. My Peacock Brand vanilla smelled like paint thinner, and when I put a match to a spoon of vanilla it exploded. I didn't buy any more vanilla from paint stores. I'd already lost a lot of weight my first few months here and I didn't need any *thinner.*

TRANSLATION SERVICES

A quality translation can make or break a deal, so don't trust your future to a hack job.

Master Translation Services, with offices in mainland China, Taiwan and the U.S., serves prestigious firms all over the planet.

Add: Unit J-I, 15 Fl., Huangda Bldg., #28 Houdaixi Rd. (后埭溪路 28 号皇达大厦 15 楼 L/M 单元)

Tel: 5188629 E-mail: frank@mts.cn

Website: www.mts-tech.com

WATER It will be taps for you if you drink tap water. Always boil first.

Bottled Water Choose water companies carefully. After much trial and severe error, we drink only Yínlù (银鹭) mineral water and purified water. Sue, a connoisseur of water, says the purified is most consistent in taste. Excellent delivery service, and as one of China's top ten food processors, Yínlù's quality is dependable.

Tel: 5811621 Website: www.yinlu.com

Supplement

Half the Sky—Get a Bǎomǔ!

(Adapted from article in "Women of China")

"A woman is like a teabag—only in hot water do you realize how strong she is."

Nancy Reagan

After life in Los Angeles, life in China crawled at a snail's pace. But even so, we had little free time, because our everyday chores took all day—until we hired a bǎomǔ (保姆， housekeeper/cook).

Unless you have a bǎomǔ, the head of the house, or her husband, must spend hours each morning haggling over every onion, carrot, head of cabbage, or block of tofu with merchants who point to enigmatic scratches on bamboo scales that haven't changed in 5,020 years, and proclaim that 4 eggs weigh a pound and a half. And once back home, the cleaning, chopping, cooking and dishwashing takes hours. No wonder that a bǎomǔ is a top priority for even poor professors.

We eventually heeded our colleagues' urges to hire a bǎomǔ. Our first candidate was a grandmother who crossed our threshold and crossed my wife in one fell swoop by instructing Susan on the errors of her ways in cooking, cleaning, studying, and raising kids.

She did not last a week. Our next time around we tried our hand with students, who were thrilled at getting paid for learning English (which is what they interpreted their job to be). Xiǎo Hóng and Melanie did little but read our English books and watch TV.

At long last a Chinese professor suggested, "Why not hire a bǎomǔ from the countryside? They are honest, hard-working, dependable, and cheap."

"Cheap" went straight to my heart, and the next day we met Lǐxī（李西), a cook's wife, never imagining that froward, silent soul would become like family.

It was an oppressively hot and muggy October day, but Lǐxī sported her entire wardrobe: long johns and striped naval undershirt beneath cotton pants and long-sleeved shirt; over that, a vintage, frayed exercise suit, topped off with a ratty gray sweater buttoned to the neck, and olive drab canvas regulation army tennis-shoes that were probably handed down from the Long March.

Lǐxī contemplated her navel while her husband, wise to the "honest, hardworking peasant" lore, extolled her virtues. The few times I addressed Lǐxī directly, she peered furtively through thick, disheveled bangs, then resumed picking her frayed cuffs with calloused fingers.

"Can she speak?" I inquired.

"Not Mandarin, just the Mǐnnán dialect," her husband confessed, "But she's smart. Just show her what to do."

"Can she cook?"

"No, but I'll teach her."

I suspected this sullen apparition was incapable of motion, either physically or mentally, but just as I sought to tactfully end the interview--she moved. Matthew was edging towards the doorway and the dangerous street beyond, and Lǐxī flew to her feet, snatched him to her breast with practiced swoop, and face aglow, bustled him off to his room. Then she retreated to her chair, donned her practiced frown, and picked at her frayed cuffs.

Her husband cried, "She's great with children!"

Enough said. Sue hired her on the spot—to my immediate regret.

If the way to a man's heart is through his stomach, Lǐxī ought never to have landed a man. More an alchemist than a wok wizard, she transmuted fine fish into blackened slabs of charcoal. Fresh vegetables, baptized in oil and pickled in salt, became mush

But how to communicate with her? Her Mandarin was worse than ours, and she could not read. Even sign language failed. I wanted to dismiss her, but Lǐxī's desperation defused my anger. Besides, man does not live by rice alone.

Though incommunicado with us, Lǐxī was telepathic with tots—especially Matthew, whom she bore on her back from dawn to dusk. But no wonder she understood children: she had four of her own before begging the doctor to tie things off down below.

Mark Twain wrote,

> "There was never yet an uninteresting life. Such a thing is an impossibility. Inside of the dullest exterior there is a drama, a comedy, and a tragedy."

Twain must have meant Lǐxī, whose plebeian dust jacket does no justice to her contents. She had labored in the field raising four children by herself until her staunch Buddhist family drove her from home after she became a Christian. She trekked over the mountains to Xiàmén, where she got a job lugging baskets of granite slung across her brawny shoulders. After two years in the school of hard rocks, she graduated and became our brawny bǎomǔ, lugging towheads with heads harder than the granite she had once hauled.

Lǐxī applied her diehard spirit to becoming a capable member of our household. She learned Mandarin and, to my chagrin, taught herself to read some of the characters that still eluded me. She even taught herself to cook both Chinese and Western food. By watching Susan she learned how to whip up a pizza, sandwiches, burgers and fries, Irish stew. Even Chinese guests begged for her recipes.

After Lǐxī had been with us two years, we moved her four children to Xiàmén to help educate and fatten them up a bit, for they were skin and bone. Her oldest son eventually took up computers, her sister opened a small shop, and Lìxī used her limited income to help those even poorer than herself, both in Xiàmén and back home in Anxi, proving that investments in the poor reap compound interest.

Give and it shall be given…

Chairman Mao claimed, "Women hold up half the sky," but I think that was an understatement. Chinese women, even with hands bound by lack of education, hold up a lot more than half.

Hire a bǎomǔ!

The 100 Chinese Names
or
Sorry, Wang Number

Chinese have about 8,000 surnames, with Han Chinese using about 3,050 of them. But roughly 87 percent of Han Chinese share the same 100 or so most common names—hence "the people" is expressed "Old 100 Names" (Lǎobǎixìng, 老百姓). The three most common surnames, Lǐ (李), Wáng (王), and Zhāng (张), are used by 250 million Chinese—almost the population of the U.S.A.. Over 100 million people are surnamed Zhāng.

Just imagine if all Americans were Lǐ, Zhāng, or Wáng. You could dial the Wáng number 1/3 of the time. Do that to your girlfriend and she might give you the old "Dear Zhang Letter" (unless she gives you some Lǐ way).

Forty percent of Chinese share the 10 most common surnames: Zhang (张), Wáng (王), Lǐ (李), Zhào (赵), Chén (陈), Yáng (杨), Wú (吴), Liú (刘), Huáng (黄) and Zhōu (周). Chinese surnames are passed down through the father, but women keep their family name even after marriage.

In old days, it was a capital crime to speak the Emperor's name aloud, or even to have the same name as the Emperor—which must have created havoc when the Emperor had the same name as 50 million others. When Liǔ Bāng (刘邦) became emperor during the Hàn Dynasty (汉朝 206 BC to 23 AD), people surnamed "Bāng" faced either a name change or a bang in the head (the Chinese Big Bāng Theory). This en masse name changing probably drove census takers out of their senses.

In more recent times, given names reflected parents' desire for their children's happiness—or for their political correctness. During the Great Proletariat Cultural Revolution, children were named "Flourishing China" (Xìngguó, 兴国), or "Build the Army" (Jiànjún, 建军), "Love Country" (Ǎihuá, 爱华), or "National Day" (Guóqìng, 国庆). And "Red", of course, was a major theme of many names. Imagine naming your little one "Face the Red" (Cháohóng, 朝红), Forever Red (Yonghong, 永红), "Red Soldier" (Hóngbīng, 红兵). No wonder so many of that generation saw red.

Nowadays parents are more likely to give names that emphasize economics over politics: Zhìfù (致富) means to get rich.

Generally, women's names have words relating to beauty, nature, jewelry, etc. Examples: "Beautiful" (Měi, 美), "Flower" (Huā, 花) or "Graceful" (Tíng, 婷). Men's names reflect strength or military bearing: "Steel" (Gāng, 钢) or "Strong Pine" (Jìnsōng, 劲松).

In my youth, I too was nicknamed after a pine: knothead.

Chapter 27

Transportation

Xiamen Sightseeing Bus

Bus routes: http://www.xm315.com/info/car01-7.jsp

The best way to see Xiàmén is from the open-air upper deck of a Sightseeing Tour Bus. Keep the one-day ticket to get off and on as often as you like; the ticket also gets you a 20% discount at many Xiàmén attractions.

> "Day Tour": 50 km., about one hour. Busses leave about every half hour from the People's Conference Hall, 8:30—18:00. The bus goes only one direction. Save your ticket so you can get on and off different busses.
>
> "City Nightscape Tour": 60 km. Leaves SM Mall at 7:30, 8:00 and 8:30. Returns to SM about two hours later. Price: 20 Yuan (half for kids under 1.4 m).

Tour Bus Tel: 5316721 Website: http://xm.focus.cn/ztdir/2275000/

City Busses Back in 1988, the asthmatic tandem buses on our 3 bus lines belched black smoke that curled up between the cracks in the warped wooden floors (nice views of the road below, though). Now we have new air conditioned buses, 20% of which run on clean LPG. They are convenient and cheap—and even cheaper with an E-card from the post office, which gives a discount for each ride.

Taxi drivers are also happy to take you for a ride. Use the meter, ask for a receipt, and have them dial 119 for free translation service if needed.

Chinese Distances

"These distances may not be accepted as entirely accurate. They are only approximate. When one comes to calculating distances in this part of China he meets with difficulties at once, chief among them being the difference in the length of the li (lee) [about 1/3 of a mile] in different parts of this district. There are long li and short li; there are mandarin li and the common ordinary country li. The difference between these two is considerable, a mandarin li being one fourth shorter."

Pitcher 1912, p.283

An Amoy "Bus" (Dukes, 1885)

Main Bus Terminals

Train Station (Huóchē zhàn, 火车站)
Harbor/Gulangyu Ferry (Lúndù, 轮渡)
Xiàmén Univ. (Xiàdà, 厦大)
Jímĕi (Jímĕi, 集美)
Húlǐ Bus Station (Húlǐ Chēzhàn, 湖里车站)
Airport (Fēijī Chǎng, 飞机场)
Exhibition Ctr.(Huìchǎng Zhōngxīn, 会展中心)
Hǎicāng (Hǎicāng, 海沧)

The first shall be last

When people push and shove to get on a bus, I step aside, happy to be last. People have commented on my saintly patience but in reality I wait only because I am too impatient to fight my way through. Besides, the first people on the bus pushed to the back, and are always last to get off. As Jesus said (perhaps after a visit to China?), "The first shall be last and the last shall be first."

Main Bus Routes

(They generally go both directions)

We used to only have 3 main bus routes, but now a full listing would add over 30 pages to this book, so please refer to the websites for a complete listing.

China's 4th busiest airport for entry & exit! Xiàmén has over 400 flights weekly to 149 destinations, including 80 abroad (Singapore, Osaka, Seoul, Penang, Kuala Lumpur, Bangkok, Manila, Yabi, Kuching, Jakarta…) We also have direct cargo flights to Hong Kong, Taiwan, Singapore, Nagoya of Japan, Los Angeles, Chicago, and Luxemburg. Our own Xiàmén Airlines serves 40+ domestic cities, and Bangkok and Seoul.

Xiàmén to HK is only a 50 minute flight but the bus is about 1/3 the cost. It is a little cheaper to fly to Shēnzhèn or Guǎngzhōu and take the train or ferry Hong Kong. The train offers a relaxing, scenic South China excursion.

Another alternative: Guǎngzhōu has daily 3-hour jet foil boats to Hong Kong, as well as a romantic overnight cruise.

Xiàmén-Gāoqí International Airport was built in 1983 and enlarged 3 times. The newest facility, built in 1996, was China's best airport—for a few days at least; then several other Chinese cities of course built better ones.

The 50+ year-old firm B+H Architects (of Canada) and East China Design Institute designed it with expansive steel-reinforced girders that curve slightly to evoke a South Fujian architectural flavour. The Canadian government gave our airport the Gold Prize for Architectural Design for its marriage of modern and traditional local architectural styles. (and no doubt also for hiring Canadian architects). But my favourite part of the airport is the display of a dozen or so brass bas-relief representations of very early Wright brothers-era aeroplanes.

B+H Architects website: www.bharchitects.com/

Flight Times

Běijīng: 2.5 hr.
Seoul: 2.5 hr.
Tokyo: 3.5 hr.
Manila: 1hr. 40min.
Guǎngzhōu: 1 hr.
Singapore: 4 hr.
Shànghǎi 1 hr. 20 min.
Hong Kong: 1 hr.

Táiwān—Xiàmén Flights Xiàmén is one of the cities with direct flights to Táiwān. Some take the ferry to Jinmen and fly from there (a bit cheaper).

Airlines in Xiamen

Xiamen International Airport Information
602-0017 (automated) or 602-8357 ×6017

Amoy Airlines There isn't one—but there should be!
All Nippon Airways Tel: 5732888
China Eastern Airlines Tel: 2130375
China Northern Airlines Tel: 5096973
China Southern Airlines Tel: 2127815 www.xmcz.com
Shandong Airlines Tel: 5139777
Shanghai Airlines Tel: 2210600
SilkAir Tel: 2053280 2053257 2053275 Fax: 2053273
South East China Airlines Tel: 5064941
Xiamen Airlines Tel: 5083666 Toll Free (800) 858-2666
Xiamen International Airlines Tel: 6022936

Xiamen Univ. Ticketing – During a family emergency, with only 1 day notice, XMU Travel booked me a RT flight Xiamen to Florida for just $1050 USD—and only 2 short layovers.
Open 7 days a week; take a translator if you don't speak Chinese.
Location: just inside large campus gate, by "Bird-Book Fountain".
Contact Mr. Zhū Ruìqiáng (朱瑞强) Tel: 2183083 E-mail: xdhk@163.com

Exit Warning! Present your Baggage Declaration Form and whatever you brought with you into China when you leave. If you had a cold when you entered, you must have one when you leave, or at least upgrade to a flu.

Train Tickets 515-4386 **Train Info** 505-4340
Xiàmén Island was isolated until the train station opened in 1957. Electric trains went into operation in 1993, the present station was built in 2003, and we now have 13 trains daily. Train service will improve dramatically within the next year after completion of a line connecting Shenzhen (by HK) with Xiàmén, Fúzhōu, Wénzhōu, etc. Train schedules are on the next two pages.

Slow Boat From China

The most convenient and leisurely means to Hong Kong used to be the "poor man's cruise," which I took at least 30 times. Buses were cheaper, but you spent 12 hours in a set watching videos of gory Hong Kong gangster movies or Karaoke tapes, and you got in at night just in time to fork out $100 U.S. on a HK hotel room.

With the boat, I was free to roam about, or relax in the cabin, and a morning arrival saved one day's accommodation. (If you go to Hong Kong, by the way—stay in the Kowloon YMCA. Great prices, great rooms, awesome view, and located next door to the Peninsula Hotel, of James Bond fame).

First class, which ran about 500 RMB, gave us a cabin with a window and a private bath--and included, at no extra charge, a cabin mate who was inevitably a chain smoker.

Second class saved us 60 RMB, and was also two to a room, but no window or bath, though we had a sink to soak our head in when the tobacco smoke got to us. Our roommate, like us, was cost conscious (that's why he too was in 2nd class), so he smoked a cheaper, more noxious grade of Chinese tobacco—like Petunia Cigarettes, or Great Ceiling.

Third class saved yet another 60 RMB and landed us in a room with 18 to 20 people in bunk beds. Smoking was not allowed while lying in bed, so everyone sat up in bed and smoked. The token foreigner was always assigned the upper berth in the corner where the smoke collected, but if you complained they just thought you were blowing smoke. Third class mattresses were a ¼" thick piece of foam laid on top of plywood; authentic "room and board."

Fourth class, the lowest you could go in our classless society, got us assigned chairs on deck. I tried it, then threw decorum out the port hole and slept on the floor like a bug in a rug (or at least with the bugs in the rug).

Dinner and breakfast were are available for a fee, and two shops sold snacks, alcohol, and cigarettes to resupply our chain smoking cabinmate.

Jesting aside, we loved the boat, if for no other reason than we could bring tons of luggage (like cheese!) and not pay a lot of overweight.

The 18 hour Slow Boat to China was a pleasant interlude in our all too busy life -- except during typhoons. Those prone to seasickness could get "seasick pills" at the front desk. Those who could not say Yūnchuán Yào(晕船药) got the message across by throwing up on the desk.

Alas, the MV Jimei, and her successor the Wasa Queen, are no more, but as of this writing the Star Pisces makes the Hong Kong-Xiamen trip once a month.

Travel Supplement One
Arcane Art of Mini-Bussing

"Get aboard! Plenty of room!"

Our first long distance bus trip, to neighboring Zhangzhou and back, was supposed to take 1½ to 2 hours, but that obviously didn't include the hour they spent packing us on the mini-bus. If only we could have figured out which bus was leaving first.

One would think the fullest bus would pull out first, but not so. Sometimes a half empty bus will race off, the strategy being to pick up more victims down the highway, while a bus that is packed to the gills like a sardine tin might wait another half hour to find some soul willing to fry their fanny on the blistering engine cover. On a 30 seat bus, they can cram 50 victims, who sit on laps, or stand, or squat on tiny bamboo stools in the aisles.

The ticket hawkers all squawk in unison, "Hurry up! We're leaving right now!" And drivers inch forward a few feet to prove time is of the essence. "Aiyah!" they scream. "Kuài Lái!"（"快来！"）

I asked one lady, "Do you have A/C?"

"Of course! See the sign? Get on quick! We're leaving!"

Amoy Bus, 1924

J. Nienhuis

Sue and I scrambled aboard and squeezed into a tiny seat in the back, between two farmers and their baskets of carrots, cabbage and Chinese celery. The ticket seller snatched my money and the driver switched off the engine.

"I thought you were leaving right now?"

"As soon as the bus is full," she said.

"It's packed now," I argued. But she ignored me like yesterday's news, and stuck her head out the window like a turtle straining from its shell for a feeble-minded fly, and she screamed at all and sundry, "Hurry up! Get on board. We're leaving now!"

Several passengers snickered, and I knew I had been had.

A youth who was obviously wiser than I eyed the bus suspiciously and said, "You've not filled up the aisle yet."

The ticket lady rolled her eyes. "Of course we haven't. We'll pick up more people down the road. The driver started his engine and inched forward. The youth puffed his chest and led his girl onto the bus, sat on a bamboo stool in the aisle, forked over his 20 Yuan, and the driver switched the ignition off.

Amoy, 1931 J. Nienhuis

"Hey, you said we're leaving now!" But the agent was again deaf, dumb and blind. I could barely keep from joining the snickers.

Twain's Duke and Dauphin would have been proud.

Fully 45 minutes after we had been told, "Hurry, we're leaving!" the van lurched off down the road. I asked the ticket lady, "Why haven't you turned on the air conditioning?"

"Open windows are cool enough when we're moving."

"But you said the bus has A/C!"

"It does!" she said, "But we don't use it when we're moving."

Snicker, snicker, all around me.

The bus slowed every few minutes as the ticket hawker poked her head from her yellow shell and screamed, "Get on board. Plenty of seats! Hurry!" One wily peasant dubiously eyed the collage of faces peering dolefully from the windows like nonAryans on the cattle car to Auschwitz. He timorously put one foot, clad in Playboy socks and plastic flip flops, onto the rusted bus step. The lady grabbed him by the collar, yanked him inside, slammed the door, and said, "Ten Yuan!"

"You said there was plenty of room!"

"There is room," she said, and pointed to the battery box, which was coated in greenish gray cottony corrosion and grease, and squeezed between the hot engine cover and the wheel well.

Those of us with enough room to expand our rib cages snickered softly.

There was no order to her people packing, so every time the bus stopped to disgorge a victim, we reshuffled the deck of dog-eared bodies; parents lost children, husbands lost wives; one lost a wallet. But we made it to Zhangzhou in one piece, more or less.

After a pleasant afternoon in Zhangzhou, we returned to the bus stop, where we saw a bus inching forward. The sweetest little granny shouted, "Hurry, we're leaving."

"Susan, this old granny can't be like the rogue on the last bus. They really are leaving." We boarded the bus, paid our pesos, and the driver cut the engine. We sweltered for 20 minutes until sweet old granny had packed her bus.

Susan snickered.

When we reached home that night we discovered that we had been gallivanting about the countryside on Friday the 13th.

Someday I'll write about Saturday the 14th.

Travel Supplement Two
Arcane Science of Darwinian Driving

Americans, who are used to traffic cops writing tickets for something as small as causing another driver to hit his brakes (for any reason), suspect driving in China to have neither rhyme nor reason. But a decade of driving in Xiamen has taught me that this is not the case. It is simply a matter of, "Darwinian Driving—Survival of the Fastest." This is immensely logical and practical—especially in a nation of 1.3 billion people, where auto warfare does double duty as population control.

You just need to know the rules...

The Rules of Darwinian Driving

1. First has right of way—whether driver or pedestrian. This explains why buses, cement trucks or 18-wheelers will careen blindly out of side streets, neither looking nor slowing down, right into the path of oncoming traffic. If they are hit by another vehicle, they are innocent because they were there first (obviously—or they would not have been hit). Of course, if they hesitate, the oncoming traffic with the so-called 'right of way' will speed up to cut them off. This is logical. Even as we must take every opportunity to cut in front of others, it is imperative we also prevent them from doing the same to us. It is a matter of the Golden Rule: do unto others, but do it first. For example, if your car breaks down, be sure to stop in an intersection—preferably diagonally to block as much traffic as possible. After all, you're not going anywhere, so neither should the competition. And when making left turns, do it from the far right lane—but do it fast, because of rule #2.

2. He who hesitates is lost. Physics plainly teaches that only two objects may occupy one space at a time. Of course, sorting out who is first can get sticky, especially when five cars abreast try to enter a two lane road. If none hesitate, all may usually merge nicely using the **Zipper Tactic**, though at times this formation does come unzipped. To insure the zipper moves smoothly, it is crucial to avoid hesitation, as well as that peculiar Western weakness known as 'defensive driving.'

3. Drive offensively, not defensively. General Patton said, "A good offence is always the best defence." It gives you a psychological edge. I learned this the hard way. When I edged to the right to let large trucks pass me on mountain roads, they literally forced me off the road. Now I hog the middle till the bitter end. (Chinese call this 'hero car;' Americans call it 'playing chicken'—though here, no one is playing).

4. Don't pander to pedestrians; you'll get them killed. Pedestrians have no qualms in stepping right in front of a car without looking. Indeed, they will deliberately not look, or even look the other way. This is because they know that 1) First has right of way, 2) Only one object can occupy a space at a time, and 2b) If they occupy that space first and you run them down, they will retire on the lawsuit. If they are killed, their entire extended family will retire on the lawsuit, and worship their ashes forever on the ancestral shelf. This explains why pedestrians ignore wide sidewalks and walk down the middle of busy streets. They seek retirement. Hence rule 5…

5. Avoid so-called Courtesy or Caution—especially with pedestrians, lest we get them killed. In my formative years, I often stopped for old ladies and women with babies. They invariably hesitated, suspicious of my motives. The few who did get the nerve to cross were nearly run down by the vehicles that raced around me from behind. So give no quarter. But in all you do, avoid looking the opponent in the eye.

6. Face is foremost. It is hard for Americans to fathom how Chinese drivers and pedestrians keep so calm while waging war on each other. In America, road rage is so endemic that people get shot simply for tapping their horn or looking the wrong way at an opponent. But Chinese avoid such extremities by avoiding direct eye contact. This keeps warfare impersonal, allowing both parties to save face during no-holds barred battle. It is a unique ability, honed over 5,015 years by hundreds of millions of people co-existing in cramped quarters.

Lesson? Relax, enjoy, and don't take it personally. Once the rules of the road are understood, driving in China is as easy as in America—and lots more fun. With cars, who needs Nintendo or Gameboy?

Chapter 28

Xiàmén Hotels

Millennium

As with all else in Xiamen, hotels change constantly. Our posh 5-star French Sofitel shut its doors, but we now have a 6-star Kempinski. My personal favorite remains the Millennium Hotel. Xiamen's oldest international hotel (1992), it is a block from downtown Zhongshan Rd. or the Gulangyu Ferry, and has several of my favorite restaurants (see International Cuisine chapter). It also has some of the most professional and consistent service, thanks to management that has stayed with the hotel through 20 years of change. I've learned the hard way that the secret of a fine hotel is not the dog and pony show put on in the posh foyers but the planning from the drab back offices.

A 56-year-old Millennium Hotel dishwasher, fresh from the countryside, proudly told me of his "team member" training, and the importance of his job. That struck a chord with me. Only a week earlier, at a 5-star international hotel just north of Shanghai, several of the "clean" buffet plates had remnants of dried food and what looked like motor oil. I showed them to the lady in charge, who managed to look down her nose at me even though she was a foot shorter, and curtly replied, "Well—get another plate!" and stalked off.

Beautiful premises—but I won't stay there a second time.

Seeing Stars? Xiamen's thousands of quality hotels range from the inexpensive "Home Inn" chain (like a Motel 6 in America—small but clean and inexpensive) to the elegant resort hotels. And the star rating may not adequately reflect their quality, value or desirability—and location means a lot.

On the following pages I share a few unique hotels. For more suggestions, visit www.amoymagic.com or the China hotel websites.

> "Arthur Smith's renowned Chinese Characteristics has a chapter on 'The Absence of Comfort and Convenience,' recounting his experience and observations of Chinese dress, houses, pillows and beds, which all European readers find amusing. I wager it is ten times more amusing to Chinese readers to learn of Arthur Smith's account of his sufferings and discomforts. The white man's nerves are undoubtedly degenerate."
>
> Lin Yutang

Useful Chinese Terms for Addresses

Lóu (楼) = building
Lù, Jiē & Dào (路,街,道)= street, road, etc.
Dàdào (大道) = literally "big road"; a main street, avenue, blvd., etc.
North = Běi (北) South = Nan (南) East = Dōng (东)
West = Xī (西) Central = Zhōng

Useful Phrase for Hotel Check-out

"Not enough money! Can I sweep or clean windows and dishes for a discount?"
Qián búgòu. Rúguǒ wǒ cā bōlǐ, dǎsǎo wèishēng, xǐ pánzi, kěyǐ gěi wǒ dǎzhé?

A Few Select Xiamen Hotels

Note! Check reviews on such sites as Trip-Advisor. Hotels change!

Millenium Harbourview Hotel Xiamen (Xiàmén Hǎijǐng Qiānxī Dàjiǔdiàn, 厦门海景千禧大酒店) 4 Stars. Xiàmén's 1st "international" hotel, best downtown location. Great Int'l buffet (different cuisine each night) Hollywood Bar, Portofino Italian restaurant (my favorite). Reservations: 800 830 3608 Front Desk: 2023333

Add: 12-8 Zhēnhǎi Lù (镇海路 12-8 号) www.millenniumxiamen.com

Xiàmén Airlines [Jīnyàn] Hotel (Xiàmén Hángkōng Jīnyàn Jiúdiàn, 厦门航空金雁酒店) On Yuándāng Lake; only –in-hotel airport check-in service.

Tel: 2218888 Add: No. 99 South Húbīn Rd(厦门湖滨南路 99 号)

E-mail: jyhotel@xiamenair.com.cn www.jinyan-hotel.com

Asia Gulf Hotel, Xiàmén (Yàzhōu Hǎiwān Dà Jiúdiàn, 亚洲海湾大酒店 5 Stars On Island Ring Road (Huándǎo Lù, 环岛路) ; seaside swimming pool. Tel: 2198888

Add: #98 Huángcuò, Island Ring Road (黄厝 98 号, 环岛路中段)

E-mail: hotel@gulf-hotel.com.cn www.gulf-hotel.com.cn

City Hotel, Xiàmén (Xiàmén Bīnguǎn, 厦门宾馆) 4 Star Elegant garden setting; great Mǐnnán cuisine; Thai consulate on hotel grounds. Tel: 2053333

Add: 16 Húyuán Lù(虎园路 16 号) http://www.cityhotelxm.com

Mandarin Hotel (Yuèhuá Jiúdiàn, 悦华酒店) 5 Stars—Xiàmén's flagship hotel; facility's supposedly cover 50 acres! Tel: 6023333

Add: 101 Yuèhuá Lù (悦华路 101 号) Hǔlǐ District, Xiàmén 361006

E-mail: mandarin@xmmandarin.com www.xmmandarin.com

Marco Polo (厦门马哥孛罗东方大酒店) 4 Stars. One of our finest; facing Yuandang Lake; 15 min. from airport. A favorite Lǎowài hangout.

Tel: 5091888 Add: 8 Jiànyè Lù 建业路 8 号 Xiamen, 361012

E-mail: xiamen@marcopolohotels.com www.marcopolohotels.com

Mǐnnán Hotel (Mǐnnán Dà Jiúdiàn, 闽南大酒店) Rocket-shaped Xiàmén landmark; revolving restaurant; 5 min. from train station, 10 min. from airport.

Tel: 5181188 Add: 26-34 Húbīn Nánlù Yīlǐ(湖滨南路一里 26-34 号)

E-mail: xmmnhotel@163.com Website: http://www.xmmn.com/

Overseas Chinese Hotel (Huáqiáo Dàshà, 厦门华侨大厦) Famous Mǐnnán cuisine. Tel: 2660888 Add: 70-74 Xīnhuá Lù (新华路 70-74 号)
E-mail: webmaster@xmhqhotel.com.cn www.xmhqhotel.com.cn/

Hilford Hotel Xiàmén (Xiàmén Xīěrfú Jiúdiàn, 厦门希尔福酒店) "Aqua-gym" fitness and recreation center (but often closed); reasonably priced rooms have kitchens and, believe it or not, **soft beds!** (Chinese beds are generally hard as boards—hence the term "room and board". Tel: 2082222
Add: 495 S. Sīmíng Lù (思明南路 495 号) www.hilford.com.cn/en/main.asp

Home Inn -- 24 Xiamen locations. Small rooms but clean, inexpensive. Breakfast is 15 Yuan. The website www.homeinns.com has an English tab but locations and booking are only in Chinese.
Best location: #291-293 South Siming Rd (1.2 block from the Millennium).

Hometel –"Youth Sunlight Service Apartments" (Xiàmén Qīngnián YángguāngZìjù Gōngyù, 厦门青年阳光自助公寓) 128-158 Yuan per day; at least nine convenient locations in Xiamen, including:

- **Hometel Xiàhé Lù Branch**: (厦禾店) Tel: 2110038 Add: #143-717 Hòudài Xī Lù Yínlóng Guǎngchǎng (后埭溪路银龙广场 143 号 717 室)
- **Hometel Dōngdù Branch** (东渡店) Tel: 5611115 Add: #69 Dōngdù Lù Lùbīn Bldg. #1905 (东渡路 69 号鹭槟大厦 1905 室)
- **Hometel Xiānyuè Branch** (仙岳店) Tel: 55011313 Add: Xiānyuè Lù: (opposite SM) (仙岳路) (SM 对面)

Int'l Youth Hostel (Xiàmén Guójì Qīngnián Lǚshè, 厦门国际青年旅舍)
Add: #41 Nanhua Road (南华路 41 号) (Facing Int'l Book Store)
Tel: 2082345 E-mail: yhaxm@yhaxm.com www.yhaxm.com/

Lùjiang Hotel (Lùjiāng Jiúdiàn 鹭江酒店) On harbor facing Gulangyu, rooftop dining. Dimsum, Mǐnnán cuisine Add: #54 Lùjiāng Dào (鹭江道 54)
Tel: 2022206 www.fjta.com/xmlujiang

Peony Wànpéng Hotel (Mǔdān Wànpéng Bīnguǎn, 牡丹万鹏宾馆) 4 Stars.
Faces Botanical Garden (Wànshíyuán, 万石园); our favorite foot massage.
Tel: 2662888 Add: #17-19 Húyuán Lù Xiàmén 361003 (虎园路 17-19 号)
E-mail: info@peony-hotel.com www.peony-hotel.com

Sheraton Hotel, Xiamen (Xiàmén Xǐlái Dēng jíudiàn, 厦门喜来登酒店)
Tel: 5525888 Add: #386-1 Jiāhé L(嘉禾路 386-1 号)
Excellent buffets. www.sheraton.com/xiamen

Wànháo Hotel (Wànháo Dà Jiúdiàn, 万豪大酒店) Popular Cantonese dimsum.
Tel: 5580888 Add: #90 Táiwān Jiē, Xiàmén (台湾街 90 号)
E-mail: ljz@xm315.com www.wanhaohotel.cn/

Xiamen Gold Coast Hotel (Xiàmén Jīn Hǎiàn Dà Jiúdiàn, 厦门金海岸大酒店)
3 Stars, close to Xiamen Govt. and Yuándāng Lake. (Offers babysitting!).
Tel: 5303333 Add: #40 Húbīn Běi Lù, Xiàmén (湖滨北 40 号)

E-mail: goldcoast@gchtl.com.cn www.gchtl.com.cn

Xiàmén Int'l Seaside Hotel (Xiàmén Guójì Huizhăn Jiúdiàn, 厦门国际会展酒店) 5 Stars Tel: 5959999 Add: 199 Conference & Exhibit Center #2 Rd.
E-mail:home@seaside.cn www.seaside.cn

Kempinski Xiamen Xiamen's only **6 star** hotel. Tel: 258-8888
Add: #98 Hubin Middle Road (湖滨中路 98 号)

Rosewood Lakeview Plaza (Service Apartments), **Xiàmén** (Xiàmén Zūnjué Húpàn Gōngyù, 厦门尊爵湖畔公寓) Your 2nd home; spacious, fully appointed lakeside apartment opposite Marco Polo, excellent service, reasonable prices by day, week or month. Kitchens, laundry, pool and gym; free breakfast buffet.
Tel: 5112323 Add: #3 Jiànyè Lù (建业路 3 号)

Xiàmén University Hotel (Xiàmén Dàxué, 厦门大学) Convenient, quiet. Jiànwén Lóu (建文楼) and Kèlì Lóu (克立楼) are cheapest; priciest is Yìfū Lóu (逸夫楼), which has one of our favorite restaurants. Chinese Breakfast included.

All three are on the first intersection inside the old university gate near Nánpŭtuó (南普陀) Temple. Tel: 208-7988

Westin Xiamen —newly opened in May, 2012, near SM City Mall. Tel: 337-8888 Add: 398 Xianyue Rd. (仙岳路 398 号) E-mail: westin.xiamen@westin.com

Off Island

Xiamen Riyuegu (Sun-Moon Valley) Hot Springs Resort (Xiàmén Rìyuè Gŭ Wēnquán Dùjià Cūn, 厦门日月谷温泉度假村) One of the best in Asia! Excellent website: Tel: 6312222 Add: Tang'an Village, Dōngfú Town, Hăicāng District
海沧区东孚镇汤岸 E-mail: dosm@riyuegu.com
www.riyuegu.com

Getting There: Busses #804, #450 or #451; or Xiàmén – Zhāngzhōu Bus

Trithorn's "Minnan-Style Hotsprings Villas"

Best Western Premier Trithorn Hotspring Resort Xiamen (Zuìjiā Xīfāng XiàménCuìfēng Wēnquán Dùjià Jiúdiàn, "最佳西方" 厦门翠丰温泉度假酒店) Best Western's first 5-star resort in China, this 35,000 m^2 resort is delightful for an overnighter or a weekend getaway. Location: 6km. north of Tóng'ān in Tīngxī village, opposite scenic Tīngxī Reservoir (汀溪水库对面). Tel: 7159999 www.trithorn-resort.com/

Gŭlàngyŭ Accommodations

Ferry Schedule: every 15 min. by day; 20 min. by night.

Gŭlàng Villa Hotel (Gŭlàngyŭ Biéshù Jiúdiàn, 鼓浪别墅酒店) 3 Stars. Secluded beachfront location facing ferry dock on back of Gulangyu; nice restaurant. Tel: 2063280
Add: #14 Gŭshēng Lù (鼓声路 14 号)
E-mail: glvhotel@public.xm.fj.cn

7th Day Adventist Sanatorium (Měihuá Lăorén Liáoyăng Yuàn, 美华老人疗养院)—delightful inexpensive hilltop retreat; great vegetarian food. Take the alternate ferry to Gŭlàng Villa Hotel (Gŭlàngyŭ Biéshù Jiúdiàn, 鼓浪别墅酒店). Turn right, walk up the coast a bit, ascend narrow granite path behind the bust of the man who invented Pīnyīn, take left fork. It's just past the hilltop Chinese Christian cemetery. Tel: 2066517

Vegetarian Feast on 7th Day--or 8th?

7th Day Adventist Sanatorium

Bayview Inn (Wānjĭng Lŭguăn, 湾景旅馆) Near harbor, off Lóngtóu Rd.; "Old World" feel; reasonable rates (from 10 USD for dorm bed to over 100 USD for suites). Tel: 2060466 Add: #17 Lóngtóu Lù, Gŭlàngyŭ Islet (鼓浪屿龙头路 17 号)
E-mail: bayviewinn@163.cn www.bayviewinn.cn (has English)

Xiàmén Marine Garden Hotel, Gŭlàngyŭ (Xiàmén Hăishàng Huāyuán Jiúdiàn, 厦门海上花园酒店 4 Stars Gŭlàngyŭ's 1st 4-star; on back of island by Găngzĭhòu Beach. Tel: 2062688 Add: #27 Tiánwěi Rd, Gŭlàngyŭ (田尾路 27 号)
www.marinegardenhotel.com.cn/en/

Piano Island Hotel (Qīndáo Jiúdiàn, 琴岛酒店) About 60 meters to left of ferry.
Tel: 2066668 Add: #8 Lùjiāo Lù (鼓浪屿鹿礁路 8 号)

Beautiful Island Hotel, #133 Longtou Rd. (Līzhī Dǎo Jiúdiàn, 丽之岛酒店) – 5 minute walk from ferry. Small but affordable rooms. Tel: 206-3309

Add: #133 Longtou Lù (龙头路 133 号)

Bright Moon Garden Villas (Hàoyuè Yuán, 皓月园) Delightful wooden cottages in a garden setting and overlooking the sea behind the Koxinga Statue on the islet's N.E. side. My favorite retreat on Gulangyu, soothed to sleep each night by the song of the surf right below the balcony. Not cheap (from 520 to 700 a night), but worth it for a special getaway.

Tel: 2069730

Going Cheap on Gulangyu

Gǔlàngyǔ Int'l Youth Hotel (Xiàmén Gǔlàngyǔ Gújì Qīngnián Lǔshè, 厦门鼓浪屿国际青年旅舍) Only 100 meters from ferry, to the left and up the hill (by red-brick former British Consulate). Tel: 2066066

Add: #18 Lùjiāo Lù (鹿礁路 18 号) E-mail: yha@yhagly.com www.yhagly.com

Hǎihuá Holiday Cottage (Hǎihuá Dùjià Wū, 海华度假屋) They have 18 rooms with baths. Rates are lower in the off season—100+ Yuan to 500+ Yuan.

Tel: 2066935 Add: #28 Zhōnghuá Lù (中华路 28 号)

Joyful Guest Tavern (Bīnyuè Kèzhàn, 宾悦客栈) Cheapest backpacker hangout on Gǔlàngyǔ; private villa turned tavern, beside Trinity Church. Spartan facilities: toilet, public bath, small, shady garden.

Beds from 40 Yuan per night. Two-person room 80 Yuan. Tel: 2063520

Add: #44 Ānhǎi Lù, by Trinity Church (安海路 44 号, 三一堂旁边)

Public Waterworks Sanitarium (Zìláishuǐ Liáoyǎng Yuàn, 自来水公司疗养院) Just south of Bright Moon Park (皓月园再向南走). Rooms about 150 per night; discount available. Tel: 2062411 Add: Zhāngzhōu Lù (漳州路)

Chapter 29

Cradle of Modern Chinese Education

Boy Scouts, Anglo-Chinese College Amoy, 1929

It is no surprise that 11% of Xiàménese have higher education, because Xiàmén was China's greatest pioneer in modern education.

Mainland China's first Protestant missionaries arrived on Gulangyu in 1841, and over the following decades opened about 20 innovative schools—everything from China's first kindergartens and first day-school (started in 1845 by Rev. Lyman Burt Peet, 弼来满) to Fujian's 1st school for girls (about 1845, William Young, 养为霖) and vocational schools, colleges, medical schools, etc.

Foreigners got the ball rolling; wealthy Chinese made sure it didn't stop. The Amoy U.S. Consul Mr. A. Burlingame Johnson, for example, started Tung-Wen Institute（同文学院）on Gǔlàngyǔ in 1898, and succeeding presidents were U.S. Consuls, but Chinese funded the school and formed the Board of Trustees.

The investments paid off. Gǔlàngyǔ nurtured such talents as Madame Lín Qiǎozhì（林巧稚）, Mother of China's Modern Women's Medicine (she delivered over 50,000 babies herself!). Acclaimed Gulangyu artist Teng Hiok Chiu was not only the first to win Britain's Royal Academy Gold medal but also a Chinese citizen's first Olympic medal (Britain's basketball team). John Ma (Mǎ Yuēhàn,马约翰) was Father of Modern Chinese Sports. Lú Zhuàngzhāng（卢戆章), "Father of Pinyin", put the punctuation in Chinese characters. Gǔlàngyǔ also produced over 100 well known musicians, as well as internationally acclaimed writers like Lín Yǔtáng（林语堂). His New York Times obituary noted,

> Lin Yutang, poet, novelist, historian and philosopher, had no peer as an interpreter to Western minds of the customs, aspirations, fears and thoughts of his people and their country, China, the great and tragic land.①

Xiàmén's pioneering education continues even today. Read more in "*Discover*

① "Lin Yutang, 80, Dies; Scholar-Philosopher," *New York Times*, 27 March 1976

Gŭlàngyŭ," particularly Chapter 4, "Pioneering Education," Chapter 5, "Pioneering Medicine," and Chapter 6, "Pioneering Music and Arts."

Xiàmén University (厦门大学)

Note: for more info, read "*Xiàmén University, Strength of the Nation.*" It includes a map and list of 103 sites (which 100+ visiting Shanghai American School students used as an educational scavenger hunt).

XMU gets top billing in Xiamen education for three reasons:

1) China's most beautiful campus;

2) China's most strategic campus (the only key university in a Special Economic Zone);

3) XMU is my home.

I rest my case.

Photo by Mr. Pan Wanhua

XMU's 400 acres, nestled snugly between the Five Old Man Mountains and the sea, are as tranquil as the sprawling Nánpŭtuó Buddhist monastery right next door – except on April 6, when it celebrates its founding in 1921 by Mr. Tan Kah Kee (Chén Jiāgēng 陈嘉庚), an overseas Chinese with a big heart and a bigger wallet, and remembered now as the "Henry Ford of Asia."

Band of Rubber Barons At age 17, Tan joined his father in opening a Singapore rice shop. From this humble beginning he saved enough to diversify into shipping and canning, but it was rubber that really stretched his fortune.

Mr. Tan was one of four members of the rubber band that founded Malaysia's rubber industry. One of Southeast Asia's few millionaires, Tan did business in 48 countries. But rubber prices plummeted during the Depression, and never bounced back, so before Tan's checks bounced faster than his rubber he closed up shop, sold some large buildings, and put the money into a trust fund for XMU.

After Japan invaded China in 1937, Tan founded the S.E. Asian Overseas Chinese Relief Association, and spent the rest of his life raising money for China. Of Mr. Tan's many projects, XMU was the apple of his eye, or as Chinese say, "bright pearl in his palm" (Zhăngshàng Míngzhū, 掌上明珠), even when XMU was no longer in Xiàmén.

In 1937, during China's war against Japan, XMU relocated to a remote mountain town, Longyan, on Fujian's western border. After 1945, XMU returned to Xiàmén, and the new president, eminent biologist, Dr. Wāng Déyào (汪德耀), immediately set out rebuilding and expanding the campus. Tan's money and Wāng's vision paid off.

Pen & Gun About the time XMU had recovered from the Japanese, Chiang Kai Shek attacked us from Táiwāin, and XMU students adopted the motto, "Pen in one hand, gun in the other!" But XMU was one tough school, and by 1962, she was designated a key national university and has mushroomed ever since.

XMU now boasts over 32,000 full-time students and a few thousand part-time students, including over 1600 foreign students, with every degree imaginable. One student has so many degrees I call him Dr. Fahrenheit.

A brochure rightly boasts, "XMU's tens of thousands of graduates and postgraduates have been highly recognized both at home and abroad as outstanding in their fields."

Of course, our farmers are out standing in their fields too.

Visit XMU's Economics College—#1 in China—and tour the Chemistry Lab, where renowned scientists, including five in the Chinese Academy of Sciences) wield such hi-tech devices as scanning tunneling microscopes to perform research in bioelectro-chemistry, spectroelectro-chemistry, and other esoteric stuff I can't spell correctly.

外文系民兵进行高射炮兵训练。这是女高射炮班正在进行對空射击操作。

Foreign Language Dept. (1950s)
Girl Students
(Language Drills?)

Also visit China's 1st anthropology museum, and take photos of China's largest university auditorium (one of the majestic granite seaside buildings constructed in the 1950s by Mr. Tan's son-in-law, Lǐ Guāngqián 李光前).

Take a break from your whirlwind tour at the coffee shop or restaurant in our International Academic Exchange's Yìfū Bldg. (逸夫楼) Tel: 2087988.

After dinner, stroll around serene Lotus Lake (Fúrónghú 芙蓉湖), which mirrors the Five Old Men Mountains and the Oriental-flavor student dorms. The small islet's statues are of Mr. Tan and students.

By day, Lotus Lake is thronged with students standing alone, textbook in hand, memorizing English dialogues. They visit the lake by night as well, but in pairs, and they aren't studying English.

In the early 90s, university regulations forbade males and females. Even my wife and I could not hold hands! But nowadays they hold hands and everything else. And men ***still*** hold hands…

Some of XMU's Many Firsts

(adapted from "*Xiàmén University—Strength of the Nation*")

China's only key university founded by an Overseas Chinese
中国唯一一所由海外华侨创办的重点大学

China's only key university in a Special Economic Zone
中国经济特区中唯一一所重点大学

China's leading economics college
中国主要的经济学院

Mainland China's 1st to award the MBA degree
中国大陆首次授予 MBA 学位的大学

A "Cradle of modern Chinese oceanography" (1st PhD in Oceanography)
"现代中国海洋学的摇篮"（培养了海洋学的第一个博士）

A "Cradle of modern aviation"
"现代航空学的摇篮"

China's 1st Institute of Higher Education Research
中国第一个高等教育研究机构

China's first modern college for foreigners (OEC) – over 1600 foreign students
中国为外国学生设立的第一所现代大学—1600 多外国学生

China's leading chemistry department
中国主要的化学系

One of China's 1st universities to teach International Law
中国最早教授国际法的大学之一

One of China's 1st Dept. of Economics and Trade
中国最早的经贸学院之一

China's #1 State Key Laboratory in Physical Chemistry of Solid Surfaces
中国固体表面物化国家 1 号重点实验室

China's only Key Lab. in Analytical Sciences (Materials & Life Chemistry)
中国唯一的分析科学重点实验室（数学和生命化学）

China's 1st Institute of S.E. Asian and Overseas Chinese Studies
中国第一个中南亚及海外华侨研究机构

China's 1st Anthropology Museum
中国第一个人类博物馆

Mainland China's 1st Taiwan Research Center & China's 1st Taiwan Research Anthology
中国大陆第一个台湾研究所和中国第一份台湾研究刊物

Mainland China's closest university ties with Taiwan.
中国大陆离台湾最近的大学

China's largest university auditorium (overlooking the sea)
中国最大的大学礼堂（眺望大海）

China's pioneer in correspondence education (since 1950s!)
中国函授教育的先锋（从 20 世纪 50 年代开始）

China's leading mathematicians, including talents like Chen Jingrun.
中国著名的数学家，包括陈景润等天才

And the list goes on… 此列表将继续添加……

XMU's Overseas Education College (OEC) –China's 1st Modern College for Foreigners Learn a few choice phrases like "Ni Hao!"（你好！）and your Chinese hosts will exclaim, "Your Chinese is great!"—even if you've massacred both tones and pronunciation (see "Mad About Mandarin" chapter).

Exchange Chinese and English lessons with a friend, or hire a tutor. Or if you're as undisciplined as I am, study at OEC. Since its opened in 1956, OEC has taught over 20,000 on-campus and correspondence students. Courses include Mandarin, Xiàmén dialect, Chinese language and literature (2-6 years by correspondence), and Traditional Chinese medicine (1-5 years, both correspondence and face-to-face). Before you book your next appointment at the Chinese medicine hospital, remind yourself that physicians graduate faster than poets.

When we arrived in 1988, OCE was on a drive to lure foreign students (or at least their wallets). They had good plans for depositing the foreign currency but no place to deposit most of the foreigners who brought the currency, so we were housed in the building just off campus that now has the KFC. But times have changed, thanks to alumni like Lín Lianxing from Indonesia. OEC's ten-story Overseas Students' Dormitory Building has A/C, in-room phones, and a dining hall. They even have modern new classroom facilities. Tel: 2186211 2086139

E-mail: xmuoec@jingxian.xmu.edu.cn http://english.xmuoec.com/

Xiamen Univ. School of Management (SMXMU)—China's Top 10 in both *Forbes & BusinessWeek*

Our MBA Center handed out China's 1st MBA degrees (we beat Nankai Univ. by one week). In 1988, we had to beg students to study management—and pay them. Now they pay us, and we have more applicants than we can handle (a lot of classes for a classless society, though Sue says I have no class at all).

In 1987 the Canadian Int'l Development Agency helped start our MBA as a joint project with Dalhousie, Saint Mary's, and other Canadian universities. The first 30 MBAs graduated in July, 1990. Some still send me letters and cards—from Běijīng, New York, London, even Helsinki (how's that for a fine Finnish!) Graduates have included the CEO of XMU Electronics, Director of Fuyao Glass Industry, and founder of Firefly Lighting. Visit XMU MBA—and hire some of our students!

Tel: 218-6441 Website: http://sm.xmu.edu.cn

Xiàmén International School (Xiàmén Guójì Xuéxiào, 厦门国际学校) One of China's finest international schools, XIS has offered quality, Western accredited education for expat children since 1997. The school has over 130 faculty and staff and almost 400 students from 34 countries and regions.

In June, 2002, XIS moved to a modern new 33,000m^2 campus, with gym, soccer field, track, three basketball courts, and an indoor swimming pool. The facilities also include a library, reading room, science and language labs, large cafeteria, and an intranet.

Got kids? Visit XIS. No kids yet? Get some so you can send them to XIS!

Add: Jiǔtiān Hú, Xìnglín, Xiàmén (九天湖兴林厦门)

Tel: 6256581 E-mail: askxis@xischina.com www.xischina.com

> "Started in 1997, XIS offers a PreK-12th grace international English language education to the children of Xiàmén's expats. It is the only school in Fújiàn province, and one of only five in all of China, authorized to offer all three International Baccalaureate Programs (i.e., Primary Years Program, Middle Years Program and the Diploma Program).
>
> "XIS students come from over 30 nations and regions. Teachers have bachelor degrees, and many have masters. XIS is accredited with the Western Association of Schools and Colleges (WASC). "We extend a warm invitation to all expatriate families to come visit us when seeking a school for their children." Dr. John M. Godwin, Headmaster

Colleges and Universities that have accepted XIS grads

Harvard University, Ma.	University of Massachusetts, Ma.
Stanford University, Ca.	Farleigh Dickinson, New Jersey
Binghamton University, NY	University of Buffalo, NY
Syracuse University, NY	Hofstra University, NY
Michigan State University, MI	Penn State University, PA
University of Nevada, Reno, NV	Xiàmén University, Xiàmén, PRC
La Salle University, Shànghǎi, PRC	Nottingham University, Níngbō, PRC
Concordia University, Montreal, Canada	Euro-Control Maastricht, Netherlands

XIS 2012

130 Faculty and Staff, almost 400 students, 34 Countries & Regions:

Argentina	Australia	Belgium	Belize	Britain	Canada
Colombia	Denmark	Holland	Hungary	France	Germny
Hong Kong	India	Indonesia	Ireland	Italy	Korea
Macao	Malaysia	Mexico	Norway	Philippines	Romania
Singapore	South Africa	Spain	Surinam	Sweden	USA
Taiwan	Thailand	Dengdeng (Chinese for "etcetera")			

Xiamen International School

Where the World Comes Together!

(Dukes, 1885)

Jīměi University –see “Jīměi—China’s College Town” chapter

Xiàmén Univ. of Technology (Xiàmén Lǐgōng Xuéyuàn, 厦门理工学院)

XMUT is a provincial university with two campuses. Most future activities will probably be held on the new 70 hectare Jīměi campus, but the original Honeycomb Hill campus, a five minute walk up the hill from XMU, will still be used for adult education, scientific research, international education cooperation, software development education, etc.

XMUT began as Lùjiāng University in 1981, the same year as Xiamen’s SEZ was founded. The school has a faculty of about 500, and a student body of about 5500 full-time and 3000 part-time students.

Want to teach in Xiàmén? The foreigners I’ve known who have taught at XMUT enjoyed their experience.

Add: #394 Sīmíng Nán Lù (思明南路 394 号). Tel: 2189536
E-mail: xmlg@xmut.edu.cn www.xmut.edu.cn

Xiàmén Oceanography Vocational College (厦门海洋职业技术学院)
Tel: 5393508 Add: #61 Tǐyù Lù (体育路 61 号) www.xmoc.cn

Private Colleges

Xiàmén Performing Arts College (Yǎnyì Zhíyè Xuéyuàn, 厦门演艺职业学院)
Tel: 2570571 Add: #32 Gǔlàngyǔ Fújiàn Lù (鼓浪屿福建路 32 号)
www.xmyanyi.com

Xiàmén Informatics College 〔XiàménYīnghuáměi Xuéyuàn 英华美(厦门)学院〕
Tel: 2960382 Add: Wénzào Dìháo Bldg. 5/F(文灶帝豪大厦五楼)
E-mail: tom@cn-informatics.com Website: www.cn-informatics.com

Learn Chinese! Try:

Xiamen University Overseas Education College (since 1956!)
Tel: 2186211 2086139 E-mail: xmuoec@jingxian.xmu.edu.cn
http://english.xmuoec.com/

Mandarin Fun Flexible language programs, summer camps, etc.
E-mail: annexu800@hotmail.com
Tel: 5118287 http://www.mandarinfun.cn/en/

Chapter 30

Health Care in Xiàmén

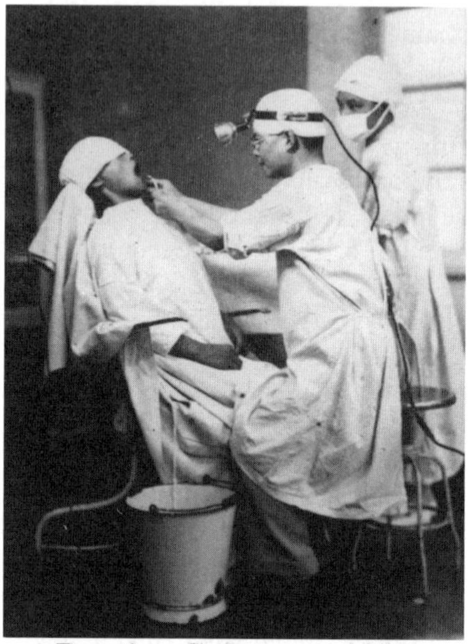

Dentist, Gulangyu, 1930s
Feels Better Blindfolded?

Gǔlàngyǔ was the birthplace of modern Chinese medicine, thanks to pioneering missionary doctors like Patrick Manson ("Father of Tropical Medicine") and Dr. Lín Qiǎozhì (林巧稚), Mother of Modern Gynecology.

Xiàmén now has over 1000 medical establishments, including an eye hospital with the latest laser surgery.

Haicang's Chang Geng Hospital, part of a Taiwan chain founded by 90+-year-old Taiwanese billionaire Wang Yung-ching, opened in May, 2008. Prices are no higher than local hospitals, but Chang Geng has English speaking Taiwan doctors, thanks to new regulations that allow Taiwan doctors to work on the Mainland without repeated tests and reviews. **Want Fast Care?** Register at the Emergency Center for very small charge.

Two of Xiamen Island's best hospitals are #1 Hospital and Zhōngshān Hospital, both of which have VIP Clinics with English speakers.

On Nov. 7, 2002, Zhōngshān Hospital doctors implanted an artificial heart in three year old Zhou Boling. Donations from local residents covered the costs of the surgery for this son of poor immigrants. They also performed open heart surgery on a young friend of ours, and two of our American friends had laparoscopic surgery to remove gall bladders (Americans must have a lot of gall).

Meds to Bring to Home

Although Xiàmén has modern hospitals, as well as a very advanced eye hospital and great dentists like Dr. Yao (named after the sounds that come from his clinic?), we still suggest you bring a medicine bag from home for basic first aid and health care. Include: thermometer, aspirin or Tylenol for fever, antidiarrhetics like Lomitil, rehydration salts, vitamins, cold medicines like Contact, a Bee Sting Kit, Pepto Bismol tablets, etc.. Bone up on basic first aid, and bring the book, "Where There is no Doctor."

The main steps for most ills, like colds, flu, food poisoning, are:

1) stop fever; 2) stop diarrhea; 3) drink lots of rehydrating liquids.

Nontraditional Chinese Medicine (NCM) may help where Western medicine does not. NCM cured an XMU American teacher's life-long asthma. But I take some claims with a grain of salt; sometimes even a whole block of salt. Consider the medicinal miracles derived from daily use of the cow horn combs sold on Gulangyu (though when I read they expel "fire-evil of the head"... I bought one for my wife):

产 品 说 明

Description of the Product

角梳在我国已有悠久的历史，采用纯天然牛角、绵羊角，经过现代科学工艺精制而成。用牛羊角梳梳理头发，去头火，除头屑，最为柔和舒适，达到润肤护发，头脑清新，调整周身气血，改善末梢血液循环。对白发、脱发者有益，亦有降低血脂调整血压之功效。

Comb having a long history in China The pure natural hotn of ox or sheep is being adopted to form the highly finished product through modern scientific technology Using comb made from ox or sheep will expel the fire-evil of the head and remove the scrap from the scalp with the most tender and comfort feeling resulting to smooth the skin and protect the hair to clear the mind to regulate the vital energy and blood of the whole body and improve the peripheral blood circulation; It is beneficial to grey hair and loss of hair and it has the effect of decreasing fatty material in the blood and regulating blood pressure

制造商：MADE IN CHINA

Xiamen Medical Website (Chinese only): www.xmhealth.gov.cn

Xiàmén Hospitals（Yīyuàn, 医院）

Chang Geng Hospital, Haicang (厦门长庚医院）English speaking staff, very reasonable prices. Avoid crowds; use Emergency Clinic.

Add: Haicang, #123 Xiafei Rd. (海沧区新阳工业区霞飞路 23 号) Tel: 6200123

Zhōngshān Hospital (Zhōngshān Yīyuàn, 中山医院）Affiliated with Xiàmén University, this is one of Xiàmén's premier hospitals. A special clinic for foreigners has English speaking nurses and doctors.

Add: #201-206 Húbīn Nán Lù （湖滨南路 201 之 206 号）

Tel: 2212328 www.xmzsh.com

#1 Hospital (Xiàménshì Dì Yī Yīyuàn, 厦门市第一医院） Add: Zhēnhǎi Lù , #10 Gǔjiē (厦门市镇海路上古街 10 号)

Tel: 2137275 www.xmfh.com.cn/default2.asp

Xiàmén Chinese Medicine Hospital (Xiàménshì Zhōngyīyuàn, 厦门市中医院)

Bring your own cow's horn comb.

Add: #12 Zhēnhǎi Lù (镇海路 12 号）(Near Millennium) Tel: 2665005

Chinese People's Liberation Army #174 Hospital (Zhōngguó Rénmín Jiěfàngjūn Dì Yībǎiqī Yīyuàn, 中国人民解放军第一七四医院). Excellent medical services, especially dental (see Dental Care, later in this chapter).

Add: #94-96 Wényuán Lù（文园路 94-96 号）(just over the small overpass from the Xiàmen City Hotel). Tel: 6335500 6335600 www.xm174.com

Xiàmén #2 Hospital, Gŭlàngyŭ Branch (Xiàménshì Dì Èr Yīyuàn Gŭlàngyŭ Fènyuàn, 厦门市第二医院鼓浪屿分院)
Add: #60 Fújiàn Lù(福建路 60 号) Tel: 2063549

Xiàmén #2 Hospital, Hăicāng Branch (Xiàménshì Dì Èr Yīyuàn Hăicāng Yīyuàn, 厦门市第二医院海沧医院) Add: Hăicāng Residential District, Hăiliù Lù (海沧生活区海六路) Tel: 6055830

Xiàmén Eye Hospital (Xiàmén Yănkē Zhōngxīn, 厦门眼科中心) You won't find better eye care anywhere—from simple prescription glasses to the latest laser eye surgery. Add: #336 Xiàhé Lù (厦禾路 336 号)
Tel: 2109795 2109793 www.xiameneye.org.cn

Xiàmén University Hospital (厦门大学医院) They've been around since 1921.
Add: #172 University Rd (Dàxué Lù, 大学路 172 号) Tel: 2186203

Húlĭ Hospital (Húlĭ Yīyuàn, 湖里医院) Western and Chinese Medicine.
Add: Huāchāng Lù (near Húlĭ government) 华昌路(湖里区政府附近)
Tel: 6038135

Xiānyuè Hospital (Xiānyuè Yīyuàn, 仙岳医院)
Add: #387 Xiānyuè Lù Tel: 5052717 5086654

Xiàmén Women's Hospital (Xiàménshì Fùyòu Băojiànyuàn, 厦门市妇幼保健院) Add: #10 Zhēnhăi Lù (厦门市镇海路 10 号)
Tel: 2662020 www.xmfybj.cn/default.asp

Liánhuā Hospital (Liánhuā Yīyuàn, 厦门莲花医院)
Add: #9 Liánhuā Běi Lù (莲花北路 9 号) Tel: 5055107 www.xmlh.net

Tóngjí Hospital (Xiàménshì Tóngjí Yīyuàn, 厦门市同济医院)
Add: Nánqiáo Lane (Nánqiáo Xiàng, 厦门市南桥巷) Tel: 2023327

Jíměi Hospital (Jíměi Yīyuàn, 集美医院)
Add: #35 Shàngnán Lù, Jíměi (集美区尚南路 35 号) Tel: 6068398

Guànkŏu Hospital, Jíměi (集美区灌口医院)
Add: Shuāngguān'ān, Jíměi (集美区双观庵) Tel: 6094143 6091025

Tóngmín Hospital, Tóng'ān (同安区同民医院)
Add: #10 Mín'ān Lù, Măxiàng Town Tóng'ān (同安区马巷镇民安路 10 号).
Tel: 7061415 7063194

Xiàmén #3 Hospital (Xiàmén Dìsān YīYuàn, 厦门第三医院)
Add: Tóng'ān District Xiángpíng Blvd. Yáng Dí 2nd Rd #2.
(同安区祥平街道阳翟二路 2 号) Tel: 7022320 www.xmdsyy.com.cn

DENTAL CARE (Yáyī, 牙医)

Yao Dental Clinic Formerly of PLA Hospital, Maryland-trained Dr. Yao (George) and Dr. Wang (Rocky) both speak English. Great service, friendly, affordable. Add: Xiahe Rd. Dihao Bldg. 22/F (厦禾路帝豪大厦 2202)

Tel: 2964399 www.yaodental.com

Tokushinkai Dental Center Xiàmén Dézhēn Association Dental Center (Xiàmén Dézhēn Huì Chǐkē Zhōngxīn, 厦门德真会齿科中心) Sino-Japanese venture. Add: #881 Héxiāng Xī Lù (禾祥西路 881 号) Tel: 2290088

Xiàmén Dental Hospital (Xiàmén Kǒuqiāng Yīyuàn, 厦门口腔医院)
Add: Dòuxī Lù, near Zhōngshān Park W. Gate（斗西路, 中山公园西门附近）
Tel: 2010277 Or: 16821168 www.xmkq.com

Historical Supplement

Classic Chinese Doctor Tales

First things first

First Things First – A Ming Dynasty Tale (1368-1644) A doctor was detained by furious relatives of a patient he had killed with the wrong prescription, but he escaped by night and swam across a wide river to reach home. When he saw his son studying medical texts, he said, "Don't be in such a hurry to study medicine. First things first. And first, learn to swim."

Quack Compensation – A Qing Dynasty Tale (1644 -1912) When a quack doctor's treatment killed a family's son, he was forced to give them his own son. He lost his daughter the same way. One day a man knocked on at his door and asked for help. "Who's sick?" the doctor asked.

"My wife."

The tearful doctor told his wife, "Sweetheart, I fear someone's taken a fancy to you."

"Anything but the hands!"

Getting the Boot A Ming Dynasty Tale A heavily laden woodcutter stumbled into the local doctor on a narrow path. When the doctor drew back his fist to hit him, the woodcutter fell to his knees and begged, "Please kick me instead."

A bystander asked, "Why would you rather him kick you?"

The terrified woodcutter replied, "Treatment with his hands is much deadlier than with his feet!"

Heal Thyself A Qing Dynasty Tale A dying doctor cried out, "If any doctor can cure me, I will give him a dose of my secret elixir of immortality and he will live for centuries!"

Someone asked, "If you have such a miraculous drug, why not take it yourself?"

He looked surprised. "A good doctor doesn't write prescriptions for himself!"

Chapter 31
Doing Business in Xiamen

"Everyone lives by selling something."
Robert Louis Stevenson

"To understand where China is heading, check out Peking University. Long a hotbed of political activism, the school these days is buzzing. But what's got students hopped up isn't politics but getting ahead....Like the rest of China, Peking University is remaking itself for a modern, market-driven age.

"...Biology major Lei Ping sums up the new spirit. 'We are not as preoccupied with politics as our predecessors, but at heart we are just as patriotic," she says. 'We are more pragmatic. After all, we're in a new era now.'"

Time Magazine (May 11, 1998)

Xiàmén—China's Mother Lode Chinese pragmatism is still alive and well, making the Middle Kingdom a gold mine for entrepreneurial Lǎowài (老外)—especially in Xiàmén, which was the ancient Gateway to China centuries before either Hong Kong or Shanghai were on the map. In the Sòng Dynasty (960-1279 A.D.), officials built the Dōngdù port inspection area between hills that formed a natural refuge.

In the late 1800s, Amoy was Germany's favorite port in Asia (the engraving from a photo on the next page filled two entire pages of a German newspaper; Germans loved their Amoy). In the early 20th century, America's "Mobil" consortium and Britain's "Asia" invested heavily to make Haicang a key petroleum transfer station and marine refueling base, and Sun Yat-sen envisioned Xiàmén becoming an "Oriental Mega-Port". Sun's vision is finally being realized today.

Xiamen Dominates Fujian Trade, 1857 The commercial enterprise of the people is to be seen in the fact that Amoy, though possessing only an estimated population of about 150,000, has three times as large a number of trading-junks as the important capital of the province itself. The people emigrate in large numbers to Borneo, Siam, Singapore, Malacca, Batavia, Samarang, and other places in Java; to which parts they resort in the hope of realizing fortunes by commerce, and returning to enjoy the fruits of their industry in their native land.

Smith, 1857

Irene. Kaiser. Prinzeß Wilhelm. Arcona. Cormoran. Iltis.

Das deutsche Geschwader auf der Rhede von Amoy (China).
Nach einer photographischen Aufnahme gezeichnet von Willy Stöwer.

Engraving of German warships in Amoy Harbor, Illustritre Zeitung, 9 March, 1896
Original about 42 cm x 55 cm

6 German Ships in Amoy, 1890s (Xiamen was 19th Century Germany's favorite harbor in Asia)

Xiamen Special Economic Zone (SEZ) was established in 1981 on 2.5 km^2 of the west side of the island, and the entire island received SEZ status after Dèng Xiǎopíng's visit in March, 1984. Today, 1,700 km^2 of Xiàmén Island and adjacent mainland enjoy Xiàmén's provincial-level autonomy and preferential policies. In 2011, Xiamen's GDP exceeded RMB 253.58 billion (more than I earn in an entire year), and fiscal revenue topped RMB 65 billion (26% higher than 2010). In 2012, the U.S. magazine *Foreign Policy* ranked Xiamen as the world's 42nd most dynamic city (our provincial capital, Fuzhou, was 68th).

Amoy's Many Assets

1. **Natural and Situational Assets** Xiàmén has one of the world's top ten natural deep-water harbors. About 1/5 of our 26 km. of coastline averages over 10 m in depth, and we are protected by a string of offshore islands that act as a natural breakwater.

All of the world's top 20 shipping companies have branches or offices in Xiàmén, and our port ranks #7 in China and in the world's top 30, with connections to over 100 ports around the planet.

In 1997, the State Council designated Xiàmén as the official port for direct marine transport between Tǎiwán and the mainland, and in April, the first container ship in over 50 years sailed to Táiwān from Xiàmén's Dōngdù Port.

Pi and Ice Cream "Necessity is the mother of invention" explains Chinese' age-old pragmatism, and why this ancient nation has invented everything from Pi to ice cream. And they're still innovating today.

In a remote Shāndōng Province town, we saw a "modern" street sweeper--a hand-welded iron vehicle twirling an iron and wood contraption with a dozen handmade straw brooms. And it worked; the tiny hamlet's main street (only street) was spotless.

Peasant or urbanite, Chinese are resourceful, resilient, and persistent, and if the future remotely mirrors the past, we can expect more marvels in coming decades--particularly in commerce.

Commerce, not Conquer Lǎowài are fortunate that ancient Chinese emphasized commerce over conquest. A thousand years ago, Chinese had land mines, water mines, and biological warfare. Seven hundred years ago, Chinese sailed the globe in the planet's most advanced ships. Watertight compartments made them virtually unsinkable, but they could have sunk barbarian boats with such advanced weaponry as gunpowder, rockets, cannon, and crossbows.

The 1,000 mile Grand Canal, earth's longest manmade waterway, led Chinese to invent suspension bridges, canal locks, and the segmental arch. China's waterways, not Twain's Mississippi, hosted the first paddlewheel ships.

Venetian blinds came from China, not Venice. So did pasta, and the use of coal for cooking. Ancient Chinese invented deep drilling for natural gas and salt. They invented the rotary crank, the waterwheel-driven bellows in steel smelting, and the seismograph.

Given their penchant for paperwork (Red China is named after Red Tape), it is no surprise that Chinese invented both paper and paper money. The world's first newspaper, Peking News, ran from A.D. 363 to 1935, and maybe Chinese reporters fought the first deadline because mechanical clocks originated not in Europe but centuries earlier in China. The first greeting cards were Chinese New Year Cards (invented so nobles would not have to visit so many people). And 1000 years ago, imperial buttocks luxuriated in 4" squares of perfumed paper, the world's first toilet paper (though a famous poet warned against using paper with writing on it). They also invented sit-down flush toilets over 2000 years ago (so why use ceramic holes today?). Chinese invented parachutes (1306), the violin (2-stringed èrhú 二胡), and the first zoos (in 1150 B.C.).

Chinese plotted the courses of sun, moon and stars, and recorded solar and lunar eclipses on bones and tortoise shells over 3,000 years ago--including all 27 Haley's Comet appearances over 2,100 years.

Chinese came up with both decimals and binomial mathematics, and about 1500 years ago, the mathemagician Zǔ Chōngzhī (祖冲之；429-500 A.D.) calculated Pi to be 3.1415926.

Last but by all means least, Chinese invented 'zero,' which is really handy in Xiàmén, now that her GDP has so many zeroes behind it…

In 2005 Xiàmén International Port was China's first solely Chinese port to go public on the HK Stock Exchange, raising US$175million.

Dōngdù Port. (东渡码头) Dōngdù Port has a 79,000 m^2 container storage yard with the latest tech, such as 300-ton gantry cranes, and is equipped with a good variety of advanced equipment. The port can handle two 50,000 tonnage vessels simultaneously, and 2.1 million tons of cargo per year. Dōngdù has direct shipping with the U.S., Singapore, Japan, and European countries; the bulk of Xiàmén's foreign trade goes through Hong Kong.

Xiàmén Port (Xiàmén Mǎtóu, 厦门码头) has five port areas and 74 berths, with twenty-three 10,000-tonnage and higher berths, the largest able to handle 100,000 ton vessels, with special terminals for containers, petroleum and coal.

Air Hub Xiamen's natural harbor, and her strategic proximity to Kong Hong and Táiwān province, as for centuries made Xiàmén the natural gateway for overseas Chinese and foreigners seeking to stake a claim in China. But nowadays, the slow boat to China isn't fast enough, so Xiàmén also has one of China's top airports, Xiàmén Gāoqī International Airport. In 2010, Gaoqi was China's 11th busiest airport, with over 13.2 million passengers. Today, 39 airlines operate 119 routes to domestic and international destinations, including Amsterdam (direct flight on KLM) Singapore, Bangkok, Taichung and Taibei, Penang, Kuala Lumpur, Manila, Jakarta, and Siam Reap (Cambodia). After the new airport is opened in 2014, we will also have direct flights to the U.S. Cargo flights are offered to cities in China, Hong Kong, Táiwān, Singapore, Nagoya of Japan, and Chicago. And planes landing at Xiàmén's new airport are a far cry from the four that landed in Xiàmén Bay way back in 1924—on the **first round the world flight.**

Round the World Thru Amoy On April 6th, 1924, 3 years before Lindbergh crossed the Atlantic, 4 custom-built built Douglas World Cruisers set out to circle the globe They must have had more layovers than a cheap Korean Air flight at Christmas because it took two full months to reach Amoy.

On June 7th, they flew from Shanghai to Amoy Harbor, refueled at the Standard Oil depot, dined with the American consul, and flew out the next day.

Modern planes no longer land in Xiamen bay. At least, not intentionally.

2. Social and Cultural Assets Gumption, more than geography, explains why over 350,000 overseas Chinese (and 70% of Taiwanese) trace their ancestry back to coastal South Fújiàn. It took unusual gumption for tradition-bound Xiamen peasants to cut their ancestral apron strings and sail to every corner of the globe in search of work. Most toiled at menial jobs, but many saved every penny, peso, and peseta to build industrial empires that even today exert great global influence. (*Time Magazine* claims overseas Chinese, not

Tokyo, wield the greatest economic power in Asia today).

Most Chinese, of course, stayed behind in Xiàmén. Maybe the prospect of capital punishment dampened their desire to depart. But they did not lack drive and initiative. They simply redirected it from rice fields into the fields of industry, and today Xiàmén is uniquely blessed by an abundance of highly motivated and qualified skilled workforce.

3. Education in Xiàmén Over 11% Xiàmén residents have higher education. We have 120 scientific research institutes, 28 higher education institutions, 45 secondary vocational or technical schools, and 66 high schools. The city's Talents Databank has info on 120,000 professionals, and the Talents Service Center holds 3 job fairs each week. The city also has an extensive program to help migrant workers.

4. Economic and political Xiàmén, as an SEZ, has Provincial-level authority and autonomy in economic administration and local legislative power. This gives Xiàmén's leadership unprecedented flexibility in development, and providing the best business environment for both domestic and foreign enterprises.

When we stepped off the slow boat to China in '88, Xiàmén was a backwater town with inadequate and unreliable water, frequent power outages, and coal dust laden air. The only tall building in town was the harbor's Seaview Building (Hăibin Dàshà, 海滨大厦), which now has a 24/f Pizza Hut, and foreign enterprises were not coming but going. Worst of all was the infrastructure

After a close encounter of the worst kind with a Xiàmén traffic jam, former Mayor Hóng Yŏngshì（洪永世）made infrastructure his priority. Our six-lane Xiàhé Road（厦禾路）was narrow than today's bike paths and virtually impassible, hawkers selling fruit, vegetables and live fowl in the middle of the road. Today, our beautiful island beltway relieves congestion while providing miles of beaches and manicured parks, and several tunnels help ease traffic without destroying our mountainous landscape. And our mushrooming skyline prompted son Shannon to say, "Xiàmén is now like a little Hong Kong."

Fortunately, Xiàmén has also retained its distinctive colonial architecture, which draws droves of Laowai and Laonei alike. But look closely because some of the beautiful 'colonial architecture' was built not in the 1840s but the 1990s. The originals were so dilapidated the government had no choice but to raze and rebuild them—but in the same style. The building to the right, for example, is on the corner of Zhōngshān and Sīmíng Roads.

Environmental Make-over Since 1997 Xiàmén has spent 3% of GDP on such environmental projects as the $50 million USD Yúndāng Lake（筼筜湖）cleanup, which the UN selected as a demonstration site for marine pollution prevention and management.

Xiàmén's environmental policy allows only low emission, low energy consumption, technology-intensive high-tech industries on the island. Labor-intensive industries are confined to the less populated and more spacious off-island Xìnglín（杏林）and Jīměi Districts, and raw material and energy industries are restricted to the Hăicāng Investment Zone. We also banned, early on, phosphorus detergents, nonbiodegradable Styrofoam fast food containers, and persistent pesticides.

Xiàmén was China's first city to offer daily air quality reports via media and internet, and today gives real-time internet environment updates, as well as monthly, quarterly, semi-annual and annual reports and bulletins.

If you have little ones, send them to one of our summer ecology camps, which are held for K-12 and college, where they can learn about the GIS databank that helps protect over 500 ancient trees. A Xiàmén 4th grader patented his environment invention!

> "And Silence, like a poultice, comes To heal the blows of sound."
> Oliver Wendell Holmes, Sr.

The Sounds of Silence. Xiàmén has attacked not just air and water pollution but also noise pollution. For years I envied the quietude of Gulangyu Islet, which forbids motor vehicles and bicycles. Many a Chinese city has tried to ban auto horns, but unsuccessfully, for every driver in China has a motive a minute for joining the raucous ranks of honkies. But Mayor Hong decreed, "No horns." and it was Silent Night overnight. (Neighboring cities still seek the sounds of silence!)

Clean air, clean water, quietude. Xiamen is finally living up to her "Garden City" reputation, and attracting not just tourists but businessmen seeking a city that's as nice to live in as to invest in. It's even nicer if we obey Xiamen Government's Ten Commandments.

Xiàmén Govt's 10 Commandments

1. Don't litter.
2. Don't spit.
3. Don't abuse the greenery.
4. Don't damage public property.
5. Don't run red lights.
6. Don't be unruly on buses.
7. Don't use coarse or inappropriate language.
8. Don't smoke in public buildings.
9. Don't honk automobile horns on the island.
10. Don't put unauthorized posters in public places.

The Ten Bu's

The list of foreign firms now in Xiàmén reads like a "Who's Who" of industry. I typed "Magic Xiàmén" on a Dell assembled in Xiàmén; the photos used film made in Xiàmén by Kodak's most advanced plant (and largest producer of single-use recyclable cameras). When my wife shops, she unloads our van, **Toy Ota**, with a Xiàmén Linde forklift…

While retaining a small town flavor, Xiamen has become a mini metropolis and host to firms such as Toyota, Hitachi, Electrolux, Panasonic, Philips, Kodak, Dell, GE,

Black & Decker, Goldman Sachs, Honeywell, Hyundai, Ikea, Marubeni, Matsushita, ABB, Swire, Boeing, TDK, and others.

Xiàmén's track record and future prospects landed her the opportunity to be China's first pilot city to introduce ISŌ4000.

Lǎowài and Lǎonèi alike have plenty of places to store all that cash they're raking in, with over 600 financial institutions from around the globe. But if you prefer 'basket banking,' (Xiàmén's traditional banking, back in the early 20th century), we have a nice basket in our XMU apartment.①

Xiamen Foreign Investment Bureau Want the latest updates on doing business in Xiamen? Visit XFIB's comprehensive website!

E-mail: xmfiecip@public.xm.fj.cn www.fdi-xiamen-cn.com

Investment Opportunities in Xiàmén are endless but not without rhyme or reason. Xiàmén government has carefully selected 4 pillar industries: chemical, electronics, power and machinery. The sprawling 100 square kilometer Hǎicāng Investment Zone has been carefully subdivided into four districts with the following emphases:

New Urban District (Xīn Shìqū, 新市区): commerce and trade, finance, real estate, tourism, recreation and leisure

Harbor District (Hǎigǎng Qū, 海港区): port facilities, energy industry, bonded facilities and warehousing & storage).

South Industrial District (Nánbù Gōngyè Qū, 南部工业区): petrochemicals

Xinyang Industrial District (Xīnyáng Gōngyè Qū, 新阳工业区): machinery, electronics, chemicals and building materials

Strike Gold at CIFIT! The best place to scout out business opportunities, whether in Xiàmén or elsewhere, is our annual **CIFIT** (China Int'l Fair for Investment & Trade, Zhōngguó Guójì Tóuzī Màoyì Qiàtán Huì, 中国国际投资贸易洽谈会).

Every September 8th, CIFIT hosts pavilions with investment opportunities in every province, from coastal Fujian to the Himalayan heights of Tibet.

CIFIT has been responsible for ***over half*** of foreign investment to small and medium enterprises, and for much of large businesses as well

In 2010, a wealthy Chinese tea exporter excitedly asked me to help him export to America, as he had heard that the entire country was now excited about holding "tea parties." He found it hard to believe the movement was political, not cultural.

① Heavy penalties for early withdrawal; offer void where prohibited by common sense

Ancient Tales of Business Conquest

Think Chinese are new at business? These ancient tales prove otherwise.

Limited Partnership (Ming Dynasty)

Two brothers planted wheat together and at harvest time the older brother said, "I'll take the top half, you take the lower."

"But all the wheat's on the top!" said the younger brother.

"Ok, if you feel it is unfair, next year I take the bottom half and you the top!"

The younger brother agreed, and the next year they planted potatoes.

If the Shoe Fits Share It (Ming Dynasty)

Two brothers saved up enough to buy one pair of shoes, which they shared. The older wore them from morning till night. The younger, to get his share of the benefit, waited till his elder brother went to bed then put the shoes on and walked all over the countryside until dawn.

When the shoes wore out, elder brother asked, "Want to buy another pair?"

"No, thanks. I need to get some sleep."

Moral: if someone says, "We're like brothers," hide your wallet!

Don't Wine About it (Ming Dynasty)

Two men decided to make wine together. One said, "You supply the rice and I'll supply the water." The second said, "If I provide all the rice, how do we divide the results?"

"I will be absolutely fair. When the wine is ready, we get back what we put in. I'll take the liquid and you keep the rest."

Mosquito Amulet—*Caveat Emptor* (Ming Dynasty) A man bought an amulet to ward off mosquitoes but when it didn't work he returned to the vendor. The vendor said, "You have to use it in the proper place for it to work!"

"And where is that?"

"Under a mosquito net!"

Eat in East, Sleep in West *On 'One Wife, Two Systems'* (Ming Dynasty)

A young girl was torn between two suitors, an ugly but rich youth who lived East of their farm, and the handsome but poor neighbor to the West. She moaned to her mother, "If only I could marry both, and eat in the East and sleep in the West."

Man of the People (ancient Chinese tale) A newly appointed official tried to impress folks with his moral virtues by writing three phrases on his office walls:

1. Don't covet money.
2. Don't desire promotions.
3. Don't fear death.

A few days later some wit added two characters to the bottom of each line.

1. in small quantities.
2. unless it's much higher than this one.
3. but I want to live as long as I can.

Chapter 32

Mad About Mandarin

"Translation is always a treason, and as a Ming author observes, can at its best be only the reverse side of a brocade—all the threads are there, but not the subtlety of color or design." Okakura, *The Book of Tea*

The language of Fukien is a greater annoyance than in any other of the Chinese coast provinces. The Foochow dialect (which is one of the most difficult to learn) is spoken only within fifty or one hundred miles of the city. At Yen-ping, Mr. Caldwell, who speaks "Foochow" perfectly, could not understand a word of the "southern mandarin" which is the language of that region, and near Futsing, where a colony of natives from Amoy have settled, the dialect is unintelligible to one who knows only "Foochow."

Camps and Trails in China, 1918.

If you're staying in Xiàmén awhile, you should pick up a little Mandarin[1] with a tutor, or full or part-time courses at XMU's Overseas College, or Mandarin Fun.

I'm still hoping to master Mandarin myself. Years before coming to China, I took college Mandarin courses. I memorized stacks of flash cards bought in Táiběi and Los Angeles' China Town. I tried the course that airline magazine advertisements promised would have me speaking like a native, and a high post in the Diplomatic Corp within 90 days or double my money back. Desperate, I even paid $500 per month for a year of private tutoring. A year later and $6,000 poorer , I could barely tell our tutor zàijiàn (goodbye). Xiàmén was my last hope. I could just imagine those enigmatic characters coming to life – if I could just survive the enigmatic enrolment.

Our college administrators had good hearts, but even as countless intellectuals were sent to the countryside to farm, I think some farmers were sent to the cities to administrate—and one of them gave the welcome speech.

The administrator began day one of our beginner's class by giving us enrolment forms typed in Chinese, and telling us rapidly, in Chinese, to fill the forms out in Chinese. When we just sat there, lost, he said, "What is wrong? Please fill out the forms now."

In my haltered Chinese I said, "Teacher, if we could already read and write Chinese, we would not be in this beginner's Chinese course."

He stalked out and returned with a translator. So began my Chinese study. I lasted all of 4 months before giving up and finding a tutor.

---

① **XMU Overseas Education College** (since 1956!) http://english.xmuoec.com/
Mandarin Fun language programs, summer camp, etc. www.mandarinfun.cn/en/

Divine Language

"The Chinese language is one of the most beautiful in the world in which to enshrine the sacred Scriptures, and there is a flexibility and grace about it, that render it capable of expressing all the tenderness, and pathos, and poetry, and sublime thought of that most wondrous book."

John MacGowan, 1889, p.17

Shanghai on Shibboleths Not to worry. Chinese are exceptionally patient, and good humored. Just talk with everyone you meet and you'll pick it up eventually. And in Xiàmén, you'll also pick up a southern accent.

The Bible recounts how the Israelites discerned friend from foe by making them say Shibboleth. The enemy could not "sh", so they invariably said "Sibboleth", and lost their tongue, and their head with it.

Likewise, Southern Chinese can't pronounce "sh", so Shànghǎi is Sànghǎi. They also can't tell *f* from *h*, *l* from *r* and *n*, or a long *e* from a short *e*. They can't hear the difference between *t* and *th*, or *c* and *ch*, or *z* and *zh*. This becomes confusing in business because it is impossible to tell "4" from "10" or "eat" (you could go by the tone, but Southern Chinese mess up tones too).

Dr. Beer If Southerners can't get the sounds right in Chinese, it is no wonder they have the same problem with English. No matter how hard most Xiàmén people try, my name "Bill" usually comes out "Beer." One Christmas, my hapless Southern students threw in the towel and their tongue and presented me with a Christmas card made out to, "Professor Beer," and a nicely wrapped bottle of Chinese Tsingdao beer (the most enduring legacy of Germany's occupation of Shāndōng Province up North).

After 18 years in Xiàmén, I too have acquired a slight Southern Chinese accent, to Northerners' endless amusement. That's why many Chinese experts recommend learning the language in the North. Go for it if you want to, but I'll take a few shibboleths over frostbite any day. So, *Ni Hao*, y'all!

English Pilot Program

During World War II an American pilot crashed in China and was rescued by villagers, who asked the local English teacher to translate. The teacher had never spoken English to a foreigner so he consulted an English phrasebook and read from page one, "Hello, how are you?"

When the badly battered pilot groaned and asked for a doctor, the teacher said to the other villagers, "I'm sorry but this man is not speaking English." "I said "Hello, how are you?" but he didn't answer, "Fine, and you?"

A Word's Worth 1,000 Pictures I often preface proverbs, whatever the source, with "Confucius said," because it's a safe bet that either he or some other ancient Chinese did say it, and probably in 4 words or less.

"A picture's worth a 1,000 words" may hold true for English, but with Chinese a word may be worth a thousand pictures. Over the past 5,019 years, Chinese have distilled their wisdom and culture into concise proverbs that not only strike to the heart of any matter but also strike fear into the hearts of foreign language learners.

Even after memorizing the 3 to 4,000 basic characters, foreigners may still not understand the meaning of characters that Chinese wield against us because no dictionary can convey the full nuances of a character. Three or four characters strung together in one of China's tens of thousands of proverbs can conjure up ancient historical incidents, or classic poems, or paintings, or deep philosophical notions. My favorite Chinese classic, "The Art of War," has influenced military, business, and diplomacy—and the entire book is only 5,000 characters. That's like fitting "War and Peace" between the covers of Dr. Seuss's "The Cat in the Hat."

Chinese have a proverb for every occasion. A Chinese businessman who squanders his capital "drains the pond to catch the fish." A public figure who thinks he can hide an immoral private life "Covers his own ears while stealing the bell." Impatient people are "rice pullers" -- like the foolish farmer who killed his rice plants when he tugged on them to make them grow faster.

"Contradiction" in Chinese is máodùn（矛盾）, or "spear-shield." It refers to the ancient fable of the weapons salesman who marketed both impenetrable shields and unstoppable spears" (he's now a lobbyist in Washington D.C.). Inappropriate public policies are like "using wood to put out a fire." People with unrealistic fears see, "a soldier in every tree and bush." A persistent person is like the granny determined to "grind an iron rod into a needle." The fawning sycophant capitalizing on others' power is the "Fox exploiting the tiger's prestige."

Every saying makes a point, but also stirs up images of the story behind it. Lao Tzu, founder of Taoism (The Way), used only 4 words to preach an entire sermon on the power of gentleness and softness over inflexibility and hardness. He said, "Teeth fall, tongue remains." (Hard teeth fall out, soft tongue and gums remain into old age). Translation: "Go with the flow!"

Mandarin is both fascinating but frustrating, yet I'm drawn to it.

Perhaps that's because I like drawing.

Drawn to Chinese The Chinese have a saying or a solution for everything except how to teach foreigners the ABCs of Chinese. That's mainly because there aren't any ABCs. No alphabet at all—just 40 to 50,000 characters to memorize.

Chinese characters are pictographs—drawings of objects or ideas. So in a sense, all literate Chinese are artists. And pictographs have some advantages over alphabets. They aren't abstract representations but concrete drawings, so any Chinese can 'read' their meaning, even though they are pronounced completely differently in Cantonese, Sichuanese, Pekinese, deng deng. Even Japanese can read them, for Japan's language, like much of her culture and religion, evolved centuries ago from ancient China.

Some Chinese pictographs so closely resemble their object that even illiterate foreign friends can figure them out. 凹 is obviously "concave," and 凸 is "convex." And if you know that "man" is written as 人, then 大, a man with outstretched arms, easily suggests "big" or "great."

刀, or "knife," looks like Yan's Chinese cleaver. Add a dot to signify a drop of blood and you get 刃, "knife's edge" or "to kill with a cleaver," and the plot of Julia Child's upcoming bestseller, "Yan Can Kill."

"Mountain" is 山, which resembles 3 peaks, and "river" is 川, which suggests a flowing river.

If all Chinese characters were so easily deciphered, beginning Chinese students would have no problem filling out Chinese enrollment forms. Yet no doubt to frustrate foreign friends, for the past 5,012 years Chinese have stylized their pictographs until today only Vincent Van Geogh could possibly see "star" in 星. And why all this:香蕉 for a banana,  when would do? And why mess with 16 strokes for apple, 苹果, when you can whip it out with two strokes and a flick: ?

And nothing is fishier than the evolution of "fish," which started out well but floundered:

First century Christian's did it well with: 

Change is afoot, though[①]. After must post-Liberation deliberation, New China decided to fight illiteracy by simplifying characters. For example, that most useful of New Chinese characters, "huì" (会)or "meeting," for Chinese spend many of their waking hours in meetings) was simplified from 13 strokes to 6—much easier to memorize and to write.

But the art of simplification can go too far. On bus signs, for example, Xiàmén's "Xià" is often written (illegally, actually) with three strokes,下, instead of twelve 厦. Taken this far, simplification robs characters of their beauty and meaning. For example, how wood Amerikans lik it if Unkel Sam fot iliterasee by simplifide speling?

(See "Euro—English 5-Year-Plan" at the end of this chapter)

A Modest Proposal Aesthetics aside, it was courageous of Běijīng to tamper with the ancient language of the most tradition-bound people on earth, and strike a blow against illiteracy. But illiteracy might be vanquished forever if Běijīng finished the job with a few of my suggestions:

Triangle: instead of the patently ungeometrical 三角形, just use ∇

Ear: who but Mike Tyson's opponents have ears like 耳朵? Just use !

Eye: the ancient's  for "eye" made more sense than 眼睛.

Fast Food: last but least, why defeat the point of fast food by wasting half a day writing it with 20+ strokes: 快餐. Two arches can do it: Deng deng.

Chinese *Ups* and *Downs* Chinese further brutalize barbarian ears by using tones (see end of chapter), and scrambling grammar and word order. "Please buy me a coke" becomes, "Please give me buy a coke." Chinese change meaning, tense, or intensity by tacking on sounds like *le*, and *ma*, and *ee*, which is why Chinese speaking English often say changee and lookee. There is no end to embarrassing mistakes Chinese can coax out of Lǎowài.

About 1890, an American missionary asked his Chinese maid to prepare chicken for dinner. The maid returned 3 days later and said, "I'm sorry, Pastor, but I couldn't find anyone willing to marry a foreigner."

① People often ask me if I've seen a lot of change in China and I say, "No change at all! The taxi drivers don't have change, the shops don't have change…"

"Chicken" (jī) sounds similar to "wife" (qī), but even said correctly, in other contexts "eating chicken" can mean dallying with a prostitute, much to Colonel Sander's dismay.

And are Chinese leftists or rightists? English is written left to right, and Hebrew right to left, but Chinese goes with the flow. Left to right, right to left, top to bottom—all are equally acceptable—and I've seen all three, plus diagonal, on the same page of a newspaper. Only context can save you.

I once told a Chinese friend, "Xiàmén University has buildings all over China and Hong Kong!" I pointed to a sign with XMU's two characters, 厦大.

My friend laughed. "You're reading it backwards!" Sure enough, 大厦 backwards is 厦大, or Dàshà, or "hotel"—from the Russian "dacha".

An excess of courtesy is discourtesy. Chinese Proverb

Titled Gentleman Even if you can communicate to a Chinese, how do you address them? Chinese honorifics are legion and lethal. Even common laborers have titles. They are called "Master," and they are, and they know it. Try to get a carpenter who is just lumbering along to finish a job on schedule and you'll see just who is master in Socialist China.

I have at least 8 licit titles and a few I'd rather not discuss. I have been called "Professor Pān," "Teacher Pān," "Master Pān" and "Mr. Pān." My Chinese elders may call me Xiǎo Pān (Xiao means little, or young), but people younger than me say Lǎo Pān (Lǎo is old, or venerable). Chinese children call me uncle—but which kind of uncle? I'm either Bōbō or Shūshū, depending on if I am older or younger than the child's father. When the child doesn't know an elder's age, then he really cries uncle.

But it all Pāns out in the end. Besides, aunties and uncles are on their way out, thanks to the one child policy. With no aunts and uncles and nieces and nephews, traditional family structures are undergoing even greater simplification than the language. Fortunately, in my wife's home I need bother with only two titles: "son" and "your highness."

But seriously, (really?) Mandarin is a beautiful language, and spending a little time on it will make your stay a lot more pleasant and profitable.

Dictionaries, Diction, and Deng Deng Whether you master Mandarin or not, a good phrasebook and dictionary are essential. The absolutely best dictionary around **is Oxford University Press's "Concise English-Chinese Chinese-English Dictionary**." It uses Pīnyīn throughout so you can look up both English and Chinese words alphabetically. Of course, if you don't know how a character is pronounced, how can you look it up?

Chinese dictionaries use several methods, not of them foolproof, even for Chinese. Some go by number of strokes: characters with 1 stroke, 2 strokes, 三 strokes, 四 strokes, 五 strokes, deng deng. This is further broken down further (very broken) according to which stroke is first (vertical, horizontal, slanting, etc.). But I've encountered characters that even Chinese professors could not find in this way. One professor who was a real character rifled the pages of my dictionary for 15 minutes, then said, "It's no problem looking this up because we know it anyway."

Well, different strokes for different folks.

"A Chinese-English Dictionary," produced by Běijīng's Foreign Language Institute, is another excellent tool—and plain fun to read! I read it through twice in four months just because I enjoyed the sample English sentences!

Bear in mind, of course, that it was printed in 1988—scarcely a decade after the unCultural Revolution, so it's not surprising that every sentence had a revolutionary bent. My favorites include:

Suppose: "I *suppose* she's gone to practice grenade throwing again."

Anew, **afresh**: "Launch a *fresh* offensive."

Barely: "When I joined the 8th Army route, I was *barely* the height of a rifle."

Be: "I want to *be* a PLA man when I grow up."

Armed with such a vocabulary, imagine the conversations that students used to strike up in Friday night English Corners!

Mandarin Chinese—a marvelous language! And it would behoove you to learn a little. After all, it's the official language of 1/5 of the planet's people. But if 40,000 pictographic characters intimidate you, start with China's official romanization scheme, Pīnyīn. It's simple, and useful—and I tell you how in "Dr. Bill's unPatented Pīnyīn Guide."

Dr. Bill's unPatented Pīnyīn Guide

Make the magic of Amoy come alive by spending a few minutes mastering China's official Romanization system, Pīnyīn. Some sounds are similar to English, but others are otherworldly. For example, how on earth do you pronounce "Xiàmén?"

Chinese words have 3 parts: initials, finals, and tone. "Xiàmén," for example, is made of two words: "Xià" (mansion) and "Mén" (gate). "*X*" is an initial, "*ia*" a final, and "Xia" is said with the 4th tone.

Pīnyīn's "X" sounds like "*sh*," so Xiamen is pronounced like "*Sh-Yah Men*," (with *Sh* and *Yah* crammed together so Xiàmén has only two syllables-something like "shaman with a *yah* after the *sh*").

With only 400 or so distinct sounds, Mandarin is a haven for homonyms, but the 4 tones (plus context) help us decipher them:

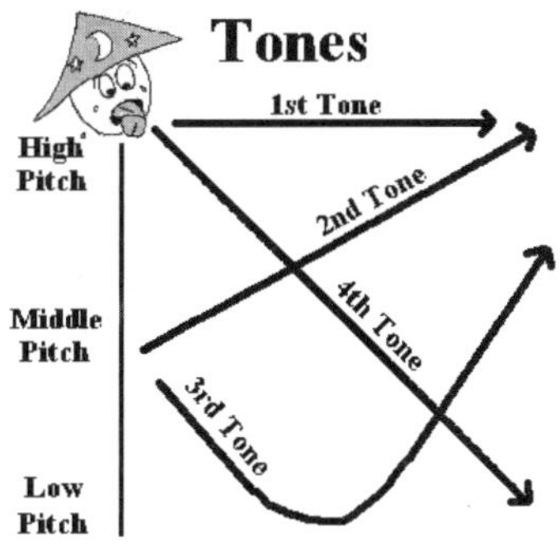

- **1st tone** is level, and at the top of one's normal vocal range for speaking.
- **2nd tone** rises from the middle of one's range to the top.
- **3rd tone** starts in the middle, drops to the bottom, and rises at the end (Susan Marie says if your chin hits your chest on the low note, you've got it right).
- **4th tone** starts high and ends low, as if you were scolding someone.

The four tones (sounds like a 60s Pop Group!) sound like this:

Tones completely change the meaning of words. Take *ma*, for example. With 1st, 2nd, 3rd, and 4th tones, *ma* means "mother," "hemp," "horse," and "to curse." Get it wrong and you might call someone's mother a horse!

Intimidated? Don't be! And don't cop out with the "I'm tone deaf" ploy because you've been using tones since you were a toddler…

"Tone Deaf" and other Lame Lǎowài Myths Frustrated Lǎowài often excuse their poor Mandarin with, "I'm tone deaf!" Sheer nonsense. All English speakers use tones—especially us married ones. I've heard all four of Mandarin's tones, and a few dozen more, from Susan Marie.

When Susan yells, "Bill!" with the 1st tone, she means, "Come here!" The 2nd tone "Bill" asks, "Where are you?" or "Is that you?" The 3rd tone "Bill" is reserved for giving me the third degree and means, "Do you expect me to swallow that?" The 4th tone "Bill," a sharp, barking descent, means I'm in hot water. But when my sweetheart drops my nickname altogether and intones with the dead calm of a Taiwan typhoon's eye, "William," it is the neutral 5th tone, a portent of dire peril, and I am not long for this world. Americans, at least domesticated ones, know tones.

Fortunately, Chinese are a forgiving people, even when you massacre Mandarin and create your own tones. A simple "Ní Hǎo Ma" will have your congenial hosts exclaiming, "You have such excellent Chinese!"

But do them and yourself a favor and master Pīnyīn.

Dr. Bill's unPatented Pīnyīn Guide

Pīnyīn Initials

Pinyin	English	Examples	Pronunciation
b,m,m,f,d,	about the same	dou	dough
n,l,g,k,j,s,	as in English	gan	gone
y,ch,sh,t,w		shu	shoe
c	Like *ts* in *rats*	cai	tseye
		can	tsahn
h	Guttural *h*, like	hao	how
	German *ch* in *ach*	hu	who
q	Like *ch* in *chick*	qu	chew
		qin	cheen
r	Between *j* & *r*	ru	roo
x	Like *sh*	xia	shee-yah
z	Like *ds* sound	zai	dzye
	in *kids*	zong	dzong

Pīnyīn Finals

Pinyin	English	Examples	Pronunciation
a	*ah* in *ah!*	ba	bah
		ta	tah
ai	Like *y* in *my*	lai	lye
		hai	hi
an	*ahn* (lawn)	can	tsahn
ng	*ahng* (angst)	mang	mahng
ao	*ow* in *cow*	zao	zow
ar	*ar* in *are*	nar	nar
e	*u* in *bush*	re	ruh
ei	*a* in *day*	gei	gay

Pinyin	**English**	**Examples**	**Pronunciation**
en	*un* in *pun*	wen	wun
eng	*ung* in *rung*	leng	lung
er	*ur* in *purr*	mer	mur
i	Like *ee* in *wee*	qi	chee
	(after b,p,m,d,t,n,,j,q,x)	mi	mee
	Like *z* after z,c,s	ci	cz
		zi	dz
	Like *r* after ch,	shi	shir
	sh, and r	chi	chir (*chir*p)
ia	*ee-ya*, in one syllable	xia	sheeyah
ian	*yen*	tian	tyen
iang	*yahng*	jiang	jyahng
iao	ee-yow (meow,in one syllable)	piao	pee-yow
		tiao	tee-yow
ie	*yeh*	tie	tyeh
in	*een* in *preen*	pin	peen
ing	*ing* in *sing*	ming	ming
iong	*eeyong* (long o)	xiong	sheeyong
iu	*eo* in *Leo*	liu	leo
o	roughly like a	mo	mwo-uh
	long *o* and short *u*	po	pwo-uh
	run together, with a *w* in front		
ong	Like *ong* in *gong*, but with long O sound	tong	tong
ou	*o* in *toe*	zhou	joe
u	like *oo* in *boo*, except	du	doo
	after j,q,x,y, and then	lu	loo
	like the French *eu*	yu	yeu
ua	*wah* (*ua* in *guava*)	gua	gwah
uai	*wye* (as in *rye*)	guai	gwye
uan	*wahn* (*swan*) except	duan	dwahn
	after j,q,x or y, when		
	it is *wen* (*when*)	yuan	ywen
uang	*wahng* (as in *angst*)	kuang	kwahng
ue	*oo* and *yeh* (yeah) said in one syllable	xue	shooeh
ui	like *way*	chui	chway
un	like *woon* with the *oo* of *book*	jun	jwun
uo	like *o* (*oh*) and *u* (*uh*) in one syllable	duo	dwo-uh

Chapter 33

Lords of Opium

Every time history repeats itself, the price goes up.[1]
Anonymous

"My goal is always the same: to invoke the past as a shield for the future, to show the invisible world of yesterday and through it, perhaps on it, erect a moral world where men are not victims and children never starve and never run in fear."
Nobel Laureate Elie Wiesel, in *A Personal Response*

Why "Lords of Opium?"

If you've waded this far through "*Amoy Magic*" you'll understand why Susan Marie complains, "Bill is never serious!" But my study of the Opium Era sobered me—though most Westerners know little about it. An American professor in Xiamen actually said he thought the Opium Wars were fought to keep China from *exporting* opium; it was, of course, the reverse.

I love magical Amoy's beaches and hills and colonial architecture, but sadly, it was a much darker magic that opened Amoy to the West.

For an entire century, Western nations trafficked in opium on a scale that dwarfs any modern Colombian multi billion dollar drug empire. By the 1920s, fully half of Europe's Asian profits derived from opium, even though most foreigners, by far, opposed the trade. Even the entire British parliament opposed the second Opium War; the Prime Minister simply dissolved parliament and called the nation to war "for the honor of the crown (carefully avoiding the mention of opium).[2]

Just Say No? In the 1840s, China started the world's first "Just Say No!" anti-drug program. Chinese leaders appealed to our sense of morality and justice, and the "Way of Heaven." The West responded with a "Just Say Yes!" campaign and two wars to implement it, and America's ex-President Adams complained that China's refusal to engage in "trade" (carefully avoiding the word opium) was a violation of 'the rights of men and nations.'

Chinese, fortunately, have pretty much put that sordid century behind them, but they *have l*earned from it. That we too may learn, this chapter is a quick but sobering overview of how our nationalized drug trafficking almost destroyed China.

① He who sacrifices conscience to ambition burns picture to get ashes. Chinese Proverb

② On Feb. 23, 2006, Harry Gelber wrote in *The Harvard Crimson* about "The 'Opium War' that Wasn't,' arguing like the British 150 years ago that the war wasn't about Opium. I can understand the British' self-delusion, but what motivated Gelber?

The Opium Den

(Rev. Macgowan, *The Story of the Amoy Mission*, 1889, p. 180)

Opium Smokers (Smith, 1908)

"The shops today are all busy, for customers crowd into them during the busiest hours of the fair. But how is it that, interspersed amongst them, there are so many houses with bamboo screens hanging in front of the open doors? Let us enter one, for it is not a private house. It is an opium den. We put the screen aside, and come into a dimly lighted room, with a broad bench running round the sides of it.

"Little lamps are placed at various intervals, and men are reclining beside them. Some are asleep, and most ghastly do they look with their haggard, opium-hued faces. They are stretched on their backs, and they seem as if they were corpses. They don't appear like men whose spirits are wandering in fairy land, and are entranced with gorgeous scenes of beauty, such as the opium smoker is said to enjoy… One man smiles at me [and says], "This comes from your country, doesn't it?" I feel distressed, for I know he does but express the common opinion that all opium comes from England. But this opium den is an unsavoury place to be in. The close, horrid smell, the ghastly figures ranged along the benches, and the sense of being in the midst of some of the very lowest of the population, are oppressive. We hear the sounds of voices outside, and we see the rays of the bright sun shining upon the bamboo mat, and we rush out of the dim, fetid place, with a sense of deliverance, into the open air. But there was no deliverance for those inside."

Birth of the Opium Trade European opium smugglers flirted with China's death penalty as early as 1729 because opium's immense profits were more addictive than the poppy. The only problem was supply, which Britain solved in 1756 by conquering Calcutta.

Clive marveled at India, the "rich and flourishing kingdom." Within decades that rich kingdom was pauperized as farmers were forced to abandon traditional crops and to grow what became the Crown's primary cash crop, and China's main import—opium.

Warren Hastings, India's first governor-general, wrested control of the Dutch opium trade, rapidly expanded poppy production, and dispatched two opium-laden ships to Canton on a trial run. One was shipwrecked, but the other evaded Chinese officials and sold 200,000 pounds of opium in Huangbo.

After an English census of China revealed 300 million potential "clients," the Crown awarded the "Honorable" East India Company a monopoly on the 'trade,' carefully avoiding the use of the word 'opium'—a face-saving subterfuge employed right into the 20th century. (For the record, most British merchants and missionaries protested, albeit uselessly, against Britain's foray into drug trafficking).

On Dec. 2, 1799, a distraught emperor penned an anti-opium edict, noting:

> "The infirm and weak perish gradually from want and hunger, while the strong and vigorous become thieves and robbers, the ultimate ruin of all being thus equally certain and inevitable."

But Britain saw not ultimate ruin but a 2,000% profit on each 130 pound chest. The Company sold 3,000 chests in 1790 and 30,000 chests in 1836. Between 1820 and 1835 alone, China's addict population grew 50 fold.

Lord Hastings maintained that Britain's opium smuggling was carried out 'in compassion to mankind', but the Emperor wrote that foreigners,

> "smuggle in prohibited opium, which flows and poisons the land. When this conduct is referred to the heart, it must be disquieting; when referred to reason, it is contrary to it."

After the Dao Guang emperor's 3 sons, including his heir, died of opium addiction, he ordered the viceroy at Canton to tighten up controls. He lambasted Britain as "a Christian nation devoid of four out of the five Virtues." Indignant opium smugglers demanded that Britain redeem her honor, but parliament urged patience, reasoning that the Emperor would give in when he saw the magnitude of the profits to be made. But the Emperor refused the part of Judas. He wrote,

> "It is true that I cannot prevent the introduction of the poison; gainseeking corrupt men will, for profit and sensuality, defeat my wishes; but nothing will induce me to derive a revenue from the vice and misery of my people."

As the stakes grew, so did the smugglers' audacity. In Feb. 1832, Lord Amherst sailed up Canton's coast to seek opium markets. He assured Fujian harbor officials that his ship was on its way to Japan from Calcutta and had been driven ashore by the storm, but he was hard pressed to explain away his crates of Chinese leaflets advertising for coastal trade outlets.

Chinese protests in Canton were fruitless. The indignant British protested they'd never heard of such a ship – technically true, since Lord Amherst had used a fake name on the vessel. Arthur Waley, in *The Opium War Through Chinese Eyes*, concluded, "It is not surprising that during his Canton days Lin worked on the hypothesis that nothing the English said could be relied upon."

London lauded Lord Amherst's escapade, and the House of Commons sanctioned opium's production and sale. Lord Shaftsbury later said the government not only encouraged opium's use but even carefully studied the tastes of Chinese addicts to "inflame the temptation so as to ensure an ample demand."

In 1836, the angry Emperor issued yet another edict ending in "Tremble." An indignant Lord Napier ended his reply with, "Therefore tremble, Governor Lu, intensely tremble." Governor Lu dispensed with diplomacy, blockaded the river above and below the foreign merchants' ships, and a humiliated Lord Napier conceded defeat. When Napier fell ill, Governor Lu sent him to Macao, where he died, becoming a martyr to the opium cause.

Furious Westerners demanded revenge for Napier's death. Matheson, the premier opium merchant, lambasted the unwavering Chinese mandarins as "imbecile, avaricious and obstinate," and demanded that Britain force open more ports for free trade. Jardine and Matheson built sleek teak ships, armed them to the teeth, and sailed the coast, plying what Matheson persisted in calling the harmless "merchandise China needs."

Even as Britain promoted opium in China, she passed several laws forbidding its use in England. Western medical experts supported this dual standard by arguing that was, for Chinese, "a harmless social family luxury," on a par with tea. The Deputy-Surgeon-General of Bombay later claimed that Chinese find in opium "a source of enjoyment, of comfort, of necessity, and of even a blessing." He added, "Opium is especially suited to the Chinese constitution, habits, and to the small pecuniary means of the masses."

A Western writer in the "*Chinese Repository*" (Nov. 1836, vol. V., p. 300) had different views. He accused traffickers of murder and,

> "the perpetuating and encouraging and engaging in a trade which promotes idleness, disease, poverty, misery, crime, madness, despair, and death."

An Assam tea plantation superintendent wrote that to obtain opium, addicts "will steal, sell his property, children, the mother of his children; and finally even commit murder." Walter Medhurst, the London Missionary Society's tireless opponent of the opium trade, described the 'harmless' drug's effects:

> "In proportion as the wretched victim comes under the power of the infatuating drug, so his ability to resist temptation is less strong; and debilitated in body as well as in mind he is unable to earn his usual pittance. Shut out from his own dwellings, either by angry relatives or ruthless creditors, they die in the streets, unpitied and despised."

Britain was unmoved. In fact, she transformed her sordid traffic into a moral crusade, arguing that opium was China's salvation, for without it the over-populated Chinese would grow poppies instead of food.

The Way of Heaven In a poignant letter to Queen Victoria, Imperial High Commissioner Lin Zexu wrote,

> "I am told that in your own country opium smoking is forbidden under severe penalties. This means that you are aware of how harmful it is. So long as you do not take it yourselves, but continue to make it and tempt the people of China to buy it, such conduct is repugnant to human feeling and at variance with the Way of Heaven."

"The Way of Heaven," Lin argued, was,

> "...fairness to all; it does not suffer us to harm others in order to benefit ourselves. Men are alike in this all the world over: that they cherish life and hate what endangers life. Your country lies 20,000 leagues away; but for all that the Way of Heaven holds good for you as for us, and your instincts are not different from ours; for nowhere are there men so blind as not to

distinguish what brings profit and what does harm..."

But for Britain, the profit justified the harm. On April 6, 1843, the *Times* would sum up Prime Minister Robert Peel's position:

> "Morality and religion, and the happiness of mankind, and friendly relations with China, and new markets for British manufactures were all very fine things in their way; but that the opium trade was worth to the Indian government £1,200,000..."

Commissioner Lin gave the British a 3-day ultimatum, and after waiting a full week for a response, he blockaded the harbor. During the foreigners' confinement, Cohong merchants carefully preserved the Westerners' property from harm, and insured that their foreign prisoners wined and dined in comfort. Lin reasoned that if he treated his foreign prisoners with respect and courtesy, they would recognize the error of their ways, abandon the opium trade, and turn to legitimate pursuits. But Western newspapers trumpeted China's barbarous treatment of Europeans, and stoked up the war propaganda machine.

Up in Smoke Captain Elliott surrendered 20,283 chests of opium, valued at £2 million. It took Lin six weeks to destroy it, and as gray smoke clouded Canton's sky, Lin noted of foreign observers, "I should judge from their attitudes that they have the decency to feel heartily ashamed."

But anger, not shame, reddened their faces. In July 1839, the British destroyed and scattered 29 Chinese war junks. Unsuspecting peasants rushed to greet British ships off Tinghai on July 5th. Lord Jocelyn described the British greeting in "Six Months with the Chinese Expedition" (1841):

> "The ships opened their broadsides upon the town, and the crashing of timber, falling houses, and groans of men resounded from the shore...We landed on a deserted beach, a few dead bodies, bows and arrows, broken spears and guns remaining the sole occupants of the fields."

City officials chose suicide over submission. As Waley wrote,

> "It had not from the first any chance of withstanding the concentrated fire of fifteen warships; as well might one expect Hiroshima to have hit back at its attackers."

British troops launched a protection racket ("security placards") by which families purchased immunity from plunder if they voluntarily surrendered their livestock. "The Chinese Repository" (1840) recorded:

> "They [the Chinese] have in a thousand instances received great injustice at our hands. While we have been issuing proclamations, talking sweet words...our soldiers and sailors have been plundering them and forcibly carrying off their poultry and cattle..."

On October 10, 1841, British forces captured Chen-hai, on the mainland opposite Ting-Hai. Ningpo was taken 3 days late. On June 22nd, Cao Sheng recorded in his diary his experiences in Shanghai: "The foreigners have contented themselves with loot and rape, but as the city fell without resistance, there has been no general slaughter." The 'general slaughter' came July 9th, in Chinkiang, where the poet Chu Shiyun recorded in his diary:

> "Corpses litter the town...is the horror ever going to end? Will our family ever be reunited...For days women have been raped or carried off."

The soldiers consoled their victims by plastering the town with proclamations encouraging the survivors to flock to Sui-Shan, where "opium is on sale very cheap—an opportunity not to be missed."

Surrender A devastated China surrendered. Under the *Nanking Treaty* (June 26, 1843), China agreed to pay an indemnity of £6,000,000 for the destroyed opium (three times its value) and cede Hong Kong to Britain. This settlement infuriated Lord Palmerston, who complained that six million did not cover the cost of the destroyed opium or the punitive expedition. The Times ridiculed this claim, arguing that Britain owed China compensation for "pillaging her towns and slaughtering her citizens in a quarrel which would never have arisen if we had not been guilty of an international crime."

The Crown countered critics by arguing that the war was over free trade, not opium. And Sir John Davis, who became governor of Hong Kong in 1844, declared that the Chinese weren't sincere about prohibiting opium, and that Britain had never forced the issue. He protested that Britain "only supplied the poison, which the Chinese were not obliged to take."

Since the Nanking Treaty studiously avoided the word "opium," the drug technically remained illegal. Britain even promised in a supplementary treaty that British officers would end the smuggling entirely. Empty words. When Captain Hope of the H.M.S. Thalia prevented several opium-laden ships from proceeding past Shanghai, he was criticized for interfering with British subjects in the course of their "trade," relieved of duty, and packed off to India.

When a large vessel has opened a way it is easy for a small one to follow.
Chinese Proverb

Hitchhiking Imperialism Western nations unanimously applauded Britain's victory. Ex-U.S. President Adams declared the war was caused solely by China's 'insulting and degrading' attitude towards foreigners, and averred:

> "The fundamental principle of the Chinese Empire is anti-commercial. It admits no obligation to hold commercial intercourse... it is time that this outrage upon the rights of human nature, and upon the first principles of the rights of nations, should cease."

America rushed envoy Caleb Cushing to China, where he announced America's intent to conclude a treaty of "everlasting friendship." He took three gunboats to help underscore his friendliness, and Cushing reminded the humiliated Chinese,

> "The late war with England was caused by the conduct of the authorities at Canton, in disregarding the rights of public officers who represented the English Government."

Cushing added that if China had not learned her lesson, "it can be regarded in no other light than evidence that she invites and desires [war with] the other Western powers [America]."

A French diplomat followed on Cushing's heels with seven French warships in tow and similar demands for everlasting friendship and trading rights. This "hitchhiking imperialism' lasted right up until Liberation in 1949.

Though Britain waged war to protect her opium trafficking, opium was opposed by most merchants, manufacturers, government leaders and missionaries on both moral and economic grounds. One merchant proved statistically that the opium trade had destroyed legal commerce and in "supplying the Chinese with an intoxicating drug, we are drying up their natural capacity to consume our manufactures."

Pottinger coined a stock answer: "If India does not produce it, other countries will." He added smugly that if the Chinese were truly such a virtuous people, they "would neither use the opium nor permit it to be smuggled."

China continued to resist the opium trade, and in the 1850s, Lord Palmerston warned, "The time is fast approaching when we shall be obliged to strike another blow in China." He explained, "these half-civilized governments such as those of China, Portugal, Spanish America…require a dressing down every eight or ten years to keep them in order."

Dressing Down China – The Arrow War The excuse for China's "dressing down" came from Hong Kong, which teemed with Chinese criminals and pirates luxuriating under the protection of the Crown. Commissioner Yeh seized the Chinese ship "Arrow", and convicted twelve of its notorious Chinese pirates. The British furiously demanded the criminals' release, arguing they had been taken from a British ship entitled to British protection. Lord Derby ridiculed the charge:

> "Chinese built, Chinese captured, Chinese sold, Chinese bought and manned, and Chinese owned. And that is the British vessel which is said to be entitled to claim the protection of a treaty by which British ships are exempted from the visits of the Chinese authorities."

Commissioner Yeh surrendered the pirates, but refused Sir John Bowring's demand for an apology. Britain now had her excuse for China's "dressing down." With characteristic hyberbole, Palmerston denounced Commissioner Yeh as "one of the most inhuman monsters that ever disgraced a nation." On Feb. 3, 1857, Britain declared war because of China's "acts of violence, insults to the flag and infraction of treaty rights."

Parliament unanimously opposed the second Opium War, agreeing with Lord Derby's sentiment that the war was "the shedding of the blood of unwarlike and innocent people without warrant of law and without the warrant of moral justification." Lord Palmerston furiously accused the dissidents of disloyalty to the Crown, dissolved Parliament, and went to war anyway.

When the Chinese refused to ratify the Treaty of Tiantsien, British and French forces attacked Beijing and burned the Summer Palace to the ground. Besieged from all sides, China succumbed, ending a full century of resistance. Opium was finally legalized, and imported at a lower duty than England, the proponent of "free trade," levied on Chinese silk and tea.

Scapegoat The English now intensified a two-decade effort to convince Western public opinion that Britain had never forced opium on China. Mr. Gladstone, in the opium debate in Parliament on May 10, 1870, argued that the Chinese government had 'wisely' decided to deal with opium as a commercial commodity. He praised the opium trade as not only a source of revenue but of great benefit to China and India:

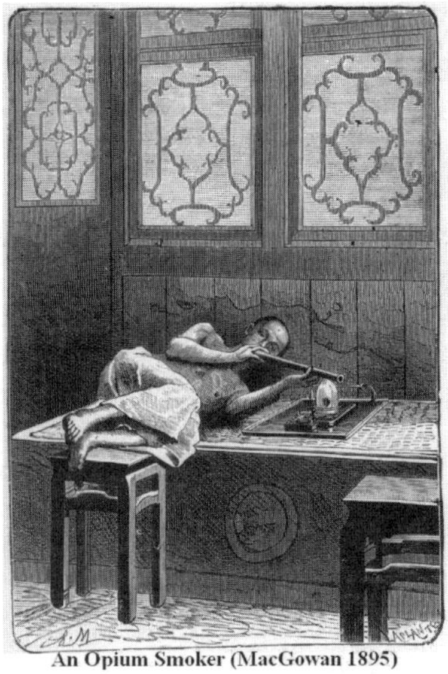
An Opium Smoker (MacGowan 1895)

> "This is one of the most remarkable cases which the whole fiscal history of the world presents. I do not suppose there is, or ever has been, a country…in which £6,000,000 of its revenue has been derived from a particular article [he still evades the word 'opium'], of which you could say with so close an approximation to the truth, without any violation whatever of political justice, that the 6 million was virtually and substantially paid by the inhabitants of another country who did not complain of the burden."

The London Times (Oct. 22, 1880) claimed that "the Chinese government admitted opium as a legal article of import, not under constraint, but of their own free will, deliberately." Lord Curzon, later Under Secretary for India, "denied that England had ever forced opium upon China; no historian of any repute, and no diplomatist who knew anything of the matter, would support the proposition that England coerced China in this respect."

Born & Bred to the Opium Pipe Gross atrocities can be sustained only by dehumanizing our prey and by canonizing ourselves. Before the Opium Era, Westerners had idealized the exotic, ancient kingdom of Cathay. After the Chinese lost the Opium Wars, they were beneath contempt, mere creatures born and bred to the opium pipe. Britain argued that Chinese not only wanted opium by that their physical constitution required it, and that the British opium monopolies throughout Asia were a humanitarian service for the Chinese.

As the dragon sank into opium dreams, Shaftbury's prophecy was fulfilled: easy money killed honest money. In 1877, Mr. Samuel S. Mander wrote that of China's £12 million in imports from India, the 85,000 chests of opium counted for £10.5 million, leaving £1.5 million for legitimate trade." Legitimate merchants suffered as China's moral and economic foundation foundered, and private bankers in London warned, "The purchasing power of China seems paralyzed by the opium trade." Sir Arthur Cotton, a well known

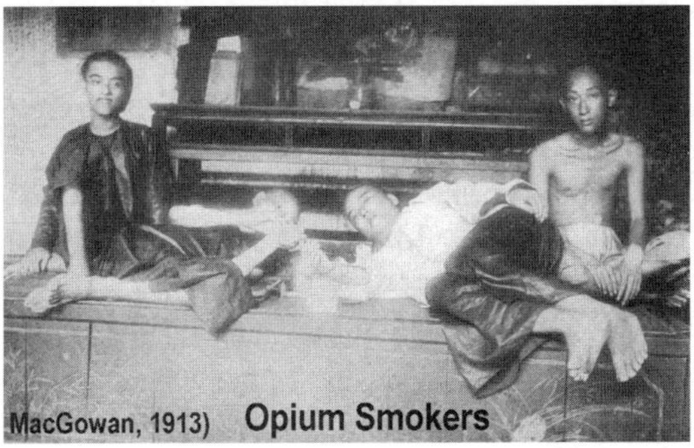
MacGowan, 1913) Opium Smokers

authority on India, argued in a letter to the Anti-Opium Society (May 6, 1882), "...there is not a shadow of excuse for our continuing this trade..." He affirmed,

> "the astonishing fact that we are perfectly independent of the opium revenue, having a clear surplus of £3.5 million without it, and that revenue increasing at the rate of £500,000 a year!"

Opium apologists argued that Indian farmers needed opium profits, but Sir Cotton proved that the farmer could make 4 times as much profit from an acre of sugar as he could from an acre of poppies. But like Chinese opium addicts, Britain's Indian poppy farmers were expendable. And expended they were.

Britain's mandatory substitution of poppies for traditional food crops ended with Indian mothers feeding their emaciated children opium to ease the gnawing hunger that plagued them from their beleaguered birth to their premature death.

In 1838, 800,000 Indians died in the Agra famine. Over 500,000 starved in 1860 in the Northwest. From 1865 to 1867, one million (1/3 of the population) perished in the Orissa Famine. From 1868 to 1870, 1/3 of the Rajputana population starved to death.

Embarrassed by the public outcry in Europe, Britain adopted a simple famine relief program. Only 28 died in the Bihar Famine of 1873-4, but at one dollar per life, Britain abandoned the program as too costly. Two years later, India's British masters idly watched the South India Famine destroy 5.25 million people in British territory alone. Another 750,000 starved in the 1896-7 famine, and in 1899, 2.5 million perished. But the poppy prospered.

Fighting Fire With Fire China reluctantly decided to destroy the Western opium trade by flooding the market with domestic opium. It was a painful decision, for Chinese rulers held that production of opium, for any reason, would "provoke the judgment of Heaven and the condemnation of men."

It certainly provoked Britain's condemnation, which resented China's infringement upon her private opium monopoly. By 1876, China was earning over 1.5 million annually from opium, but Sir R. Alcock told the House of Commons that China would gladly abandon the trade if Britain stopped her own trafficking.

Five years later, Sir R. Alcock, the stalwart anti-opium crusader, sold out.

Turncoat In December 1881, Sir Alcock shocked anti-opium advocates with his article "*Opium and the Common Sense*." He claimed that opium was no more harmful than alcohol and insisted:

1) "In early years, the Chinese were insincere in prohibition..."

2) "The British government never had forced opium on China; the Chinese were always eager to take more than India could supply."

Mr. B. Fosset Lock explained Sir Alcock's betrayal in his article "The Opium Trade and Sir Rutherford Alcock (Contemporary Review, April, 1882). It turned out that only one month before publishing "Opium and the Common Sense," Sir Alcock had been made a director of the British North Borneo Company, an affiliate of Dent, the premier opium trading firm. Alcock proved to be an even better opium trafficker than moral crusader. By the 1920s, fully 100% of Britain's income from North Borneo came from the opium trade.

China's Death Rattle The ranks of addicts now swelled with women and children. In 1889, Mr. Samuel Smith declared before the House of Commons, "one thing is certain: unless the vice is combated, China will commit something like national suicide and her population will succumb to pauperism, famine and death." He asked Britain to make a sacrifice by ending the trade, for "nothing ennobles a nation more than to make sacrifices for a great cause."

Britain's ennobling response was the Royal Opium Commission's 2,556 page report, which concluded that opium was no worse than alcohol and, furthermore, "there is no evidence from China of any popular desire that the import of Indian opium should be stopped."

> **On Deadly Statistics** "When the officer inquired whether after the war people would not ask what happened to the millions of Jews, Eichmann [Hitler's right hand man] replied: 'A hundred dead is a catastrophe. A million dead is a statistic.'" Nuremburg war crimes trial witness

China's Viceroy, Chang Chih-Tung, begged to differ. In 1896, he wrote in "China's Only Hope":

> "Cast out the poison! The foreign drug is debasing the homes and sweeping away the lives of our people.
>
> "It is not foreign intercourse that is ruining China, but this dreadful poison. Oh, the grief and desolation it has wrought to our people! Opium has spread with frightful rapidity and heartrending results through the provinces. Millions upon millions have been struck down by the plague...The ruin of the mind is the most woeful of its many deleterious effects. The poison enfeebles the will, saps the strength of the body, renders the consumer incapable of performing his regular duties, and unfit for travel from one place to another. It consumes his substance and reduces the miserable wretch to poverty, barrenness, and senility...Many thoughtful Chinese are apprehensive that opium will finally extirpate the race..."

In 1901, French writer and Naval officer Pierre Loti wrote, "China is dying of this poison." In 1906, a memorial to the Emperor claimed,

> "China can never become strong and stand shoulder to shoulder with the powers of the world, unless she can get rid of the habit of opium smoking by her subjects, about one-quarter of whom have been reduced to skeletons and look half dead." (*China Times*, Jan. 16, 1906)

Cold Turkey In 1907, the Dowager Empress vowed to eradicate the opium scourge within ten years. By June, all 700 opium dens in a Chinese-controlled city had been closed, and by mid 1910, China had reduced by 70 to 85 percent her domestic production of opium.

Meanwhile, Britain continued to insist that China had started the opium problem and was insincere about ending opium use.

Ironically, when impoverished Chinese farmers voluntarily torched their poppy fields, they actually boosted the profits of wealthy British traffickers by creating an opium shortage. Still, Britain mourned its alleged losses and complained about unsold stocks of opium in Shanghai and Canton warehouses. Chinese officials in Shanghai responded by purchasing 1,200 chests of opium, worth $25 million, and consigning it to the torch, evoking memories of Lin Ze Xu's conflagration a century earlier. China declared solemnly that, from that date, opium could no longer be imported legally into China. The British, old hands at smuggling, were unfazed.

On Feb. 26, 1924, a steamer hauled 180 cases of opium to Shanghai. Thousands of cases more were never discovered. Even John Campbell, representative of the Indian government, confessed that most smuggled opium "came in steamers from Liverpool and London, and steamers from the latter port arriving with 3,000 pounds of opium." He said,

> "The statistics showed beyond a shadow of a doubt that hundreds of thousands of ounces (in one year, almost 800,000 ounces) had been sent to the Far East for illicit introduction into China. China did not produce an ounce of morphia herself..."

"The pleasure of what we enjoy is lost by coveting more."
Chinese Proverb

New Markets As China tightened her borders, Britain pinned her hopes on her other Asian colonies. Opium production in the Straits Settlements (Singapore, Penang, Malacca, Labuan) rose from 353,938 pounds in 1916 to 370,688 pounds in 1920, in spite of Britain's promise at the Hague Convention to limit opium sales. In 1918, 60% of Britain's Asian income was derived from opium sales. In 1925, opium accounted for 48% of Singapore's revenue, and 100% of North Borneo's. At the 1923 Opium Conference, Mr. Campbell admitted that the British Indian government was determined to maintain high levels of both internal consumption and export, and that they,

> "controlled the production, distribution, sale, possession – every possible practical question which could arise in connection with opium—in the strictest possible manner—They had built up a complicated and highly efficient administrative system which started from the time the poppy seed was put into the ground, and did not relinquish control of the drug until it was in the hands of the consumers, or till it was actually exported."

Some wits noted wryly that the Crown did all but light the addicts' pipes.

When Indians begged Britain to abandon the opium policy, Britain responded that her opium monopoly was a humanitarian service to India (as it had been to China), and that to end the trade would be "a mockery; to many millions it would be sheer inhumanity."

> "History teaches us that men and nations behave wisely once they have exhausted all other alternatives." Abba Eban, Israeli politician

Coming Home to Roost Lin Zexu had warned a century earlier, "For so long as your subjects make opium, who knows but they will not sooner or later take to smoking it?" Lin was a prophet.

Even as she expanded her opium trafficking abroad, Great Britain struggled to curtail growing domestic consumption by passing the Dangerous Drugs Acts of 1920 and 1923. The desperate Western nations convened two International Opium conferences to debate the causes and cures of the worldwide opium epidemic—this when fully half of Europe's Asian profits were derived from opium trafficking!

Although Britain exported 700 tons of opium annually, and sold 500 tons to Indian addicts, she and other Western nations held that their mammoth opium monopolies were 'legal' and hence blameless, and that the sole cause of the growing global opium problem was Chinese opium producers, whom Lord Cecil piously called, "one of the most worthless sections of the human race."

Hong Kong – Opium's Last Stand In 1924, in a show of goodwill, Britain began an intensive campaign in HK to stop illegal (i.e., non-British) opium trade. Simultaneously, Britain expanded her own opium production. In 1922, Hong Kong's government handled 30 tons of opium, and reaped enormous profits from selling confiscated contraband opium. In spite of Hague Convention promises, in 1923 Britain asked permission to double opium imports from India, and then mounted a massive sales drive in Hong Kong to compensate for lost mainland profits. The sales drive was successful.

In 1924, a committee found that 20 to 25 percent of the Chinese adult population in HK had used opium, and the percent had been increasing for 6 to 7 years. Britain's stock response was, "It's not possible to stop opium use amongst the Chinese." But the Japanese knew better.

The Japanese Opium Experience Japan was the only colonial power to execute faithfully the principles of opium suppression set forth at the Hague Convention in 1912, for Japan had been fighting opium addiction, at home and in her colonies, for decades. Japan persistently argued that drug trafficking was not only immoral but, in the long run, unprofitable.

One of Japan's top priorities after taking Taiwan in 1895 was to end opium use. European smugglers were impotent against the Japanese' efficient police organization and tight surveillance and investigation. Opium-related deaths in Taiwan plummeted from 215,476 in 1908 to 38,000 annually by 1923. Japan also suppressed opium smuggling into Korea.

At the Second Opium Conference, Mr. Sugimura of Japan complained that it "was beneath a nation's dignity to derive so much revenue from opium," and he urged Western powers to view the problem not just from a humanitarian viewpoint but from an economic one, noting that in Taiwan,

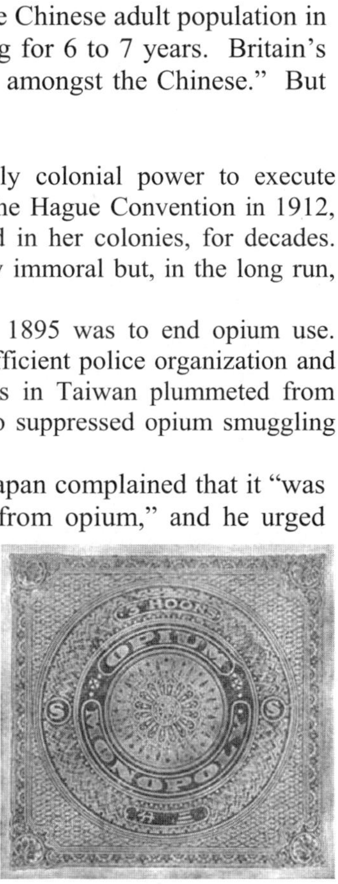

> "Even from the economic and financial point of view, a sacrifice of revenue from opium was in reality a gain, since the productive power of the nation increased."

Britain protested Japan's attacks on 'the justice and fairness of the British government," but the Polish delegate agreed with the Japanese. He said that because of the smokescreen of rhetoric clouding Western opium monopolies, the world was further from eliminating opium in 1924 than it had been in 1913.

Lord Cecil finally dismissed mounting criticism by arguing that opium was "purely an Indian question…it does not appear to me to be a matter for international interference at all."

Britain clung to her Hong Kong opium monopoly right up until 1945, when postwar profits no longer justified the embarrassment.

Thankfully, opium trafficking is behind us, but not so the arrogance born of opium's easy wealth and power.

> "Mankind loves to hate. It makes us feel good and right. People feel so appallingly righteous about ideologies and faiths they have been conditioned to believe in. We need scapegoats, objects outside ourselves so that we can project our own anger and hostility. If we are to understand how we can commit barbarities, we have to analyze this need and question the whole process of demeaning and devaluing others." Professor Ron Baker, Holocaust survivor.

What You See Scientists say what you expect of people is pretty much what you get. Maybe it's the same for nations. 'Japan' conjures up images of Mount Fuji, Japanese gardens, quality cars and electronics – not of the rape of Nanjing, or the bombing of Pearl Harbor, or the enslaving of Amoy. We put Japan's atrocious past behind us and helped her rebuild.

Germany evokes images of Beethoven and BMW, of engineering excellence – not of millions of massacred Jews and Gentiles. We put Germany's past behind us and helped her rebuild.

Time and economic success have exonerated Japan and Germany, but we continue to view China only from the perspective of the Great Leap Forward, or the Cultural Revolution, or Mao's dental hygiene.

Some people demonize China, others deify her. She is neither demon nor deity, but a nation with the same frailties, faults, hopes and dreams as others. The Chinese are a carnival glass through which we see darkly images that, however distorted, are of ourselves.

Opium Smoker (Dukes, 1895)

> "Blessed are the peacemakers, for they shall be called the children of God."
> The Prince of Peace

Excerpts from some Readers' Letters

We've reprinted the book in spite of them

07 July 2001, Dorothy Aksamit, "Dear Dr. Bill, You have shattered my husbands peaceful retirement. Even before I reached Gulangyu and before I found the round houses and long before I found *Amoy Magic*, I knew I had found a special place. Am still working on my husband who is not enthusiastic about that looooong flight. Amoy Magic. Congratulations! That's the best guide to a town I've seen.

"Appreciated your 'Lords of Opium' essay."

Oct. 3, 2006. Joanne C. "Hi Dr. Bill, The first time I found your "*Amoy Magic - Guide to Xiamen*" English version, I was so happy. I went through just a few pages, then I bought some to take back home. I told myself, you really do a great work for Xiamen...

You can't imagine, when I sent the books to my relatives in Singapore and Malaysia, so happy they were. My uncle, he was born in Gulangyu, grown up in Nanyang. Although he can speak Chinese and Xiamen dialect, he can't read Chinese. He always wanted to get to know more about his hometown, but he can't communicate with his relatives in Xiamen. But your *Magic Amoy* helps him and also he can use it to teach his children, and let those "white bananas" get to know some about Amoy. I was so happy when I got the phone call from my grandaunty, who had not returned to Amoy after leaving for Singapore over 60 years ago. She told me it is a good book, and a few copies were not enough for her family. The young generation all want to read it.

20 Mar. 2007, Jean Marc "We are a French family...an old lady selling souvenirs ran to me with your book "*Discover Gulangyu*", which I bought immediately... and read straight away the same evening.... We have very little information in French about this beautiful area of China, even in travel guide as *Lonely Planet*, Petit Futé or Guidee bleu Hachette. Moreover, I appreciate your sense of humour. So I wanted to say you a big thanks for having written these books, it makes our trip much more interesting..."

Jan. 17 2002, Karl R. (author). "On the trip back to VT I got a chance to read your book. I started to just read through it, but your humor was like a magnet; I wanted to see what your next witticism was going to be. It was particularly fun reading about a place that we had visited and seeing what your take on it was. Well done. So here's a book in return. It is #4 in a series..."

Nov. 21, 2006, Yong Ming. "I read your *Amoy Magic* many times. I am a Singaporean working in Hong Kong. My purpose of this e-mail is just to express my gratitude and I wish you many more happy years in Xiamen."

July 31, 2006, On a personal note, thanks for writing about Xiamen. Your writing style, for an ADD person like me, is easy to read, put down, pick up. I marvel at your ability to synchronize so many small chunks of information with wonderful historical research and personal/family exploration. Your writing is entertaining, irreverent, practical, whimsical, and full of useful information for newcomers and oldies alike. Thanks. C. Parker.

Feb. 24, 2003, K.R, Ph.D., Center for Atmospheric Chemistry Studies, Graduate School of Oceanography, "I got your book while in Xiamen and read it from cover to cover. Nice to meet the guy behind the book. I appreciated your sense of humor."

14 Mar. 2003, James and Norma Mason (Washington), "Your book brings extraordinary excitement to our minds and spirits.... We study your uniquely Chinese graphics, and "travel" about in Amoy Magic; we discuss the universe in which you live; each time, I have a hankering to book flight and experience Xiamen, the University, Amoy."

02 April 2003, David R. (Xiamen), "bought your book Amoy Magic shortly after I arrived in Xiamen about six months ago...I just wanted to say I appreciated your book and it helped me discover a little bit of Fujian Province."

27 Jan 2000, Ma Jun (Chinese in Xiamen), "After reading "*Amoy Magic*" tonight, I surprised found it to be a great help to my work. You came up with many useful comments on various Xiamen places."

17 Feb. 2000, Jonathan Raiti, (Middle East), "Last week your book, Amoy Magic, was shown to me by some mutual friends. I was catching a ride up to Fuzhou and enjoyed reading through the whole trip. Afterwards I mentioned this great little book to a few friends who work up there. We would all like to get some copies. How much are they?"

18 Feb 2000, Joy J. "For the past several days I went through **Amoy Magic**...it gives vivid descriptions and detailed information of Xiamen and the surrounding area —at almost each aspect —location, geography, history, culture, local customs and festivals, food, shopping , sight-seeing... What grabs me is not only the kaleidoscope of the introduction of Xiamen, but also the sense of humor. And the pictures from your hand are lovely, fresh, humorous, just like your words. In general, it's a good mixture of knowledge and fun...it looks that your book is very popular among Kodak's Laowai."

23 Feb 2000, Cindy W. (IKEA Corporation), "I know of this book from one of my Laowai colleague, and gladly read it. It's very useful guide not only for foreigners but also for Xiamenese like me. It gives me more information .Do you know that I even didn't know how the Mooncake Gambling was invented until read this book?"

07 Mar 2000, Hugh B. "*Amoy Magic*" is a really good book for foreigners who want to come/stay in Xiamen. Also a wonderful book for our Chinese, especially researchers and students who want to study Xiamen from a foreigner's eyesight. It is the #1 among Xiamen guidebooks. books It is obvious that you had spent a lot of time & done a lot of work to investigate, study, deep into the local people. I could not imagine all the toil."

31 March 2000, Martin R. (German), "Hello Dr. Brown, I'm Martin, a German who lives now since 1 1/2 years in Xiamen and I like it so much. its one of the best cities in china. I was living in Beijing, Shanghai and Hong Kong and Xiamen is the best. Today I finally bought your book and from the first look into it, I have to say, ITS JUST GREAT.
"I thought, that I know Xiamen quite well, but in this book is so much information inside, which I didn't know. This weekend I have to read the book and then I have to check out everything."

26 July 2000, Tracy M. "Dr. Bill Brown, I came across your book by accident several weeks ago. A local man (he could not read English) gave me a copy. I really enjoyed it. Where can I purchase extra copies? I have lived and worked in numerous areas of China the past ten years. I left Beijing in 1997 and arrived in Xiamen. Like you I fell in love with Xiamen and I now call it my home.."

01 Aug. 2000, Dave H. "write to tell you that yesterday I was given your *Amoy Magic* by someone from Utica, NY, who taught at XiaDa last semester, and last night I read it from cover to cover. I had your earlier, shorter pamphlet version when I came to China. Wish you were older—or I was younger—and this book had been available when I was there. Just your summary of where the bus lines go is worth the price! ...Well, enough of this. Just wanted you to know how much I enjoyed *Amoy Magic* —and what a wonderful thing it is for those like me who come to China. Dave"

17 Oct. 2001 Agnes (Kodak), "I've read the book of *Amoy Magic*. It's very good and I learn much from it. I also heard from Ms. Lee that you would write a book about Fujian. I hope you will have a success too!"

08 Nov. 2001 Pistachio, "Good Morning, Bill, I'm so excited to read your Book *Amoy Magic* given by my friend... I just browse several pages of your book, haven't finish your book yet, But I believe It will be very helpful to me and also to my American friends. I can't wait to E-mail you. I know I have to E-mail you right away, letting you know me."

19 April 2001, Cindy Friend (U.S.) "Ni Hao Dr. Brown, By way of introduction, my name is Cindy Friend and I am a fellow Laowai (from Towanda, KS) who will be staying in Xiamen for the next 5 1/2 months. I am here with my husband John who is on assignment at Taeco (for Boeing) to modify a couple of airplanes... John and I have read and enjoyed your book and are looking forward to experiencing the magic of Amoy....Since I am not working I will have more time to experience the "magic of Amoy."I look forward to hearing from you, Dr. Brown. Xie xie!!"

23 April 2001, Yu B., "Dear Sir, I just recently pass through Xiamen and thanks to your book, my visit to the city was all the more memorable. Despite Xiamen's potential as a tourist destination, the city suffers a lack of tourist publications. Nothing to tell us where to go, what to do, where to eat, I couldn't even find a single postcard of the city! (Friends later help me buy some Xiamen University postcards.) "

26 May 2001, Jenelle L. Nevada City, California, "I was loaned a copy of your book and find it delightful. I'm currently teaching reading and writing English in Fuzhou at Wha Nan Women's College with plans to return to my home in CA in June."

11 July 2001, Nellie C. Sales Manager, Holiday Inn, "Dear Dr. Bill Brown, I saw your book *Amoy Magic* blue trial volume some years ago but I didn't take time to read.Last weekend, my cousin Zhang Li asked me to check the page 55 about an article you wrote about him during Culture Revoluation Period, I bought the 2001 version in the book store, I can't put it down till it is all been finished. As a Sales Manager in Holiday Inn Xiamen, my job need to take care the expatriates who long stay in hotel, it is the first time I feel how helpful is your guide to expats. You really have done a lot for Xiamen."

06 Sep. 2001, Max B. "Dear Dr Brown, Your book, *Amoy Magic*, has made my first few days here in Xiamen much more comfortable than they would have been without it.

"I've come to teach English Writing and British and American culture at Jimei University. This is my second year teaching in China. I live, here, in a hotel which serves a buffet lunch for 5 Yuan, which is just fine. At dinner I am confronted with a large Chinese menu with the instructions, "order anything you want." Fat chance. But Amoy Magic saved me from starvation—all 250 pounds of me. I sit down with the helpful waitress and we pore over pages 178 to 187. She previously marked with a check the dishes they offer. I'm making my way through them, marking them with stars to remind me which ones I like. Many thanks for the contribution your little book has made to my acculturation here in Amoy."

10 Sep. 2001, Richard H., Washington, D.C. "My guides in Xiamen—two of your former students whose name cards are somewhere amid more than 400 that I collected at the investment seminar last weekend—gave me your book. I read it on the flight home and only regret that I did not have it on the way over. It was great fun and I loved the puns, particularly the visual puns."

10 Sep. 2001, Michelle, DELL, "Hey, Bill, I got the book, took a quick look through, to be honest, you are more Xiamenese than most of local people. You know more culture and history than local. It is a good guide and full of fun. You are a genius. "

02 Oct. 2002, Eugene K. Wilson, "Dear Dr. Brown, As a visitor here to Xiamen this week, I was fortunate enough to buy your book. Besides the useful information, I found your humor interesting and , yes, humorous. Have you written anything else about this area?"

04 Nov. 2002, Phoebe Z. "Dear Mr. Brown, It is amazing when I read the book of *Amoy Magic* you wrote. I am so surprised that you could find so many interesting things in our daily life. As I grew up in Xiamen, everything around seemed so common and I felt a litter bit boring towards the environment."

07 Nov. 2002, Lisa N. (Chicago, Illinois), "Dear Bill Brown, I've just recently arrived in Xiamen from Chicago. Although I had read Amoy Magic before leaving Illinois, I never could have estimated its value until now, as I am beginning to get settled and to learn my way around town. Xiamen is wonderful, as you say, and your book is a lifesaver. I am never without it (bus routes). Thanks for taking the tine to write it! Lisa"

25 Nov. 2002, Colorado, Dr. Nathan K. "Hi Bill. Just got your book. Great read! You do have a sly sense of humour.... I particularly enjoyed the inset piece on the Chinese Jews... I look forward to sharing this with my son,."

10 Jan. 2003 Frankie S. M.D., Houston, TX "Got your book in Shanghai two yrs ago. but got a chance to read it only a month ago. have been reading n enjoying it since then. like ur way of looking at things as a lao wai n lao nei. Is there a chance of getting your autograph when I get there sometime around the new yr (yang nian)? Another friend of mine in Texas will surely enjoy and treasure another signed copy. Their daughter in law is from Xiamen. Hoping at least to see u there. Pls. don't worry. I won't be stalking you. Sincerely, FS. "

13 Jan 2003, Anna Ong, Manila, Philippines, "I was in Xiamen a few weeks ago and got a copy of your book. I was so happy to find one so helpful since my family and I will be moving to Xiamen next month."

Bibliography & Suggested Reading about Amoy & Fujian History

Abend, Hallett, "Treaty Ports," Doubleday, Doran and Company, Inc, New York, 1944

De Jong, Gerald F., "The Reformed Church in China 1842-1951," Wm. B. Eerdmans Publishing Co., Michigan, 1992

Dukes, Edwin Joshua, "Everyday Life in China; or, Scenes Along River and Road in Fuh-Kien," London Missionary Society's Edition, The Religious Tract Society, 56, Paternoster Row; 65, St. Paul's Churchyard; and 164, Piccadilly, 1885

Fisher, Lena Leonard, "The River Dragon's Bride," Abingdon Press, New York, 1922

Gutzlaff, Karl F. A., "Journal of Three Voyages Along the Coast of China in 1831, 1832, and 1833," Frederick Westley and A.H. Davis, London, 1834.

Hewlett, Sir Meyrick, "Forty Years in China," Macmillan & Co., Ltd., 1943.

Hutchinson, Paul, Ed., "A Guide to Important Mission Stations in Eastern China," The Mission Book Company, Shanghai, 1920.

Johnston, Meta and Lena, Jin Ko-Niu—A Brief Sketch of the Life of Jessie M. Johnston For Eighteen Years W.M.A. Missionary in Amoy, China, T. French Downie 21 Warwick Lane, London, E.C. 1907

Lin, Yutang, "My Country and My People," Foreign Language and Teaching Press, Beijing, 1998.

Lowrie, Rev. Walter M., "Memoirs," Board of Foreign Missions of the Presbyterian Church, New York, 1850.

Macgowan, James, "How England Saved China," T. Fisher Unwin, London, 1913.

Macgowan, John, "Beside the Bamboo," London Missionary Society, 16 New Bridge Street, London, 1914.

Macgowan, Rev. John, "Christ or Confucius, Which?, or, The Story of the Amoy Mission," London Missionary Society, 14 Blomfield Street, E.C.; John Snow & Co., 2 Ivy Lane, Paternoster Row, E.C. 1895

Macgowan, Rev. John, "Men and Manners of Modern China," T. Fisher Unwin, London, 1912. use, 43 Gerrard Street, W. 1907

Macgowan, Rev. John, "Sidelights on Chinese Life," Kegan Paul, Trench, Trubner & Co., Limited, Dryden H

Manson-Bahr, Sir Philip, "Patrick Manson, The Father of Tropical Medicine," Thomas Nelson and Sons, Ltd., Edinburgh, 1962

Neill, Desmond, "Elegant Flower—First Steps in China," John Murray, Albemarle St., London, 1956

Werner, E.T.C., "Myths & Legends of China," George G. Harrap & Co. Ltd., London, 1922.

Williams, Edward Thomas, "China—Yesterday and Today," George G. Harrap & co., Ltd., London, 1923

Williamson, Rev. G.R., "Memoir of the Rev. David Abeel, D.D." Robert Carter, New York, 1848

(Johnston, 1907)

"PIGTAILS STICKING OUT ALL ROUND."

110 Emergency Call and Locator
Call Police from one of over 30,000 110 signs. Give them the red 7 digit number at the top and they can find you quickly (this is a national government initiative). They have volunteer translators; you can even phone them to help with taxi drivers.

120: Emergency Medical Help and Ambulance The Emergency Medical Center, at Zhongshan Hospital (s. Hubin Road) has an ICU, a couple dozen ambulances, and over 200 paramedics available 24/7. When going to the hospital, always have 10,000 to 20,000 Yuan cash on hand—or an ATM card for a local bank.

Xiamen Chang Gung Hospital 厦门长庚医院
Add: No.123, Xiafei Road, Xinyang Industrial Park, Haicang District (海沧区新阳工业区霞飞路 123 号)
Tel: 0592-6203456
Website: www.cgmh.com.cn
Buses: 804, 58, 62, 408, 458, 807, 460, free shuttle bus, stop at Chang Gung Hospital

Other Hospitals
No.1 Hospital 2137101 No.2 Hospital 2063549
Zhōngshān Hospital 2210468 Húlǐ Hospital 5622502
Jīměi Hospital 6068398 Hǎicāng Hospital 6055880

Tóng'ān Hospital 7022591 Xìnglín Hospital 6079206
Traditional Chinese Medicine Hospital 2022860

EMERGENCY TELEPHONE NUMBERS

Fire alarm 119 Police: 110
Directory inquiries: 114 Time inquiry: 117 (or buy a watch?)
Weather Report: 121 Telecom users complaints:180
Mayor Hotline: 968123
International airport inquiry: Automatic: 6020017 Manual: 6022936-6017
24 Xiàmén flight inquiry, booking service: 800 8582666
Ship transport inquiry: 2022517
Train service inquiry: 5054340
Weather bureau service: 6013031

Tourism Hotline	111858
Xiàmén Airport	96321 800-858-2666
Weather	12121
Police	110
First Aid	120
Phone Directory Service	114
Phone/Internet Inquiries	10000

Survival; Expat/Business Services

Pìzzǎ Delivery 21-PIZZA

图书在版编目(CIP)数据

魅力厦门/(美)潘维廉著.—4版.—厦门:厦门大学出版社,2013.5(2019.2重印)
(魅力·老潘)
ISBN 978-7-5615-1604-1

Ⅰ.①魅… Ⅱ.①潘… Ⅲ.①厦门市-概况 Ⅳ.①K925.73

中国版本图书馆CIP数据核字(2013)第085169号

出 版 人 郑文礼
责任编辑 施高翔

出版发行 厦门大学出版社
社　　址 厦门市软件园二期望海路39号
邮政编码 361008
总 编 办 0592-2182177　0592-2181406(传真)
营销中心 0592-2184458　0592-2181365
网　　址 http://www.xmupress.com
邮　　箱 xmup@xmupress.com
印　　刷 厦门集大印刷厂

开本 720 mm×1 000 mm　1/16
印张 23
插页 6
字数 575千字
版次 2013年5月第4版
印次 2019年2月第2次印刷
定价 48.00元

厦门大学出版社
微信二维码

厦门大学出版社
微博二维码